When Teaching Becomes Learning

2nd Edition

Also available from Continuum

FE Lecturer's Survival Guide, Angela Steward
Guide to Vocational Education and Training, Christopher Winch and Terry Hyland
Psychology and the Teacher, 8th Edition, Dennis Child
Teaching Adults, Amanda Hayes
Teaching in Further Education, L.B. Curzon
Ultimate FE Lecturer's Handbook, Ros Clow and Trevor Dawn
Differentiation in Teaching and Learning, Tim O'Brien and Dennis Guiney

When Teaching Becomes Learning

A Theory and Practice of Teaching

2nd Edition

Eric Sotto

continuum

Continuum International Publishing Group
The Tower Building   80 Maiden Lane
11 York Road   Suite 704
London SE1 7NX   New York NY 10038

www.continuumbooks.com

First published 1994
Reprinted 1995, 1997, 1999, 2001, 2002, 2003, 2004, 2006
Second edition published 2007
Reprinted 2009, 2011 (twice)

British Library Cataloguing-in-Publication Data
A catalogue record for this book is available from the British Library.

ISBN: 978-08264-8908-1 (hardcover)
ISBN: 978-08264-8909-8 (paperback)

Library of Congress Cataloging-in-Publication Data
A catalog record for this book is available from the Library of Congress.

Typeset by Servis Filmsetting Ltd, Manchester
Printed and bound in Great Britain

Contents

Preface to the Second Edition   vii

Preface to the First Edition   viii

Acknowledgements   ix

Introduction   1

Preliminaries   6

Part I   Learning   19

1   Motivation   21

2   Two Accounts of Learning   33

3   The Learning Process   55

4   Talking and Feeling   62

5   Perception   75

6   Where are the Answers?   82

7   Why Only Living Things Can Learn   87

8   Two Memories   97

9   Explaining and Experiencing   109

10   A Theory of Learning   123

Part II   Teaching   129

11   The Transmission Method and an Alternative Approach   131

12   Research into Teaching   139

13   Clarity, Enthusiasm and Variety   145

14   Indirectness, Opportunities and Fit   151

15   Theory and Practice   160

16   Reflections on Educational Technology   169

17   Planning   190

18   Communicating and Participating   195

19   Interacting   204

20   Discussing   212

21   Difficult Lessons   223

22   Learning a New Approach   233

23   Variations on a Theme   239

24   Overview   250

25   Why Teach?   254

Further Reading   275

Notes and References   279

Index   319

Preface to the Second Edition

When Joanne Allcock of Continuum invited me to prepare a second edition of this book, I had mixed feelings. On the one hand, I was pleased that this book was still in demand twelve years after it had first been published. On the other, I was no longer involved in training, and deeply immersed in other activities. After considerable hesitation, I agreed to prepare a new edition, but on the understanding that I would make only a very limited number of changes.

So much for decisions. For, once I had begun to work, I realized what I should have known, namely, that any halfway serious book is always of its time and place, and that this cannot easily be changed. As a result of this belated recognition, I was faced by the choice of either re-writing much of the book, or abandoning the project. For a variety of reasons, I chose the former option, and, after considerable juggling with budgets, the publisher was able to support this decision. The result is this new edition. The foregoing can be compared with someone who has decided to redecorate a house, but finds on beginning that, not only does the plaster need repairing, but also that some of the piping has gone rusty, that much of the wiring is obsolete, that some of the joists must be replaced, and that a new roof is required.

Four changes have been made to the first edition. One: most of the book has been re-written, especially the last third; and this includes amending hundreds of passages; deleting whole sections and adding others; changing tenses, the focus, the emphasis, and the direction; and trying to improve the writing. Two: the addition of two new chapters, one on educational technology, the other on the general aims of teaching; and I hope that readers will find that these offer more than comments on mere technique. Three: the addition of a considerable number of works to the Notes. And four: a radical change in the layout of the book. That is, when I submitted the original manuscript, it was written in a narrative style, with short chapters, divided into sections to enable readers to catch their breath. The first publisher changed this arrangement completely (perhaps to conform to a house style), so that the published book looked more like a textbook, with long chapters divided by subheadings. I am delighted that it has been possible to return to the original layout, and I hope readers will find that this has made the book friendlier and more accessible.

Preface to the First Edition

This book is intended to help anyone who does any kind of teaching. I begin by outlining a certain approach, and then I give descriptions of classroom practice that I have observed to illustrate it.

As I try to deal with fundamentals, I believe it is possible to spread the net this wide. For example, if we really understand the basics of soil cultivation, it won't usually take us long before we know how to grow cherries in California or melons in Tashkent.

Anyone especially interested in learning might also find something in this book, and I hope that anyone interested in the various branches of psychotherapy might find something useful here, too.

It gives me pleasure to note that nearly everything I have written has come out of interacting with others, either in classrooms or in reading what they have written in their books. As for my more specific debts, one of the rewards of writing a book lies in the pleasure one gets from being able to state them. I have indicated my debts in the Notes at the end of the book, and I have added a reading list.

My biggest general debt is undoubtedly to the many taxpayers who have supported the various schools and colleges in which I have worked. That has enabled me to earn a living in a challenging but interesting way, and to these people my warm thanks.

Godshill Pottery
Fordingbridge
Hampshire, England

Acknowledgements

I should like to thank Rosemary Aikens, Herbie Goldberg and Dr Robert Ward for taking the trouble to read and comment on early drafts of chapters. I am obliged to Fanny Baldwin, David Griffith and Stephanie Pollard for reading and commenting on an early draft of the manuscript. I am very grateful to Professor Tony Becher for reading a late draft from cover to cover and making many detailed and encouraging comments. I am very pleased that my daughter, Leora, read and commented on some of what I wrote.

My ex-student and friend John Holden did the anatomical drawings, and I should like to thank him warmly for his help. I am also much indebted to my friend Gemma Hooper for help with the proofreading.

I should like to thank the staff at Harrow College Library (University of Westminster) for their help. I thank in particular Janette Dollamore for getting me innumerable publications, and Juliette Dye and Alleyne Riley for much cheery aid in locating things. Writing a book like this one would be near impossible without such help.

Some of the best work on the book was done at Godshill. I have gained a great deal from Kate and Chris when there. I also had the pleasure of Susan's interest during one period.

The above said, I can claim all the infelicities which remain in the book as my own. Like many people who have tried to write a book, I have had certain people particularly in mind while doing so. In the case of this book, that has been very much my daughters. It is to them with much love that this book is dedicated.

For Tamar and Leora

'There is nothing as practical as good theory.'
Kurt Lewin

Introduction

When people write books, they seem to begin in one of two ways. They either begin with their topic, or they tell you how they got to their topic. I have always found the second way the more helpful, and readers might find it helpful if I begin in that way, too.

The first time I taught was in a private language school in Austria. I was a young man at that time, and got the job almost by chance. I had two qualifications: I could speak English, and I vaguely knew the director of the school. The day before I was to take my first class, she taught me the method of instruction they used. She told me it was called the 'Direct Method'. She stood tall, thin and formidable in front of her desk, pointed to a book on it, and said slowly and emphatically in French, 'That is a book.' Then she pointed to the book, and asked me in French, 'What is that?'

Although I did not know any French, I knew what she was getting at. But I felt rather stupid, because I could not remember what she had just said. She had to repeat the sentence a number of times before I could get the answer right.

Whenever I couldn't answer one of her questions, I sensed that she saw this as a slight on her teaching ability, and that made me clumsy. Fortunately, she stopped after about twenty minutes. Her expression suggested that she thought I was an idiot, but her next words, in English, were about administrative matters. So, it looked as if I had the job.

At first, I had two classes. Then I got some more classes. Sometimes I even came in during a morning to teach a single student. I liked meeting the students, but I did not care for being a teacher. I felt it put me too much out front.

Things improved when I got to know a few of the women students. There was one that I particularly liked. She came in for private lessons, so she must have had plenty of cash. She never mentioned a husband, lover or partner, or any family, but she seemed to have lots of time and plenty of money because she was always beautifully dressed, and had a swish sports car. She greatly intrigued me. She had a bright mind, a warm laugh, and a delicious body, and we reached a stage when I spent quite a bit of each lesson kissing her hand and sometimes her cheek, and discussing in which language we were better at using the direct method. Unfortunately, I couldn't get any further than that. But those were my favourite lessons. The director of the school also let me know that she warmly approved of the work I was doing with this customer. And those lessons helped to cheer me up when news came in about a new government regulation to the effect that everybody with a job like mine had to take an examination and acquire the official status of 'English Teacher'.

I had never sat a serious exam before, and it soon looked as if I would not have to sit this one either. A colleague discovered some small print which stated that you could keep your job, provided that you registered for the final examination, paid the examination fee, and sat the examination within a year – and I had no intention of staying that long.

But I did. Instead of sitting under the plane trees in the Beethovenplatz each morning, with the pigeons, the pensioners, and the young women and their prams, reading a one-day-old *New York Herald Tribune* (Paris edition), I sat in the grandly housed Nationalbibliothek. There were lots of books in English on education there, and I read about people like Pestalozzi and Montessori. At other times, I practised translating from English into German, or from German into English. None of this was related to what I did in my classes, but I did not even notice this at that time. The important thing was to pass that exam; and, after about ten months, I sat that exam; and to my surprise and not surprise, I passed. A month after that I left, and thought I'd never teach again. But I did. This time it was in Israel. I was farming at the time. I had got married, a second child had been born, we worked hard, crops grew and got sold, but we were never sure that there would be enough money for essentials. So, when I heard that a few hours of English teaching were required at a local school, I applied for the job, and I got it.

I taught children of twelve and thirteen. Very few children of that age see much point in learning a foreign language, and most of the ones I taught thought it an awful waste of time. They also showed this! So, it wasn't enough to woo them, and to teach well. One also had to be coercive, and I hated that. But a small monthly cheque came in, and this helped to tide us over between the cauliflowers and the aubergines. Then, about ten months later, we moved. I began managing citrus groves, and I thought I'd never teach again.

But I did. This was because the citrus job ended after a few years, and some temporary teaching seemed the best next step. I saw an advert for a teaching job in a nearby town, and applied for it. At my interview, it came out that the post had become vacant because the previous teacher had not been able to control her classes. It also came out that I had once been a sergeant in an infantry company. It was that which impressed the man who interviewed me; and he offered me the job, and I took it.

That was a part-time job. I had another part-time job, in another school, in an immigrant town, miles away; and for a greenhorn like me, just controlling those classes required a very great deal of effort. I didn't know which job I hated more. But the teaching day in Israel begins at about eight, and ends at about two, and my plan was to use the afternoons to look for another job. But I didn't find one. However, as time passed, I found I could cope better, and I even began to see some advantages in teaching as a career. There were two things I particularly liked about teaching. One was that I did not *have* to be nice to anyone. The other was that the amount I earned was not directly related to how well I did my job. If I tried to do well, it was because I felt I should, and because of the inner satisfaction that this afforded me.

Controlling the classes was my main problem. However, at the same time, I was very slowly also developing a teaching technique that seemed to work. I will describe that in a moment. First, I should like to mention something I did not even notice at that time, something that comes to the heart of why this book came to be written.

Here I was, a part-time, temporary teacher, who had had a little experience, who possessed a kind of certificate, but who actually knew next to nothing about learning and teaching. Nevertheless, I had been given a responsible job, and let loose in a classroom. At that time, this seemed normal to me. The people who gave me the job must have thought it normal, too. They must have thought that teaching is a kind of art form which you either have, or do not have, and which, if you have it, you can develop through experience. Such an attitude implies that we can all learn the fundamentals of sepsis from experience, and that, whether we wash, or do not wash our hands before we perform an operation is our own business. That, after all, was precisely the attitude in medicine for hundreds of years when so-called 'doctors' maimed more people than they cured. I shall be discussing the extent to which we can learn from experience later. Before that, I should perhaps note that things slowly began to improve for me. I found I was managing to keep order with less and less effort, and my pupils seemed to be learning some English as well. Perhaps I should now say a few words about the method I used.

In a previous lesson, I would give out some homework. That would usually involve completing a few exercises, and reading a short story. In time, I learnt to give as little work as possible, but to ensure that that little was properly done. I began the next lesson by checking that the exercises had been done, and that the answers were correct. As time passed, and as my confidence grew, I found I could do that briskly. Then I'd start asking questions, in English of course, on the story I had set; and I tried to involve as many pupils as possible. I'd also use answers as part of an ongoing assessment, and I tried to get a proper conversation going whenever I could.

And that is what we would do for most of the lesson, and it seemed to work. By the end of a year, most of my pupils could speak some English; and, if I had them for two or three years, they were usually able to speak, and often also able to read and write English quite well. It might be noticed that, in this approach, there was a little explaining, a little correcting, but very little rote learning. Mostly there was a maximum of doing in a meaningful context. At the time, I did not see the full implications of this, and I shall attempt to explain what I think was happening in the pages that follow.

Eventually there came a time when controlling a class ceased to be a problem. That wasn't because I was doing anything in particular. It was more that I was beginning to take it for granted that there would not be many problems. Also, we were usually so busy doing things, that there wasn't much time for many problems. I even began to feel that I was doing a useful job. I still didn't like what seemed to be an essential element in teaching: being up front, in charge of the show; and I often thought about finding something else to do. But nothing came of that. So the years passed, the better job became a permanent one, my pension rights accumulated, and I even made it to head of department. Then I left.

The details are not relevant here. I returned to the UK, and I discovered that the qualifications I had acquired after I had begun teaching would not entitle me to 'recognized teacher' status in the UK. However, without such a status, I could not get a decent teaching job. I seemed to have one of two options: Either move into another occupation, or apply for a place at a teacher training college and obtain the qualification that was required. I did the latter. After all, I had had ten years of teaching and a degree behind me by then. I certainly did not want to go back to being trained. But I had to; and I found doing that very difficult.

One of my difficulties was that I felt I had to do extra well, and I wasn't at all sure I could. Another difficulty was money. I considered myself lucky to be in a country that (at that time) gave students a grant, but there was a huge drop in income. Nevertheless, I began, and I very soon discovered that I knew very little about learning and teaching! I could put it like this: I discovered that my previous ten years of teaching had mostly confirmed me in the kind of teaching that was all around me. But, so all around me, I had not really noticed it. I had been like that proverbial goldfish: the last creature on earth to discover water. That is one of the problems about learning from only experience: It doesn't take you out of your experience.

I came to none of this because the training course I was attending was particularly good. We had lectures on language in the classroom, comparative education, philosophy of education, language in the classroom, a professional course (in my case the teaching of English), the sociology of education, and more about language in the classroom.[1] But fortunately, I learnt as much from what we were not taught, as from what we were taught. For example, I was powerfully struck by the fact that our teachers were no better than any other teachers I had ever had. Some of them were worse. The fact that they had been trained to teach, and were training teachers, did not seem to make them one whit better than any other teachers I had ever had.

I hope I shall not be thought petty if I write like this. I often had teachers on that course who clearly knew a great deal about teaching, but who did not teach well. (The man who taught us educational psychology once gave us a lecture on the inefficiency of lecturing as a teaching method.) To put this another way, those tutors did not seem able to use what they knew. Why not? How can somebody know something, yet not know it?

I also began to wonder about how much learning results from being taught. This occurred to me because, here I was on a course many of us thought poor, yet I felt I was learning a great deal. (Some of the students felt it was such a poor course they organized a protest about it.) This experience got me speculating about the relationship between learning and teaching, and it came to me that there did not seem to be much of one! The nature of the material we were asked to study also raised questions for me. I had always enjoyed reading, but I thought that many of the books we were asked to read, downright poor. Reading some of them felt like swimming in treacle.[2] Worse, I was seldom able to relate what I was reading to the many years I had spent in classrooms. It took me some years to grasp that this was because many of the people who wrote those books and papers did not write them for practitioners, but for other academics, for that was how to get ahead.[3]

I also noticed that, when we had to write assignments, many of the students went about this by lifting chunks out of a textbook, and embellishing them with a few 'famous' names. Quite a few said that this was the best way to get by, and they did get by. They were a mixture of amused and cynical about it. Others did not set foot in the library the whole time they were on that course. It seemed to me that there was something amiss here, and I was strengthened in that belief by the writers from whom I did learn. These tended to be people who were not academics, or academics who did not work in education.[4] That seemed a very striking situation to me, and I shall return to it later.

The most important thing that this course did for me was to raise questions. The teaching staff on the course framed a few of them for me, but others I stumbled on myself; and what I indirectly discovered thereby, is that learning, real learning, is much more a matter of seeing a question than acquiring an answer.

After that course ended, I went back to teaching: first in a school, then in a technical college; and then in a training department. Eventually, my job became trying to help a wide variety of people engaged in various forms of teaching; and these people ranged from tutors and instructors who taught computing, to those who taught horticulture. Perhaps because the range was so wide, I found that the questions that had arisen for me while I had been at my training college came back to plague me even more. Of course, I did not manage to arrive at any final answers. There are no final answers. However, I would hope that reading this book might help anyone engaged in any kind of teaching to make better sense of his or her experiences.

Preliminaries

In my Introduction, I noted that I encountered two main problems in my teaching. The first arose when I began to teach in a school, and it was how to maintain discipline. The second arose ten years later in my training college, when it dawned on me that many of the things I had taken for granted about teaching needed to be examined. I should first like to consider the problem of maintaining discipline for a few paragraphs, but readers not concerned with schools might like to know that these comments will be very brief.

I found it very difficult to maintain discipline when I began to teach. What seemed to be required was a man who could silence a class with one look, and, in those days, I used to wish I were such a man. Today, that strikes me as much less attractive than it did then, but, either way, I am not that kind of a man. So I felt I had to act in a way that wasn't remotely like me, and I was very unsure of my ability to keep up that pretence for long.

I would walk into a difficult class and try to be friendly. And it didn't work. It wasn't that the children in that school were particularly rowdy. Problems of discipline take different forms in different societies. Where I found myself, at that time, the youngsters didn't jump around much, or do anything remotely vicious. They simply talked loudly to each other and ignored me. For them, going to school consisted mainly of sitting quietly behind desks. But they were bright and energetic. So, in the time it took one of their teachers to walk out, and the next one to walk in, they talked. At the top of their voices. And when a greenhorn like me walked in, they ignored him. And when I raised my voice, I continued to be ignored.

What does one do? I hated shouting. I hated imposing anything on anyone. But there didn't seem to be any choice. So I shouted. And there was quiet. But only for a short time. There were no detentions, so I gave out lines. It turned into a battle, and I hated it. Years later, when I became involved with training people to teach, I realized that it is impossible to teach anyone how to maintain discipline. It isn't something 'out there', which can be learnt like a chemical formula. It is something that relates much more to who one is, mostly to how secure one feels. Qualities like that cannot be taught. They can only be developed in a supportive environment.

The above creates a problem. On the one hand, I am aware that many people who intend to teach are keen to gain information on how to maintain discipline.

However, on the other hand, I have come to realize that the problem of maintaining discipline (in a difficult class) hides an even larger problem. That problem, as I have already noted, is that a great deal of what we tend to take for granted about teaching needs to be examined. Under these circumstances, it seems best to begin by discussing, not the question of discipline, but how the experience of teaching has the odd effect of hiding the main problem that all teachers have.

⅋

When I first began to teach, it often struck me that the teachers around me seldom talked much about how they taught. I regretted that, because I was new to the job and often felt lost. Years later, I grasped that most teachers are concerned about how they teach, but that they seldom express that concern. I believe one reason for this is related to the fact that one's teaching involves who one is as a person, and that is not so easy to talk about. So, instead of talking about their teaching, teachers tend to follow roughly the same approach that was used on them. That is, they tend to walk into a classroom, perhaps ask a few questions, perhaps give out some material, but when it comes to their own input, they tend to do that by 'explaining'.

This 'explaining' is sometimes called the 'transmission method' of teaching.[1] In adopting that approach, teachers sometimes use a handout, an overhead projector, or a model; and of course, they also do other things, like set an exercise, or have a discussion. But anyone who has observed teachers at work, including those who say that they use a 'student-centred' approach, will know that a great deal of teaching is done by explaining. This method has certainly been going strong for a long time, and it was extensively used in Europe during the Middle Ages. In those days, all books were hand-written, and therefore very expensive, so they were far beyond what most learners could afford to buy. The main method of conveying knowledge to a group of people was therefore by word of mouth. Also, as paper was very expensive, learners couldn't afford to take many notes, so they had to try and remember a good deal of what they were told. Now we have pens, paper and print, but 'teaching by explaining' is still very common.

In my Introduction, I noted that I took this way of going about things so much for granted that I hardly noticed it. But it is also the case that I often felt an underlying unease. Sometimes this unease took a concrete form, as when I felt uncomfortable about being 'out front'. Other times I wondered what it was about me that had got me into teaching.

Sometimes, I experimented with a cassette recorder. I asked my learners if they would mind if I brought one in, and, when they said they did not, I recorded a lesson. Back home, I'd listen, and try to work out how I could improve. There would be my voice, sounding strange at first, and sometimes there would be the voices of some learners. Occasionally, there would be a few things I wished I had said or done a little differently; but there was never anything solidly 'there' that gave me any clues about how I could improve.

Much later, I realized that my trouble was that I didn't really know what would be 'better'. All I had was a vague notion that my lessons could somehow be 'better'. To put it a little more precisely, I would say that I had no analytical tools with which to examine my teaching. I was like a quack doctor examining a patient. The patient says he has a headache, but the 'doctor' hasn't got any concepts like 'blood pressure' that might help to explain the ache. At other times, I asked my learners what they thought of my lessons. I tried to convey that I was sincere; that I was not – as far as I could make out – on an ego trip; and to save them from embarrassment, I asked them for written comments and suggested that they leave their names off the page.

I have to report that I never got anything really useful by doing that. Whatever was said, was always either friendly or peripheral; things like, 'We reckon your lessons are OK'; or, 'You could have told us so-and-so in an earlier lesson.' Of course, those learners had the same problem as I did. They did not have any analytical tools with which to make perceptive suggestions.

☙

Occasionally, I heard another teacher express the same kind of doubts. But more often than not, another teacher would then say that ours was a 'tried and tested' method; that is, a method that produces high examination pass rates. I used to find that comment unconvincing. Both personal experience and research had shown me that the single most important factor contributing to exam pass rates is what the learners themselves bring to their studies. Other factors could be the learners' previous teaching, the teaching of another teacher in another subject, or the general atmosphere in a school.[2]

During those discussions, I also remembered that the way teachers frequently learn is often quite different from how they expect their students to learn. A good example is teachers who begin their career teaching one subject, then move into teaching another. Some go on courses for this, but many teach themselves. Yet, they use quite a different method when they teach others. I could not but ask myself: Why use one method on oneself, and another on others? Years passed like this, and I did not resolve any of these questions. I think that this was partly because I was only half aware of them, and partly because I was gaining more confidence in what I was already doing. It was only later that I realized that teachers use whatever method they do, not because they have systematically studied it and found that it generates good pass rates, but because it was used on them.

Teachers are sometimes accused of being rather conservative. I don't think that they are any more so than the members of any other occupational group. But I often noticed a strong resistance, among many teachers, when an alternative approach to teaching was mentioned. That is, when the topic of 'alternative methods' came up in a discussion, one of the teachers present was sure to say, 'We have to cover the syllabus.' That is no ordinary statement. It is a magic statement! When it is made, you sense that the person who has made it considers that the discussion has come to an end. But there came a time, in my own case, when I began to wonder: '*Who* covers the syllabus?' I mean, what is the point of a teacher covering a syllabus in class, if the learners have to cover it at home? Furthermore, if one recalls one's own experiences as a learner, one soon remembers that the bulk of what one learnt took place outside the classroom. This suggests that a teacher's contribution is an incidental but important one. It seems to be largely a matter of conveying a certain attitude, and serving as a model of competence. But I can't say that I began to see the implication of such thoughts to my own teaching. That came later, when I became involved with training. But even then, the change came piecemeal, as the rest of this section will show.

☙

When we have something complicated to do, we often have to spend some time studying how to do it. We might decide to go on a course, or we might try to find out what has been discovered about the matter by others who have done some research. But my experience of teachers suggested that most of them were sceptical about the value of research. Here is a typical example: 'My attitude to educational research was antagonistic. I was irritated by the negative tone of many of the research reports, and suspicious of the methods used to collect data. The reports were often couched in jargon and statistics, and were published in journals that rarely reached staff-room shelves. . . . We seemed to live in separate worlds. A prestigious research industry seemed to be thriving at the expense of school practitioners rather than in support of them.'[3]

Readers might here recall the critical comments I made in my Introduction about the material we had to study in my training college. But there came a time when I began to have doubts about that as well. For, all around me, there were people doing a variety of jobs, and it was clear that some were happy to coast along on their personal experiences, while others went off and did some systematic study. What I could also usually see was that those who did some systematic study usually gained a better understanding of what they were about than the others. Furthermore, what I increasingly could not understand was why teaching should be considered so different.

Many people believe that, to become an effective teacher, one must have a certain flair, and that this must be followed by gaining some experience. Experience is often considered especially important, and that was certainly the way I had seen things for many years. But here, too, I was becoming doubtful. Readers might recall that, in my Introduction, I noted that I had felt considerable unease about the way I had been teaching, but that nothing much had come of that. I also noted that I had had to go to a training college ten years after I had begun to teach, and that the main effect of that had been to make me question the experiences of teaching that I had had 'til then. The question that I then found myself asking could therefore be put like this: If personal experience is so important, why hadn't I learnt more from my personal experience? After all, by then I had had about fifteen years of experience as a learner, and another ten years as a teacher!

By about this time, I had also begun to do some reading, and it was becoming clear to me that one of the main effects of personal experience is to corroborate for us what we expect to experience. In other words, it looks as if, once we have got used to doing something in a certain kind of way, our experience often has the effect of reinforcing the way we already do it. It was also becoming clear to me that what we can learn from personal experience is limited. Would personal experience ever teach us that water is a compound of two gases? Or that the earth is a ball? We could walk the earth for a thousand years and still think it flat. In fact, the more we walked, the more sure we would be that, aside from ranges of hills and valleys, it *is* flat. Those kinds of considerations suggested to me that we must often escape our immediate experiences if we are to make progress.[4]

I often thought of the above when taking part in a 'teaching workshop'. At first, I welcomed the opportunity that such meetings provided to get together with other teachers. I enjoyed some of the contacts, and sometimes picked up an interesting idea. But I seldom gained any powerful new insights in that way. Indeed, if I am to be honest, I should say that I found that a great many platitudes tended to be expressed in such workshops. For my part, I have found that I tend to make substantial progress in one of two ways. One is when I begin to have fundamental doubts about what I am doing. The other is when I come across a new way of seeing things which puts my personal experiences into a new perspective.[5] In other words, I would say that, before we can reflect on our experiences in a powerful new way, we usually have to view them from a new frame of reference. That seldom happens when we meet with others, discuss our experiences, or reflect on them on our own.[6]

I could put the above a little more technically like this. Although it is fashionable to say that theories grow best out of practice, and reflection on practice, my own experience has shown me that things are not quite like that. In short, I believe that we tend to see our practice largely in terms of our past experiences, that is, in terms of a theory we already possess. Indeed, I believe that we tend to view everything we do in terms of an existing 'theory'. How could we do anything, even stretch out an arm, unless we had some kind of 'theory' or model, no matter how tentative or unformulated, to guide us somewhere in the back of our mind?

In the case of teaching, our theory will be made up of all our past experiences of being a learner; and we will tend to view teaching from that frame of reference, and mostly without being clearly aware of it. In short, I am suggesting that our theories often come before our practice; and not only do they then help to determine our practice, they also shape how we see our practice. Of course, none of this is to deny the importance of experience. On the contrary. As readers will see, in this book I shall frequently argue for the importance of experience. Here I am only suggesting that our personal experiences tend to be limited.

Another problem I encountered when teaching was being discussed, was the variety of topics that can arise. Teaching touches on so many issues! Topics that often arise in such discussions include resources, race, gender, equal opportunities, minority interests, political influence, methods of assessment and, especially, administrative matters. These are important topics. But knowledge of them must not obscure the need to study the learning process. Unfortunately, the former topics are often of a pressing nature, so they tend to shift attention away from the learning process, with the result that teaching remains largely a matter of going into a classroom and learning from experience.

I could sum up like this. I believe that it is very important to have experiences, and to reflect on them. But I would argue that that is not enough. I would argue that, if we wish to make substantial progress when dealing with a complex task, we must also do some systematic study. Earlier I mentioned the disappointment I felt with the bulk of the material on learning and teaching that I was asked to study at my training college. But that cannot mean that all research into learning and teaching is useless. It simply makes no sense to believe that research can be useful in everything except in teaching.

⁖

For a long time, there has been a great deal of controversy about how one should teach. In recent years, there has been considerable talk about such things as 'student-centred learning' or 'resource-based workshops', and I happen to believe these approaches have their merits. However, if one observes teachers actually at work, one soon discovers that there are almost as many interpretations of these approaches as there are teachers. Moreover, I was often troubled to find that some teachers did not appear to know much about the origin of these approaches. Being so-called 'student centred' is one example. Few of the teachers I observed who used this term came even near to implementing this approach in the manner intended by Carl Rogers, the man from whom this approach stems.

Perhaps such ambiguity is understandable. Many writers on teaching maintain that it is the kind of subject, or the kind of learners that one has, that should determine how one teaches. Others argue that, as teaching is such a complex activity, there is no one effective way of doing it. Others say that, as people are all different, one must find a way to teach that suits one's particular learners. Others point out that there is still a great deal of controversy among researchers about what constitutes good teaching. Some maintain that research can be helpful, but only if teachers themselves do it, while others argue that research is out of place in such a personal matter. Another view is that learners themselves should determine how they are taught. Given all this conflicting advice, it is difficult to know where to begin if one would like to improve one's teaching.

Perhaps in reaction to this kind of controversy, many of those engaged in the training of teachers take a practical approach. They maintain that teaching is a skill, and can be compared with skiing. If you want to learn how to ski, the best thing to do is to get on to some snow and go. That is, you learn best by practice, with perhaps an expert alongside to give you some tips. I believe that there are at least two things fundamentally the matter with this approach when it comes to teaching. Consider surgeons. They also have to be skilled. They have to be able to use a knife and catgut with dexterity. But the 'skill' required to mend a damaged knee is obviously only a part of the expertise a good surgeon possesses. Such a skill is practised under the control of a much higher-order ability. In the case of a surgeon, that must include, at the very least, a powerful understanding of physiology and anatomy. Is mastery of that kind of knowledge also a 'skill'?

We speak of a 'skilled' or an 'unskilled' craftsman, and the word 'skill' carries a distinct and very important meaning here. It refers to an ability to carry out a complex task efficiently, and often in an almost routine kind of way. Usually, too, the parameters are not too wide, and the subject matter does not require systematic study. If so, what do we mean by the words 'an unskilled surgeon'? A person who is clumsy with knife and catgut? It is as if terms like 'knowledge', 'understanding', 'insight', 'scholarship', 'expertise' and 'skill' have all become interchangeable now. The increasing use of the word 'skill' seems to be part of an attempt to make anything that requires systematic study easily digestible. Instead of trying to understand 'what is', you concentrate on 'how to'.[7] That may be good for computer maintenance, but it is surely an un-educational way of going about things.[8] The degeneracy of the word 'skill' is perhaps best seen when it is used in a phrase like 'social skills'. In this instance, manipulation has replaced things like empathy, fellow feeling, curiosity, friendliness and charity.

Commerce and the mass media also come into the matter. All over the world today, there is an ideology of competitiveness, and, from commerce, it creeps into all occupations, including teaching. This ideology favours the 'fast solution', and hence action is preferred to reflection, and knowledge to understanding. Moreover, solutions come by the dozen, often driven more by changing fashions than deep reflection. In the mass media, we have chat shows, quiz shows, sound bites, and hence slick superficiality. As a result, we get an ever-increasing trivialization of everything. How can people carry out a complex task, unless they first study the nature of that task? In the case of skiing, one does not have to understand much about the physics of acceleration, or the chemistry of snow. But in the case of car mechanics, for example, it isn't enough to know how to wield a spanner. One must also spend a few years studying how cars function.

But if one believes that teaching is a 'skill' or a 'competence', it can hardly follow that it is necessary to systematically study how human beings learn before one teaches them. 'Skill' in teaching usually includes things like being able to conduct a discussion, stand at a blackboard, show a DVD/video, use a computer, or draw up a lesson plan. Not surprisingly, all these 'competencies' are easy to demonstrate. But how can one be *sure* that these are the important factors in teaching, if one has not first studied how people learn? Or how can one be sure that it is these factors that distinguish a mediocre teacher from an excellent one? I could put this matter in another way. I believe most educators would agree that one of the most valuable abilities anyone can learn is the ability to question the validity of anything, including a 'competence'. But is such an ability a 'competence'? Everyone agrees that the ability to pass a written exam need not indicate a competence to do an actual job, but is there not a danger, in going in the opposite direction, in emphasizing demonstrable competences, that one trivializes the educational process?[9] Notice here that to learn a 'competence' is to learn a technique, and a technique is a method that has been standardized in order to achieve a certain end with a minimum amount of individual initiative.

When people begin to teach, they tend to like the 'skills' approach. It seems straightforward, and that seems a blessing when one is trying to master the highly complex activity of teaching. To teach, one must first master a subject, and then acquire the ability to convey that subject to others. And one has to work with the most complicated things on earth: other people. In such circumstances, it isn't surprising that people should want tools that will help them, and immediately. This brings me to my second worry about taking a practical approach too quickly. Is there not a danger that, in stressing the practical, we might apply the practical in the service of a half-baked, perhaps even a vicious, fad? Everyone who has worked in education for more than ten years will know that what most powerfully drives a new approach is seldom a carefully worked-out conception, but often no more than a kind of flavour of the times, or a bunch of slogans.

I suggested earlier that the experience – the demanding experience – of teaching, has the odd effect of hiding the real problem that all teachers have. And that problem, it seems to me, is to understand how people learn. If that is broadly correct, it follows that it might be best to ignore teaching altogether initially. In other words, it seems to me that deciding how to teach, without first having studied how people learn, is like deciding to use a screwdriver before one has understood the nature of the job.

There is another attitude towards teaching that should be considered. It is the one that holds that a teacher's job is to 'meet the needs of students'. This belief is often coupled with the idea that students, especially adult students, 'know what they need'. It sounds almost perverse to question such an attitude, especially if one remembers that it arose in reaction to the absurd belief, held for many years, that learners are empty vessels that teachers know best how to fill. But I found that, when I acted on such attitudes, I often ran into trouble. For example, when I asked my learners what they need, they nearly always voiced immediate needs. But these are often in conflict with long-term needs. Here is just one example.

When I asked instructors or teachers what they needed, they often said, 'Ways to motivate learners.' That was exactly the kind of thing I used to say when I began to teach! Many years later, it dawned on me that wanting to know how to motivate learners is a mistake, because it takes one in completely the wrong direction, – the wrong direction, because it places an emphasis on teaching rather than on learning. More on that later.

I am of course aware that to suggest that learners often do not know what they really need runs the risk of making them sound childish, and me condescending. But there is nothing unusual about teaching in this respect. In every profession, one will hear thoughtful practitioners say that their clients often do not know what they really need. One hears doctors and nurses say that they must sometimes work hard to convince patients that they do not really need what they think they need. Solicitors will tell you that they often have a hard time convincing some of their clients that they should not do what they feel they need to do. And counsellors and psychotherapists soon learn that one thing is for sure: Whatever a client might initially say, it is seldom what he or she ultimately needs.

None of this is to suggest that 'experts' know best, or that one should not listen to a client. Such notions are so absurd that they do not merit discussion. I am only suggesting that the question of 'needs' is a complex one. It is also the case that one of the best ways to describe learning is to say that it implies change, and we all know that change can be very difficult. So, if learning implies change, and if change is often difficult, then learning must also sometimes be difficult.

Furthermore, the more powerful the learning, the greater the difficulty. A good teacher will try to minimize that difficulty, but there is no such thing as significant learning without considerable difficulty. That is why, on looking back, we often find that our best teachers were challenging, so challenging that they sometimes upset us. Such observations are not easy to square with the belief that it is a teacher's job to 'meet the needs of students'. Much current writing on teaching, especially the teaching of adults, makes inexplicable the fate of Socrates and Jesus – the fact that teachers can be put to death for their teaching.

There is also the problem of standards. For example, a learner might want to be an electrician. That is his or her 'need'. But how is a teacher to act if a learner needs an electrician's certificate, but is not prepared to put in the work required to become a competent electrician? What about the community that needs competent electricians? It is possible to read current books on teaching, and find a hundred references to 'the needs of the student', and not even one to 'the needs of the community'. Yet, in all the humanities (anthropology, sociology, politics, economics, history) a common theme is the frequent tension between the needs of the individual and the needs of the community. Unfortunately, in especially the west today, we live in a climate of phoney democracy, bogus equality and mistaken relativity, and one of their effects is to generate a devaluation of standards in the interest of pseudo fulfilment.

This increasingly strong emphasis on self carries with it an unexamined assumption that happiness or satisfaction is a matter of achieving 'one's potential'. It is a kind of 'cult of the self', and in developed countries it increasingly pervades life from the factory to the family.[10] One would have to look for a long time to find some expression of the idea that many of our needs, and their satisfaction, are profoundly social in nature. It is even rare today to find an expression of the idea that there is a deep reward to be found in working towards something that transcends one's own needs. It is a sign of our times that this idea only surfaced in Britain during the last war. It is as if many people are blind to essentials 'til the chips are down. I would not want to pretend that these are simple matters. I raise them here only to indicate why I sometimes take an approach that might not be fashionable at present.

⅋

There is one more aspect of training I should consider, and it is whether teaching is a profession or an occupation. This is a large and complex topic, and it would take one beyond the remit of this book to consider it in detail.[11] I shall return to this topic at the end of this book, but, before that, there is one aspect of this topic that is immediately relevant. I have in mind the fact that, in every profession, one must master a certain body of knowledge to become a member of it; but that is not the case in teaching. That is, one does not have to study teaching in order to become a teacher. It is true that, in order to teach, one must first study a subject like chemistry, computing, cooking, carpentry, or oceanography. But it isn't knowledge of one of these that makes one a teacher. After all, one can be a chemist and not be a teacher.

I should perhaps add here that, in most countries, to become a 'qualified' *school* teacher, one has to study for a Certificate of Education. But the course of study for this qualification does not usually include the systematic study of an agreed body of knowledge. And there are many educational establishments where no teaching qualification whatsoever is required before one can teach in them. A remarkable example of this is universities. An essential characteristic of university lecturers is said to be their quest for evidence, but they seek no evidence whatsoever for one of the things in which they are most engaged: teaching. They can ignore this requirement because they are said to be engaged primarily in research. But a high proportion of them produce no research, and in the case of the majority who do, this work sinks into oblivion soon after it has been published. In any case, it is a simple fact that teaching is one of the prime activities for which many lecturers are paid. The same situation holds in medical education. Yet, no study of teaching is required of those engaged in this enterprise, presumably because they consider teaching either a self-evident activity, or below their dignity. Interestingly enough, tutors in schools of nursing often hold a teaching qualification; so the global picture is one in which the higher your status, the less you believe in the need for some training in order to teach effectively. Here I have mentioned just a few institutions in which teaching takes place, but of course there are dozens, from police training establishments to schools of librarianship, and in none is there a requirement that those who teach in them should have had any training in teaching.

So, teaching is quite different from all other 'professions'. Earlier, I mentioned car mechanics. Car mechanics are not usually considered to be in a 'profession', but they have to study how cars function before they are considered competent to work on them. But teachers are not required to study how people learn before they teach them. One assumes that those who hold such a view must believe that people are a good deal less complicated than cars. We consider a person 'a professional' because a professional has learnt both the 'practice' *and* the 'theory' of a subject. As a result, such people are usually able to tackle a practical task with a greater likelihood of success than a person who has had only experience. The best way I have heard that observation expressed is by the statement that 'there is nothing as practical as a good theory'.[12]

I would summarize my arguments in this section like this: people who teach, and have a sense of responsibility about it, must surely study *two* subjects. One is the subject they teach; and the other is how to teach it.

☙

There are a great many books on teaching. On closer inspection, one will often find that some of them are not about teaching, but about education; and the best of these help one to see that education is about more than only teaching. However, some books on teaching consist of no more than slogans. I find this practice irritating, and the books that contain the slogans, that express the ideas with which I am most in sympathy, often irritate me the most. Examples of such slogans are 'empowering students' or 'student-centred teaching'; and my irritation stems from the fact that the writers who use those slogans the most, tend to provide the fewest practical clues as to how one might achieve such aims.

As for factual material on teaching, there is no lack of it. There are many textbooks, a great many research papers, and lots of accounts of practical teaching on offer. I have found some of these helpful, but I don't think that they are enough. I believe that a general theory of learning and teaching is required that would embrace the most useful bits of information we already have.

At this point, I should perhaps comment on my use of the word 'theory'. Consider, for example, what happens when we take a car to a garage to be mended. We drive in, and perhaps tell a mechanic that the car isn't stopping properly. The mechanic will probably ask for further information, and we might say that the car pulls to the right when we put on the brakes. The mechanic will then probably say something like, 'Ah, I see . . .' Then, as he or she continues talking, or booking the car in, or being rude, he (if it is a man) will be looking inside his head at the model he has of the total braking system of that car. What we have said isn't enough. The mechanic has to slot our information into something larger.

For example, no mechanic would start by dismantling the right front wheel in the circumstances I have outlined. If anything, when a mechanic begins to work on such a car, he will probably dismantle the left front wheel first. This is because, if the car pulls to the right, it is probably because the brake on the left front wheel is not functioning properly. In other words, when one goes about a complex task, it isn't enough to know a few facts. One must also have something in one's head that holds those facts together. This 'something' is provided by a model. And by looking at this model inside one's head, one can get a picture of how the various facts of a matter hang together.

In the above, I have used the word 'model' to describe the sort of picture that experienced people have inside their head when they are considering how to tackle a complex task. Another word that I could have used is 'theory'. But that word 'theory' is a little problematic because it is used in several ways. For example, the word 'theory' is often used in the same way as the word 'idea' or 'notion'. Thus, people might say, 'I have a theory it is going to rain tomorrow.' In that sentence, the word 'idea' or 'notion' could have been used instead of the word 'theory'. A second example, of how the word 'theory' is often used, is when, for instance in medical education, people say, 'This morning the students will have three hours of "theory", and in the afternoon they will have two hours of "practicals" on the ward.' In this example, the word 'theory' is being used to denote something done in the head rather than practically or physically.

Notice that, in both the above examples, the word 'theory' might convey something a little vague; and, by implication at least, that what really counts is practical knowledge. But it is clear, from the example of the car mechanic given above, that practical knowledge, in the absence of a sound theory, isn't just useless, it is downright dangerous. Imagine having a car fixed by a mechanic who is good with a spanner, but has no clear understanding of how the total braking system of the car works.

In other words, if one wishes to carry out a complex task, it isn't enough to have several bits of information. One needs an overall picture that helps to integrate all the available information into a coherent whole. Such a picture is called a 'theory', and that is how the word 'theory' is used in these pages. And, as was illustrated with that car mechanic, it isn't only scientists who use theories. Everyone has some sort of a general picture or theory in his or her head when they go about a complex task. The main difference between people in general, and scientists, is that scientists try to state their theories as precisely as possible. They do this because that helps other researchers to amend or question those theories; and, in this way, progress is sometimes made. For, unlike what is sometimes assumed, a theory isn't a bit of waffle engraved in stone. Having a theory is important because it is a clear statement, and that allows people to examine it, amend it, or scrap it. It is for these reasons that this book has, near its beginning, the sentence: 'There is nothing as practical as a good theory.'

It doesn't of course follow from the above that teaching is like car mechanics, or physics. Unlike the case in the latter two subjects, the personal is often very important in teaching; and the personal is difficult to encompass in any theory. Indeed, it is often impossible to do that. But how one teaches is not just a personal matter. It also involves the more objective matter of the process of learning. And, as there is a good deal of evidence available on how people learn, it would be irresponsible to ignore it.

In short, and as I see the matter, what teachers need is a theory of learning and teaching, in which everything I have learnt, and which has been discovered about learning and teaching, hangs together to make a reasonably clear and coherent picture. That should provide anyone engaged in any kind of teaching with something solid they can use practically, and that is surely better than everyone doing their own thing.

At this point, I should perhaps also mention that a theory does not grow out of an accumulation of facts, as is sometimes assumed. Popper notes that progress, in both our general understanding and in science, is thought to come about in one of two ways: either when we acquire new evidence, or when we manage to better organize the evidence we already have. He goes on to say that, although such a view is not wrong, it misses the point. It is, he writes, 'too reminiscent of Bacon's induction: too suggestive of his industrious gathering of the "countless grapes, ripe and in season", from which he expected the wine of science to flow; of his myth of a scientific method that starts from observation and experiment and then proceeds to theories. This legendary method', he notes, 'still inspires some of the new sciences which try to practise it, because of the prevalent belief that it is the method of experimental physics.' That is, Popper notes that progress in science does not come about because more and more evidence is accumulated. He writes instead, 'bold ideas, unjustified anticipations, and speculative thought, are our only means for interpreting nature'; and it is these that lead to fruitful theories. These theories, in turn, must of course be tested. In that way, more evidence is also accumulated, – evidence that either corroborates or refutes our 'bold ideas'.[13]

Here, someone might want to object that, although the above sounds plausible, people who teach should not be in the business of simply applying a theory that has been handed down to them. In any case, when something is simply handed down, it is seldom used intelligently. This suggests that people are more likely to be favourably disposed toward considering a certain theory if they are reminded that, as they are not robots, there must be some sort of a theory, or notion, or idea, already in their head when they set about doing anything of some complexity. And if that is the case, it would probably be a good idea to express one's existing ideas, because, in doing that, one might see what is sound and what could be improved in one's ideas. Two things would then ideally follow. One would be that the notorious gap between theory and practice might begin to narrow; and the other might be that one would begin to compare the ideas, or rudimentary theory at the back of one's head, with the kind of theories that are on offer. Whatever the case, as I do not know of a book which contains the kind of theory of learning and teaching I have in mind, I have decided – so help me – to try to put one together myself.[14] And I am encouraged to do this in part because of what has been discovered about the difference between teachers who find their work satisfying compared with those who do not. The Swiss investigator Huberman, for example, noted:

'Put briefly: teachers who steered clear of reforms or other multiple-classroom innovations, but who invested consistently in classroom-level experiments . . . were more likely to be satisfied later on in their careers than most others, and far more likely to be satisfied than their peers who had been heavily involved in school-wide or district-wide projects . . . an early concern for instructional efficiency was one of the strongest predictors of ultimate satisfaction. Inversely, heavy involvement in school-wide innovation was a fairly strong predictor of "disenchantment".' And this writer concluded:

'. . . there emerges an image of the harmonious teaching career that is perhaps surprising in its simplicity. It would seem that the . . . teachers in our sample thrive when they are able to tinker productively inside classrooms in order to obtain the instructional and relational effects that they are after. . . . To do this, they appear to need manageable working conditions, opportunities to experiment modestly without strong sanctions if things go awry, periodic shifts in role assignments, access to collegial expertise and external stimulation, and a good shot at significant learning outcomes for their pupils.'[15]

The present book takes the more modest route. It seeks to find what is common in 'instructional efficiency' rather than to urge 'school-wide innovation'. That is not to argue that innovation is unimportant. However, although the word 'innovation' is frequently used with respect to organizations, and has highly positive connotations, on closer examination one notices that this word has about the same status as the word 'new' in advertising. That is, it takes only a moment of reflection to recall that 'innovations' seem to come and go. For example, anyone who is at all acquainted with the educational scene will have heard about the new mathematics, teaching by objectives, and language laboratories; but these things tend to come and go like fashions in clothing. They sound exciting when first introduced, become repetitious, and then boring. I suspect that such talk often suggests a search for solutions that are superficial and avoid a more serious consideration of the real nature of the problem. In short, it seems to me that 'innovations' are likely to work best when considered in concrete detail, in the context of real teaching situations, and in an attempt to build a testable theory.[16]

What I have noted so far, then, suggests a certain format for this book. It suggests that the first half should contain material on how people learn, followed by a second half on how that material might serve as a guide for teaching practice. And I would hope that readers who have examined both halves might then be in a better position to make some informed choices.

Part I

Learning

Chapter 1

Motivation

A question that teachers often ask themselves is how to motivate their learners. That is an understandable concern, for it is commonly held that teachers must be able to do this. But this must also be a troubling concern, for I think most of us would be hard pressed to name more than one or two people whom we know who are genuinely stimulating, and hence able to motivate others.

The questions we ask determine the answers we get, and to ask a question that takes one in the worst possible direction must surely be a bad way to begin. I say this because I shall try to show that no one can motivate anyone. It took me a long time to reach that position. For years, I took it for granted that it was my job to motivate my learners. Many textbooks on teaching outline a hierarchy of human needs, followed by suggestions on how, once the learners have had a good sleep and a decent breakfast, one can motivate them. And after I became involved with training, I became even more aware that many teachers are concerned with this matter, so it seems best to begin with it. In short, the central issue, it seems to me, is this: Everyone is already motivated.[1] To try to motivate someone is like trying to breathe their air for them.

At this point, some readers might want to throw up their hands (or their latest meal) and say something like, 'Don't make me laugh. You should see my lot. About the last thing on earth that they are, is motivated! And if I didn't try to motivate them, they'd fall asleep.' It isn't difficult to imagine the kind of learners that such a speaker might have: Rows of unresponsive faces, even if that teacher tries to do handstands. What does one do in such circumstances?

I have just suggested that everyone is already motivated, in the same way that everyone is already breathing and digesting. If so, when one of those functions does not work properly, we do not immediately set about carrying out that function for that person. We try to find out what is impeding it. In other words, if being motivated is like breathing or digesting, then being motivated is intrinsic to being alive.[2] And if that is so, it is the absence, not the presence of motivation that needs investigating. Notice that, in comparing being motivated with breathing, I take what might be called a biological orientation.[3] I invite readers to explore this way of viewing things in the next few sections to see where it might take us.

A lesson usually begins when a teacher greets the learners, announces the topic of the lesson, and begins to teach. But one could begin differently. To illustrate, perhaps I could describe what I sometimes do. Having greeted the learners, I give out the following case study.

Case study: Simon Winch

Please read the following account. Then, after discussion with your neighbour, jot down your answer to the question at the end.

For many years, Simon Winch had an old-fashioned jewellery shop in Deansvale High Street. He retired last year, and soon found that he did not always have enough to do. Being an active man, that upset him. Then, one day, his daughter Mavis, who teaches in one of the town's schools, put him in touch with the local adult education officer. Simon met her, and it was arranged that he teach 'jewellery making' one evening a week to an adult education evening class, beginning the following September.

Simon had no qualifications, but he had always been interested in jewellery and he had read widely. He was also a good craftsman. In fact, with the spread of chain stores, most of his trade in the years before he had retired had been in repairing jewellery and clocks. Simon put a lot of work into preparing for his class. He went to the Victoria and Albert Museum in London several times during the summer, and he bought many slides. He did a good deal of careful reading, and he made many notes. The education officer was able to let him have £50, and with this, he bought a few tools and a small stock of silver. He was told that at least twelve people would have to enrol for his class for it to run, so he was rather apprehensive when September finally arrived. On the day of his first class, he was excited, and then delighted to find twenty-three people there. Simon greeted the students warmly; and then he launched into a history of jewellery making. He was pleased he had the slides; they illuminated very well what he wanted to say. The slide-projector worked like a charm, and he felt he held his audience well. He found that teaching came naturally to him. But then, he had always known that teachers were born not made.

After a twenty-minute break, he began the second part of the lesson. For that first evening, he had decided to talk about precious stones: their physical properties, and what this implied about working with them. He began confidently enough, but, after a short while, he began to feel uneasy. Some of the students did not seem to be listening. As there was so much to explain, Simon began to hurry. And, what with the way time was passing, and the rather bored look on the faces of some of the students, Simon finished the second part of that lesson in rather a fluster. For the next lesson, Simon decided to show more slides. He felt that these had held the interest of the students well. And, as he showed them, he would talk about the physical properties of stones. He had heard that it was important to use visual aids in teaching, and his first lesson had proved that.

At first, the lesson went well. But, after about half an hour, he again sensed that not all the students were listening. That bothered him. He decided to change his plan for the second half of the class. Instead of talking about stones, he would take a practical tack and talk about the kind of tools that were used in his trade and the need for safe practices. Then he would show the class the tools he had bought, and tell them that they would soon be using them. And that is how he began. But, after about five minutes, one of the women said, 'I came here because I wanted to learn how to clean and rethread some pearls. Forsters want £35 to do the job. I think that's too much. I'm sure I could do it if I had a little help.'

The comment annoyed Simon. He said, 'It takes a lot of experience to clean pearls properly. Threading them isn't that easy either. But we'll come to that. I've got "Pearls" down as a topic for a fortnight today.' Before he could continue, a man called out, 'I'm interested in old clocks. I've always found them fascinating. I'm retired now. I'd like to get my hands on a few old ones, and mend 'em. I was told this class would be about that.' Simon said, 'We can't do everything all at once. I was an apprentice for five years, and I worked at cleaning watches for two years before I ever mended one! But we're going to look at clocks and watches soon.' Another man called out, 'Things go faster today. I really did hope we'd be making a few things by now. Do we really have to wait two years?' For the first time, there were a few smiles.

Then a young man with an earring spoke. Simon was surprised he spoke so well. He said, 'I have a friend who makes modern jewellery. You may not call it jewellery.' He smiled. 'You know, it's made of wire and various beads. I rather like it, and it sells quite well. I don't care much for the present job I have. My friend sells in markets, and I'd like to spend some time out of doors like that. I wonder if we could do something that would help me? Others might be interested?' He looked around. Several people nodded. Simon said, 'Well, I must say . . . it hadn't crossed my mind.' He was thinking of the boxes of slides he had prepared. He said, 'Let me think about it?' The young man nodded.

Simon brought out the tools. He was a little worried they might disappear. But they came back very quickly, much more quickly than he had anticipated. The students didn't seem particularly interested in them. He had a few precious stones in his pocket, 'just in case he needed to motivate the students'. He held up a diamond, and said something about carats. He thought he sensed some interest, but was relieved when the end of the lesson came.

On his way home, Simon felt bad. The notes in his pocket seemed to mock him; the time and effort he had put into their preparation seemed childish; and he had always suspected that there were a lot of stupid people around. Still, that young man with the earring obviously wasn't stupid. Simon decided gloomily that teaching wasn't for him. But he didn't know how to get out of his commitment to teach for two terms. Deansvale was a small place. He couldn't just chuck the teaching after twenty-three people had paid to do the class. As soon as he got home, he phoned Mavis. Perhaps she would have some advice.

Question: If you were Mavis, what would you say to Simon?

This case study usually generates some discussion. A few participants nearly always suggest that Simon should have consulted his learners much earlier. If the matter does not arise during the discussion, I ask whether Simon could have motivated his learners more. The participants usually shrug their shoulders. They clearly consider the question irrelevant. Several are likely to suggest that Simon should have enabled his learners to tackle practical tasks much sooner. This is an important point, and I shall return to it.

In the above, the course is a non-vocational, adult, evening class. Can one extrapolate from that, to a class of children learning mathematics, or to medical students in a teaching hospital? I believe one can. I believe it makes sense to begin by greeting the learners, then to say something like, 'We are here to study biology (music or business administration) and I wonder how you think we should begin?' In the case of young children, the content would obviously be different, but the orientation could be the same. In a nutshell, it would be a matter of coming down from an accepted format, and meeting the learners on their ground. Quite possibly, having begun like that, a teacher might end up doing a good deal of what she or he had intended to do; but it would be done with the students' concerns in mind, and that could make a very big difference. Matters would obviously be more complicated on an examinable course. What learners might want to do might not be what it is necessary to do. Nevertheless, it seems safe to assume that learning is likely to be encouraged if a collaborative atmosphere is fostered from the beginning.[4]

I would not want to suggest that beginning a lesson in the way just outlined is some kind of magic formula. That would be absurd, and it has been my experience that, no matter how much I have consulted learners, many problems remain. I would only suggest that, by beginning in this collaborative kind of way, teachers are less likely to inhibit their students' motivation to learn.

&

When we find ourselves in a room with other people, we usually talk to some of them. We might not want to talk to everybody there, and we might not begin to talk immediately, but most of us will feel like talking to some of the people in the room to some extent or other. This inclination to communicate seems to be true of most mammals. Sheep, goats, cows, horses, monkeys, seals – all these tend to seek the company of their own kind; and each communicates with others of its kind in one way or other. We consider this 'normal'.

Compare this with what happens in many classrooms. In most classrooms, the learners don't talk much, and it is usually the teacher who does the talking. But how appropriate is this? Consider the work of Vygotsky. This man did his work some seventy years ago, but he is still one of the most respected researchers in this field. In one of his experiments, this man placed a desirable object in a cupboard so that a child would have some difficulty reaching it. He then found that a child not only *acts* in its attempt to get at that object, but that it also *speaks*, and that this speaking arises quite spontaneously. He also discovered that, when a child is prevented from speaking, its *actions* tend to be inhibited.

None of this will surprise parents. Most will have heard their children doing exactly what Vygotsky described. However, because a child talking, as it is trying to do something, seems so artless, we may not grasp its significance. After repeating such experiments many times, Vygotsky concluded: 'A child's speech is as important as the role of action in attaining a goal. Children not only speak about what they are doing; their speech and action are part of *one and the same complex psychological function*, directed toward the solution of the problem at hand.' (Vygotsky's emphasis throughout.) He therefore went on to say that children, '*solve practical tasks with the help of their speech, as well as their eyes and hands.*' And he added that, when such speech is allowed normal scope in childhood, it eventually becomes internalized, and evolves into our ability to think.[5]

In the Preface, I noted that I hoped that all kinds of teachers would find this book useful, so it might be appropriate to recall here that the process outlined above does not cease when we become adults. I have often found myself talking to someone and, while doing so, realized that the matter we are discussing has suddenly become clearer to me. I have then sometimes pretended that the matter has always been clear to me. At other times, I have found myself saying, 'As we were talking, I realized . . .'

Teachers probably have this experience more than anyone. If so, it is rather odd that they often adopt an approach to teaching that prevents their learners from doing something that would help them to learn. I should perhaps add here that one might agree that learning is helped when we are able to talk, but that it is difficult to know how to facilitate such talk in a large class. Detailed descriptions of how this might be done will be found in the second part of this book. In the mean time, it might be helpful to continue by recalling what happens in a typical place of work when something new has to be dealt with; for here, too, we see that people often talk to each other when they are trying to understand something. Indeed, solving problems in a place of work without talking would be impossible. Yet, it is still uncommon to see such an approach in many classrooms. Perhaps that is why people sometimes say that they learnt most after they had left school. I think it was George Bernard Shaw who once said that the only time his education had been interrupted was when he had gone to school.

What else is there about classrooms that might demotivate the learners in them? Consider what pupils and students mostly do in them. Everyone agrees that we learn best when we are actively engaged. If you want to learn how to ride a bicycle, you have to ride a bicycle. If you want to learn how to bake a cake, kiss a girl, understand thermodynamics, or kiss a boy, you have to do those things. Explanations from somebody who already knows can help. But, no matter how good the explanation, the best way to learn is to be actively engaged. If so, it follows that, if one can establish what people mostly do in a given situation, one will also discover what they are mostly learning.[6] What do learners mostly do in a classroom? In many classrooms, they mostly sit and listen. It follows that they learn:

- to sit and listen
- to believe that learning is a matter of sitting and listening, and
- that answers come out of a textbook or a teacher's head.

How is one to get out of such an absurd situation? In the second part of this book, there will be some practical suggestions. In the meantime, I return to considering why learners often seem de-motivated; and another reason might be that most people do not like to sit and listen, for hours at a time, when they are trying to learn something. Imagine you have just bought a new kitchen gadget. Imagine further that somebody tells you to sit down, and begins to read the instruction booklet to you, – for the next hour. How would you feel?[7]

I have just noted that, in many lessons, learners mostly sit and listen. I also implied that most of them would prefer to be actively engaged.[8] Is that true? That is surely an important question; for, if learners would rather be actively engaged than passively listening, that is almost the same as saying that they are inherently motivated to learn. Some interesting experiments have been carried out on this question; and one of the most striking was done many years ago at McGill University in Montreal.[9]

Three researchers offered undergraduates $20 a day (big money in those days) to lie on their backs on a couch, with their ears and eyes muffled, in a soundproof room, but with access to plenty of food and water. If they wanted some diversion, they were able to get old stock market reports piped in via earphones. Those experimenters reported that, after about six hours, the students began to feel very uncomfortable. Some began to hallucinate, and all gave up taking part in this experiment after two days. One is reported to have got a job on a building site at $8 a day instead!

But the above cannot mean that teachers must attempt to motivate their learners. On the contrary: If it is true that we learn best when we are actively engaged, it follows that, the more a teacher is actively engaged, the more that teacher will learn. It further follows that, instead of trying to motivate learners, teachers would help their learners if they could devise an approach to teaching that enabled their *learners* to be actively engaged.

So far, I have drawn attention to two constraints on motivation: one, that teachers often do most of the talking in a classroom; and two, that, in many classrooms, learners tend to be rather passive. I am suggesting that both not only inhibit motivation, but that they also prevent optimal learning.

&

This section contains some findings that have come from research on animals. As animals are not humans, one should perhaps begin by asking whether one ought to be interested in such research. A comparison with medicine might be helpful here. When we become ill, we are sometimes prescribed medicines, and many of these are tested on animals before they are given to humans. Some people might not like this idea, and I happen to be troubled by it. However, it is clear that animals have the same basic biological processes as we do, so, technically speaking, such testing might be appropriate. In the same way, it is well known that animals and humans share many basic psychological processes. So here, too, it seems safe to assume that, provided that experiments on animals are humane, they might further our understanding.[10] I trust readers will notice my hesitations here, and that they will make up their own minds. With those provisos in mind, here, then, are a few accounts of experiments with animals that might help to shed some light on the nature of motivation.

Imagine a laboratory, and in it, a small, white, tame rat inside an enclosure. It has two paths leading to food. One path leads directly to the food. The other path is longer, variable, indirect, and involves searching for the food. Which path does the rat take? The researcher reports that, very often, the rat will choose the longer and more difficult path. Why? One assumes that rats, like many humans, are inclined to explore their environment when they have a chance to do so. Here, now, another experiment. A well-fed chimpanzee is put in a cage, the walls of which are covered with cardboard. However, in one place, there is a covered window, and the chimp can lift the cover, and, in this way, can look into the laboratory. But the cover is so built that, each time the chimp lifts it, it soon falls shut again. What does the chimp do? The researcher reports that it raises the cover repeatedly in an attempt to look out. Why? Why not just lie back and snooze?

Here is another experiment, and again there is a cage with some chimpanzees inside it. They have all had plenty to eat and drink, and into their cage the experimenter places a contraption consisting of a padlock, bolt and chain, all put together so that it can be taken apart again. What do the chimps do? This researcher reports that they spend hours fiddling with it. Why? It must be immediately obvious to them that fiddling with it will provide nothing to eat or drink, nothing to copulate with, nothing they could use, not even something to scratch with. Why fiddle with it, and for hours? Again, one assumes that they do so because animals are often active, not in order to reduce some drive like hunger, or to gain some reward like status, but because being active is intrinsic to being alive.

Does the above also hold true for humans? A great deal of research has been done on that question, and here is a typical finding from the work of Hanus Papousek on infant development.[11] This researcher wished to learn how infants vary in their response to different kinds of conditioning, and, in doing that, he was struck by the following. He had arranged things so that when the infant he was observing did something relatively simple, like turn its head to the right, he rewarded it with milk. Papousek then discovered that infants as young as two months old, were soon able to learn that turning their heads to the right got them some milk. However, he also discovered that infants would go on turning their head in the correct direction, refuse the milk, and smile their pleasure when milk was offered to them! This showed that, having got all the milk they wanted, they gained no further reward from obtaining milk. Their reward now lay in being *offered* milk; that is, in gaining control of something.

In later experiments, Papousek found that an infant, as young as four months old, could learn to turn its head first to the right, then to the left, then back again to the right, in order to get a light to go on. But the remarkable thing was that it was clear from the infant's evident pleasure, and the direction of its gaze, that it did not gain a reward from looking at the light. The reward lay in the fact that the infant had itself managed to get the light to go on. That is, the main reward derived from mastery of the task.

With results such as these in mind, Papousek proposed that, in acting like this, an infant is matching the information coming to it with its actions; and, in doing that, a model of the world is built up in that infant's brain. That is, the infant's main reward lies in sensing that its actions bring about results that square with this model; and this is rewarding because having such a model helps it to gain mastery over its environment. Only a moment of reflection suggests that gaining such mastery must have enormous survival value.

The implications of what has been noted so far could be summarized like this. When not resting or asleep, animals and humans are often active. Not in order to reduce some drive or to gain some reward, but partly because, through such activity, models of the world become established in our brain. These models will include things like objects, attitudes, colours, movements, people and words; and, having such a model in the brain enables people to respond appropriately to the world around them. And quite clearly, having an accurate model of the world is likely to have survival value.[12]

Take finally a few everyday examples. Consider a child that has just been put to bed, having had all the food and drink it wants. As most parents know, that is precisely when it will often be most active. A child of three will often lie in bed and say a word it has just heard repeatedly. Why? It seems safe to assume that it does this in order to achieve mastery. But notice that there is no one around doing any motivating. Parents also know that young children are forever 'into things'. Fragile objects have to be kept out of their inquisitive reach; cupboards have to be kept latched; and dangerous objects hidden away. At this early age, a child's curiosity manifests itself mainly physically. But soon a child will begin to ask questions. Endlessly! Where does this propensity to ask questions come from?

From 'reinforcement'? Clearly not. Children often continue to ask questions even when their parents hardly answer. Who then is doing the motivating? Probably thousands of years of evolution. Tizard and Hughes found that, when young children interact with their parents (as compared with their teachers), children ask about twenty-six questions an hour; and they suggest that one of the main purposes of those questions is to enable a child to fill out its understanding of the world.[13] Moreover, this tendency clearly does not cease when we become adults. The more we know about the world, the better will we be able to cope with it. We can see how strong this inclination is when we consider the experiment with the McGill University students reported earlier.

To sum up: The findings to which I have drawn attention in this section suggest that living creatures are naturally active and motivated to learn when they find themselves in an environment that enables activity and learning to take place. If that is roughly correct, it again suggests that teachers need not be concerned with motivating learners. The problem is rather: First, to find a way of teaching that does not inhibit motivation; and second, to find a way of teaching that is in line with the motivation already present in learners.

Some readers might well be thinking here that the latter is easier said than done.

Ⅎ

It seems fair to say that we like what we are good at.[14] If we are very interested in something, but cannot master it easily, our failure might spur us on to try again. But, if we keep failing, we will tend to give up. We then often justify our giving up by reminding ourselves that we cannot be good at everything.[15] We also know that a complex task requires time and effort; and, the more complex the task, the greater the effort. Hence, if we succeed, we tend to feel good; but, if we fail, we tend to feel bad. So, before we tackle a complex task, we usually ask ourselves how likely we are to succeed.

In this section, I shall consider the experience of being, or having been a pupil in a school in England. Many readers will not be concerned with pupils in schools; but the experience of having been a pupil in a school must be relevant to all learners; for this experience will probably colour one's attitudes to learning for years to come. In the same way, some readers might not be concerned with the experience of having been a pupil in a school specifically in England; but here, too, I think that my comments are likely to hold broadly true for people in most countries. Until about ten years ago, to have done reasonably well at school in England was to have obtained what used to be called five O-level examination passes (O = ordinary). How many pupils left school in England having obtained five O-level examination passes? The relevant government statistics indicated that not more than about 25 per cent did so. It follows that, until quite recently, 75 per cent of pupils failed to do reasonably well in schools in England.[16] These figures are surely remarkable.

The examinations noted above have now been replaced by others, and recent reports indicate an improvement in examination pass rates. However, it is unclear to what extent this is due to changing standards, a change in emphasis, or a different way of going about things. What is clear is that schooling has remained problematic in many developed countries, and it therefore seems safe to conjecture that one of the things that some pupils learn during their years at school is that they are bad at learning.[17]

I draw attention to the above because it seems safe to assume that one feature of such a system is that it will demotivate many of those who are in it. These are complex issues; I would not want to trivialize them; and they take one beyond the remit of this book. I raise them here only to suggest again that there are certain features of schools that de-motivate the pupils in them, and that this must have implications for learning. If there is some truth to that conjecture, it must follow that teachers of all age groups would be wise to keep it in mind.

Here I should perhaps note the truism that it is seldom possible to teach in a way that will enable *all* learners to pass whatever examination might lie ahead. But good teachers usually know how to structure the material to be learnt so that the *majority* of their learners are able to master it. And if this cannot be done, then there is clearly something the matter with the curriculum, and teachers should protest. What is for sure, is that good teachers have no need to make their learners feel small so that they can feel big. Good teachers know intuitively that an atmosphere of fear is bad for learning; and they know this because they are not afraid to look inside themselves and remember what it was like to be a learner.

As for the question of the relevance of the material to be taught, I don't think that that can be simply a matter of teaching material that is 'useful' in the real world, for it is difficult to determine exactly what is going to be 'useful'. Nor can 'being relevant' be a matter of trying to make unreal things seem real. I am sure I am not the only one who squirmed when a teacher began, 'Your team has decided to re-mark the borders of its football field. Now, if the vertical measures . . .' In contrast, there are teachers who can make the wars of the Romans seem very real, and they manage to do this because they have a realistic outlook. They are able to show that all wars have certain things in common; that intelligent study is a matter of seeking patterns; and that looking at the past can provide clues about the future. Nor do these kinds of teachers teach something because 'it is likely to come up in an exam'. Being realistic, they know how to make most of what they teach relevant to the real world, and in that way they also help their learners to pass exams. Again, these are complex issues, and a serious consideration of them would take one beyond the remit of this book. I have raised them here only to suggest that they are relevant to the question of 'motivation'.

&

Consider next, the qualities that are assessed in most schools and colleges. The most common is how well a learner answers a question on a piece of paper. It is obviously important to be able to do that if one is a learner in a developed country; but, when learners are assessed in *only* that way, many of the abilities we most admire in people are ignored. I have in mind qualities like courage, integrity, ingenuity, empathy, perseverance, generosity, initiative, responsibility, kindliness, flexibility and independence. Or consider the ability to cook a meal, fix a machine, deal with a wound, or contribute constructively to the efforts of a team. In schools, abilities of the latter kind can sometimes be demonstrated in games, but many learners find themselves in establishments other than schools; and these seldom afford any opportunity to use and display such highly important abilities. These things being so, it is hardly surprising if some learners appear indifferent.

Consider further the subjects that afford the most prestige. For example, by common consent there is more prestige to studying medicine than plumbing. But why? No logical argument can be mounted that will show that one of these is more valuable than the other. True, more time is required to study medicine than plumbing, but a developed country needs both to function effectively. And anyone who argues that the practice of medicine is more difficult than the practice of plumbing has never tried to replace a pipe behind a kitchen cupboard. Whether a thing is, or is not difficult, obviously depends on the ability of the person concerned.

A subject has prestige because that is what a given society has determined; and my guess is that, the more insecure a society, the more will it value occupations that enable people to avoid getting their hands dirty. There isn't room in this book to discuss the likely economic and social effects of devaluing manual work. I would only argue that many people like to work with their hands. This inclination is deeply rooted in human nature, and is probably related to how the human brain developed in the way it has.[18] However, this inclination is subtly undermined in many learning establishments; and in this way, human dignity and the motivation to learn is also undermined. In some countries, a craftsman is still afforded some respect. But it is not to be compared with that to be gained from advising clients on how they might pay less tax. At least two results flow from such an attitude. One is that the so-called educated classes in many parts of the world become effete; and the other is that many learners become alienated. And if the foregoing is even roughly correct, it would not be surprising if some learners become de-motivated.

Notice something else about the subjects most commonly taught, and how they compare in prestige. For example, compare chemistry and economics, with child development and home economics. The first two carry much higher prestige than the second two. Why? It cannot be because of their usefulness to oneself or to one's society. Nor can it be a matter of complexity of subject matter or scarcity of talent. The higher prestige of the first two is probably related to how examination passes in them are passports to jobs. This suggests that a culture, that confers a higher prestige on the first two subjects, is a culture in which it is believed that the primary aim of learning is to enable people to earn cash. Earning cash is obviously important, but is living a sensible life less so?

The fact that the first two of the above subjects have a higher prestige than the second two, also suggests that, in our culture, the impersonal is often preferred to the personal. And if that is roughly correct, and if many people have a strong interest in the personal, it isn't surprising if some learners should find being in many learning establishments de-motivating.

Notice also that, in most learning establishments, most esteem is gained by working on one's own. In schools, one usually sits behind a desk, and one works on one's own; and, on examination day, one produces one's own answer. The situation with older learners is more complicated; but here, too, most kudos is gained by individual achievement. It is important that each learner knows what he or she is supposed to know. But must there always be such an emphasis on individual achievement? It is true that human beings are often competitive and sometimes produce good work that way. But recall here that, outside of learning establishments, more often than not people tend to work as part of a team. However, it is still unusual for assignments to be so designed that they require learners to work in a team.

Individual teachers cannot change such a value system even if they would want to. As in most such situations, it is anyway best to do what one individually can. For example, one can, through an occasional humorous aside, convey that one does not share the values noted above; but that, life being as it is, one must sometimes put up with nonsensical values. At the least, when teachers act like that, they might help to counteract the effect of a value system that many learners must find de-motivating.

&

By now, some readers might have become impatient. They might have found the comments on motivation noted above moderately interesting, yet they might wish to insist that many learners do not want to learn very much. I agree. So, what does one do? Try to motivate learners? The trouble is, when one tries to do that, the learners sit back and expect a performance. If the performance is good, the learners are pleased. If it is poor, they are bored. Unfortunately, that happens quite often, for, after all, teachers are not entertainers. Moreover, very little real learning results from being entertained. The end result of such a situation is that teachers in this way become the victims of an impossible position. Teachers believe that they must motivate; learners expect to be motivated; and I am arguing that no one can motivate anyone! No wonder teachers and instructors are sometimes heard to say, 'They don't seem to have any motivation at all. I don't know what they come here for.' Is there a way out of such a situation?

Notice first that, when teachers speak in this understandable way, it is clear, on reflection, that their learners *are* motivated – that is, they are motivated *not* to learn.[19] That comment might sound perverse, but I don't think it is. For, when some teachers say that their learners are not motivated, it might be that what they are really saying is that their learners are not doing what they want them to do, – namely, to sit and listen, and for hours at a time. But this is not a criticism of teachers. It is a criticism of a method of instruction; and I emphasize this point because I believe that the only way out of this vicious circle is to grasp that, what goes on in many classrooms, is based on a false perception of learning and teaching.

One could put the matter like this. Because we can teach someone, we risk slipping into the belief that we can also 'learn' someone. But we know that this cannot be done. All one can do is to try to arrange conditions that might enable people to learn. Unfortunately, that sounds rather passive, for many teachers feel that they must teach. Isn't that what they are paid to do? But when we focus on teaching, we tend to produce a performance. Can a performance generate learning? Surely teaching has to stop before learning can begin?

&

I have tried to show that no one lacks motivation. Motivation is like breathing. If we are alive, we will be motivated, – to learn, or not to learn. And if that is roughly correct, two things follow. First, teachers must be alert to factors that might inhibit their learners' motivation to learn. And second, teachers must work with whatever motivation is already present in their learners. Broadly speaking, I believe that the latter is largely a matter of creating situations that enable learners to become actively engaged, and I know from my many failures that this is much easier said than done. But what is for sure, is that such an approach brings about a shift in focus away from teaching and on to learning.

Some readers might wish to object here. They might wish to say that there is no real difference between setting out to motivate, and setting out to create interesting learning situations. Such an objection misses an important point. When a teacher sets out to motivate, the focus is on the teacher. But when a teacher sets out to create a carefully structured and inherently interesting learning situation, the focus is on the learners. And the effect of such a shift is to lift a burden from teachers, and to give learners a chance to do some learning.

For thousands of years people learnt 'on the job'. If they were not motivated to do that, they went hungry. This soon made them motivated! Then learning moved into institutions called 'schools'; and, in these, a method of instruction evolved (the transmission method) which inhibits motivation. The idea then arose that learners need to be motivated. That is surely like first putting cotton wool down people's throats, and then pumping air into them because they are not breathing. Perhaps I could illustrate this point for the last time by once again comparing the motivation to learn with the motivation to eat. Can we motivate anyone to eat? Surely not. What we can do is provide a decent meal and some convivial company; and, when we do that, the other person usually falls to it. And if they do not, there is not much else we can do. If that is roughly correct, the idea that learners have to be motivated must be a misconception. What clearly does require careful study is the conditions under which people best learn. That is the topic of the next few chapters.

Chapter 2

Two Accounts of Learning

In the previous chapter, I suggested that it makes little sense to decide how to teach before one has spent some time studying how people learn. In line with that belief, I next outline some research on learning. To make the presentation as orderly as possible, I report this research according to two psychological approaches. Of course, life is not ordered along the lines of any psychological approaches! However, in later chapters, I hope to show that, when one takes what is most valuable in these two approaches, one obtains the beginnings of a reasonably clear account of learning.

⅋

The Behaviourists

I begin with a group of researchers who called themselves Behaviourists. Their work quite rightly attracts much less attention today than it once did, but I believe that they discovered a few important things about the process of learning.

I begin by recalling that behaviourists believed that, if one wants to find out how people learn, asking them how they do this is unhelpful. They took this view because, as is well known, the reasons people give for their behaviour are often mistaken. Behaviourists therefore maintained that the only kind of evidence on which one can rely, is observable evidence; that is, when researchers can themselves see the way a person *behaves*. Such evidence, they held, is objective; for a person's actual behaviour can be recorded and measured. This will allow other researchers to check those findings, refute them, or extend them; and in that way progress might be made.[1] This approach has many shortcomings, but, rather than discuss them now, I think it would be more helpful to examine the kind of work that these people did by considering one of their experiments.

Imagine a laboratory. In the middle, there is a table; and on the table, there is a small cage. The cage has a door at one end, and a bar at the other. When the bar is pressed, a pellet of food drops into a food-trough below it. A small, white, tame rat is put inside the cage. The researcher now has a reasonably simple situation to investigate. He or she wants to find out how that rat will learn that pressing the bar can get it food. Notice that, in this arrangement, the researcher is able to observe the actual *behaviour* of the rat.

Although this rat has never been put into such a cage before, it has been reared in a laboratory, so it will not be afraid of the cage or the researcher. Probably, it will first sniff the air. Then, as it won't have been fed for quite a while, it will begin to move around to look for food. The researcher and the rat don't talk to each other. Even if they could, the researcher would not be interested. As noted, this is because the researcher would consider such oral evidence unreliable. So, the rat runs around, and the researcher sits there with pad, pencil and stopwatch in hand, and observes the behaviour of the rat.

A word about what is intended by the term 'learn' might be in place here. By 'learn' is meant the ability to do something that one could not previously do. It follows that 'learning' results in 'a change'. Notice the implication of that state-ment. Unless a change has taken place, how is one to determine that learning has taken place? By what a person says? That could clearly be ambiguous. Consider for example a certain girl who has acquired a dog. Every time she puts food out for it, she shouts. Very soon, the dog learns to associate the shout with its dinner, and comes running. Previously a shout hadn't meant much to it. So it has 'changed'. Or a person might move from Honduras to Hungary and learn to speak Hungarian. That is, he or she will have changed from not being able to speak Hungarian, to being able to speak that language. Here again we see that 'learning' implies a 'change'.

To continue with that rat. It runs around, and the researcher watches. As can be imagined, there will come a time when, half by accident, the rat will touch the bar. A pellet of food will then drop into the trough. The rat will notice it, and eat it. At this stage, it will probably not have registered any connection between the bar and the pellet of food. However, pretty soon, it will again half by accident touch the bar, and again a pellet of food will drop into the trough. This process will occur several times, and, sooner rather than later, the rat will be pressing that bar and obtaining all the food it wants. It has 'learnt' that bar pressing produces food.

Behaviourists explained the above like this:

- the rat *acted on the environment*; that is, first it ran round the cage looking for food, then it touched the bar, and then it pressed the bar; and
- its actions were *reinforced by being rewarded* each time it did something that got it what it needed.

That is, the rat's bar pressing was rewarded by it obtaining some food. Some researchers add that a connection was set up in the brain of that rat which links bar pressing with obtaining food. When that connection is solidly established, so that the rat presses the bar every time it wants food, 'learning' will be said to have taken place.

Behaviourists maintained that the above account also holds good for humans. They held that we are all driven by internal biological drives like hunger, thirst, or the need for sleep; and that these drives make us act on our environment. And when we reduce those drives by acting appropriately, our acts are reinforced by being rewarded.[2]

Behaviourists also argued that this account of learning can be applied to learners in general. That is, they maintained that teachers can reinforce those of their learners' behaviours that they consider desirable by rewarding them; and, if teachers do that, learners will repeat those actions, and thereby learn what they need to learn.

On the face of it, this shift – from acting on the environment and being rewarded by *it*, to acting on the environment and being rewarded by a *teacher* – does not seem very large. In the next section, I shall show that this shift raises important questions about the process of learning.

&

The behaviourist approach to learning was once extremely influential in the training of teachers. However, one of the most prominent behaviourist researchers, B.F. Skinner, once stated categorically that the findings of the Behaviourists cannot be used in a conventional classroom to aid learning, and his reasons still merit examining.[3]

Consider again the illustration with that rat. The rat was said to have learnt because:

a) it was *active*, and
b) each time it did something that brought it a mite closer to learning that pressing a bar produces food, its action had to be *reinforced by being rewarded immediately.*

So, according to the Behaviourists, learning is generated by two fundamental factors:

a) the need for the learner to be *actively* engaged, and
b) the need for the learner's appropriate activity to be *reinforced by being rewarded immediately.*

Consider what would happen if the rat sat in a corner of the cage and just watched the researcher. As the rat wouldn't be doing anything, none of its actions could be reinforced. This must be an important consideration for, in a conventional classroom, the learners will probably be sitting on their backsides and listening, or perhaps taking notes. Either way, there would be very little in their behaviour that could be reinforced.

The strange thing is that, although the Behaviourist theory of learning was once widely discussed, it seldom affected the way anyone actually taught. I say this remembering an occasion in my training college when I heard a man give a *lecture* on the Behaviourist theory of learning, – that is, he taught in a way that was completely at odds with the theory of learning he was explaining. I mention this episode to add a rider to my previous assertion that it makes no sense to set about teaching without first studying how people learn. The rider is that, having studied how people learn, one must find ways of teaching that take on board what one's study of learning has shown one.

The Behaviourists' method of teaching – which was in line with their theory of learning – was to introduce programmed manuals (or teaching machines).[4] Readers who have never seen one of these might like a brief description.

Programmed manuals had a paragraph of text, followed by a question on that text, then a blank for the learner to write an answer. Then came the correct answer. If the learner's answer was correct, she was given praise. If incorrect, she was instructed to begin again. Then came the next paragraph of text, then a question, followed by a space for the learner's answer. Then the correct answer. Then praise if the learner's answer is correct. And so on, till the manual had been completed.

In this way one got:

a) the learner's *activity*, and
b) an *immediate* reinforcement each time the learner made a correct response.

Teaching machines worked on the same principles. They consisted of a box, with a roll of paper inside which a learner could turn. As she turned the roll, a text appeared in a window. She read the text, responded to a question, turned the roll of paper, an answer appeared, and the rest was as previously described. Computer programs have, of course, superseded such machines, and I mention the latter because readers might notice that the principles on which computer programs work are often similar.

At one time, this Behaviourist teaching/learning method was much in fashion, and many thousands of programmed manuals and teaching machines were sold and bought. However, except where routine skills are to be learnt, they have now all been discarded. Nor is their fate surprising. As will have been seen, the Behaviourist approach to learning was simplistic.[5] Yet the Behaviourists were right to insist that, in order to learn, an animal or a human has to be actively engaged.[6]

At this point, some readers might wish to protest that this emphasis on the need to be actively engaged is based on work done with animals; that is, with creatures that do not possess the gift of language. Human beings, however, do possess the gift of language, and, with its aid, it is possible to *tell* learners what they need to know. Surely, such a reader might wish to continue, it is precisely our possession of language that has enabled human beings to accumulate so much knowledge from one generation to the next, and in this way to outstrip all other living creatures? Such an objection is obviously along the right lines. We certainly do not need to learn everything from scratch. But does our ability to understand a language release us from the need to be actively engaged if we wish to learn?

Consider the following illustration. On a drive home, I sense that there is something the matter with my car. That evening, I go to a neighbour who is more knowledgeable than me, and describe the symptoms to him. He nods, and begins to explain how the fault can be repaired. He is using language to teach me. How well does this work?

I have noticed that one of two things always happens in such a situation. If I have a working model of that which is being talked about already inside my head, I am able to follow what is being said. But, if I do not have such a working model, I find I may understand the individual *words* said to me, but I do not really understand their full *meaning*. The result is that I begin to lose track of what is being said. I might then ask the speaker to repeat what he or she is saying, but, pretty soon, I usually find I am lost again.

The same happens if I consult the car manual. I can pore over it for an hour at a time; but, if I have never manipulated the actual parts before, I do not really *understand* what I am reading. In short, until I have the car in front of me, have the faulty section in front of my eyes, push it this way and that with greasy fingers, look back at the manual (or my neighbour) – that is, until I am in this way actively engaged – I do not really learn.

The above illustration is of a practical task. Do we need to be 'actively engaged' when it comes to more abstract things? For example, how can one be actively engaged in the study of history? The discussion here turns on the meaning of the words 'actively engaged'. Of course, it is not as easy to be *practically* engaged in the study of history, as in the study of car mechanics. But there is an important difference between simply listening to a teacher talking about history, and doing research on a historical topic. To illustrate what is involved, I describe a history lesson in a school, but readers will immediately see that this illustration could equally be set in any institution in which learning and teaching take place. Let us say that the lesson begins with a teacher saying, 'Now, most of you live around here, and most of you live in a house that was built some years ago. But how did that house get there?' Lots of answers will probably be forthcoming. But a good teacher won't leave it at that. A good teacher will initiate a disciplined 'activity'. Pupils will be asked to make a search in local archives, investigate local authority plans, consider the structure of local commerce and industry, and study the development of the local community. Compare that with a teacher who talks for fifty minutes about how the houses got built in that area. In short, the argument is that real learning is not a matter of being *practically* engaged, but of being *actively* engaged.

Consider last a very common illustration of the above. When someone drives us to a new locality, we are seldom afterwards able to remember much about the route. But, when we ourselves do the driving, we usually can. So one can say that we do not have to work out everything we want to learn from scratch. That would be absurd. We can consult a manual, or question someone who already knows; and these can save us a great deal of time and trouble. However, *unless we already have a working model inside our head of that which we wish to learn, it isn't usually enough to read or listen*. If we wish to *really* learn, we must physically expose ourselves to situations; and if we do that, models will become established inside our head; and that happens most aptly when we are actively engaged.

Readers might notice how these comments relate to the research on child development noted earlier. There, too, models of the world were built up in the mind of an infant as it engaged actively with its environment.

But being 'actively engaged' is clearly not enough.

&

In the previous section, I noted that programmed texts and teaching machines were once bought in their thousands, but are almost never used today. That again suggests that the Behaviourists made some serious mistakes, and are best forgotten. However, over the years I have realized that one can sometimes learn a good deal from trying to understand why someone is wrong. Let us embark on such a journey, and begin by examining the way in which B.F. Skinner once famously stated his position:

'The practice of looking inside the organism for an explanation of behaviour has tended to obscure the variables which are immediately available for scientific analysis. These variables lie outside the organism, in its immediate environment and in its environmental history. . . . The objection to inner states is not that they do not exist, but that they are not relevant in a functional analysis.'[7]

Notice that those words describe well how that rat learnt that pressing a bar got it food. Recall first that the rat was said to have learnt because, each time it pressed a bar, its action was reinforced by being rewarded; and notice second, that all those factors refer to that rat's environment, and how it responded to it. There is nothing here about any 'inner state'. In other words, learning is said to take place as a result of the automatic forming of associations. (In the case of that rat, an association between bar pressing and obtaining food.) So far, then, Skinner appears to have been right. But consider the following experiments.

A researcher named Hunter placed a rat in a maze, and eventually it found its way to the exit. As one would expect, on subsequent trials the rat found its way to the exit more quickly. A Behaviourist would say that, each time it took a correct turning in the maze, the movement of turning was reinforced with the reward of getting out of the maze. Or they might have said that the rat learnt the physical layout of the maze through a process of associations. Next Hunter flooded the maze. When the rat was put back inside, it still found its way to the exit quickly by swimming. So what had the rat learnt during its previous visits to the maze? Clearly, it must have been more than the details of the route. For, if that were all it had learnt, then changing the details of the route by flooding the maze should have prevented the rat from reaching the exit quickly. In another experiment, a researcher named Lashley trained a rat to reach food by carrying out certain movements. That is, when it performed certain movements, they were reinforced with food; and in that way, it learnt that it was able to obtain some food by making those movements. Lashley then removed certain parts of the rat's brain, and this operation prevented the rat from carrying out those movements. Nevertheless, the rat obtained the food by going head over heels! So what had that rat learnt? Clearly not only that certain movements would get it food. For, if that were all it had learnt, then it would not have performed completely different movements to obtain food after the operation.[8]

Consider next the following experiment reported by Tolman.[9] Rats were placed inside a maze so that they were able to run along a path to reach food. The path was then blocked, a series of quite new paths were made available, and each pointed in a different direction. When the rats were placed back inside the maze, the great majority quickly chose one of the new paths that led most directly to the food. This suggests that, on their first visit to the maze, the rats had learnt, not only the details of the first path, but also the direction in which the food lay.

Readers might now see what has been gained from considering in what ways Skinner was wrong. In short, these experiments make clear that to explain learning by talk of 'reinforcement' and 'associations' leaves too much out.[10] But what? One way to consider that question might be to ask what would happen if the rat in these experiments had been offered a waterproof, resin-strapped, illuminated, digital, quartz watch as a reward. A behaviourist would say that a watch would not act as a reinforcer for a rat, so it isn't a reward. This is because, according to Behaviourists, a reinforcer is defined as that which causes a behaviour to be repeated. This sounds rather circular, but, instead of questioning such a definition, one might ask why a watch is not a reinforcer for a rat.

Behaviourists would have replied that that question is unhelpful, and the reason for their objection is clear: it would have fallen completely outside their terms of reference. But perhaps their terms of reference were too narrow? Most people would say that a watch would not *mean* anything to a rat. Behaviourists would, of course, have rejected such an explanation, for a 'meaning' is related to having an 'inner state', and Behaviourists wished to exclude explanations given in terms of unobservable inner states.

Here it might be an idea to pause and ask: 'What is a "meaning"?' Only a moment of reflection is required to sense that this is a difficult question to answer, so one might ask instead: 'What is a watch?' In response, one could say that a watch is a mechanism that turns two hands, so that they sweep in a circle over a number of figures. (A digital watch shows numbers on a dial.) To a rat, all this is double Dutch; and we only understand such statements because we already know what watches 'mean'. One could fill 10,000 pages with descriptions of watch mechanisms, their chemical and physical properties, and a detailed analysis of our concept of time, and one would still not have got near its 'meaning'. Yet, by the age of seven or eight, a child will know what is *meant* by 'time'. This is because we human beings grasp the 'meaning' of something *intuitively*. To put the above in another way, notice that, if we fed all the information in the world about watches and time into a computer, that computer would still not *understand* the 'meaning' of time.

This is because, ultimately, a 'meaning' isn't the sum of a number of physical properties. I shall have a few suggestions to make about some of the characteristics of a 'meaning' later. For the moment, I suggest that a meaning is a compact, living, abstract 'something' inside our mind, and that it has to be *experienced*. In other words, I am suggesting that meanings are a property of life. And, if that sounds vague, well, I am only saying that, at least for the present, 'meanings' are no more amenable to a final description than life itself is![11]

I could sum up like this. It is quite possible for a man born blind to obtain a PhD in perception. However, this would, unfortunately, still not give him any real idea of what it is like to see.

The following might further illustrate the limitations of the Behaviourist approach. Behaviourism was once used extensively in the health services to modify behaviour, both among adults who are mentally troubled, and among infants who may trouble us. And today, variations of this approach are still in use. So, here is a passage by a student who had some training in this technique: 'I spend much time discussing with parents how to cope with problems like sleep refusal, potty training, temper tantrums, etc. in their children. For instance, in the case of a child who refused to eat the food put in front of him, most parents are so terrified that he will starve, they will try and persuade him to eat, will try to feed him, threaten him, and probably end up getting very angry. The child sees his parents are very concerned about this and, although it is bad attention he is getting, at least it's some, which is better than none at all.

'My advice to these desperate parents is to sit the child at the table with his meal, and if he refuses to eat, to remove the food without comment and to let him see you couldn't care less. Give him nothing to eat or drink except water until the next meal and then repeat the whole procedure. The odds are that, after two or three meals, the child will think it is not worth the trouble and, anyway, he's hungry and so he'll eat. This is the time for the parents to show their praise, although not over-praise. It is important to be consistent, and for all the family to co-operate and not to give in at any step till the situation improves. The praise is gradually reduced.'[12]

The above is rather unsophisticated. An academic Behaviourist could point to several inaccuracies. However, this student has grasped the essentials of the matter; and the simplicity of her outline again enables us to see the limitations of the Behaviourist approach.

It is this. The person giving advice in the above ignores what the child's behaviour might *mean*. It might be that the child is unwell; or it might be that the child is not getting suitable attention; or something else might be the matter. What is most unlikely is that a healthy child would simply refuse food. But it is impossible to discover why a child refuses food by simply observing its *behaviour*. One must try to understand the *meaning* of its behaviour. And to understand that child, one must consider its 'inner state'. But the 'behaviour modification' approach – as illustrated above – sets out to modify only behaviour. Occasionally, as with the severely mentally troubled, such an approach might serve a useful end. But often it does not. This is because, as noted earlier, this view is too narrow. It tends to take things at face value; it is mechanical; it ignores *meanings*. Behaviourists tried to get away from a nebulous something we call a 'meaning', and went in search of something that was concrete, like behaviour. Such an approach has merit in a world bedevilled by mere opinions. But being concrete has nothing to do with being scientific. What is concrete about the notion of gravity? Here is Newton himself talking about it:

'that one body may act upon another at a distance through a vacuum without the mediation of anything else, by and through which their action and force may be conveyed from one to another, is to me so great an absurdity that, I believe, no man who has in philosophic matters a competent faculty of thinking could ever fall into it.'[13]

One of the most striking characteristics of the Behaviourist account of human behaviour was the absence of any sense of mystery about it. They seem to have believed that human behaviour is essentially a straightforward affair, and that, given the painstaking application of the appropriate technology, it could be understood. They appear to have believed that human behaviour is a simpler matter than the mechanics of moving planets. But recall here that *eminent* scientists often speak about the mystery of things. They hold it constantly in mind. They try to understand the little things about the mystery first. But they do not, in doing that, ignore the main mystery. And they never use trash phrases like 'demystifying' something.

A science should help us to understand things, and hence also to do things more effectively. More exactly, it should provide theories that can be used in practice, modified, extended, or scrapped. In short, the first test of a science of learning is that it should put a person who has studied it in a position to help others to learn. But programmed manuals did not work, and this was because they were based on a weak theory.

Consider a last and everyday example that indicates that much learning cannot be accounted for by the notion of 'reinforcement'. Consider the widespread practice of prayer. People have learnt to pray for rain, a bicycle, the absence of rain, and many other things, and they continue doing this even when they get the opposite of what they have prayed for. That is, they continue certain behaviours when there is no reinforcement for them whatsoever. Behaviourists had explanations for these things, but they sound contrived. Because their theory left out the 'inner state' – something all of us experience vividly – their theory could not account for a large number of things.[14]

Fortunately, there is an approach that accounts for certain things about the nature of learning, things that the Behaviourists left out, and I have in mind here those studies of infants noted in a previous section. Those infants did not respond automatically to a stimulus, and repeat their previous actions because they were 'reinforced'. As is the case with all living creatures, an infant's behaviour has been shaped by millions of years of evolutionary pressure. Hence, already at the age of a few days, infants try to make *sense* of the world. In short, they 'strive after meaning'.[15] And they do that because that enables them to interact with the world around them.

 ⚓ 

As noted, the notion of 'rewards' played an important part in the Behaviourist approach to learning. And, as was the case with other aspects of this approach, an examination of this concept might throw some light on the general nature of rewards.

I first draw attention to the work of Mark Lepper and his colleagues.[16] They began by selecting two comparable groups of nursery school children. Then they visited one group, and put out attractive new drawing materials for them to play with. They also told the children that they would get a 'good player's award' if they played with the materials. (The award consisted of an impressive certificate with a blue ribbon and a gold seal.) And when the children had finished their drawings, they were presented with their 'award'. Then those researchers visited the second group of children, and put out the same kind of drawing materials for them to play with. However, they did not promise these children any kind of reward, and when the children had finished their drawings, they were not given anything.

Two weeks later, these researchers returned to the children they had visited. They went first to one group, and then the other. As before, they put out the same attractive drawing materials for them to play with; but, this time, nothing about rewards was said to either group. Instead, the researchers sat around and recorded the amount of time each group of children spent using the drawing materials. Lepper's results were clear-cut. The children who had not been rewarded spent twice as much time with the drawing materials compared with those who had. This suggests that, when an activity is associated with an extrinsic (external) reward, the activity ceases when the extrinsic rewarding stops. In short, it looks as if extrinsic rewards undermine intrinsic (internal) ones. What may be the reason for this? There is a good deal of evidence that suggests the following. In short, it is that we enjoy a task most when we feel that we ourselves have chosen to do it. In contrast, when we are extrinsically rewarded for doing a task, we seem to feel manipulated.[17] And, as most of us don't like that, we stop doing the task as soon as we can.[18]

Some readers might want to object here, and suggest that the first group of children played less with the drawing materials on the second occasion because they were disappointed with the reward they had received. This explanation might be correct, but it would not contradict the point at issue. For, even if the children had been given a more substantial reward, and had played more with those drawing materials, their motive for doing so would have had nothing to do with those materials.

Consider next the following finding. It has been found that, when a chimpanzee is given the opportunity to use drawing materials, it will do so; and it will often show pleasure in doing so. Also, its productions are often indistinguishable from those of a young child. In an attempt to encourage a chimpanzee to draw more intensely, an experimenter bribed it with food.

Interestingly enough, he then found that, 'the animal took less and less interest in the lines it was drawing. Any old scribble would do, and it would then immediately hold out its hand for the reward. The careful attention the animal had previously paid to design, rhythm, balance and composition was gone.'[19]

Consider further the following finding. Condry and Chambers introduced learners to a problem-solving task.[20] They let them work on it for a while to get practice, and then they divided those learners into two groups. They asked those in the first group to work on several tasks similar to the ones that they had just dealt with, and they promised them a payment for each problem correctly solved. Then they set the learners in the second group the same kind of task, but did not offer them any kind of reward.

These researchers then recorded the problem-solving strategies used in each group. They found that the learners who were paid to solve the problems tended to be more 'answer-oriented' than those who were not. For example they began to guess at the answers before they had managed to obtain sufficient information to do so intelligently. Furthermore, what information they did obtain, they used inefficiently. The result was that they tended to make guesses that contradicted what they already knew. In contrast, the learners in the second group, the ones who were not promised an extrinsic reward, tended to be more thoughtful in their approach. In short, the extrinsically rewarded group, the group that was paid, focused on the answer. But the learners in the second group – the ones who gained an intrinsic reward by solving the problems – were more concerned with discovering the nature of the task before them.

The above research was done with pupils in a school. Here, now, the results of similar research done with students at a university. First, and as is well known, it has been found that some students are happy with a superficial understanding, while others try for a deeper one. It has also been found that one factor that tends to generate a superficial understanding is the anticipation of an extrinsic reward. These researchers therefore conclude that, if we value deep understanding in learners, 'every effort must be made to avoid . . . conditions which rely mainly on extrinsic motivation'.[21]

The findings noted above can be summarized like this. Extrinsic rewards not only tend to undermine intrinsic ones, they also tend to generate poor learning. If so, these findings suggest that, instead of worrying about 'reinforcing' or 'rewarding', teachers would be better advised to try to devise learning tasks that enable learners to gain intrinsic rewards. This does not, of course, imply that teachers should not express appreciation for work well done. It implies that the attempt to motivate learners extrinsically can have damaging consequences.

Is it possible to make learning intrinsically interesting, so that external rewards are not required? Consider the work of a researcher named Rainey.[22] Rainey selected a group of 124 pupils in the upper forms of a secondary school. All attended the same chemistry lessons once a week, and were divided into two groups for laboratory work. In the latter, each pupil had to perform sixteen experiments. Those in the first group were given detailed directions, while those in the second group were asked to do the same experiments on the basis of their lesson notes. At the end of the year, the pupils were tested. No difference was found in the examination results of the two groups. However, the following differences were found:

a) the pupils in the second group took longer to get to work, and they expressed some resistance to being asked to work in a non-directed way; however, once they had got going, they expressed pride in their work;

b) the pupils in the second group produced better write-ups of their experiments; and

c) at the beginning, the work of the second group tended to be unsystematic, even chaotic; however, by the end of the year, it became necessary to hurry them along because they wanted to spend extra time checking work that was already good.

These findings suggest:

a) if a task is organized so that learners find it intrinsically rewarding, nobody needs to 'reward' (or 'motivate') anyone;

b) one of the main characteristics of a learning task that offers an intrinsic reward, is that the learners are actively engaged in it; and

c) the more responsibility the learners have for their learning, the greater is their intrinsic reward likely to be.

At this point, readers might like to compare what has been noted above, with the comments made on motivation in an earlier chapter. They might also recall that it was then noted that one of the attributes of a good theory is that it integrates the available evidence.

Above, I drew attention to the conjecture that the more responsibility learners have for their learning, the greater their intrinsic reward is likely to be. Is there any further evidence for such a claim? Consider the following finding. A researcher named Kavanau put some deer mice (very small mice) in a cage.[23] In it, there was a running-wheel, and the mice used it a great deal. He then arranged things so that the wheel could be activated by a small electric motor, and he placed a switch inside the cage so that either he, or the mice, could set the wheel in motion. He then found the following: When the mice had learnt how to control the motion of the wheel by using the switch, they would run on it only if they had initiated its movement themselves! That is, if he set the wheel running, the mice would stop it, restart it, and only then begin running. That is at the level of deer mice!

For those still sceptical about the effect of allowing people as much responsibility as possible for their learning, here is another finding. A researcher named Langer visited two large firms to sell $1 lottery tickets to their employees.[24] He sold the tickets in one of two ways. He either *gave* purchasers a ticket in return for their cash, or he invited purchasers to *choose* a ticket in return for their cash. On the morning of the lottery, he went back to the people who had bought tickets from him, and asked them if they would sell their tickets back to him. He found that the people to whom he had *given* a ticket wanted $1.96 on average for it, while the people who had *chosen* a ticket wanted $8.67 on average!

So far, I have drawn attention to the effects of giving extrinsic rewards on the process of learning. But giving extrinsic rewards also has other effects, for example social ones. Consider first the work of Garbarino.[25] This researcher paired a number of children so that an older one taught a younger one. In some pairs, the older child was paid to teach; while in other pairs, the older one was not paid to teach. He found that the 'teacher' in each kind of pair tended to treat the 'learner' differently. For example, where the older child was paid to teach, she tended to see the younger child either as someone who was helping her to gain payment, or as someone who was hindering her. Hence, when the younger child in this situation did not catch on quickly, the relationship between teacher and taught tended to become hostile. In the other kind of pair, where the older child was not paid to teach, the quality of the relationship tended to be better. The focus was more on the task at hand, and the learners in that kind of pair made fewer errors.

This is hardly surprising. We know that we learn best from a person who sees our attempts to grasp something with interest and good humour. We are not usually at our best when we have to learn from someone who sees our endeavours as something that will, or will not get them some cash.

As teachers' incomes in most countries are not directly related to their learners' progress, this piece of research might be thought of doubtful relevance. Unfortunately, some people would like to make such a link, and one would hope that the above finding would make them think again. I believe that there is another implication in the above research.

Though most teachers' incomes are not directly linked to their learners' progress, their self-esteem often is. That is, some teachers tend to see their learners' failure to grasp something as a slight on them. Garbarino's finding suggests that the more that teachers see their role as that of a 'reinforcer', the more are they in danger of seeing their learners' natural and necessary failures as their own.

Garbarino's findings are of interest for another reason. It is often claimed that, unless people are extrinsically rewarded for doing things, nothing will get done. That must be true to some extent, – but only to some extent. Consider the following scenario. I once worked in a college. At the head of such a place, there is a principal. Also working in a college are people like caretakers, and these people earn a lot less money than the principal. The mythologies prevalent in much of the world hold that this difference in income is necessary for reasons to do with the nature of the duties these two kinds of people perform. That is, it is commonly believed that, if we do not pay principals more than caretakers, the principals will take their talents elsewhere. Is this true?

My friend Albert Einstein used to perform what he liked to call a 'thought-experiment'.[26] (He never carried out a practical experiment in his life.) Let us do the same. Imagine a law is passed which states that, in a given college:

- nobody is able to leave their employment for employment elsewhere
- everybody in the building is paid the same, and
- everybody can switch jobs inside the building.

In the above circumstances, would principals immediately elect to become care-takers? Probably not. If they did, it would suggest either that they could not really cope with being a principal, or that they were doing their job only because of the money they were being paid. I would have thought that in neither case would they be doing a good job.

College principals not only get the satisfaction of being paid lots of cash, they also benefit from a host of other things like power, interest, and doing something useful. And it is surely because of these *intrinsic* rewards that no healthy and able principal would exchange jobs with a caretaker, even if that meant they would earn the same amount of money as a caretaker. Now, if we extend this thought-experiment over the whole world, it is easy to see that nobody would drop a job that affords intrinsic rewards for one that doesn't, if all jobs were paid the same. The trouble is that many jobs do not afford any intrinsic rewards. So extrinsic rewards – mostly in the form of money – have to be given in their place. In other words, extrinsic rewards are often given to people when they are asked to do what they would rather not do. If that is roughly correct, it follows that, when teachers offer learners extrinsic rewards, the hidden message that could be picked up by learners is: 'What I am asking you to do is boring, I know you would rather not do it, so I am offering you an extrinsic reward.' Having conveyed that message each time a reward is given, how can anyone expect learners to want to learn anything except when they are given an extrinsic reward?

Learning establishments reflect the values of their society. If there is an empha-sis on extrinsic rewards in schools, that is not because of established facts about how people best learn. Behaviourism didn't arise in Borneo in 1928, because the value system of Borneo in 1928 could not have produced it.[27] But the value system of the USA in 1928 did produce it, just as it produced cheap automobiles, a painfully rising crime rate and a science that turns human beings into machines. Everything, but everything, in a given society is a part of a seamless web. The prevalence of extrinsic rewards in our society is probably not the only reason for the prevalence of extrinsic rewards in our schools. Another reason might be related to the fact that the teaching method most commonly used – the transmission method – destroys many of the intrinsic rewards that learning can itself provide.

Some readers might wish to object here. They might wish to say that, although some learners are motivated to learn, many are not. I agree! The extent to which learners are motivated to learn depends to a considerable extent on factors that lie outside the classroom, and teachers have no influence on these.[28] What teachers can do, is to try to create learning situations that are intrinsically rewarding, as well as a climate of learning that is friendly and supportive. When teachers have managed to do these things, and learners still do not wish to learn, there is not much else teachers can do. Teachers are not magicians! As for using extrinsic rewards, these offer a short-term solution with many long-term costs, – in as well as out of school.

At this point, an additional comment is called for. It is commonly agreed that there is much amiss with schools in some western countries, and it is clear that not all teachers are as good as they might be. However, a developed society needs an educational system, and this can only function reasonably effectively if both learners and teachers agree to abide by certain rules. I would include the following rules: Being willing to curb one's desires in the interest of the group; being prepared, and reasonably cheerfully so, to put up with a certain amount of routine; understanding that learning often requires sustained work and is not the same as entertainment; that there is a virtue in civility and some decorum; that it is best to treat all people with honour; and to recognize that there is a need for there to be a teacher who is ultimately responsible for what happens in a classroom.

If the above is considered a reasonable view, it requires only a moment of reflection to see that people must learn such rules long before they enter a classroom. Unfortunately, a society, in which the focus is almost only on the individual, and which is bedevilled by serious malfunctioning, often imposes the role of surrogate parent on teachers; and this role often prevents teachers from concentrating on teaching. Furthermore, as it is difficult, and sometimes impossible to impose rules of the above kind, teachers and educational establishments are often the recipients of a great deal of criticism. And perhaps the worst aspect of this criticism is that it is motivated by an unwillingness to place responsibility where it belongs, that is, on the value system of one's society, and especially on how its culture shapes attitudes towards children and the family. And as if that were not enough, the status of teachers has fallen very considerably in recent years.

❧

The Gestaltists

I turn next to another approach, this one associated with a group of researchers who worked in an orientation commonly called 'Gestalt psychology'.[29] The word *Gestalt* is German, and it can be roughly translated as 'pattern'. These people believed that the kind of topic typically studied by psychologists does not simply consist of facts, but of facts, *and* the pattern in which those facts are located. The argument is, in short, that the pattern has an importance no less significant than the facts, and indeed to a considerable extent determines the nature of the facts. It is rare to find anyone working in this orientation today, but I believe that it has much to teach us, and I now summarize some of the findings of this orientation.

Think of a tune, any tune, and whistle or hum each note separately. Pause the same amount of time between each note, and stress each note in the same way. Those are the separate notes of the tune, and they could be said to be its 'facts'. If you have whistled or hummed in the way I have just suggested, the sounds will not have produced a melody.

However, if you whistle or hum the melody in the way that the composer intended, that is, with all the pauses and the right beat, a *melody* becomes recognizable; and this result comes about because the notes are now arranged in a pattern. In short, it is not just the notes that make the melody, but also the way in which the notes are arranged. This example might illustrate what was noted above, namely, that the pattern is no less significant than the facts out of which the pattern is made. Gestalt psychologists like to explain this effect by saying: 'The whole is greater than the sum of the parts.'

The following example might further illustrate this point. About a hundred different elements make up everything on this planet. Those elements are separate entities. But what millions of very different wholes they produce! For example, water is a compound of two gases. But how unlike any combination of gases water feels!

Consider another effect of pattern. I am writing these words with a word processor. One of its facilities can tell you how many words you have used in a given chapter. This facility can also tell you the number of *different* words you have used. Whenever I use this facility, I am always surprised to discover that, however long a chapter, and although I favour a simple style of writing, there are seldom more than about 600 *different* words in it. For example, there are about 2,000 words in this section, but only about 560 different words.

How can a few hundred words (and just twenty-six letters) do so much? It is because we can produce millions of different *patterns* with that number of words (and letters). Again, 'The whole is greater than the sum of the parts.'

Incidentally, the above suggests that, in order to learn how to speak a foreign language, the important thing is not to know a lot of different words. As just noted, one can make oneself perfectly well understood with not more than about six hundred different words. The important thing is to know how to put those words together in a meaningful pattern.

Consider next these two strings of words:

- cable a clutch on a replacing Beetle is a job of a broken hell.
- replacing a broken clutch cable on a Beetle is a hell of a job.

The above two strings contain exactly the same words. However, in the first string, the words have been set down arbitrarily; in the second string, the words have been set down in a meaningful pattern. This kind of pattern is called a sentence. A pattern makes sense. A non-pattern seldom makes sense.

Next, compare these two sentences:

- The gnat bit the woman.
- The woman bit the gnat.

The above two sentences contain exactly the same words (or separate 'facts'); yet they have very different meanings, and that difference is, of course, caused by the different arrangement (or patterning) of the same items. Notice also that, because of the pattern, each word has an effect on the others.

The importance of pattern can be seen everywhere in nature. Look at a leaf, a rock, a piece of bark, a patch of skin, a raindrop. Always one sees a pattern. In nature, nothing is ever 'untidy'. Look at the outline of a tree against the sky. Notice how balanced it is. Pattern is everywhere. The following might again suggest the importance of pattern. A brick can be used to build a wall, smash a window, warm a bed, or prevent a car from rolling. In each case, it is a brick. But, in addition, it is also something else; and this difference is due to the context in which it is used. In this instance, one could say that a fact (in this case a brick), gets its *meaning* from its context. That is similar to saying that facts get their meaning from how they fit into a pattern.

In an earlier Chapter, I noted that I would attempt a definition of 'meaning' later. A moment of reflection now shows that everything gets its meaning from everything else around it. Or, one could say that the world is an interdependent whole, and that the separate things in it get their significance from how they fit into that whole. Note here how the latter comment also helps to describe a good theory. For one of the attributes of a good theory is that it will indicate how the various facts of a topic – especially the seemingly disparate facts – hang together, and make 'sense'. Note here that none of this is to say that the separate words of a language, or the facts of a topic, are unimportant. It is rather that the parts gain their significance from the whole.[30]

Consider a last example. Imagine you go into your garden one day, and find a creature from outer space admiring your geraniums. It stands 35 cm high, its upper part looks like a dish of blackcurrant jelly floating on spun sugar, and it has several antennae sticking out of it. Having been suitably radiated, it can speak a little English. So it says, 'Hello.' When you get over your surprise, you begin to chat; and, after a while, you find that you rather like the creature. So, you ask it into your house, and the surprises then continue.

For example, just inside your door there is a picture. The creature floats up to it and asks, 'What is that?' You say, 'A picture.' The creature repeats the word till it has the pronunciation right. But you can see from the way that one of its antennae is twisting that it hasn't really understood what it is saying. So, you begin to explain that humans like to have pictures in their houses. 'Why?' asks the creature. Now you realize that you really are in deep water! Why have a picture on a wall? You realize that you would have to explain about a thousand other things before you could get this creature to understand the *meaning* of the word 'picture'. That is because, to begin to understand what that word means, one has to have a few thousand connections inside one's head.[31] Or, as I was saying before, a fact gets its meaning from the way it fits into a whole.

Teachers should find the above helpful for a number of reasons. Consider the following example. Teachers are often told to give their learners one fact at a time, and perhaps that advice is based on the belief that knowledge is like a wall made up of separate bricks. Hence, if learners are given one brick at a time, they will be able to place them next to each other, and then perhaps on top of each other, and then, when they have the last brick, they will 'have' the topic.

But if the Gestalt approach is on the right tack, then a topic does not consist of only separate 'bricks', but also of the way in which they are held together. In other words, to understand a topic, one must understand the way in which its facts fit together to make a certain kind of pattern. If so, it follows that, when a teacher begins to explain a new topic by stating a series of new facts, the learners will not really understand those facts till the teacher has finished. Put that way, it sounds as if one must begin at the end. But that is impossible. What one can do, is to give a rough outline of the topic first. That might help the learners to see how the various bits, of which the topic consists, hang together.

It is interesting to recall here that learners who really want to understand a topic always feel that they don't really understand anything when they first begin to study. Unlike the kind of learner who is content to memorize facts, real learners tend to feel inadequate. They sense intuitively that knowing only facts is nothing, and that it is only when one sees the pattern into which the facts fit that one begins to understand the facts.

These are the learners who ask the awkward questions. Or don't say much in class. These are the learners who find that the notes they take in class are mostly a waste of time, because they are taken before one has grasped the pattern. These are the learners who read around their subject. And these are the learners who find, to their surprise and deep pleasure, that, when they persist in this way, there very slowly comes a time when the material they are trying to understand begins to take on a shape, a pattern, – that is, *a meaning*. These are also the learners who can freewheel through questions at an examination, and note implications where others see nothing. Even an unintelligent examiner will see that they understand, not just remember.

Reading around a topic is particularly important. The best thing to do, when one wants to learn something theoretical, is to try to find a good 'gist' book. A good 'gist' book will provide an outline of a topic, and it will be written by a person who knows the facts inside out. Then one must get hold of a book that has all the necessary details, – what might be called a 'list' book. Having read a good 'gist' book, one will be able to cope more easily with a 'list' book, and this is because one will have a rough idea of how the various facts of the topic fit together.

Notice how the above shows that learning is not the same as remembering. This distinction becomes clearer when one compares the kind of learner I have described above with participants in a quiz show. These inanities are often given grand names like *Brain of Britain*. However, if one examines what is actually said in them, one soon sees that the participants are seldom required to do more than recall two or three words. The deeper implications of an answer are never discussed. For example, a participant might be asked the date of a battle, but never what justification there was for fighting it. Snappy answers are preferred. Compare the notion that intelligence is a matter of remembering 'facts' – as in quiz shows – with the following two comments made in a widely used textbook on economics:

- If all farmers work hard, and nature cooperates in producing a bumper crop, total farm income may fall, and probably will.
- Attempts by individuals to save more during a depression may lessen the total of the community's savings.[32]

On the face of it, these two statements might sound absurd. But anyone who knows a little economics will know that they express a basic *understanding*, and such understanding is not a matter of knowing facts. Knowing facts is important, but only to the extent that knowing them enables one to understand a total structure. In a quiz show, participants merely reproduce facts. But in real learning, the facts are merely the building blocks out of which one constructs a meaning that helps one to understand the world.[33] To equate remembering facts with having understanding, is like believing one can cook because one can put a potato in a microwave oven. This section has been on one element in the Gestalt approach, namely, the importance of 'pattern'. There is another element in this approach that is also important, and it is called 'insight'. It, too, is related to the importance of pattern. But it is an important topic in its own light and deserves a new section.

&

During the First World War, a German psychologist named Wolfgang Köhler spent about four years at an animal research station on the island of Tenerife. We do not know how Wolfgang felt about being on that island for so long, but he produced a book called *The Mentality of Apes* while he was there which, I believe, has some very important things in it for a better understanding of learning, and hence teaching.[34]

Consider first the following experiment that this man carried out. Imagine an empty room, and in it a chimpanzee named Sultan. To the ceiling is tied a bunch of bananas, and Sultan cannot get at them by climbing. Inside the room there are also two large boxes, and the researcher wants to find out whether the chimpanzee can learn how to place one box on top of the other, climb up them, and get at the fruit. As Sultan has never made a ladder out of boxes before, there is potentially a learning situation here: that is, a case of moving from not knowing how to stack boxes to make a ladder, to knowing how to do such a thing. Some scholars have objected that Köhler's account does not constitute a clear change in behaviour.[35] They argue that Sultan is likely to have encountered box-like objects before. I believe that this argument misses an essential point, and I shall turn to it in a minute. Here now is Köhler:

'Sultan drags the bigger of the two boxes towards the objective, puts it just underneath, gets up on it, and looking upwards, makes ready to jump, but does not jump; gets down, seizes the other box, and, pulling it behind him, gallops about the room, making his usual noise, kicking against the walls and showing his uneasiness in every other possible way. He certainly did not seize the second box to put it on the first; it merely gives vent to his temper. But all of a sudden his behaviour changes completely; he stops making a noise, pulls his box from quite a distance right up to the other one, and stands it upright on it. He mounts the somewhat shaky construction, several times gets ready to jump, but again does not jump; the objective is still too high for this bad jumper. But he has achieved the essential part of his task.'[36]

I read this, and I know how Sultan must have felt. There is the aim, in this instance of getting at those bananas, and I just cannot do it. That makes me feel very frustrated. So one kicks at a tyre, or one stares out of a window. Or, if one is a chimpanzee, one may tear around a room dragging a box behind one. And then, as if out of nowhere, the way to solve the problem seems to become clear. A Gestalt psychologist would explain what has happened like this. He or she would say that the various facts of the situation have become organized in the animal's mind in the form of a pattern, and this imparts certain meanings to those various facts.

In that illustration of a brick in a previous section, I noted that a brick could be used as a missile, a bed-warmer, or a wheel-chock, and that, in each of those instances, it is the context that determined the 'meaning' of the brick. Or one could say that an object 'affords' a meaning depending on its context.[37] In the present instance, one could say that the room, the bananas, and the boxes turned into a meaningful pattern in Sultan's brain, and in terms of the circumstances in which he found himself. Translated clumsily into words, that pattern would convey something like: 'boxes-on-top-up-go-to-fruit-you-want-eat'.[38]

Earlier, I noted that some researchers have maintained that the mental process that an animal undergoes in such a situation is best explained in terms of associations. That is, that the objects before the animal trigger off appropriate action, based on associations established by past reinforcements. Such an explanation may sound more concrete than the one suggested above. But is it really more concrete? What is an 'association'? Two specific nerves linked together? If so, such a link has yet to be found. And even if such links were found, precisely what is it that determines which links are activated and which not in a given situation? After all, each situation could activate many of the millions of links that are present in a brain.[39] What does the organizing? The circumstances in which Sultan found himself provided literally thousands of possible clues as to what he could do next. What determines which clues are relevant and which not? In other words, how was Sultan able to decide what was relevant, and what not, before he knew what to do?

Notice also that the information Sultan was able to pick up could not have registered itself in his brain in the form of words. As Sultan was an ape, he did not have any words. This suggests that the information must have been registered in his brain in an abstract form, that is, in the form of 'a meaning'.[40]

I am aware that the above might sound fanciful, but the comment by Newton quoted in a previous section showed how inherently absurd he himself considered the notion of 'gravity' to be. Nevertheless, that notion enabled tremendous strides to be made in fields like mechanics and astronomy, 'til Einstein came along and improved upon it. I make this observation thinking that a notion like 'a meaning forming in a mind' may also sound absurd. But its value should not, I think, be judged by how it sounds, but initially at least by how useful it is in offering a tentative explanation, and guiding practical action.

I noted earlier that some researchers objected that the description provided by Köhler does not suggest a clear case of learning. They maintained that Sultan must have encountered box-like objects before. But, even if this objection is correct, it misses an essential point. This is because it is clear from the description Köhler gave us that the facts before Sultan became organized in his brain 'spontaneously'. It is certainly possible that Sultan had encountered box-like objects before. But it is also quite clear that the implications of the situation in which that ape found himself were new to him; and that the meaning of that situation did not become clear to him for some time. Moreover, when that meaning *did* become clear to him, it did so in a flash. It is true that conscious thinking preceded this flash; but Köhler showed that this conscious thinking was fruitless. It produced only frustration.

As I see this matter, the above suggests that understanding is a spontaneous activity of the mind, in the same way that breathing or digesting are spontaneous activities of the body. That is, just as we do not consciously need to do anything in order to digest or breathe, I suggest that we do not consciously need to do anything in order to understand. Indeed, seen in evolutionary terms, it seems to me inconceivable that nature should leave it to our fallible thinking to produce understanding. As that suggestion might seem fanciful, perhaps the matter should be considered in a little more detail. After all, the ability to teach effectively must depend – at least to some extent – on having some understanding of the relationship between thinking and understanding.

❦

In the previous section, there was a description to illustrate the process of insight in a chimpanzee. Here now is a description to illustrate the same process in a man. The person in this instance is the once well-known mathematician Henri Poincaré,

and in the passage to come he describes how he came upon one of his mathematical insights. Readers whose knowledge of mathematics is as scanty as mine can
ignore the mathematical jargon and still make good sense of the passage. Here is
Poincaré:

'Having reached Coutances, we entered an omnibus to go some place or other.
At the moment when I put my foot on the step the idea came to me, without anything in my former thoughts seeming to have paved the way for it, that the transformations I had used to define the Fuchsian functions were identical with those of
non-Euclidean geometry. . . . On my return to Caen, for conscience's sake I verified
the results at my leisure. Then I turned my attention to the study of some questions
apparently without much success and without a suspicion of any connection with
my preceding researches. Disgusted with my failure, I went to spend a few days at
the seaside, and thought of something else. One morning, walking on the bluff, the
idea came to me, with just the same characteristics of brevity, suddenness and
immediate certainty, that the arithmetic transformations of indeterminate ternary
quadratic forms were identical with those of non-Euclidean geometry.'[41]

The above is typical of how Poincaré described his mathematical insights, and it
is also typical of how many other creative scientists have described how they
achieved their insights.[42] Consider now some salient points in the above description. First, Poincaré tells us that there was nothing in his previous *thoughts* that
paved the way towards his discovery. In fact, it is clear from his description that he
stopped *thinking* before he came upon his discovery. When first heard, that last
statement might sound absurd. But a moment of reflection soon shows that,
although thinking often precedes or accompanies understanding, it does not
follow from this that thinking brings about understanding. Indeed, the opposite
might be true: thinking could be what happens when we do not understand.[43]
Indeed, that is precisely what a careful reading of the descriptions of Sultan and
Poincaré suggests. Those descriptions indicate that both had to *stop* thinking. But
why? An answer might suggest itself if one considers the nature of thinking a little
further. If one examines what happens when we think, it looks as if thinking is a
matter of consciously considering what there is in our mind; and what there is in
our mind is largely the sum total of what we have experienced to date. So thinking seems to be a matter of bringing our memories to bear upon the present. If
that is roughly correct, it follows that, when our present circumstances are similar
to ones we have encountered in the past (and when we are able to consider these
consciously), then thinking is helpful. For then we will usually be able to find a
match between something we have experienced, and dealt with successfully in the
past, and our present circumstances. However, if our present circumstances are
quite different from any we have encountered in the past, then thinking might be
a hindrance. For then, we will not be able to make a match between what we have
experienced in the past and our present circumstances. If so, it would follow that
we must stop thinking (i.e. bringing the past to bear upon the present), for such a
tool would be inappropriate.

Consider again the situation in which Sultan and Poincaré found themselves.
They wished to understand something that was new to them, so it made no sense
to try to bring the past to bear upon it. This view of things is borne out by the fact
that, when they did, they got nowhere. In fact it produced only frustration. In
short, they had to stop thinking, for how else could the new come to them?

One could rephrase the above like this. If we must deal with a situation quite new to us, it is helpful if we can come to such a situation with a fresh mind. For, if we don't, we might well go round and round in circles. But if we go off and do something else, or go to bed and have some sleep – that is, if we can stop thinking – then a solution might *come* to us. Of course, we must then check that solution against our present circumstances, and here thinking will be important. In solving something like a mathematical problem, the situation is more complex. In such a situation, it is obviously important both to know a great deal about mathematics, but also to be able to come to the problem with a fresh mind. In other words, an agile and flexible mind is required, a mind that is able to move from knowing, to not-knowing, constantly back and forth, 'til a solution slowly presents itself.

At this point, recall that we don't always want to accept a solution that manages to present itself to us. This is probably because that solution is in conflict with our desires. So we go on thinking! At such times, our thinking is caused by our wish to reconcile that which cannot be reconciled. But when we can immerse ourselves in a new situation, when we can allow it to come to us freshly, not through the screen of our past experiences, expectations or desires; and when we are able to allow it to unfold itself before us, so that all its facets become clear, we might be able to understand it.

In the West, especially, we tend to find such an approach odd. We tend to believe that, unless we consciously *do* something, nothing will get done. Yet, it is clear that we do not have to do anything (consciously or unconsciously) for our lungs to breathe or for our stomachs to digest. In the same way, I am arguing that we do not have to do anything in order to understand. All we have to do is come to that which is to be understood with an open mind; to immerse ourselves by degrees in it; to be patient; and to allow the situation to unfold itself. After that comes the need to check whether what we think we have understood corresponds to reality.

I believe that such a description helps to explain what happened to Sultan and Poincaré. To explain the process of discovery by reference to the 'unconscious' is unhelpful. What is rather required is a keen but passive alertness.[44]

Consider the following passage by another mathematician, Spencer Brown:

'To arrive at the simplest truth, as Newton knew and practised, requires *years of contemplation*. Not activity. Not reasoning. Not calculating. Not busy behaviour of any kind. Not reading. Not talking. Not making an effort. Not thinking. Simply *bearing in mind* what it is one needs to know. And yet those with the courage to tread this path to real discovery are not only offered practically no guidance on how to do so, they are actively discouraged.'[45]

Compare the above with the following passage by the poet John Keats:

'I had not a dispute but a disquisition with Dilke, on various subjects; several things dovetailed in my mind, and at once it struck me, what quality went to form a Man of Achievement . . . I mean *Negative Capability*, that is, when a man is capable of being in uncertainties, mysteries, doubts, without any irritable reaching after fact and reason.'[46]

Descriptions of how discoveries have been made often sound dramatic. They sound that way because Westerners are steeped in a mode of thought that tends to place them outside nature. Westerners tend to believe that they have to *make* things happen. But when a researcher 'makes a discovery', he or she isn't making anything happen; it is nature that is 'happening'! When a discovery is made, a human mind and nature get in touch. Nature unfolds its secrets to a mind that is keenly receptive to it. Or one could say that one of the properties of mind is that it can resonate to nature.[47] After all, mind must be an integral part of nature. More on this in a later chapter.[48] In the meantime, consider again the stages through which that chimpanzee passed when solving his problem:

a) He recognizes that he has a problem.
b) He attempts to solve it.
c) He is unable to do so (because he is 'thinking', i.e. bringing his past experiences to bear upon it).
d) He becomes frustrated.
e) He becomes detached from the problem (i.e. he stops 'thinking').
f) There is a spontaneous reorganization in his brain of the facts before him 'til they assume a meaningful pattern.
g) This leads to appropriate action.

I believe that that mathematician went through a similar process. Recall also that when the solution to a problem that has perplexed us for some time eventually comes to us, that solution often seems almost self-evident. It is then also sometimes difficult to understand why it ever constituted a problem.[49]

But now it is time to dig potatoes and consider how the two accounts of learning described above might help one to understand the general nature of learning a mite better.

Chapter 3

The Learning Process

The psychological literature contains many descriptions of people trying to learn something in a laboratory, but I know of only one or two systematic reports of people trying to learn something in a real-life situation. One of these is by John Carroll and Robert Mack, and I believe one can learn a good deal from it.[1]

These researchers describe how ten office temporaries tried to learn how to use a word processor. They report that one of the difficulties that these learners had was that they often had too much information to deal with at any one time. This is a problem most learners have! Carroll and Mack give an example of a learner who wants to delete a word. She presses what she thinks is the correct key, and sees a number of things come up on her screen. She looks at the manual, remembers a few things, and presses another key. But instead of the word being deleted, the screen assumes a completely different configuration!

What's gone wrong? She has no idea. So, she tries to get back to the previous screen. When she succeeds, she finds that she has forgotten what she did a moment ago. But Carroll and Mack report that, even when learners do not understand what they have just done, they usually try to press on. They often act on the flimsiest kind of hunch, and we know what the result of doing that is likely to be: even more confusion! When teachers observe such a situation, many are inclined to tell a learner what to do. But such interventions seldom help in the long run, for, unless one understands how each 'fact' is related to the next one, simply knowing one fact will not help very much. In other words, unless a task is a very simple one, it isn't possible to master it by learning one fact after the other in rote fashion. In line with what was noted in the previous chapter, one has to learn how the whole thing hangs together. In short, one has to see the pattern.

The foregoing illustrates why it is possible to follow a set of instructions exactly, obtain the required result, – and learn nothing. The above might also help to explain why some children can stay in school for ten years, and leave without having learnt very much. They learnt by drill and practice. They might remember certain things, but remembering is not the same as understanding. That is why people who really want to learn, strike out. They latch onto whatever they think they do understand, and act on that. In short, they test their hunches. Of course, in doing that, they often get into a frightful muddle. But, in acting in this way, they also very slowly come to see how one thing relates to the next. In short, they begin to understand.

The above is an illustration taken from the learning of a relatively simple skill, word processing. Here, now, an illustration taken from a university setting. Nobel prize winner Richard Feynman spent a year teaching physics at a university in Brazil, and readers whose knowledge of physics is as sketchy as mine will not have much trouble following the gist of what he has to say. I paraphrase him like this.[2]

Feynman began by noting that his students had already had many courses, and that his was to be their most advanced in electricity and magnetism. He went on to say that, as he taught, he discovered something odd. That is, he found he could ask a question, the students would know the answer; but the next time he asked more or less the same question, they couldn't answer! For example, he was once talking about polarized light, and gave out some strips of Polaroid. He noted that Polaroid passes only light whose electric vector is in a certain direction, and he explained how you could tell which way the light is polarized from whether the Polaroid is dark or light. Then he got the students to take two strips of Polaroid and rotate them till they let the most light through, for, by doing that, one could tell that the two strips were now admitting light polarized in the same direction. But when he asked the students how one could tell the absolute direction of polarization, from a single piece of Polaroid, they hadn't any idea. He noted that, as answering that question takes a certain amount of ingenuity, he gave them a hint. He said, 'Look at the light reflected from the bay outside.' Nobody said anything. So he said, 'Have you heard of Brewster's Angle?' One of the students said, 'Yes, sir! Brewster's angle is the angle at which light, reflected from a medium with an index of refraction, is completely polarized.' He therefore asked, 'And which way is the light polarized when it's reflected?' The answer came pat: 'The light is polarized perpendicular to the plane of reflection, sir.' Feynman notes that even he has to think about this, but they knew it cold! So, he said, 'Well?' Still nothing. He went on, 'They had just told me that light reflected from a medium with an index, such as the bay outside, was polarized; they had even told me which way it was polarized! Yet they couldn't answer my question.' So he said, 'Look at the bay outside, through the Polaroid. Now turn the Polaroid.' 'Ooh, it's polarized!' they said. And Feynman concluded that the students had memorized everything but that they didn't know what anything meant.

Feynman reports that, at the end of his stay at that university, he gave a talk to the staff and students, and in it tried to explain that, although he had been struck on his arrival in Brazil by the widespread interest in science, nobody at that university was learning any real science. Interestingly enough, that is what many eminent scientists say about the study of science in many places. And that isn't surprising, for it is due to the style of teaching commonly found at many universities. It is also commonly found in many schools, and readers might here recall the lesson described at the beginning of this part of this book.

Learning, real learning, isn't what happens when we are fed information. Learning is what happens when we realize that we do not know something that we consider worth knowing, form a hunch about it, and test that hunch actively. In doing that, we might also have to seek information, but notice that finding information is only a part of that process. And notice that the process begins when we realize that we don't know something.

The above seems so self-evident, one hesitates to say it. But, if correct, it surely has some very important implications. For example, it suggests that the prime function of a teacher isn't to convey information. It is, first, to help learners to realize that they don't know something (worth knowing). Second, to encourage conditions that will enable learners to pick up information to test their hunches about it. And third, to manage these things so that the learners can learn what they need to learn, with as few redundancies as is sensibly possible.

Notice again that nearly everything we wish to learn exists in the form of a system, not an isolated 'fact'. It could be a word-processing system, a judicial system, a circulatory system, or a play. At a more basic level, it could be how to build a fire, or how to catch a fish. In even these two 'simple' tasks it is not enough to know isolated 'facts'.

It is also important for teachers to remind themselves that, to anyone who has a grasp of the pattern that makes a system, that system is likely to be a model of clarity. But a learner will only achieve such clarity *after* he or she has come to understand how the various facts of a system hang together. And the only way of finding out how something hangs together, is first to take it apart, and then to put it together again. In the case of learning how to use a word processor, it is often a case of looking at a manual and pressing a key. When you do that, the static array of information on the screen before you is moved. You then get a chance to glimpse how one fact is related to the next. You might then consult your manual again, or the 'help' screen, or a teacher. But having done that, you must try out the information you have just obtained. And then the process begins once more. In learning another subject, it will be necessary to do other things, but the basic process remains the same.

The above illustrates a number of things to which I drew attention in previous chapters. Examples are:

a) the importance of active engagement
b) the need to *immerse* oneself in a problem if one wishes to solve it
c) that intrinsic rewards are the best motivators
d) that human beings strive after meaning
e) how parts or facts get their meaning from the way they fit into a whole
f) that one is helped to see the foregoing when one tests hunches, and
g) how, in the above way, models slowly become established in one's brain.

Notice two other things at this point.

I earlier noted that, in what was to follow, I had to present each section one after the other; but that I hoped that readers would soon see a coherent pattern emerging. And two, that one attribute of a good theory is that it brings a whole series of data together into a coherent pattern.

&

I noted above that we cannot learn how to use something as mechanical as even a word processor in rote fashion. A word processor consists of a set of procedures designed to produce a written text, and how it works is governed by a set of rules. What could be more mechanical? And yet, rote learning is useless in even such a task. Even when we try to learn the most mechanical of things, we never simply say,

'First this, then that, and then that, and then that . . .' In saying that, I am of course noting again that learning is not the same as remembering. In real learning we always try to make inferences. We say to ourselves, '*If* I do this, *then* that seems to happen.' Readers who are still not convinced that learning isn't the same as remembering might like to consider the following two sentences. Which is easier to learn?

- When a boat faces directly into the wind, and its sails flap, it is said to be 'in stays'.
- Up so in so in up in we in so so than in than we so we.

The first sentence is longer than the second, and contains longer and more varied words. Yet, most people would find the first sentence far easier to remember. If asked why, most people would say that the first sentence has a *meaning*. A good deal of research has been done on this matter. For example, Sacks found that people do not remember the exact words – or the sentence construction – used to convey a message. What they remember is its meaning.[3]

Or consider the following experiments reported by Jenkins.[4] Two groups of people were asked to memorize a list of words. One group was also asked to rate whether the words were pleasant or unpleasant, while the second group was asked to note whether the words were spelled with an 'e'. The results showed that the first group – the group that was asked to consider the *meaning* – recalled twice as many words as the second group.

Another experiment went roughly like this. Two groups of people were read a series of sentences about animals. One group was also asked to arrange the animals in terms of size, while the second group was simply asked to memorize the sentences. Here, too, the people in the first group, the group that was asked to consider the meaning of the sentences, remembered the sentences better than the second group.

In a searching review, Craik and Tulvig conclude: 'what determines the level of recall or recognition of a word . . . is not the intention to learn, the difficulty of the task, the amount of time spent . . . it is the qualitative nature of the task', that is, the amount of *meaning* it contains. They even found that their subjects remembered more when the task was meaningful, than when the task was meaningless and they were paid to learn![5]

Rote learning is not about understanding. In rote learning, we drill and practise until we remember. Interestingly enough, when we repeat a word frequently, it loses its meaning. But when we see the same word in a variety of contexts, its meaning for us increases, and we are then able to remember it more easily.[6]

Some teachers (or writers of a manual) expect learners to read instructions, and then to practise a task until they have mastered it. I have tried to show that such an approach rests on a fundamentally mistaken view of learning. People seldom read through a set of instructions. They don't, because instructions:

a) don't pose a problem, and
b) don't enable a learner to find an answer.

So normal people try to work things out. They probably do that because that is how the human brain evolved over the 50,000 years that humans have been on this planet; and, during this time, they have had 'written instructions' for only about a hundred years. When people are given a set of instructions, they usually first try to follow them passively. Then they put the instructions beside the thing they want to understand, read the first two lines, and begin to experiment. Some teachers get exasperated when their learners ignore their instructions (or manuals) and begin to experiment. Such teachers also become annoyed because their learners then make all sorts of mistakes. These exasperated teachers then say, 'Why don't they follow the instructions?!' I hope I have managed to indicate that such exasperation is quite misplaced. To use instructions intelligently, one has to understand them. And to understand them, one *must* experiment. Carroll and Mack note that this process 'looks much more like slightly unsystematic scientific research than drill and practice'.

Unfortunately, the experience of going to school makes many people equate learning with remembering. So, if their teacher gives them a string of instructions, and they don't learn anything from that, they blame their memories. They should blame a form of instruction based on ignorance. None of this is to say that there is no room for rote learning. There is no other way to learn the alphabet or the formula for sulphuric acid. But such remembering constitutes no more than a small fraction of what we need to learn; and it is useful only to the extent that it enables us to understand a 'whole' or a 'gestalt'.

&

The example of learning given in the previous section was of a relatively straightforward, practical task: learning how to use a word processor. But I believe that the description of learning given there holds broadly true for many kinds of learning, including the learning of an experienced practitioner. Consider, for example, what happens when a physician is confronted by a sick patient and attempts to understand the nature of an illness. Research into how physicians go about such a task shows that they do not gather a great deal of data. Instead, they very soon begin to consider a small number of provisional hypotheses, all based, of course, on their theoretical knowledge and past experiences. Then they test these hypotheses. One researcher, Elstein, describes the process like this:

a) attending to initially available cues
b) identifying problematic elements
c) switching between long-term memory and the present instance
d) generating hypotheses and suggestions for further inquiry, and
e) informally rank-ordering hypotheses as to their likely correctness in the present instance.[7]

Notice that, although this list describes experienced physicians at work, much of it also holds true for novices trying to learn how to use a word processor. I note this in part in support of my claim in my Preface that, if we understand the basics of soil cultivation, it won't usually take us long before we know how to grow cherries in California or melons in Tashkent.

Consider next what happens when we try to understand a page of text. Many readers will have had the experience of having read a page, thinking that they have understood it, – only to discover, when they are asked a question about it, that they have not really understood it. One then often finds that one has to re-read the page, try a tentative answer, compare this tentative answer with the text, and then reformulate the answer. If the page contains complex information, one must sometimes repeat this process several times.

Readers might have noticed that there was no mention of a teacher in the previous chapter. In a practical subject like word processing, people are often able to learn by themselves. But in many subjects, for example medicine, there is a large theory component, and having a teacher for such a subject seems important. I mention medicine again because this chapter has contained some findings from medicine, and the following quotation is also from medical education. It is by Michael Polanyi, and he was once a medical student:

'Think of a medical student attending a course in the X-ray diagnosis of pulmonary diseases. He watches in a darkened room shadowy traces on a fluorescent screen placed against a patient's chest, and hears the radiologist commenting to his assistants, in technical language, on the significant features of these shadows. At first the student is completely puzzled. For he can see in the X-ray picture of a chest only the shadows of the heart and the ribs, with a few spidery blotches between them. The experts seem to be romancing about figments of their imagination; he can see nothing that they are talking about. Then as he goes on listening for a few weeks, looking carefully at ever new pictures of different cases, a tentative understanding will dawn on him; he will gradually forget about the ribs and begin to see the lungs. And eventually, if he perseveres intelligently, a rich panorama of significant details will be revealed to him: of physiological variations and pathological changes, of scars, of chronic infections and signs of new disease. He has entered a new world. He still sees only a fraction of what the experts can see, but the pictures are definitely making sense now and so do most of the comments made on them. He is about to grasp what he is being taught; it has clicked.'[8]

That last sentence might remind readers of the descriptions of Sultan and Poincaré solving their problems. In their cases, there was first puzzlement, then frustration, then detachment, and then a sudden tentative grasp of how the problem could be solved. That is, the leap from not knowing, to knowing was large. In the case of these medical students, the leaps in understanding are much smaller, but Polanyi's description indicates that such leaps are often present nevertheless. Perhaps all understanding is like that. It seems to come in jumps, as more and more connections are made. And, like those office temporaries, the medical students must also have become aware that they did not know something that they needed to know; and they must have found that frustrating. They probably also made tentative guesses. It is true that, in the lesson just described, they were not able to test their hunches practically in the same way as the office temporaries. However, they must have been constantly engaged in the process of trying to find out whether they had grasped what they needed to know. Recall also that, in line with what was noted earlier, the chimpanzee, the mathematician, those people trying to learn how to use a word processor, and the medical students, all had to immerse themselves in that which they wished to understand, and to allow the information to *come* to them.

As Polanyi's description of learning is a rich one, it might be possible to use it to ask a central question: What essentially happens when we find ourselves trying to learn something in a classroom? Aside from the more general factors, like being in good health and awake, the following factors appear in Polanyi's description:

- discovering that there is something that one does not know, which one needs to know
- immersion in the problem
- puzzlement
- active engagement – especially obtaining information, and testing hunches
- repeated exposure to the learning situation
- the presence of an expert – who sets up the situation, acts as a model of competence, and can answer questions
- the inherent capacity of the human mind to understand
- periodic insights
- pleasure in gaining insights
- doubt that one will ever fully understand
- faith that one will eventually understand.

Notice that the above list also holds true for those office temporaries.

I would draw attention to two other features in the above list. One is the absence of a teacher doing much *talking*; and the other is that many of the above items refer to the way the students were *feeling*. I emphasize those two words because they will be considered in the next chapter.

Chapter 4

Talking and Feeling

One of the things that teachers often do, is to explain the topic of a lesson. That is a rather trite observation, but it might be helpful to examine it for a moment. A practical way of doing so might be to consider another passage by Polanyi. This one is a little technical, but readers should have little trouble with it:

'Unless a doctor can recognise certain symptoms, e.g. the accentuation of the second sound of the pulmonary artery, there is no use in his reading the description of syndromes of which this symptom forms a part. He must personally know that symptom, and he can learn this only by repeatedly being given cases for auscultation in which the symptom is authoritatively known to be present, side by side with other cases in which it is authoritatively known to be absent, until he has fully realised the difference between them and can demonstrate his knowledge practically to the satisfaction of an expert.'[1]

I don't think anyone will find anything remarkable in this passage, except perhaps the clarity and elegance of the language. (But then, people born overseas sometimes write especially good English.) Polanyi reminded us here that a learner must often make repeated attempts at a task, until he or she has 'got it'. A few sentences later, Polanyi sums up the point he wished to make, and I believe that what he stated here really is remarkable. He noted:

'The large amount of time spent by students of chemistry, biology and medicine in their practical courses shows how greatly these sciences rely on the transmission of skills . . . from master to apprentice. It offers an impressive demonstration of the extent to which the art of knowing has remained unspecifiable at the very heart of science.'

What does Polanyi precisely mean with the words: 'the art of knowing has remained unspecifiable'?

When we go to school or college, and study a subject like biology or electronics, we have some lessons in a classroom and some in a laboratory. But why have practical lessons in a laboratory? Why should a teacher not 'explain' everything that needs to be learnt? Laboratory lessons are expensive. They require space and equipment for each learner. It would be a great saving if they could be discontinued. But no serious teacher would be prepared to do away with practical lessons. And learners often say that they learn the most from a practical lesson. What is the exact reason for this?

When I asked students this question, they tended to say something like, 'Because practical lessons strengthen what is learnt in theory lessons.' But Polanyi went much further. He stated that one simply cannot convey that which learners pick up in a practical lesson by 'telling' them that. And further, that this is because a good deal of what is learnt in a practical lesson *cannot be specified in words*. He called this kind of knowledge 'tacit'.

If Polanyi was right, the implications for teaching are surely very great. At risk of seeming repetitious, I note again that Polanyi claimed that a great deal of knowledge *cannot* be stated in words. And he was not referring to emotional things, which most people agree are often difficult to state in words. He was referring to practical knowledge, a problem that I described in a previous chapter when noting my attempts to learn how to fix a fault on my car. I then stated that, if we do not have *a model of the thing with which we are concerned, already in our brain*, having somebody explain a matter to us will not usually help very much.

Consider next a more general example than fixing a car. Many readers will remember having been told something important about life by their parents or friends when they were youngsters. They will probably also recall that, until they had had some actual *experience* of the matter, they often did not really understand the implications of what they had been told. This again suggests that 'telling' has serious limitations. The trouble is, we often think that we have conveyed the meaning of something when we have said something. But we only manage to convey a meaning when the person to whom we are speaking already has that meaning. We can give someone the words that stand for a meaning, but we cannot give someone a meaning by using words. Meanings cannot be given. Meanings are a part of life, and, like life, they have to be experienced. Many tests of learning hide this limitation of language. They assume that learning has taken place when a person can write or say something. This illusion is often exploded the minute that this person has to *do* something. With a practical task, that is often soon seen. But with a theoretical task, learners can often get by with words, – until they have to apply those words in a practical situation.

This limitation of language has long been recognized, and I write this book at a time when the reaction to 'theoretical' knowledge has become so strong that there is now a growing attempt to test all knowledge via 'competences'. The trouble with this approach is that, just as the ability to pass a written exam does not show evidence of being able to do a task, so being able to do a task shows little evidence of being able to understand a task. But even with the current emphasis on practical abilities, a good deal of teaching is still based on the belief that one can convey a new meaning by 'explaining' it. This belief is seldom examined. Sometimes it is glanced at, as when a teacher says, 'I went over that topic last week, and they still don't seem to have a clue.'

Many years ago, John Holt expressed the above like this. He noted: 'We teachers – perhaps all human beings – are in the grip of an astonishing delusion. We think we can take a picture, a structure, a working model of something, constructed in our minds out of long experience and familiarity, and, by turning that model into a string of words, transplant it whole into the mind of someone else. . . . Most of the time explaining does not increase understanding, and may even lessen it.'[2]

When I was on my teacher training course, a great deal of attention was paid to the use of language, and I suspect that this emphasis was related to the

widespread use of the transmission method of teaching. When we see the limitations of language, we also see the limitations of that method.[3] It is obviously
important to use the right kind of language when one teaches. There are teachers
who talk in a way that is quite unsuitable for their learners, and a few seem to be
oblivious of the fact that half their learners do not understand what they are
talking about. But the problem here is not one of language, but of attitude.
Teachers who have a sense of empathy take on the perspective of their learners,
and speak so that their learners can understand. But even when teachers have a
sense of empathy, and speak so that their learners can understand, they will still
not be able to convey new meanings a good deal of the time, and this is because
this is beyond the scope of language.

Of course, none of this is intended to suggest that language is unimportant.
Language is obviously very important, and readers might recall the comments I
made on language when I referred to the work of Vygotsky in an earlier chapter.
That is, it is only with the help of language that we are often able to gain a
clearer understanding of something that we have experienced. Most readers will
have heard of the little old lady who said, 'How do I know what I think 'til I've
said it?'

So language is two-edged: it can help us gain a deeper understanding, but it
can also create an illusion of understanding. The latter happens when a teacher
believes that, if she gives us a word for something, she has also given us the thing
for which the word stands. It is probably because of this illusion that learners often
find lessons either entertaining or boring, but seldom the source from which they
really learn. And it is probably because of this, that an unknown learner carved the
following legend into a certain classroom desk:

> Here I sit bord as hell
> Waiting for the bloody bell. (T. S. Eliot)

&

I could paraphrase what I have noted above by saying something with which, I
think, most people would agree. It is that there is an important difference between
learning something verbally, and learning it experientially. For example, we all
know people who seem to carry around chunks of prefabricated thought, and
when an appropriate slot appears, they slide the chunk in. Other people make
quite a different impression. What they say seems theirs, and it seems alive. The
latter kinds of people also seem able to use their knowledge in varying circumstances, and they are sometimes even creative.

I am beholden to several people for helping me to understand the above a mite
better than I might otherwise have done. The work of one of them, Michael
Polanyi, was noted above. Another was Carl Rogers. The work of Carl Rogers is
much less fashionable today than it once was, but I believe that he had some very
perceptive things to say on this matter. Consider, for example, his belief that it is
impossible to teach anyone anything of any real consequence, – if by 'teach' is
meant what we commonly mean thereby. Of course, this belief *sounds* absurd,
and Rogers thought so, too. He wrote: 'That sounds so ridiculous I can't help but
question it at the same time as I present it.'[4]

When I first came across Rogers' work, I felt I had made an important discovery; and I would hope that people who have not read his work will be encouraged to do so if I quote a few more lines. For example, Rogers also wrote:

'self-discovered learning, truth that has been personally appropriated and assimilated in experience, cannot be directly communicated to another. As soon as an individual tries to communicate such experience directly, often with quite natural enthusiasm, it becomes teaching, and its results are inconsequential.'

He went on: 'When I try to teach, as I do sometimes, I am appalled by the results, which seem little more than inconsequential, because sometimes the teaching appears to succeed. When this happens I find that the results are damaging. It seems to cause the individual to distrust his own experience, and to stifle significant learning.'

I used to distribute photocopies of these statements in my classes, and ask the students what they thought of them. At first, many of the students used to smile and nod their heads in thoughtful agreement. Then a few would object. They would say that they had learnt a great deal by listening to a teacher. Others would echo this sentiment; and then objections would come so thick and fast that Rogers was soon buried. After such discussions had continued for some time, I would ask how we could summarize the position we had reached. Somebody would say that Rogers was right to some extent, but that he overstated his case; and many of those present would nod their heads. One or two would disagree, but they appeared to find it difficult to justify their support for Rogers.

I never quite knew what to do next. I believe that Rogers was broadly right. But, if he was right, that is, if 'telling' is often a waste of time, even damaging, then it would be contradictory for me to *tell* my students why I think so. I should perhaps nevertheless add that I sometimes tried to explain why I think Rogers was right. But when I did, I often found that some learners would repeat my comments in their assignments, and I then had the strange experience of seeing Rogers vindicated. For the way in which students did this strongly suggested that they had not 'really' understood what Rogers had intended. In short, they conveyed that they had learnt merely verbally, that is, that they were repeating something.

But it would be a mistake to exaggerate. I found that quite a few students understood beautifully what Rogers was getting at, and it was then a great pleasure to see their thinking develop powerfully. But, in the case of quite a few students, a dilemma remained. Immediately after a lesson on Rogers, in which the theme had been the danger of 'telling', they complained that I did not explain enough.

As I noted earlier, the work of Rogers is much less fashionable today than it once was, and that is of course to be expected. It is also the case that some of Rogers' findings have not really stood the test of time. Nevertheless, I think it is safe to say that Rogers' basic orientation towards counselling has been adopted by a large number of counsellors, and that he has probably had more effect on the practice of counselling than any other writer in the last fifty years. He also contributed frequently to discussions on educational matters, so it might be helpful to re-consider some of his basic premises.

Very briefly put, Rogers took a very concrete position, that is, he came to most of his conclusions while working with clients who had come to him in distress. These were people who found that they kept falling out with their spouse; or that they were making a mess of their studies; or that their personal lives were unrewarding. In the process of discussing these things with such clients, Rogers discovered, among other things, three things that can be summarized like this. First, that even when he was able to discover the causes underlying his clients' difficulties, telling them these causes seldom helped them to change much. Second, when he was able to establish the right kind of conditions, his clients were sometimes able to work out for themselves why they had difficulties. And third, when they made such discoveries for themselves, a change for the better sometimes followed.[5]

At this point, some readers might well be wondering what relevance findings such as these have for the process of learning in a classroom. They might be willing to concede that clients in therapy and students in a classroom are both engaged in learning, but the similarity seems to end there. For it is clear that clients in therapy are engaged in trying to learn how to conduct more rewarding lives, whereas students in a classroom are engaged in trying to learn new material. In response to such an apparently obvious difference, consider the work of Gertrude Hendrix on learning mathematics.[6] Among other things, she discovered that the ability to transfer what one has learnt from doing one kind of mathematical task, to doing a similar one, is more likely when:

a) learners have been helped to discover the rule for doing the first task, and when
b) the rule so learnt remains unverbalized until it is completely mastered.

She also found that:

c) giving learners a rule before they have been helped to discover it, or asking them to verbalize a rule before they have mastered it, interferes with their ability to transfer their learning.

Readers will immediately see the similarity between the Rogers and the Hendrix findings. Some might find them odd, and they certainly go clean against widespread belief and practice. But then, that is a characteristic of many discoveries. It is easy to imagine how people must have felt when they were first told that the sun does not move.

What is the explanation for the Rogers and the Hendrix findings? I believe that the following might offer a start. When we discover something ourselves, we have direct experience of it. This knowledge is then encoded inside us in a compacted, abstract, living form; and that enables us to grasp its meaning. We don't then see the items bit by it, word after word. We dimly see the matter as an integrated whole. We also sense how it interconnects with the thousands of other things that we already know; and this kind of learning permeates our being. However, when someone tells us something, we do not need to strive to grasp its total *meaning*. We can memorize the words. That often gives us the illusion that we have understood something; but we have seen that the words that describe something, are not the same as that thing itself. They are symbols that stand in lieu of that something.

Consider an everyday example. A friend of yours visits Boston, comes back and tells you enthusiastically about his visit, and shows you some excellent photographs. By chance, the following week you see a fine film about life in that city. All this whets your interest, and that summer you decide to visit the place. Now, anyone who has had this kind of an experience, will know that there is seldom much of a relationship between what one expects to see, and what one experiences when one actually sees a place. This is because, as suggested, an experience cannot be communicated.

Looking back on it now, I must add that I did not find it easy to apply such a view of learning in my classes. Moreover, Rogers' clients differed in one very important respect from many learners in most classrooms. Clients do not come to a therapist in order to obtain a certificate; they come because they are in distress. But many learners come to a classroom precisely in order to obtain a certificate. After all, that is one very common way of getting a job.

I believe Rogers underestimated the importance of this difference. He maintained that people learn best when they find themselves in the right conditions to do so, and are encouraged to make their own way. The latter assertion might well be correct. But the question that then surely arises is: Learn what? Few people are happy to spend a lot of time and effort to master a certain body of knowledge. There is only so much time in any one day, and many people want to do other things besides study. This can create a conflict between what an individual learner might want, and what a community needs. In other words, an individual might need a particular certificate, but not be prepared to put in the work required to master the knowledge to merit being granted that certificate. A community, however, needs competent practitioners. In short, although a client in psychotherapy, and a learner in a classroom, are both engaged in learning, their aims might be very different.

At this point, it might be helpful to recall that there is a great deal in Rogers' work about the needs of the individual, but very little about the needs of a community, and the possible conflict between the two. His work is very much the product of a certain Western outlook, with its emphasis on the individual, and it seems to me that, although this outlook can confer certain advantages, it also has some very important disadvantages.[7] Nevertheless, I believe that Rogers was broadly right in what he noted about the effect of didactic teaching. I also believe that his observations remain broadly correct for the process of psychotherapy, and I shall return to this matter later. If so, the problem I noted earlier, again arises: How does one teach without too much telling?

I shall consider that question in some detail in later chapters. Before that, I draw attention to the fact that this is not a new problem. Many of the most thoughtful religious teachers have wrestled with it. They appear to have known intuitively that preaching seldom results in significant learning.[8] We all know religious people who are scrupulous about keeping to outward observances, but whose personal lives are far from moral. We also know that, for centuries, all over the world, people have been taught by religious teachers, yet the actions of both teacher and taught have often been in direct contradiction to that which has been taught. In short, it is not enough to know the truth; *one must also act on it in order to learn it*. The foregoing is not intended as a criticism of religion, only as another example to suggest that didactic teaching seldom results in significant learning.

'Real' learning is never a matter of listening to a teacher, religious or otherwise. Such listening merely runs us along grooves of pleasant reassurance. Real learning only comes about when we have had an appropriate experience. And the more we have to struggle during that experience, the more powerful is our learning likely to be. It is only when my knuckles are bruised, oil is dripping into one of my ears, sweat is beading on my forehead, the wrong spanner is in my hand, and I can't wriggle out from under my car, that I begin to learn how to fix a fault on it. In short, when computers can sweat, they will learn.

❧

One of the topics most often discussed in the literature on learning is the way in which people solve problems. Unfortunately, I am unable to make much sense of most of this literature.[9] Three things especially tend to trouble me about it. The artificiality of the tasks set; the clumsy and illogical way that the people described in it often act; and the absence of any comment about how the people involved feel.[10] I have the same reactions to accounts of computer simulations of problem solving, for these also seem completely artificial to me. For example, although computers can be programmed to solve a problem in calculus, they cannot be programmed to recognize a cucumber, and there is never any reference to how the computer feels. In view of these difficulties, I shall try to describe my own experiences of problem solving; and, although this is likely to be subjective, it will be ecologically valid. Readers should also be able to see whether my experiences tally with theirs.

The example of problem solving I should like to consider, is the experience of writing this book; and I choose this example because I have often recalled times when I have been a student while engaged in this task. That is, I have often found myself faced by the need to solve a series of problems, and I have not been at all sure I can. The office temporaries and medical students described earlier must have had the same kind of doubts. Next come other feelings. For example, the wish to establish professional competence, to make a contribution, to argue a point, to make some money, to gain the esteem of friends, to get a new job, perhaps even to override death.[11] Most students must have at least some of those feelings. If so, how to simulate them on a computer?

Another very powerful feeling I often have, while writing, is that I do not really understand. It is as if there is an air of mystery about everything; as if almost all topics under discussion are somehow different from what seems immediately apparent. Then, occasionally, when I manage to pierce the fog of mystery, there is a feeling of pleasure. That is similar to how I have often felt as a student. How does one program a computer to have a sense of mystery?

The next thing that strikes me is that, whenever I write something that I later consider useful, it is seldom my thinking that has produced it. Rather, my thinking is what happens *after* I have had an insight. Whenever I have tried to force myself to gain an insight, my mind has gone blank. Useful insights have always *come* to me; and they have usually come in one of two ways. One is when I am engaged in an activity other than actually thinking. Typical activities include having a shower, or going for a ride on a mountain bike. That is, thinking has to stop before insights can begin. Readers might recall that I made this comment when describing how Sultan and Poincaré solved their problems. How does one program this on a computer?

It has also been long established that progress in science dos not come about as the result of the accumulation of facts, but when someone glimpses a discrepancy between what is commonly believed to be the case, and what might actually be the case. Then come hunches as to how such an anomaly might be resolved, followed by tests of those hunches.[12] Readers will immediately see that such an account echoes what I have written about the process of learning in general. The above raises an intriguing question: What causes a productive hunch to come about? If that could be made clear, then we could all have a productive hunch fifty times a day. But, if we cannot specify how such a hunch comes about, we cannot program a computer to have one. It certainly hasn't been done to date; and this again draws attention to the huge difference between computers and humans.

Another way in which insights sometimes come to me is in the process of writing. Until I began to consider how this book got written, I had not realized to what extent the very process of writing has such a powerful effect. For example, I want to draw attention to a piece of research. So, I start writing about it. In the process of doing that, something else will suggest itself to me. So, I'll write about that. Then, while I am doing that, more modifications will suggest themselves. None of this would have happened unless I had begun writing. Notice here how this process occurs to a much lesser extent while speaking, and this is a very important matter to which I shall turn in a later chapter.

Another characteristic of the material that occurs to me while writing is that it comes in the form of compacted hunches. At first, those hunches seem clear enough, – but only until I try to write them down. Then they sound clumsy. I have to have many, many attempts at writing before a hunch becomes reasonably clear to me. Even then, the moment another hunch comes along, the previous hunch, which had seemed reasonably clear till then, either becomes increasingly clear, or less clear. Notice that this is similar to how the office temporaries and medical students learnt. I have also noticed that the thousands of strands, out of which this book is constituted, get put together in a decidedly piecemeal way. I'll write a few paragraphs on a topic, come to the end of a third or fifth paragraph, and then find I have to rewrite the first paragraph in the light of the third. Several weeks later, I have another idea, or come across another research finding, and another strand will suggest itself to me. When I try to add this to the network I already have, I find I have to rewrite many of the strands around it. Quite often, whole sections have to be rewritten. It is as if meanings come in compacted kernels, and that these have to be clarified and expanded until they mesh with each other to make up a coherent whole. Readers will immediately see how these observations relate to the comments made in an earlier chapter on the way parts get their meaning from a whole. And again, readers might notice that this is all very different from what happens when we speak about something.

None of this is like how a computer program works. All the information in a computer program is held in the form of discrete items. And when a program contains a great deal of information, that information has to be organized in segments or hierarchies to allow for processing. In writing this book, the opposite happens. I begin by using things like sub-headings. But, as I continue, these organizational strategies blur, and it is only when I can see all the details of a topic as one coherent whole, that I begin to feel it makes sense.

The above suggests that one of the main characteristics of a powerful understanding of a topic is that the person concerned can see all its details as one integrated whole. How would one program a computer to see a thousand details as one aesthetically satisfying whole?[13] I also believe that the word 'aesthetic' is very important here. Whenever I have found myself struggling to get the various strands of this book to mesh together, I have often been struck by the way I have been prompted as much by aesthetic as by intellectual considerations.[14]

For example, I find I keep asking myself whether a section now 'sounds' or 'feels' right. This reminds me of a period when I was a boy, and became interested in painting. A few strokes here, a few strokes there, until a picture was built up. It also reminds me of more recent times when I have tried to establish a garden. There is the same digging, planting, weeding, pruning, staking, replanting and thinning. Guiding such an enterprise there is always an indistinct but potent sense of aesthetics.

Another thing I discovered while writing, is that I am often far from clear about the implications of what I am writing. For example, after many revisions, I will complete a chapter and leave it at that. I feel I just cannot improve on it further. Weeks, months, even years later, something I had not considered before will suddenly strike me. Or I will come across another bit of evidence, or another person's insights, and these will throw what I have been trying to say into a new light. It is then as if I suddenly understood much better what I had been trying to say. Other times, I realize I have been on the wrong track. It is as if I were heading towards a goal, that I am unable to specify clearly beforehand, but that I am able to recognize when I reach it.

How to explain this? It seems to me that there is only way. It is to say that what I am trying to do is related to life. I am alive, I can therefore experience life; and in writing this book, I am trying to make sense of those experiences (more specifically, my experiences of learning and teaching). And this process will never end, for always the goal is as complex and indistinct as the nature of life itself. It follows that, when we are engaged in a complex and new task, we are never able to determine the goal exactly beforehand. We can only recognize it – often mistakenly – when we get close to it. If that is all roughly so, it follows that a computer could never simulate human problem solving because computers are not alive. But more importantly, I trust it will be seen that what I have attempted to describe in this section is similar to what happens in much learning.

At other times, I become aware that what I have known tacitly has become conscious. For example, I find myself saying, 'Ah, that's how it is . . .' And colouring all these processes, there are often intense feelings. These can be painful or pleasurable, and everything in between. For example, I sometimes doubt whether anything will ever come of all the work I am doing, and I then groan at the implications of this. At other times I feel hopeful, even elated. There must also be a strong inclination to persevere, for, without this, the job would never get done. Royston helps to make clear the extent to which feelings play an essential part in all intellectual activity. He notes that, when people find reflecting in the way I have attempted to illustrate difficult, new material tends to sit outside their mind in the form of a shapeless mass. And when they manage to reproduce it, it tends to take the form of slogans. In Royston's words, 'dynamic complexity lapses into truism or formula, and the originality and aliveness of the work leaks away'.[15] A typical example, in discussions of a psychological nature, is the use of phrases like 'person centred' or 'significant other'. In politics, a favourite word is 'terrorist'. That is, naming replaces understanding. There is one more factor that plays an essential part when one is trying to write a book, and it also plays an important part in many learning tasks. This is trying to make what one wishes to say clear, both to oneself and to other people.

There are plenty of tips on how to write. For example, we all know that we must try not to use the same words too often, and that it is helpful to vary the length of sentences. But knowing these things will not save a person from using ten words where six would do. I find I have to rewrite things many times, sometimes hundreds of times, before I am half way satisfied with them. In short, good writing cannot be reduced to a set of instructions. If so, how does one program a computer to write simply and clearly? But the difficulty goes further, and I would put it like this: The main difficulty in writing is to get the meaning one is trying to convey past the screen of language in which one must say it. How is one to program such a factor into a computer when the basic element of a computer is language, not meaning? I raise these questions in part to suggest that expressing what one wishes to say in writing can be difficult, that good teachers are sensitive to this, and that they will sometimes encourage their learners to go over things many times.

In the above, I have drawn attention to mainly two things. One, that the distinction often made between feeling and thinking is misleading. And two, that problem solving is not a matter of using appropriate 'strategies' (as is often claimed in the writing of those who base their findings on laboratory tasks), but depends greatly on the quality of one's exposure to the problem before one. Indeed, I would argue that the fewer the strategies, the better the exposure. And so it logically must be. For I am unable to specify the goal until I have reached it.[16] Nor could those office temporaries or those medical students.

If I reflect further on what I have written in this section, I am also forced to conclude that, although the urge to write is somehow mine, it would be more correct to say that the book got written through me. I fear that this may sound mystical when I am trying to be accurate. For I do not believe that we solve problems by mystical forces (whatever that might mean). I believe rather that thought processes are as open to rational investigation as our respiratory processes; that is, in terms of an integration between organism and environment. However, in artificial intelligence, there is no environment. There is only a disembodied 'brain' working in a vacuum. In short, I can see no sensible similarity between the way in which this book got written, and how a computer program works. The essential feelings are entirely missing, as are also many of the most important intellectual features.

So far in this book, I have drawn attention to the nature of motivation, the effect of intrinsic and extrinsic rewards, the importance of active engagement, the way in which a part gains its meaning from a whole, the phenomenon of insight, the nature of thinking, the process of understanding, the power and limitation of language, the need to experience, and the part played by a sense of aesthetics. I summarize like this, because I am thinking about the need to have a theory if one's practice is to be guided by some coherent conception.

The next section is a kind of interlude. After that will come a new chapter on how we see.

For about fifty years, the Behaviourist position was the dominant one in psychology, and by far the strongest when learning was under consideration. In educational circles, only the work of Jean Piaget was studied to the same extent.[17] Today, the Behaviourist position has been superseded by the 'Cognitive' approach, and Gestalt psychology gets as little attention as before.[18] Actually, the study of psychology has almost disappeared from many training courses, and it is usually only mentioned when fashionable peripherals like 'individual differences' are brought in. On the rare occasions when psychology is mentioned on a training course, it is in terms of the cognitive approach, and it might therefore be an idea to consider it briefly.

First, in Cognitivism, the focus of attention is not restricted to an outside stimulus and the resulting behaviour, as was the case in Behaviourism, but rather, attention is directed at the mental processes that are thought to take place inside a person. As a result of this shift, fifty years of Behaviourist research appears to have been scrapped. For example, there is no mention of 'reinforcement' in the research published today in the cognitive style. That is, with the appearance of Cognitivism, it is as if, in physics, concepts like mass and velocity were not just seen differently, but as if they had ceased to have any relevance. Or, as if in medicine, the notion of metabolism and respiration were now considered outmoded. There is surely something odd about a discipline that can change as dramatically as this.[19]

One of the main topics of interest to a Behaviourist was learning. Today, one can read research in the cognitive style and find no mention whatsoever of learning. This is probably because many Cognitivists like to compare humans with computers, and it is difficult to program a computer to learn. So, the focus is on 'information processing'. More exactly, in Cognitivism, there is a fundamental assumption that action follows thought, and that thought, or thinking (conscious or unconscious) is a matter of the brain or the mind manipulating symbols. In other words, one does not begin with a problem – I would say the problem of the relationship of the mind to the rest of nature – but with an orientation, and it is that orientation that determines what one looks at, and therefore sees. All this is very different from the approach taken in this book. In this book, an intimate link is assumed to exist between individual minds and nature. In brief, that the location of consciousness is in the world, not in individual minds, and that individual minds are linked to this larger consciousness. More on this later.

What is perhaps most striking about the move from Behaviourism to Cognitivism is not the alleged difference between them. For example, just as was the case in Behaviourism, the focus in Cognitivism is also on the individual. That is, people are seen largely as isolated entities, encapsulated in a bag of skin. Hence, there is seldom much of a suggestion that humans are profoundly dependent on, and affected by their physical, social and cultural environment. In other words, Cognitivism might best be seen as one of the symptoms of a culture in which there is a focus on 'the individual'. For in Cognitivism, all attention is focused on what goes on inside one person's head, and this is perhaps best seen in cognitive therapy, which is guided by the fundamental and implicit belief that the problem that troubles clients lies inside their heads. But recall here that, with the help of an appropriate gadget, we are able to see that, around each organism, there is a layer of warm, moist air, and that this moves regularly up the surface of the body. This layer is the result of the production of heat and water by metabolism, and it is only when a sharp wind blows this layer away – the so-called 'wind-chill' factor – that we sense how cold it really is. This example might illustrate the close interconnection between organism and environment.[20] If so, the problem that a person who consults a psychotherapist might have is likely to lie in the interplay between that person and his or her environment, rather than inside that person.

Moreover, just as was the case in Behaviourism, so also in Cognitivism, these 'individuals' are often studied as if they were automatons. Thus, an examination of the cognitive literature indicates that many Cognitivists are even more inclined than Behaviourists to compare humans with machines. More exactly, whereas Behaviourists often compared humans with animals, Cognitivists prefer to compare them with computers. In short, Cognitivism is like the rebellious son who often reminds one of the Behaviourist father.

Critics of Behaviourism used to say that, with the advent of Behaviourism, psychology became the study of people who had lost their minds. Today, it would be appropriate to say that, with the appearance of Cognitivism, psychology has become the study of people who have lost their bodies.[21] In Behaviourism, feelings were mostly ignored. In Cognitivism, feelings have almost entirely disappeared. As a result, everything we most associate with being human and alive, things like joy, worry, hope, shame and fear, tend to have little place in the Cognitive scheme of things. Thus, the things that most often give rise to our feelings – other people, and especially relationships – have little place in the electronic switchboard model of humans that is fashionable in much Cognitive psychology.

When I read the writings of some of those who work in this tradition, I often feel that the writer failed to get into a school of engineering. I used to read such work from the perspective of a journeyman teacher, as a man trying to understand how human beings learn. And I found that I could read a great deal of this literature, and not find much in it that tallied with my experience of learning.[22] In the search for usable evidence, method appeared to replace insight.[23]

At this point, I should perhaps note that I am aware that a cognitive approach is the one most favoured today in psychotherapy, and, very briefly put – for this book is not primarily about psychotherapy – I have three main reasons for doubting its alleged efficacy.[24] One is that much dysfunctional behaviour is learnt very early in life, that is, before the acquisition of language, and hence before cognitive structures have become established. Two, I believe that most substantial learning, both before and during psychotherapy, is experiential and hence only secondarily cognitive. Or to put this another way, as much of our behaviour is governed by schemas in our procedural memory system, and hence often beyond conscious awareness, an approach based on cognition is unlikely to tap into, and modify such schemas. And three, as the schemas in our brain are strongly interconnected with our sense of self, it is not enough to attempt to change cognitive schemas in order to change behaviour.[25] A substantial change in one's sense of self is also required, and this is again very unlikely to come about if the focus is cognitive.

There is, however, considerable research that indicates that some people in severe emotional distress are helped with cognitive therapy. If so, I believe that the explanation for this is roughly as follows. One, being with someone who listens attentively to one's distress, and who responds in an encouraging and thoughtful manner, is likely to raise one's hopes. Two, one's own best endeavours are likely to be stimulated when one is with a psychotherapist who considers cognitive therapy validated.[26] And three, cognitive therapy does not seek to enter into deeply painful experiences, so is unlikely to be experienced as threatening.

The above is a large and complex topic; these comments do not do it justice, and I would urge interested readers to consult the references I cite. However, I trust that what I have noted is enough to suggest that, if cognitive therapy is sometimes beneficial, it might be for reasons other than what its advocates claim.

Chapter 5

Perception

There does not seem to be much of a connection between how we see, and how we learn. However, if one recalls that the word 'see' can refer to our ability to see with our eyes, and also to our ability to understand with our brain, one might be prompted to examine how we see. Consider the following illustration.

A little girl is out for a walk in the country with her parents. The child is two years old, and, as they walk, they see a cow, the first this girl has ever seen. Rays of light are reflected off the cow, reach the child's eyes, and cause chemical changes and electrical charges inside them. These things travel along the child's optic nerve, reach her brain, and stimulate certain nerve cells inside it. The child then 'sees' a cow. In other words, as the child looks, 'pictures' of a thing called 'a cow' are traced upon, or coded in the millions of nerve cells that make up the seeing part of that child's brain.[1]

I have used the words 'picture', 'traced' and 'coded' above, but an examination of a person's brain does not show any such things. The people who study the process of perception use other, more technical terms; and the one often used to correspond with a 'picture' in the brain is 'schema'. The plural is 'schemas' or 'schemata'. But these are also only words, and exactly how images are coded in the brain is still rather unclear.[2]

So, the child walks along, and thousands upon thousands of schemas of 'a cow' are coded in her brain. I write that 'thousands' of schemas are coded in that child's brain because, after all, next time that little girl is out for a walk, she might catch a glimpse of a cow's backside in the shade of a big tree. As her eyes take this in, the thousands of images (or schemas) she already has inside her brain that remotely resemble anything that looks like the backside of a cow in deep shade, are reeled off automatically. If the new images coming into her brain from the outside match any of the thousands of schemas already inside it, she will recognize what she is seeing. It follows that what we call seeing is better called recognizing. In short, every time we look at something, it is matched against the models we already have in our brain.

Notice that this description is similar to the description, given in a previous chapter, of infants moving their heads in order to control a flow of milk; and the similarity lies in this, that those infants were also testing the model of the world they already had inside their brain, against the world around them. Moreover, the same is true of those office temporaries learning how to use a word processor. That is, in their learning, those people were also testing what was happening on the screens in front of them, against the schemas inside their brain. From this it looks as if it is after all not far-fetched to say that how we see is reminiscent of certain features of how we learn. Readers might also notice that, here again, a number of seemingly very different strands mesh, and that this is a characteristic of a good theory.

But it does not follow from the above that there is a one-to-one correspondence between the things in the world around one, and the schemas inside one's brain. As usual, things become more complicated when one examines them closely.[3] However, the above account provides a rough working model with which, I think, one can get along, 'til a better model is put forward. So one could sum up like this: When we 'see', we test what we take in with our eyes, against the schemas already inside our brain; and, if there is a match, we recognize what we see. Here, now, is some evidence on this matter.

If you look at Figure 5.1, you will see either a duck or a rabbit. This raises an interesting question: How is it possible for a drawing to be recognizable as two so very different things? Notice also that there is no in-between kind of image. One never sees a picture that looks a little like both animals. How can a drawing remain the same, and yet what one sees be very different from moment to moment?

The answer is of course that 'seeing' is not just a matter of taking something in, but rather a case of matching what is out in the world, against what is already inside one's brain. Hence, the act of looking is something like the act of picking up clues; and the clues one picks up cause one's brain to reel off the millions of schemas stored inside it which resemble what one happens to be looking at. So, as in the above example, at first an image of a duck pops up in one's brain, then an image of a rabbit. Of course, it could be the other way round. Which way round depends on the general context, or in which animal one happens to be more interested.

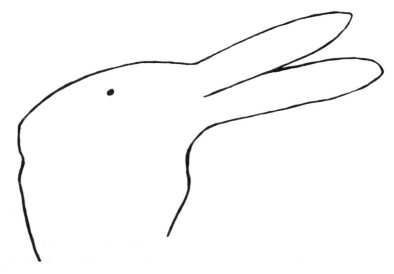

Figure 5.1

Figure 5.2

Notice that the previous comments indicate that seeing is an active process. That is, we nearly always have expectations (based on our previous experiences), and these influence what we see. Notice also that we see with our brain, not our eyes. To say that we see with our eyes is like saying that we hear with our ears. Both of the latter are, of course, merely receptors. Consider next some of the implications of what has been noted so far.

Look at Figure 5.2. If you have never seen this picture before, you will probably not 'see' (better, 'recognize') anything. It probably looks like a mass of blobs and patches. Perhaps it reminds you of a badly drawn seacoast; and if you go on looking, you might 'see' all kinds of other things. But notice what happens if you are given a few clues. For example, towards the left, there is the head of a cow. The cow is standing broadside on, with its head turned at 90 degrees toward you. It is standing half in deep shade, and half in bright sunlight. Perhaps you have now 'seen' it? If not, Figure 5.3 provides an outline of this animal.[4] If you now look back at the unclear picture, you might recognize (i.e., 'see') the cow. Notice also that, when one first sees (that is, recognizes) the cow, it comes in a rush. First, there is nothing. Then, seemingly of a sudden, one 'sees' a cow. How is this possible? The drawing on the page has not changed.

The answer is clear. As was noted, whenever we look at something, thousands of schemas are reeled off in our brain, depending on the clues we pick up as we look. Then, as we pick up more clues, the possibilities are narrowed. Increasingly, what comes up in our brain begins to match what we are looking at. Finally, there is an exact match; and at that point, we *recognize* what we are looking at, and say, 'Ah!'

Figure 5.3

Of course, all this usually happens extremely quickly, so quickly there seems to be no gap whatsoever between our looking and our seeing. It is only in unclear instances, as in the case of that cow, that there is a slight gap. Whatever the length of the gap, like our circulatory system, the process takes place completely beyond conscious awareness.

To sum up: 'Seeing' is primarily a matter of testing what we perceive of the world around us, against the schemas already present in our brain; and readers might again notice the connection here with what has been noted in previous chapters.

&

It sometimes happens that a person is born with impaired vision. Such impairment might be due to cataracts, or to an opacity of the cornea, and people with one of these impairments might grow up quite blind. However, many advances have been made in medicine and technology in the last fifty years, and it is now sometimes possible to correct such impairments with an operation. The cataracts are removed, or a corneal graft is made, and the person concerned obtains a corrected visual system. There are researchers who have investigated how people react to gaining sight after such an operation, and one of them, Richard Gregory, provides us with a striking account of a man who was blind, and in the way just noted gained sight in middle age.[5]

Gregory reports that, immediately after the man's bandages were removed, he turned his face in the direction from which the voices of the nurses and surgeon around his bed were coming, but he was unable to see anything except a blur. That will not surprise us when we remember that, to see, we must have appropriate schemas in our brain. A few days later, things had much improved. The man was able to walk along the hospital corridors, and tell the time from wall clocks. But this man's sight developed in selective ways. That is, if the man had had an experience of something via touch before the operation (e.g. telling the time by touch from a pocket watch), then his sense of sight in that respect developed reasonably well. But, if he had not had such an experience, things were problematic. For example, the man learnt how to read words written in capital letters by sight without too much difficulty, and that was probably because he had learnt how to read those kinds of letters in Braille when he had been blind. But he found it much more difficult to learn how to read words written in lower-case letters by sight, because these he had not learnt to read by touch. In fact, he never did manage to learn to read anything other than the simplest words written in that form. A more dramatic example came to light when the man began to draw. Gregory found that he was able to draw the back of a bus, but not its front, by sight. That was probably due to the fact that he had often touched the back of a bus in his blind years, but never the front of one. (Gregory was, of course, referring to certain buses in Britain that are entered from the back.)

Notice that the above example demonstrates that one has to *learn* how to see, just as one has to *learn* how to walk or speak. Or, to rephrase this in the terms used before, learning how to do these things is partly a matter of laying down appropriate schemas. The above example also indicates that to lay down schemas late in life is not easy, and we are given some indication of how difficult this is by the following. Gregory reports that, although the man's sight continued to improve slowly, he unfortunately became so depressed that he appeared to give up the wish to live, and died three years later. Depression is, apparently, quite common in such cases; and Gregory suggests that this is perhaps because some of these people feel a deep sense of pain at what they have missed in previous years.

The above also illustrates what is already well known, namely, that it is difficult to learn how to do certain things in middle age that one can learn how to do almost without effort when one is a child.[6] More exactly, if one has the necessary basic experiences when one is young, one's abilities in those respects can develop further all through one's life. However, if one has not had a chance to have certain basic experiences when young – as was the case with this man's sense of sight – then there can be trouble in later years.

So far, this chapter has been mostly about the process of seeing. But, just as one must have the appropriate schemas in one's brain before one can recognize what one is looking at, so must one also have the appropriate schemas in one's brain to understand the words a person might be saying.[7] Consider what happens when somebody speaks to us in a language that we do not understand. It sounds like noise; and the reason is clear: we do not have the appropriate schemas in our brain that would allow us to 'recognize' what we are hearing.

What has been noted so far might also help to explain why it is that new ideas are often rejected out of hand, even if they are later shown to be sound. That is, when we hear something that does not match what is already in our brain, it does not usually make much sense. Or, in the language used in this chapter, if we do not already have a schema for something in our brain, we tend to find that something puzzling, even nonsensical. Many readers probably found the picture of that cow nonsensical when they first looked at it; and the same is often true for new ideas in music, physics or cooking.

ꬷ

I noted above that a child learns how to 'see' cows, when thousands of schemas for cows are laid down in its brain. In the same way, a child will 'understand' the things it hears, if it has had opportunities to lay down schemas of them. That comment might help to explain why children who have homes that offer rich experiences, tend to be 'brighter' than children who live in impoverished homes. That is, among other things, the former children will have more schemas in their brain. We can sense some of the further implications of the concept of 'schemas' if we consider the extent to which our experiences – especially our earliest experiences – often have a powerful effect on the way we 'see' things for the rest of our lives. Notice also that we will usually be no more aware of many of those experiences than we are aware of having schemas for cows in our brain.

I turn now to a consideration of how these comments on schemas might relate to a lesson. Imagine a classroom. The learners are nine-year-olds, and this is one of their first lessons in biology. The teacher is up front, and he is giving a lesson on plant cells. He is using an overhead projector, and has thrown an image of a magnified picture of a plant cell (Figure 5.4) on the wall behind him. Now he is talking about it.

The children look at the picture, and of course, they 'see' (i.e. recognize) very little. Some of them might think that they see craters on the moon. We know that they don't really 'see' much, because there are no schemas in their brain that

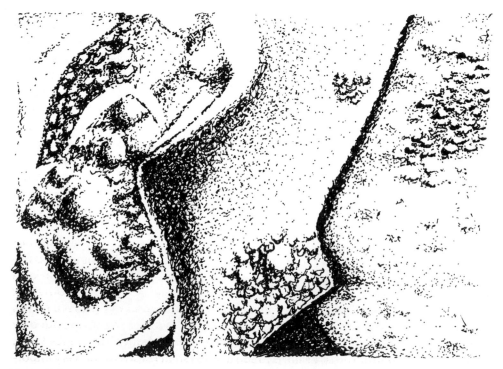

Figure 5.4.

would match what they are looking at. Hence, they are unable to make much sense out of what they are seeing. But not only will they be unable to 'see' much, they will also be unable to 'understand' much. For, when this teacher talks about 'cells', many of them will not really understand what he is talking about. Again, this is because they are unlikely to have a schema for the word 'cell' in their brain.

Compare the above with a better teacher. She would first ask the children to bring some leaves to school. Then she would get them to look at those leaves under increasingly powerful magnifications. She might then ask them to draw what they were seeing; and only after that, would she tell them that the shapes they were drawing are called 'cells'. Later still would come an explanation of how cells work. In that way, slowly, relevant schemas would become established in those children's brains. They would then be able to 'see' cells, and 'understand' how they work.

What this brief account of perception might imply for learning and teaching might be summed up like this:

- If a thing outside one's head is the same as the thing inside one's head, one will be able to make sense of it.
- If a thing outside one's head is completely different from the things inside one's head, one will usually not be able to make much sense of it.
- If a thing outside one's head is a little different from the things inside one's head, one will be unsure what one is perceiving – one might even see the things inside one's head.[8]

It follows that, if a teacher talks about something quite new, and the learners just listen, there is no way of knowing whether what the teacher is saying is what the learners are hearing. We also see from the above that the human brain is not some sort of blank tape, able to assimilate any input provided that it is loud and clear. *The brain is an organ that processes, and it processes information in terms of the schemas already inside it*. That is why, after twenty-seven people have listened to one person talk for ten minutes, there might be twenty-seven versions of what the speaker has said. That is why eyewitnesses can be very poor witnesses.[9] That is why human memory is often subjective; and why proof-reading requires a certain kind of attention. One of the most striking manifestations of the fact that we always process the information around us in terms of the schemas already in our brain is provided by the landscapes that Chinese painters have painted of English scenes: they look like pictures of China! It is surely sobering to realize that we always think in terms of the schemas we already have in our brain; and it is even more sobering to realize that we are usually quite unaware of that.

But here I must emphasize, and as strongly as I can, that the above does *not* imply that 'everything is relative'. The above only implies that everything *looks* relative. For example, it does not follow from the fact that eyewitnesses can give several different versions of an event that there really were several different events. And that is the case even if 'an event' requires a brain to achieve such a status. Nor does the above imply that there is no such thing as 'the truth', but only varying constructions of what we call true. I believe that reality, and hence truth, is in *principle* absolute. The problem is to see it; and I shall return to this very important matter in a later chapter.

Chapter 6

Where are the Answers?

Although it isn't elegant, I shall begin this chapter with a list.

1) It is often said that teaching must begin from where the learners are at. The notion of 'schemas' might help to explain why that is so. That is, if everything one sees and hears is processed via the schemas already present in one's brain, teachers must obviously attempt to find out what schemas are present in their learners' brains; for, if they don't, their learners might well not be able to follow them.

2) As people tend to have different experiences, they will also have different schemas inside their brain. It follows that people will process information differently. From this it also follows that people will make connections between any new set of facts, and the facts that they already know, in their own way. If so, good teaching cannot be a case of simply 'telling'. It must be a case of creating situations that will enable learners to tackle manageable chunks of new material directly and in their own way, for that will enable them to make links between what they already know, and the new material to be learnt.

3) Before one can learn something new, one must often un-learn something old. This is because new information is always processed via information already present in the brain. But getting rid of inaccurate schemas can be very difficult. For example, many people will have had the experience of speaking to someone, but sensing from the other person's reply that they have been misunderstood. So one tries again; but again it might become clear that one has been misunderstood. That can be frustrating, even painful!

   In the terms used in this chapter, one can explain such a state of affairs by saying that, the person to whom one is speaking, is using a set of schemas to hear one, that do not match one's own schemas. It follows that mutual understanding will only come about when the schemas causing the misunderstanding are dealt with first. In the same way, learners might continue to misunderstand something, *until they are able to grasp why they misunderstand*, and a good teacher is sensitive to such things. She will allow many opportunities for learners to say what they think they understand, and she will 'really' listen. That will provide her with an entry into her learners' frame of reference (their schemas), and might enable her to clarify things.

4) As noted, the human brain does not simply take in new information, but always *processes* it. And further, as each person has had different experiences, each person will process information in a different way. It must follow that the only way one can know for sure whether what one has taken in is what is actually out there, is to *test* what one has taken in.

    Notice first that the previous comment describes what the people trying to learn how to use a word processor were doing. And notice next that we are often able to check whether we have grasped something correctly, when we are able to talk about it and hear someone agree or disagree. That is, of course, what people frequently do, especially in places of real learning, like research laboratories. However, this does not usually happen in many classrooms. But then, sadly, in many classrooms there is a great deal of teaching and not much learning.

5) Many people will have noticed that learning is not always a matter of picking up something new. Sometimes it is a matter of seeing what one already knows in a new way. When that happens, it is as if the schemas in one's brain had been reshuffled into a new pattern. That new pattern will then give the old facts a new meaning. Readers might here recall what was noted earlier about the importance of pattern, or gestalt.

6) I have repeatedly noted that real learning often requires testing and interpreting, not simply recording. That observation complements the many comments that have been made on how 'real' learning is an active rather than a passive process.

7) When we look at something, we have the illusion that it is 'out there', not inside our brain. One of the effects of the transmission method of teaching is that it tends to reinforce the allied illusion that answers are also 'out there', either in a textbook, or about to come out of a teacher's mouth. But, just as seeing takes place inside our brain, so also does understanding. In the next section, I shall try to indicate what that claim implies.

&

I noted above that we must ultimately find answers inside our own brain. When I first came across that notion, I whistled with pleasure. I felt it was packed with implications. I also thought it new. Then someone drew my attention to the fact that Plato had made it in his *Meno* more than two thousand years ago.[1] In this short work, Plato describes how Socrates manages to get an uneducated boy to state the proof of several geometric theorems, and Socrates does this by asking the boy a series of questions. It could be argued that Socrates simply leads the boy by the nose, and I doubt whether the boy fully understands his own answers. I certainly do not think that Socrates demonstrates a good teaching technique here, but these doubts are beside the present point.

The important point is that, in this passage, Plato attempted to demonstrate that, although the boy appears not to have the foggiest notion about how to solve geometrical problems, with Socrates there to guide him, the boy is able to find all the answers inside his own head. Does that mean that the boy had those answers in his head all the time; and that all Socrates had to do was to help the boy find them there? If so, it would follow that Plato had in mind the notion that under-standing is not something entirely new, but a *recognition* of something already in one's mind. At first blush, such a notion seems decidedly odd, but that is exactly what Plato did argue. In short, Plato maintained that we never learn anything; that we already know everything; and that, what happens when we say that we 'learn', is that we recognize something we have always known. Such notions seem decid-edly odd; but, some two and a half thousand years later, here is Spencer Brown saying something similar when discussing the process of discovery in mathematics: 'Even the analogy of seeking something cannot, in this context, be quite right. For what we find, eventually, is something we have known, and may well have been consciously aware of, all along. Thus, we are not, in this sense, seeking something that has ever been hidden. The idea of performing a search can be unhelpful, or even positively obstructive, since searches are in general organised to find some-thing that has been previously hidden, and is thus not open to view. In discover-ing a proof, we must do something more subtle than search. We must come to see the relevance, in respect of whatever statement it is we wish to justify, of some fact in full view, and of which, therefore, we are constantly aware.'[2]

Consider next the following research on memory.

If we want to store beans, we put them in a jar. But if we want to store infor-mation, things are more complicated. We then have to write that information down. In the case of an image, we have to draw it, or take a photograph of it. And if we want to store sounds, we have to use electric gadgetry. In other words, when it comes to storing *information* (in the form of words, pictures or sounds), some kind of physical change must be made in a medium. That may consist of marks on a piece of paper, chemical changes on a photographic plate, physical changes in the magnetic particles on a cassette ribbon, or other changes in silicon chips.

What happens in our brain when information is stored in it? What kind of change in the medium takes place? One researcher in this field, Colin Blakemore, writes that, as just noted, having a memory of something must involve some kind of physical change occurring in the brain. How else is the memory to be stored? To illustrate, Blakemore reports the following experiment.[3] A rat is placed in a maze, and allowed to run around inside it, until it has learnt how to get to the exit quickly. It is then *immediately* cooled down to about 5°C. That stops all electrical activity in its brain. Shortly after, when it has thawed out again, it has been found that the rat will be none the worse for wear. But, if the rat is then put back inside the same maze, it will run around in a way that shows it has not learnt anything about the maze from its first visit to it. In other words, its behaviour shows that it does not have a memory of having been there.

Now consider what happens when that same rat is cooled down to about 5°C *several minutes* after it has run around inside a maze. It has then been found that it will retain the knowledge that it gained from having been there because, when the rat is put back inside the maze, it shows by the way it gets to the exit that it learnt the topography of the maze from its previous visit. In other words, it now has a memory of having been there.

This experiment suggests that cooling a rat down to 5°C *immediately* after it has learnt to run a maze prevents a physical change from taking place inside its brain.

That is, it prevents the establishment of a memory trace (or schema) in its brain. The next thing that would interest a researcher like Blakemore is to identify the molecules in the brain that are changed when a memory is stored inside it.

Blakemore (University Lecturer in Physiology, and Fellow and Director of Studies in Medicine at Downing College, Cambridge, giving the Reith Lectures in 1976, some 2,500 years after Plato had given one of his lectures) concludes that no such molecules exist in the brain. And he goes on to note that such a conclusion leads to one of two possibilities: Either memory does not have a physical basis in the brain, or, in his words: 'every memory is innately within us, in our genetic make-up'. And further, that this supposition is 'curiously reminiscent of Plato's nativist theory that all human knowledge is derived by the soul from a previous existence'.

Well, well, well! So the answer might be in the learner's head after all!

Not quite in the case of that rat, perhaps. For readers may be prepared to agree that *answers* must be found inside our own heads, but surely not specific facts. That is, we might be prepared to agree that an answer is obtained when schemas are rearranged so that they produced a meaningful Gestalt. But the topography of a given maze can only be learnt by having some actual experience of running around inside it.[4] So perhaps Blakemore was right to say that the problem he faces is 'curiously reminiscent of Plato's nativist theory'. That is, 'reminiscent' only. For that rat could not possibly know anything about the topography of a certain maze before it had actually run around inside it. But this is running too far into mere speculation. The important question is what happens at the interface between brains and the rest of nature. That said, readers unacquainted with Plato's view of learning might like to hear a little more about it.

Plato maintained that all human beings have a soul. Nobody quite knows what a 'soul' is. Whatever it is, it is commonly held that souls are immortal. It is also held, by those who believe in souls, that each time a person is born, a soul enters that person's body; and each time a person dies, that person's soul goes to a place called 'heaven'. It follows, Plato maintained, that each time a soul enters a person's body, it will carry with it the knowledge that it gained from its many previous visits to this planet when it inhabited another living body. Plato therefore argued that, when we learn, we discover what our soul already knows from its previous visits to this planet.[5] I noted earlier that many people are likely to find such an account absurd. However, it is clear that a living body and a dead body are very different things. It is also clear that it is impossible to describe this difference in only physical terms. From this it seems reasonable to conjecture that there is more to being alive than having a beating heart. So exactly what happens when a person 'dies'?

People have various answers to that question. Some believe in souls, others do not. I find at least one widespread belief about souls (whatever they are) unsatisfactory. Rather than each one of us having a soul that continues living after we die, it seems to me more plausible to assume that the thing we call a soul is a part of a general 'something' that permeates the whole universe. Perhaps a comparison with water is possible here. That is, our bodies contain a good deal of water, in the form of various fluids, and those fluids will be a little different in each person (depending on what they eat and drink). But when people die, those fluids reduce mainly to water, and go back to being a part of all the water on this planet. In the same way I am suggesting that, while we are alive, we all have an individual soul, and that soul is likely to be a little different from person to person (depending on our individual experiences). But, just as the water inside our bodies is a part of all the water in the universe, so might all our souls be a part of a larger soul that permeates the whole universe. And when we die, our soul might go back to being a part of one large 'soul'. I don't think it matters what we decide to call this general 'soul-something'. We could call it God, Tao or Nature. I quite like the word 'consciousness'. Whatever word we use, the advantage of the above account is that it suggests an intimate link between the world outside our bodies and what we call 'a soul' inside our bodies. Or perhaps I could put the matter like this. There is obviously something called 'life', 'soul' or 'consciousness' in this universe; and this consciousness only manifests itself through a living creature. Now, if this 'thing' some people call 'soul' is ultimately not only the private affair we usually take it to be, and if it permeates the whole universe as well as our brain, then that which we call 'understanding' might not be a case of processing the stimuli that come to us from the outside world. It might rather be a matter of being open to the world, and becoming consciously aware of what our brain receives from the world.

All this might well sound rather 'unscientific'. However, it is a line of thinking one frequently encounters among many eminent scientists. Consider the following comment by the biologist Sinnott: 'Mind itself, at least in essence, seems to be coextensive with all of life, and grows out of that self-regulation and goal-seeking which is life's distinctive quality. Mind and life are essentially one.'[6] Or consider this comment by Schrödinger, one of the scientists most responsible for the revolution in modern physics: 'The same elements compose my mind and the world. This situation is the same for every mind and its world, in spite of the unfathomable abundance of "cross-references" between them. The world is given to me only once, not one existing and one perceived. Subject and object are only one.'[7] Or consider this comment by the psychologist Gibson: 'Instead of postulating that the brain constructs information from the input of a sensory nerve, we can suppose that the centres of the nervous system including the brain, resonate to information.'[8]

These are speculations, but readers inclined to dismiss them might first like to consider some criticisms of contemporary accounts of learning.[9] For my part, I have found such comments liberating; but some readers might well be thinking that, although the above is moderately interesting, and has some relevance to the question of how we find answers inside our head, it rather strays from what the title of this book conveys. Not so, for I shall return to this topic when I consider the more general aims of teaching. In the meantime, it is enough if I have managed to suggest two things: One, that learning is to a considerable extent a matter of being open to the world. And two, that answers must be found inside one's own head.

Chapter 7

Why Only Living Things Can Learn

In earlier chapters, I drew attention to the nature of motivation, the importance of active engagement, the effect of various kinds of rewards, and the abstract nature of meaning. I also drew attention to the phenomenon of insight, the effect of pattern, the scope of language, the importance of experience, and the concept of schemas. And in the previous chapter, I drew attention to the need to look inside one's own head if one is to find an answer. But there is one element in learning to which I have not yet drawn sufficient attention, and it is the importance of personal involvement. Here is a true account to indicate what I have in mind.

For many years, it was a part of my job to visit student teachers and observe them teach. After the lesson, the student teacher and I would discuss how the lesson had gone, and there was always some concern in such discussions because, no matter what I had said beforehand, student teachers usually saw such a visit as an assessment. Teaching is a very personal matter, and very difficult to do well. Hence, anything but generalities, praise, or the mildest suggestion for improvement will tend to be seen as criticism, at least initially. Hundreds of such visits showed me that many people find them a threatening experience, and I therefore came to see that it is wise to be as unobtrusive and gentle as possible. I am sure that no one who has done any teaching will be surprised by any of this. That said by way of an introduction, here is a description of how one of these visits typically went.

The day has come, and I am to visit a student teacher. This particular student teacher is a tutor-librarian. As usual, this first visit is made towards the end of the first term, and, by this time, the student teacher will have examined and discussed the materials presented in this book so far. This particular student teacher – let us call her Betty – has herself determined a date for my visit. (My diary goes around the class, and people put in a time when they would find it convenient for me to visit.) Betty has chosen this afternoon, and she has decided to have a lesson on the topic 'Using a library'. She has placed eighteen chairs in a horseshoe, and when the learners come in, she welcomes them, and announces the topic of the lesson. She talks about the library organization, the various indexes, and the many things that library officials believe that users should know. Betty is a knowledgeable, pleasant, conscientious, middle-aged woman, and she speaks about these things in a systematic manner.

Betty talks for about forty minutes. Her voice goes up and down, the learners sit and listen, glance at their notebooks, move in their chairs, look around, look at each other, sit and listen, and look at Betty. At the end of her talk, Betty gives the learners a sheet of paper on which there are half a dozen questions. Very soon, the learners settle down and write their answers with good cheer. Occasionally they get up to consult a catalogue. Sometimes they exchange a few words. It takes them about ten minutes to do this work, and then they sit in the horseshoe again. Betty asks for their answers, these are read out, and it is clear that they have caused few problems. Next Betty asks if there are any questions. A girl asks what should be done if someone wants a book that isn't in the library. A boy says he can never find a book when he needs it. Another asks if there are any fines. Betty is conscientious and answers these questions in detail. Some of the learners look restless. Finally, Betty asks if they have learnt anything that afternoon. As we stand up to leave, one of the girls says that she has.

Betty takes me back to her office and offers me some tea. There is the usual touch of nervousness in her manner. She smiles and asks, 'Well, what do you think?' I say I thought the lesson had gone well, and ask how she felt about it.

Betty tells me that she wished she had had more time, that there was so much to get through, and that it is difficult to hold a lesson in a library. I say I can appreciate all of that, but that I had the distinct impression that she enjoyed her job.

And so we chat. And when I feel it is appropriate, I mention the course she is doing with me, and the material on learning and teaching we have considered so far. Then I ask her whether she has found any of it useful. My question clearly makes Betty feel uncomfortable. From things she has said, and things she has written in her assignments, and from the way she has sometimes smiled in class, she has given the impression that she has usually found the material, and the approach to teaching we have discussed in my classes, useful.

It also becomes obvious, from the next few things Betty says, that she believes that she has used this material in her lesson that afternoon. She says that she employs quite a few of the techniques I use: things like getting the learners to sit in a circle, and using a worksheet. But, as we continue talking, it becomes increasingly obvious that her lesson that afternoon had remained largely untouched by anything of any real substance that we had considered in my classes. So I say with a smile, 'For ten weeks you have been examining material in my classes which strongly suggests that simply telling people does not help them to learn very much. You have certainly shown that this is broadly correct this afternoon.'

I wish I knew how to describe Betty's face. For it only took her about twenty seconds to work out what might be stated like this. If little she had considered in my classes, over the past ten weeks, had had much practical effect on her; then it would be unlikely that anything she had said, over the past fifty minutes in her class that afternoon, would have much practical effect on her learners either.

So Betty took a sort of breath and said, 'Well, you seem to be talking yourself out of a job!' I replied as mildly as I could, 'How about devising a question sheet in which everything you said this afternoon, except for your welcoming comments, appears on it in the form of a question? That way you could get your learners doing practical things right from the start? Do you remember . . . .' But I was wasting my breath. I could see that Betty knew exactly what I was getting at. I could see from her face that, for the first time, the material she had been studying in my classes had *come alive for her*. And this was because she had begun to identify with it. Betty had come to my classes. She had spoken about things she found problematic in her teaching. She had heard others do the same. She had heard me mention things that thoughtful people had suggested in response. She had examined research findings on learning and teaching. She had discussed them in small groups. She had written assignments that invited her to reflect on her experiences, and to consider the relevance of the material she had studied to her experiences. On the face of it, Betty had done my classes. But had she really 'done' them? I believe that Betty had been a good deal more active in my classes than she might have been in some. And yet, it was still not enough to generate real learning, that is, learning that can be used practically. Until today, the material she had examined in my classes had been something 'out there', perhaps 'mine'. But when it comes to learning, 'out there' means that it has no real substance. It is just so many *words*.

Recall here that learning isn't a process that exists on its own. It is obviously a part of a much larger process. Breathing isn't a process that exists on its own either. Just as breathing cannot be found on this planet on its own, neither can learning. On this planet, breathing and learning can only be found in a *living* organism. Computer simulations of learning are like artificial lungs: very odd things in the absence of a living person using them to stay alive.

If one takes this kind of an approach, an approach I earlier called a biological one, one can understand why Betty had 'really' learnt so little in my classes. Until she *felt* that the material she was studying in my classes could further her own needs, she didn't 'really' learn. For learning, like breathing, must have evolved on this planet to further *felt* needs. In short, until Betty deeply *felt* she had a need, she had learnt at a level that would get her by: that is, verbally. I put the matter like this because, from what Betty was able to *say*, it appeared that she had learnt a good deal.

As the above is, I believe, of fundamental importance, I risk rephrasing it. My point is that learning isn't something disembodied that goes on in the head, as some of those who carry out experiments in laboratories appear to believe, but is closely related to *living on this planet*. Readers might here recall my earlier noting that language is two-edged: Through it, we can communicate; but through it we can also create an illusion of communication. That is, a teacher might ask a question, a learner might answer, and there is a suggestion that some learning has taken place. But actually, nothing of any real *substance* has often occurred in such an exchange. And so, over the years, I discovered a fact. It was that next to nothing my students discussed or studied in my classes had much of an effect on the way they actually taught – even when they said that the material is apt and interesting – until two things happened:

a) they strongly *feel* its relevance to their personal needs, and
b) they repeatedly *act* on those felt needs.

When I discovered that what we did in my classes had next to no *practical* effect, I was greatly upset. Here I was, encouraging them to exchange experiences, showing them all this rich material, – and none of it had much of a practical effect! Even in those who were enthusiastic about it! It took me several years to realize that my disappointment was quite misplaced. This dawned on me when I realized that it had taken me years of struggle to work out an approach to teaching that half way satisfied me. And the critical element had been my *felt* need.

I can now ask a question, and my reason for again referring to computers is to highlight what I consider is distinctively human. The question might be phrased like this. When one feeds information into a computer, it can be said to 'know' that information if, when it is made to perform a function, it performs that function correctly. When a computer responds in this way, some people maintain that it has simulated a human being; and this, they say, is interesting because it tells us something about how human beings function.

Now, I noted earlier that I had introduced Betty to certain information in my classes; and, whenever I had asked her a question about that information, she had usually been able to respond in a way that indicated she 'knew' it. However, I showed above that she did not *really* know it, for she was unable to act on it. Nor would it have made any difference if Betty had been introduced to that information a hundred more times, each time in a somehow clearer manner. And I went on to say that, until Betty began to make that information hers, because she *felt* its relevance to her *personal* needs, she had really learnt mainly words.

I had better add here in parenthesis that it took Betty many practical endeavours until, to some extent, she was able to act appropriately on the information that she had supposedly learnt; and this was partly due to the fact that this information was in conflict with her existing habits. Or, to use the language of a previous chapter, this new information had to supersede the schemas already present in her brain; and, as was then noted, the replacement of old schemas by new ones can be very difficult. These things recalled, I am now able to ask my question: How can one tell when a computer knows, as distinct from *really* knows?

My question here is, of course, rhetorical, for it is impossible to program such an effect on a computer, and this is because computers are dead. The simple fact that they are dead also explains why it is easy to replace old information with new information on a computer. For, as computers are dead, they have no sense of self; but the information we have in our brain, especially that which is most salient to us, is closely bound up with our sense of self, and there is more to changing our sense of self than merely changing the information in our brain. At this point, readers might recall that I touched on this matter when I considered the nature of Cognitivism.

As this is such an important matter, it might be helpful to consider it again in a completely different context. While discussing her work as a translator, Barbara Reynolds describes a visit she and some Italian friends made to a British war cemetery in Italy. She writes that it was a beautiful place, and it is clear from her evocative description that she was greatly touched. She notes that she was talking to her friends, in Italian, and goes on to say that, a moment later, she read a notice, also in Italian, which told visitors what the place commemorated. She continues: 'suddenly I walked a few paces on, and there was another notice, saying exactly what the Italian notice said, but in English. The shock was astonishing. I knew then that only my brain had taken in the meaning of the Italian words; my sympathies had been stirred, but only faintly. I realized this when I read the words in English: "Here lie the bodies of British soldiers killed in action in the Asiago campaign during the War of 1914–1918." I knew then, with all my powers of knowing, as I had not known before, that British soldiers were buried there.'[1]

Here again two forms of knowing: one verbal, the other felt. How does one model this difference on a computer? I pose this question again in an attempt to explain why I believe that much psychology (especially cognitive psychology) is misconceived. For, as noted earlier, a great deal of academic psychology ignores the biological fact that human beings are *alive*. In the next section, I propose to consider the implications for learning and teaching of that striking fact. But before that, I must admit to a dilemma.

№

Many times in this book, I have noted the limitation of 'telling'. However, this book is inevitably based on 'telling'. If so, there must be a serious doubt about its value. The matter could be put a little more technically like this. If the theory of learning I am putting forward in this book is roughly correct, it follows that reading this book will not have much of an effect on established practice.

As the above might sound fanciful, I add the following in support of my contention. I once had a colleague who asked to see a copy of this book. As I liked and esteemed this woman, I was a little apprehensive about this, so I was the more pleased when she expressed considerable enthusiasm for the book when she returned it. A few weeks later, it so happens that she and I taught a class together (i.e., we did some team-teaching), and it was then soon obvious that her reading of this book had had next to no effect on the way she actually taught.

I found this experience distressing and embarrassing, especially when this woman talked to me about her teaching afterwards. For it then became apparent that she was distressed and embarrassed, too! Being candid but human, she both criticized and defended herself; and the more she did so, the more contradictory she became. I fear I made matters worse when I hesitantly observed that, if my theory of learning was roughly correct, then reading this book was unlikely to have much of an effect on her established practice.

I suppose it was in an attempt to cheer myself – especially as I feared that I might have lost this woman's affection – that I came to think that perhaps some good had come out of her reading after all. For, although her actual practice had not changed, she had obviously been troubled, and this might have the effect of encouraging her to view her teaching from a new perspective.

As noted, I have described this episode, first, in order to buttress my contention that reading about something is unlikely, on its own, to change established practice. But second, because it might also illustrate a way out of my dilemma. That is, although I do not believe that reading any book is enough to change a person's established practice, it just might plant a seed in that person's mind that might grow, and eventually come to affect practice, – provided, of course, that it falls on hospitable soil and gains some support from a sustaining environment.

But now to return to this matter of feeling.

№

Human beings are made of flesh and blood, bone and sinew. They *feel*. If they did not feel, they would do very little. They would certainly not want to show that 'humans are essentially machines'. What would be the point? Who would *care*?

Imagine you felt nothing. Your arm would burn to the bone every time you touched a fire when you hadn't noticed it. Nor would there be anything to prompt you to eat, for you would never feel any hunger. It follows that you would be unlikely to go out and grow some food, or to earn some cash, to ease that hunger. In short, if you did not feel, you would be as good as dead. You really would be a machine!

Some centuries ago, the philosopher Descartes famously stated, 'I think, therefore I am.' He wanted to begin with fundamentals, with things about which one could be *sure*. It seems to me that the way he began also typifies a European tradition. I put the matter like this because it seems to me that seeing things like this confers on thinking a pre-eminence it does not have. Consider the fact that we are aware that we are alive. However, in some people, the *feeling* that they are alive is absent. They say that they *know* that the things around them are real, but that nothing *feels* real to them. Such feelings cause anguish, and the people who have them often seek a priest or a therapist because they are in such pain.[2] One researcher, Weckowicz, described such people like this: 'they think, but they do not exist'. He went on: 'It is as if there were two kinds of knowledge; one supplied by . . . experience, and the other by rational judgements.'[3] Notice the use of that word 'experience'. Experiences are felt, but these people do not feel. Notice also that there is nothing the matter with the ability of these people to make a 'rational judgement' – that is, with their ability to think – yet they are in anguish. Why?

It must be because, if we *feel* that life is 'not real', then life does not *seem* to be real, no matter how much we are able to *think* it is. It follows that to say that we know we exist, because we can *think*, must be misleading. It is the kind of thing typically said by a person who spends a great deal of time inside his or her head.

I believe that the above raises a most important question. Simply put, it is: From where do we get the *feeling* – as distinct from the knowledge – that we exist? This fundamental question takes us far beyond the aims of this book, so I shall restrict myself to suggesting that it derives from our *sensing*, when we were small children, that we *exist* in the mind of another person, and in particular the mind of a parent. This is also the reason, I think, that many adults find the withdrawal of affection from someone who is important to them intensely painful. In short, I suggest Descartes was wrong, and on two counts: First, to place such an emphasis on cognition; and, second, to place such an emphasis on the individual. He should rather have stated: '*They* think I exist; hence *I feel* I am.'[4]

The above raises another important question: Where do feelings end, and thoughts begin? When I try to determine this in myself, I find I cannot; so I fall back on the vague notion that thinking is perhaps best seen as an extension of feeling. But at least one thing is clear. It is that creatures existed perfectly adequately on this planet for millions of years before thinking – in the usual sense of that word – arrived on it. If so, it seems plausible to conjecture that a good deal of what we do is at least initiated by a feeling.[5]

Consider, for example, what happens when a topic like capital punishment is being discussed. Participants will usually put forward a variety of reasons for whatever position they hold. However, if the discussion continues for long enough, we often come to suspect that these reasons are really justifications for the way that the participants happen to *feel*. Here is some support for this way of seeing things.

Place a Martian in front of a bicycle, and he will smile and scratch his antennae. Never having seen a bicycle before, he has no idea what it is for. In other words, whenever we do or think something, it is usually based on past experiences. In what form, then, are our experiences of riding a bicycle coded inside us? Or, to use the terminology introduced in a previous chapter, in what form are these kind of schemas encoded? Clearly not in a verbal form. Imagine setting out on a bike to go to the post office, and having to verbalize every muscle contraction required![6] So only some of our past experiences will be coded inside us in the form of words. The rest will be coded in what I have been calling a 'felt form'. This felt form must also be the form in which are coded the experiences that infants have, before they begin to acquire a language. In short, there must be a felt, pre-verbal state 'behind' language.[7]

Take next a simpler example than riding a bicycle or learning a language. When a baby first stretches out an arm to reach for an object, it tends to be clumsy. However, after a few months of practice, it becomes proficient at such an action. This suggests that a kind of coding must become established in the brain of a baby before it can carry out such an action, but that coding cannot have a verbal form.

Or consider Sultan, the chimpanzee noted in an earlier chapter. He eventually grasped that he could reach some bananas by stacking boxes on top of each other. To say that he 'grasped' seems clear enough, but it actually says very little. One might well want to know in what form his grasping or understanding was coded. In response, one must first recall that an understanding is something abstract; and second, that apes do not have the gift of language. If so, and in the absence of a better word, it seems fair to assume provisionally that Sultan must have *felt* that 'grasping'. What better word could one use?

Consider further the case of completely deaf people.[8] Many of these people do not possess the gift of language (as we usually understand that word), yet they are usually able to take perfectly good care of themselves. It is true that they are not always able to perform as well on certain mental tests as people who possess natural language. But it is obvious that their brain must nevertheless contain a wealth of complex schemas, and that few of these could be in the form of words. If so, these, too, must be in the form of abstract, living, '*felt* experiences'.

Consider next what often happens when we are faced by a problem. We tend to say to ourselves, 'Well, if I do "this", then "that" is likely to happen.' We do not say to ourselves exactly what the 'this' and the 'that' stand for. We know what they stand for. They are whole chunks of compacted 'felt meanings' and we usually leave them unsaid.[9] At other times, we might wish to convey some of those chunks of compacted, felt meanings to someone. When we attempt to do this, our listener will often be heard to say: 'I'm sorry, I don't quite understand what you are getting at.' We will then tend to pause and reflect. Because, if we are to make ourselves understood, we often find that we must first clarify those 'felt meanings' deep inside us. That can be difficult; and this suggests that it is only when we are able to gain a reasonably clear pre-verbal sensing of those feelings that we are able to translate them into words.

William James described something similar in 1893 when he described what sometimes happens when we try to remember a name, and cannot. He noted: 'The state of our consciousness is peculiar. There is a gap therein; but no mere gap. It is a gap that is intensely active. A sort of wraith of the name is in it, beckoning us in a given direction, making us at moments tingle with the sense of our closeness and then letting us sink back without the longed-for term. If wrong names are proposed to us, this singular gap acts immediately, so as to negate them. . . . And the gap of one word does not feel like the gap of another, all empty of content.'[10]

Notice that James used the word 'feel' in his last sentence, but then, what other word could he have used?

This passage again alerts us to the likelihood that there are a variety of thinking and memory processes in the human brain. This is a complex matter, but, from what has been noted so far in this book, it seems safe to assume that, at bottom, human beings have been provided with a basic 'feeling' process, or experiential process, and that they share this with all other living creatures. Then, tacked on to that basic feeling/experiential process, there appears to be another, more elaborate process commonly called 'thinking' which is closely related to the use of language. At this point, it might be helpful to digress for a moment, to recall work that MacLean published some years ago. MacLean suggested that, in the course of evolution, the human brain developed in a hierarchical fashion, based on the development of three brain structures. He named the first structure 'reptilian' because it is found in the simpler kind of animals that first inhabited the earth. The second brain structure he named 'paleo-mammalian' because in complexity it approaches that found in somewhat more advanced animals. And the third brain structure, the most advanced, he named 'neo-mammalian'. In evolutionary terms, those three structures are, of course, eons apart, and MacLean's researches indicated that those three entities differ in chemistry and structure. However, they are extensively interconnected; and, in view of this interconnectedness, he calls the human brain a 'triune' brain. That is, although each of those three parts has its own form of intelligence, memory and motor functions, each is connected to the others making one larger whole.

Very briefly put, what MacLean called the reptilian brain is responsible for the simplest motor behaviours, and those behaviours that are wired into the simpler animals, such as finding suitable territory, hunting, breeding, imprinting and so on. In more advanced animals, there is a limbic system that enables a creature to learn simple things from its experiences, and in this way to go further than what is wired into it. It is also involved in all emotional behaviour. And then, as evolution continued, the neo-mammalian part of the brain, or the neocortex, became larger in the more advanced animals; and, in human beings, it became relatively speaking very large indeed. This neocortex (or what I have called simply 'cortex') provides its possessors with a vast neural network in which planning and organizing, often through language and abstract thought, is able to develop, making human beings what they are.

The sketches below might help to illustrate MacLean's proposals. I do not possess the training to evaluate them, and it would anyway make this book unwieldly to go into further details. I add these comments in general support for the position outlined in this chapter, namely that, although our mind appears to work as an integrated whole, it is based on brain structures that function independently at least initially.[11]

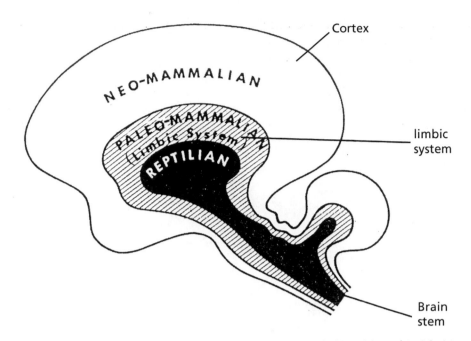

Figure 7.1 In the course evolution, the human brain expanded in a hierarchical fashion, as shown by the three entities named above. First the spinal cord and brain stem, then the limbic system, and then a neocortex in more advanced animals.

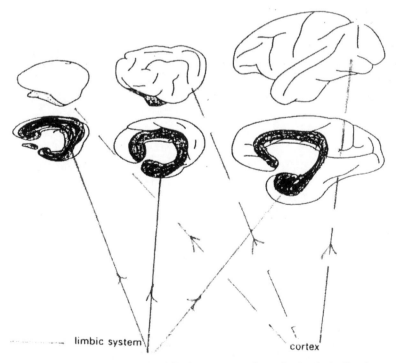

Figure 7.2 The brain of three mammals (the lower one when the brain is sliced to provide an internal view). From left to right: rabbit, cat, monkey. The shaded area shows the limbic system that all mammals possess, and then in more advanced animals there is the neocortex. Notice the relative size of the neocortex in each animal.

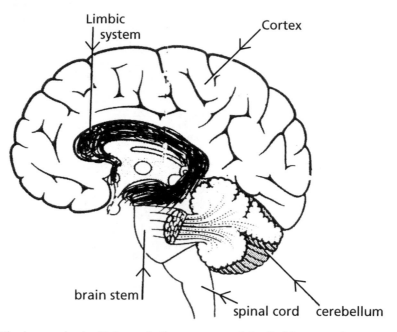

Figure 7.3 The human brain. Note again the presence of the limbic system; but compare the size of the cortex with those shown in Figure 7.2.

Chapter 8

Two Memories

At several places in previous chapters, I suggested that human beings possess at least two different mental processes:

a) a basic feeling/experiential process, and
b) verbal/thinking process.

I now present some evidence for the above suggestion that is quite independent of any material cited so far, and which comes from several sources. The first that I would invite readers to consider is that which derives from research on memory. But I had better note here that this is not some kind of digression. I think readers will find that what I report below has powerful implications for all learning and teaching.

Briefly stated, the people engaged in research on memory have concluded that there are two forms of it. One form is commonly called the 'procedural memory system', and the other the 'declarative memory system'. It has also been established that these two systems are located in different parts of the brain.[1]

I begin with the procedural memory system; and, in this, is coded the schemas that enable us to *do* things. Two examples might be: a) walking down a flight of stairs; or b) forming sentences in our native tongue. Another characteristic of this kind of memory is that we have no conscious knowledge of the schemas that enable us to do the things we are able to do with its help. For example, we have no conscious knowledge of all the muscle contractions necessary to walk down a flight of stairs, and indeed, were we to try to do such a thing consciously we could easily end up breaking our neck. The same holds for how we form sentences in our native tongue. That is, unless we have studied the matter, we have little conscious knowledge of the rules that govern how we form correct sentences. Hence, most native speakers of English are unlikely to know why they usually say, 'I like to swim in the sea', and not, 'I like to swim in a sea'.

The second form of memory that human beings possess is the declarative memory system; and in this is stored all the *knowledge* we have of the world. This might include things like one's address, and what size shoes one wears. It might also include our knowledge that the Amazon is a big river in South America; that tomatoes are a fruit; that our immediate neighbours are a pain in the neck; and, after a moment of hesitation, we can usually recall what we did yesterday. In short, we can 'declare' all this knowledge, and it therefore follows that this knowledge is coded in schemas that have a conscious and verbal form.

From what has been noted so far, it follows that the knowledge coded in the procedural memory system can usually only be demonstrated, whereas the knowledge coded in the declarative memory system can usually be communicated to others. For example, we can *demonstrate* how to ride a bicycle, and we can *tell* a friend our address. Notice also that, whereas the knowledge coded in our procedural memory system requires practice before it becomes sufficiently established for us to be able to use it, the knowledge in our declarative memory system is frequently acquired by a single act, for example by reading or hearing something just once.[2]

To summarise so far: Human beings possess at least two rather different memory systems, and they are located in different parts of the brain. In the one system is stored our knowledge of how we *do* things; and our knowledge in that system is mostly coded in a non-conscious form. In the other memory system is stored our *factual* knowledge; and that kind of knowledge can usually be recalled consciously and communicated to others.

One gets an increased sense of some of the implications of the above if one pauses for a moment to consider the following.

For example, from what has been noted so far, it is clear that there is likely to be a good deal about ourselves that we do not know well. This is because our earliest experiences – and hence the ones that are likely to be most formative – will have been laid down in our procedural memory system, and long before we acquired the ability to speak. From this it follows that we will not be consciously aware of those experiences, and their effect on us; and the quality of our relationship with people, especially ones to whom we feel close, might well be affected by those schemas. As this might seem fanciful to some readers, consider two infants. When one of them cries, it is attended to reasonably promptly, deftly, affectionately and sensitively. When the other infant cries, it is attended to after a long delay, clumsily, rejectingly and with little sensitivity. And these infants experience those responses a dozen times a day, for 365 days in a year! Such experiences will be coded in the procedural memory system, and it is most unlikely that they will have no effect in later years.

Considerations such as the above take us beyond the aims of this book. However, they might indicate some of the very powerful implications of the fact that human beings possess at least two different kinds of memory; and due to the nature of one of them, people are often prompted to act in part by experiences coded in their brain in a non-conscious form.

Many researchers have also concluded that memory is hierarchical. That is, that our procedural memory system lies at a more basic level than our declarative system. This is in line with the finding noted at the end of the previous chapter, namely, that the brain evolved in the course of evolution. That is, that the human memory is an elaboration of an earlier form that existed before human beings arrived on this planet. This is clearly seen when we recall that creatures, other than human beings, do not possess language, and hence do not possess what was earlier called a declarative memory system. It further follows that they are unable to declare their knowledge, and hence are unable to reflect on it. It is interesting to note here in parenthesis that, in diseases of the brain, it is the higher levels that tend to be damaged first. Thus, people so afflicted might be unable to reason clearly, or recall their uncle's name, but they will nevertheless be able tie a shoelace and comb their hair.[3]

At this point, I would urge readers to recall something else I noted earlier, namely, that one of the characteristics of a good theory is that it accommodates a wide range of data. Notice that, in the above comments on memory systems, I have drawn attention to data that has come from research on memory, from evolutionary theory, and from diseases of the brain; and all this evidence, from quite different sources, dovetails well together. I would also hope that readers who have persisted with this book so far, and who had not previously considered the material outlined above, will be in a better position to understand what I had in mind when, near the beginning of this book, I noted the following.

I noted that, in my training college, I had had the odd experience of encountering members of staff who clearly *knew* a great deal about learning and teaching, yet seemed unable to *act* on what they knew; and I therefore asked myself how it is possible to know, and yet not know. What I have reported in this chapter might help to answer this seemingly paradoxical question. In short, I believe that those members of staff acquired their knowledge in a verbal form only – that it was hence coded in their declarative memory – and could hence not be used practically (or one could say 'procedurally'). Or readers might recall my noting in the last chapter a colleague of mine who had read this book, who had been generous enough to speak approvingly about it, who had taught a class with me, and whose teaching in that class had not been even partly affected by her reading of this book. Again, the most plausible explanation for this outcome is, I think, that her experience of reading this book had been coded in her declarative memory, so it had not been available to her when practical action – that is, teaching – was required.

To summarise: The evidence that has accumulated over the years from research on how our memory functions indicates that human beings are endowed with at least two different kinds of memory, the procedural and the declarative. Although there is often an overlap between them, our experiences will tend to be encoded in either one or the other – depending on whether the experience is experiential or verbal – and will hence support different kinds of actions: For example the ability to *drive* a car, or the ability to *talk* about cars. It is the fundamental thesis of this book that considerations such as these have very important implications for learning and teaching.

&

As the thesis outlined in previous chapters, and in the above section, is so fundamental, it might be helpful to approach it from a different angle, that is, by considering some of the differences between what I have been calling our feeling process, and our thinking process.

First, it has already been noted that many of our feeling processes are nonconscious. (And when we can make them conscious, they will tend to be generalized, because it is impossible to make all the details conscious.) Our thinking processes, in contrast, tend to be mostly conscious, i.e., we can usually consciously reflect on our thoughts (and in some detail). This enables us to do things like review a matter, modify it, or plan ahead. But our feeling (mostly non-conscious) processes also have advantages. For example, they enable us to do several things at the same time, such as drive a car, suck a gumdrop, chat with a passenger, scratch an ear, and take in a new route.

The latter point indicates that our feeling processes can often be 'on automatic', and this frees our limited capacity for conscious thinking for those things that require our conscious attention. Recall here that, the moment we begin to think consciously, we can deal with only one thing at a time. That is of course also how language works: one word after the other, not holistically.

I have just noted that we can sometimes become conscious of our feeling processes. That is the same as saying that it is not *always* possible to do this. I should therefore have said that we can sometimes become conscious of an experience, but all depends on the nature of that experience. One can more easily state the converse, that is, that what we consciously think is only very rarely encoded in our basic feeling process. I attempted to illustrate the latter point when, in an earlier chapter, I noted that hearing a description of Boston does not have the same effect as going for a walk in that city. That is, a *feeling*, or an *experience*, does not become encoded in our brain when we are *told* or *read about* something. Only the *words* become encoded in our brain, and, as was earlier noted, the words that stand for something are not the same as that thing itself. Experiences have to be experienced; they have to be felt. Readers might here notice that what I am stating now parallels what I noted earlier about the difference between the procedural and the declarative memory system.

As these considerations are fundamental, I turn now to evidence of a quite different kind, and I have in mind findings that come from research done with split-brain patients, that is, people who have undergone an operation to ease epileptic seizures. In this operation, the two halves of the brain are surgically severed, and this is sometimes done because it has been found that such a separation can help people so afflicted.

Note first that a brief examination of the figures in this chapter indicates that, in most people, the language centre of the brain is located in the left half (or the left 'hemisphere') of the brain. This language centre is very important, for it enables us not only to understand and use language, but also to reflect consciously about what we have understood. In view of these attributes, it is hardly surprising that no other creatures aside from human beings possess a language centre in the brain. The right hemisphere of the brain in most people, in contrast, is responsible for global feelings; that is, it is in this half of the brain that most of our felt experiences are encoded.[4] I recall here in parenthesis that, when people have what is commonly called 'a stroke', that is, when the blood supply to the brain is temporarily halted (or when a flooding of blood takes place in the brain), and when this results in damage to the brain, it is usually one of the hemispheres that is afflicted. It follows that, when the right hemisphere is damaged, one kind of result ensues; and when the left hemisphere is damaged another kind of result ensues; for example, the person concerned might manifest difficulties with speaking.

These figures also show that the two halves of the brain are closely connected via a bundle of thick nerve fibres called the corpus callosum. In consequence of this anatomical arrangement, most of what is processed in one half of the brain is immediately communicated to the other half, so that the two halves of the brain

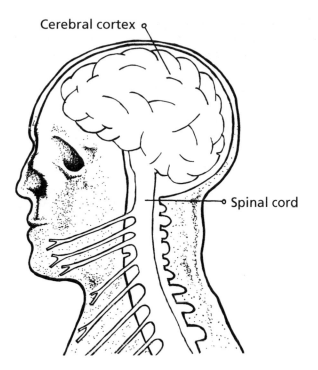

Figure 8.1

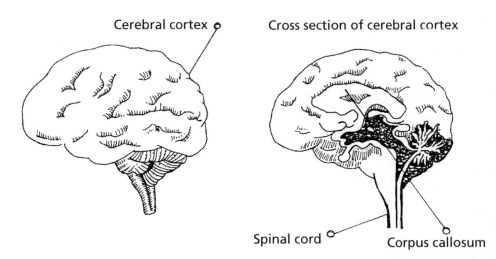

Figure 8.2

work as if they were one. However, and as I noted at the beginning of this section, there are people who suffer from epileptic seizures, and in whom the nerves between the two halves of the brain have been severed; and studies of such people have shed some further light on the working of our brain. Among other things, such studies have shown that the two halves of their brain can work independently. For example, when such a man (it could equally be a woman) receives information that is registered in his right hemisphere – the half where there is no

View from top

Corpus callosum

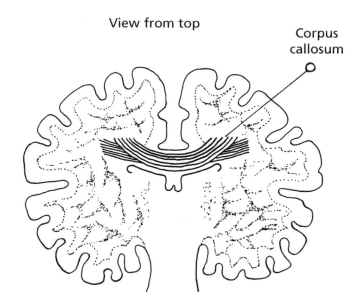

Figure 8.3

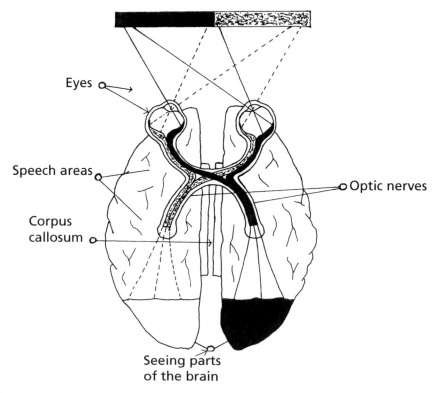

Eyes

Speech areas

Corpus callosum

Optic nerves

Seeing parts of the brain

Figure 8.4

language centre – he may be able to *act* on that information, but he will be unable to *say* what that information is.

In a moment, I shall report an experiment that has been carried out with such a man that illustrates the above. But, before that, it might be helpful to recall the

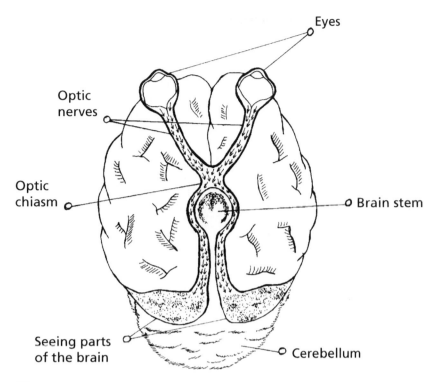

Eyes

Optic
nerves

Optic
chiasm

Brain stem

Seeing parts
of the brain

Cerebellum

Figure 8.5

following. Figure 8.4 shows that the structure of the human nervous system is such that, whatever a person picks up in his or her left visual field is registered in that person's right hemisphere. And whatever a person picks up in his or her right visual field is registered in that person's left hemisphere. In anticipation of the experiment I am about to report, it might also be helpful to note that a person in whom the bundle of nerve fibres that link the two halves of the brain has been severed, usually retains the ability to *recognize* single words registered in his or her right hemisphere. However, like most people, such a person will usually be unable to *state* what those words are by using that hemisphere, and this is of course because there is no language centre in it.

Now for the experiment.

Figure 8.6 shows a man in whom the two halves of the brain had been severed to ease epilepsy; recall here that, after such an operation, the two halves of the brain will tend to work separately. A picture of a claw was presented to his right visual field, and was hence registered in his left hemisphere, that is, the verbal and conscious one. At the same time, a picture of a snow scene was presented to his left visual field, and was hence registered in his right hemisphere, that is, the non-verbal and non-conscious one. In response to a request that he select a picture to match what he had seen, this man chose a picture of a chicken with his right hand, and a picture of a shovel with his left hand. If one recalls that the two halves of this man's brain were working independently, it requires only a moment of reflection to see that these choices make good sense, for 'claw' relates to chicken, and 'shovel' relates to snow. But it is the next part of the experiment that produced a most interesting result.

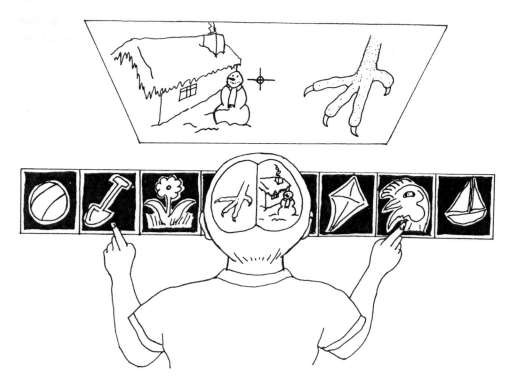

Figure 8.6

Source: Adapted from Gazzaniga, M. and LeDoux, J., *The Integrated Mind*. Plenum Press, 1978.

This occurred when the man was asked why he had chosen these two pictures. He answered as follows. He said that he had seen a claw, so he had chosen a picture of a chicken; and that, as you have to have a shovel to clean out a chicken shed, he had chosen a shovel with the other hand! What is interesting here is that this man's reply shows that:

a) he was not consciously aware of the content of the non-verbal, non-conscious part of his brain, – the part that had registered a snow scene, and
b) the verbal and conscious part of his brain gave an explanation for his behaviour *on the basis of his outward circumstances, that is, what he had said.*

I trust readers will agree that this experiment suggests some further support for one of the main arguments of this book, namely, that there are two forms of knowing, one experiential and the other verbal.

Here, now, another experiment of the same kind. In this, there is again a man in whom the two halves of the brain had been severed to ease epileptic seizures, and this time a picture of the word 'Laugh' was shown to his left visual field. In line with what has been noted about the anatomical structure of the brain, this image reached this man's right hemisphere, that is, the non-verbal, non-conscious half. The man acted on that request and laughed. The experimenter then asked him why he had laughed. His reply was that the experimenter was funny!

I draw attention to such experiments for two reasons. One, they suggest that, when people act on the basis of promptings from their non-verbal, non-conscious, or only partly conscious part of their brain, they tend to offer an explanation for their actions that is in line with their outward circumstances. In other words, they do not offer an explanation that indicates that they are aware of the schemas in the non-conscious, non-verbal part of their brain, the part that has actually prompted them to act as they have. And two, I believe that the results of such experiments again indicate that we possess two rather different forms of knowing: experiential, and verbal.

Consider next the following experiment. In this, the left half of a normal person's brain – the half that usually houses the speech centre, and hence the part that is conscious – is anaesthetized. Such an effect is achieved by injecting sodium amytal into the carotid artery, the artery from which blood flows into the left half of the brain. That person is then asked to handle with his or her *left* hand an object, say a toothbrush, lying under a blanket, and hence unseen. As a result of such an arrangement, the nature of the object handled will be registered in the *right* hemisphere, that is, in the non-verbal, non-conscious half. When the anaesthetic has worn off – and thus when the left half of the brain is again functioning normally – that person is asked to name the object that he or she handled. It has then been found that people are unable to do this. They *say* that they do not know. However, they are able to *point* to the correct object when shown a number of different ones. Such a result again suggests that information coded, or processed, in the non-verbal part of the brain can be *acted* on, but that it is often inaccessible to conscious introspection and hence *verbal* expression.

At this point, it would seem appropriate to pause for a moment to consider again, in what form information could be coded in the non-verbal parts of a brain. Clearly, it must be in a non-verbal form. But how? My best guess would be to say what I have already noted, namely, that it is coded in a 'felt' form, the form in which information is coded in the brains of most other living creatures.

I next draw attention to a finding reported in a medical journal that, I believe, sums up neatly, and possibly ironically, the material presented so far in this chapter. Having undergone an operation, a certain woman patient developed a strong reluctance to see the surgeon who had operated on her. Her reluctance was surprising, for, prior to her operation, she had liked the man. Moreover, she was unable to furnish a reason for her dislike. However, under hypnosis, the woman quoted her surgeon as having said, during her operation, 'Well, that will take care of this old bag.' This, together with similar findings, suggests that:

a) a level of anaesthetic which enables surgery to be performed without pain to a patient may not prevent certain patients from overhearing things said during their operation, and
b) as such patients are not *consciously* aware of having overhead anything, they are unable to *state* it.[5]

This finding again suggests that information processed non-consciously often remains inaccessible to conscious awareness. Or, in the language of a previous chapter, schemas that are laid down in a non-conscious form cannot easily be made conscious.

The neurologist Kurt Goldstein discovered something similar many years ago. In reporting his work with soldiers who had sustained injury to their brain during the

First World War, he noted: 'a phenomenon which is not experienced in conscious form, can never subsequently become directly conscious; and, conversely, a conscious phenomenon can never work directly upon attitudes and feelings.'[6]

Readers will immediately see that it is easy to rephrase these observations in the form of 'schemas', and I have still not got over my astonishment at Goldstein's finding. In part, this is because they explain one of Freud's clinical observations in a way very different from how Freud sought to do so. I recall here as an aside – for some readers might be interested in such things – that, after listening to his patients hour after hour, Freud concluded that there were things in their mind they were unable to confront; and he called this phenomenon 'repression'. As is well known, he came to the conclusion that these things were 'repressed' because they consisted of experiences which that person found too painful to allow into conscious awareness. As has been noted, Goldstein's explanation is rather different. He maintained that, 'things experienced in a non-conscious form can never subsequently become directly conscious'. But here I must emphasize that this is an aside, and my reason for drawing attention to these observations is again to draw attention to the distinction between experiential and verbal knowledge.

At this point, I would urge readers to notice that I have not attempted to offer a series of experimental findings. Instead, I have attempted to offer as much evidence as I have thought appropriate in support of a theory, a theory that seeks to explain some aspects of how our mind works, and especially the distinction between experiential and verbal learning. In other words, in this book, unlike many others, theory is treated as primary.

⚜

I turn last to LeDoux, a contemporary researcher who has reviewed a large number of neurological findings of the kind reported in this chapter. He typically concludes: 'When input is registered by non-conscious systems, that input is not available to the conscious self. It is coded in a way that cannot be decoded by the verbally dominant conscious mechanisms. Yet, it is as much a part of the store of information that directs our moods and behaviour as input which is initially processed in consciousness.'[7] And further: 'It is through overt behaviour that the conscious self comes to know fully the passions and prejudices that rule below.'

If all we have to go by is our outward behaviour, I would have thought it unlikely that we can ever know fully why we behave as we do. However, the findings reported in this chapter do suggest that much of our behaviour is determined by factors beyond conscious awareness; and that this is so because the sources for much of our behaviour cannot be easily accessed by the conscious, verbal part of our brain.

At the risk of diverting too much from the immediate aims of this book, but hopefully in support of one of its main arguments, I next draw attention to the finding that it is the right half of the brain that first develops in infants.[8] Then, as people develop further, and acquire language during the second year of life, the verbal, conscious left half assumes more control of actions. In short, much of our early learning is registered in the right hemisphere of our brain, and will hence be coded in a non-verbal, non-conscious form. It follows that such learning will be difficult to access consciously. It also follows that, if our earliest experiences are difficult to access consciously, this might not be due to 'amnesia' or 'repression';

but, as Goldstein maintained, because such experiences were coded in a non-conscious form.

Here is how another researcher, Josef, describes the above situation: 'In that the emerging human organism is asymmetrically arranged, with apparently little inter-action and information exchanged between the cerebral hemispheres, the effects of early experiences could have potentially profound effects . . . it is fascinating to consider the later ramifications of early emotional learning in the right hemi-sphere unbeknown to the left; learning and responding which may later be com-pletely inaccessible to the language centres of the brain even when extensive transfer is possible.'

In much the same way, Squire notes that, as what he calls the non-declarative memory is unconscious, we will not be directly aware of its contents, but we may become aware of those contents indirectly as when behaviour, prompted by it, causes us to question why we are acting as we are. It follows that, as we possess a number of memory systems, some of which are unconscious, we often possess atti-tudes, habits and preferences without being aware of their source. In other words, many of our actions and feelings are shaped by our early experiences, but, as those experiences will have been laid down in our procedural memory system, we will be unaware of those experiences and will act on them in an automatic manner – unless they have been laid down in our declarative memory system as well. However, it is also the case that the declarative memory system is imperfect. That is, it is prone to error, and this is because it is always based on a *reconstruction* of events, not the events themselves.

Notice that the above observations call into question the common assumption that we control our actions by a conscious act of will. The truth is rather that quite a few of our actions are prompted by past experiences, that many of these will be coded in a form inaccessible to conscious awareness, and that conscious thinking often has the function of merely offering a justification for those actions. Moreover, we are usually unaware of this process because the way in which we behave usually makes sense; and it is only when our behaviour is not as sensible as it might be, that we might have an inkling that things are not quite as is commonly assumed.[9]

Here is a common illustration from everyday life. We often find that a girl who has got on well with her father will tend to feel comfortable in the company of most men later in life. Likewise, a boy who has had a tense relationship with his mother often feels uncomfortable with women later in life. (Of course, matters could be the other way around.) Moreover, like all of us, these people will tend to associate with people, and to prefer situations, which corroborate their existing feelings; and, like the people in the experiments described above, they will tend to explain their feelings and reactions in terms of their outward circumstances. Again, it is as if one of the functions of thinking is often not to direct our actions, but to explain or justify them to us.[10]

The above could be re-stated like this. We commonly assume that first some-thing happens to us, and then we have a reaction. But it seems more accurate to say that, quite often, when something happens to us, it triggers off a feeling already latently inside us. That is why the same event often elicits quite different reactions in different people. In short, it is as if the world furnishes us with hooks, onto which we hang our past experiences.

What has been noted above might also help to explain otherwise paradoxical behaviour. For example, it helps to explain how it is possible to 'know' that smoking cigarettes is likely to kill one, yet continue smoking; the finding that parents who abuse their children usually have a history of having been themselves abused; and that people often behave like the one of their parents they most dislike.[11] Such seemingly paradoxical behaviour becomes explicable when we grasp that we *structure* many of our current experiences in line with our earliest experiences, rather than learn *from* those experiences.

Although these comments might sound counter-intuitive, they sound quite ordinary when applied to practical things. For example, most people would agree that we play a game in the way that we do, because we have *learnt through experience* to play in that way. What hubris to believe that the processes that determine the way in which we react to the angle of a ball are basically different from the processes which determine the way in which we react to the slant of an argument! In short, I am merely suggesting that we often know no more about our mental processes than we do about our digestive processes. But I should perhaps emphasize here that I have drawn attention to the findings noted in this section in an attempt to indicate yet again that, unlike what is commonly assumed in discussions about learning, there are various forms of it, and that it would be sensible to have that in mind when one teaches.

I would also hope that the above findings might suggest that, although a man certainly is a piece of work, he is not noble in reason, not infinite in faculty, far from an angel in action, not like a god in apprehension, and not remotely the paragon of animals. Still, if he is able to discover the kind of things about himself outlined in this section, he (or she!) possesses the remarkable faculty of sometimes being able to mirror life.

Chapter 9

Explaining and Experiencing

In several chapters I have drawn attention to findings that indicate that we often learn a good deal without being consciously aware of it.[1] One way to refer to knowledge of this kind is to use the word 'tacit'; and readers might recall that I drew attention to that term in an earlier chapter when I noted the work of Michael Polanyi. He maintained that science students must be given repeated opportunities to have practical experiences – as in a laboratory – because much of what one learns through experience cannot be conveyed in words. Readers might also recall my mentioning in the above respect the work of Carl Rogers in psychotherapy, and Gertrude Hendrix on learning mathematics.

Consider now an everyday example of tacit learning, and again something to which I referred briefly in an earlier chapter, namely, most people's ability to speak and write their native language reasonably correctly, without being able to *state* many formal rules of grammar. For example, few native speakers of English are likely to know what is meant by the term 'subjunctive', and many are unlikely to be able to explain why we use the word 'a' in English. Nevertheless, most speakers of English are able to use those forms perfectly correctly. As this tends to be a contentious issue, perhaps a concrete illustration would be in place. Consider the following two sentences:

- I like to live near the sea.
- A wave came in fast.

Most readers of this book would have little trouble writing those sentences correctly. However, many might have a problem if I were to ask: What is the function of the word 'the' in the first sentence, and the word 'a' in the second sentence? Many readers will know that those words are called 'articles', and that the first is 'the definite article', and the second 'the indefinite article'. But what is 'definite' about the use of the word 'the' in the first sentence? And what of my question about the function of these words? What does the word 'a' *do* in the second sentence? Anyone unable to answer those questions, yet able to write the above sentences correctly, must agree that he or she is able to use the articles in English correctly, without being able to state the rules that govern such usage. As some readers might be interested in this matter, I should perhaps add a partial explanation of the use of articles in English, and this is best done with another illustration. Consider the following sentence:

Ship sails tomorrow.

Most readers would guess that this sentence is a shortened form telling someone that a ship will set off tomorrow. But there is another possibility. That sentence could be a request that we send some sails. This suggests that one of the functions of the article in English might be to signal whether the next word is a verb or a noun; and this might be related to the fact that, unlike the case in many languages, in English, the verb and the noun form of a word are often the same. Whatever the case, I trust that even this incomplete explanation will illustrate that we are usually able to use our native language perfectly correctly, without consciously knowing the rules that govern its usage. If so, it must follow that we have learnt those rules 'tacitly'.

The above, incidentally, raises an important practical question, namely: Should formal grammar be taught in school? I had better note that 'formal grammar' does not include spelling or punctuation, but rather, an understanding of things like the 'subjunctive', and the use of 'articles'. Many researchers have investigated that question, and their findings point consistently in one direction. That is, it has been repeatedly found that pupils who are *not* taught grammar tend to write more accurately than pupils who are.[2] Some people might find this outcome surprising, even unacceptable. But then, evidence – in contrast to mere opinion, especially the kind purveyed by the mass media – often is. Consider how surprising the evidence that the sun does not move. No wonder it was resisted for centuries. And notice how the available *evidence* – in contrast to mere opinion – on the teaching of grammar noted here, complements the available evidence cited earlier on the teaching of mathematics.

The evidence noted above strongly suggests that native speakers of English learn how to write grammatically correct English best when they are exposed to good models, are encouraged to do lots of suitable reading and writing, and when their work is responded to in a serious and sympathetic manner. In short, when they have lots of appropriate *experiences,* – in contrast to being *told* things.

Notice also that the above observation on grammar again suggests that we often learn things of importance, and considerable complexity, tacitly; that is, without being able to state explicitly what it is that we have learnt. In fact, we have seen that the evidence goes further. It suggests that trying to apply rules – e.g. the rules of grammar – often interferes with effective action. A reader still inclined to dismiss the evidence cited in the Notes might like to consider the finding that attempting to attend to all aspects of a task consciously is characteristic of schizophrenia.[3]

None of the above implies that knowing rules is useless. Such a notion is absurd. For example, it might be very helpful to know the rules of grammar if we wish to learn a foreign language. However, it looks as if that ability should come after the rules have been mastered tacitly in one's own language.[4] Or consider the rules that govern how a house should be wired. It is obviously essential that an electrician engaged in such a task should know those rules. But the question here is not knowledge of rules, but how that knowledge has been acquired. In short, my argument here is that there is a predilection in western societies to overestimate conscious thinking, and to underestimate the importance of tacit knowledge acquired through experience.

In support of the above assertion, I note that *experiential* (or tacit) learning is powerful because, among other things, it has the following attributes. It:

a) enables us to apprehend things directly (rather than via 'rules')
b) enables us to respond to many things at the same time
c) enables us to gain a global view
d) does not require the medium of language, and
e) works in an abstract way.

Again, none of this is to dismiss the value of conscious thinking. On the contrary, I would suggest that our most powerful learning takes place when we:

- have had a suitable experience, and
- are able to reflect consciously on that experience.

Among other things, an interplay, such as the above, allows us to view the experience from a variety of angles, amend it, rehearse it for new action, dismiss it, store it in writing, and communicate it to others. And it is, of course, precisely the latter ability that makes us different from other creatures on this planet.

&

I come now to a consideration of what is required when we decide that we have learnt something that is wrong, misleading, or counter-productive. A practical illustration might help to indicate what is involved.

We often learn how to play a game, say tennis, by going on to a court with a partner and playing. In learning like that, we learn through experience. Or one could put the matter a little more technically, and say that, through the experience of playing, schemas become established in our brain, many of which will be of a quite non-conscious kind, and these often enable us to play pretty well. However, one day, we might meet a professional player who tells us that the way we hold a racket isn't 'right'. That professional might then show us a new way. Nine times out of ten, when we try that new way, it feels uncomfortable.

We get used to holding a racket in a certain way. Trying a new grip might not only feel awkward, it might also make our game go haywire. We will then be very tempted to ignore the advice that we have been given, and go back to holding the racket in the way to which we have grown accustomed. As noted in an earlier chapter, established schemas are difficult to override. But, if we admire how that professional plays, and if he or she has managed to convince us that, if we change our grip, our game is likely to improve, we might persist. And, if we do, no matter how uncomfortable it feels, and no matter how bad our game has now become, we might have the very gratifying experience of slowly learning how to play a better game. This suggests that, if we wish our behaviour to change, we must first override the schemas that have become established in our brain as the result of previous experiences. At the same time, we must expose ourselves to new experiences that, we hope, will result in the establishment of new and more appropriate schemas. Notice that these attempts will only succeed if we are able to do two things:

a) see the incorrectness of our previous learning, and
b) persist in a more appropriate way of behaving – in spite of the discomfort and failure that this might initially cause – until new schemas become established.[5]

The above is an example of re-learning in the case of a game. Matters are more complicated when it comes to things like personal relationships. Consider a person who had the frequent experience of being made to feel unjustifiably guilty as a child. It would not be surprising if such a person felt resentful, when he or she is made to feel guilty later in life. However, it is sometimes necessary to feel guilty. For example, in the course of interacting with friends, one might say something that hurts one of them. That friend will then usually indicate that he or she feels hurt, and that should make one feel guilty. If it does, one will usually try to make amends, and the friendship is then likely to continue. But, if one is over-sensitive to feelings of guilt, one might feel angry rather than guilty, and justify one's reaction by deciding that that friend is assuming the role of a victim. If that happens, one will be much less inclined to make amends, and one might then lose that friend. This illustration suggests that such a person would be well advised to try to re-learn how to respond to feelings of guilt.

If correct, the above suggests that we learn attitudes in roughly the same way we learn how to play a game. That is, our attitudes are encoded in our brain in the form of schemas, and, as noted in a previous chapter, many of them might well be coded below conscious awareness. If our attitudes are reasonably realistic, we will tend to react realistically to the things around us. If they are not, we will tend to react unrealistically. When that happens, we might become aware of it, and we might then find ourselves saying, 'Why the hell am I behaving in that way?' We may never discover the reason. As noted, many of our most basic attitudes will have been formed in our earliest years, and these may not be accessible to conscious awareness. Nevertheless, we might be able to see, from the result of our behaviour, that certain of our attitudes or behaviours are leading us astray. We might then decide that we had better try to change them; and, if we can persist in such an endeavour, we might manage to override our inappropriate behaviours, until new and more realistic ones become established.

The above suggests two things. One, that, contrary to what is commonly assumed, we should not always 'listen to our feelings', that is, that our feelings are not the infallible guides that our 'feeling age' holds. And two, that the schemas for attitudes are more difficult to override than the schemas for holding a tennis racket. However, a change in attitudes is also possible, but only when the conditions noted above are met. That is, when one is able to:

a) see the nature of one's mis-learning
b) ignore one's inappropriate feelings
c) begin to act more appropriately
d) cope with the stress that acting in a new way might initially cause
e) continue in this new way until new and more appropriate schemas become established.

One important point is missing in the above. It is that being *told* the above is unlikely to have the desired effect. On the contrary: Being *told* the above is most likely to cause resentment. Change is far more likely to come about when the person concerned *discovers* his or her mistake, and when he or she then has appropriate *experiences*, from which new behaviour can develop.[6] Readers might notice that these comments echo what I noted in earlier sections on how certain people learnt to use a word processor; and more recently, the learning of mathematics and grammar. In other words, I am suggesting that learning grammar, and learning a new way of behaving, have much in common. In short, that all learning has certain features in common.

I would summarize the above like this. There are various levels of knowing. The most powerful form of knowing comes about when one has had a suitable experience of something. That kind of knowing is coded inside one in a felt, compacted, living, tacit form; and in this way it becomes a part of one's total mental structure. In other words, it becomes a part of one's *sense of self*. With some effort, one can sometimes make this kind of knowledge conscious, and think about it verbally. That can help one do things like rehearse that knowledge, modify it, extend it, scrap it, plan ahead, or communicate it. One is able to do these things because, with the help of language, one can reflect; and in this way, one is able to link events or objects that might be far apart in space and time. Notice again the interplay between having experiences, and then consciously reflecting on them.

Consider here the behaviour of people who are good at something. They often convey a sense of effortlessness; and they often find it difficult to explain what enables them to carry out a task as well as they do. This kind of knowledge can be compared with verbal knowledge. In verbal knowledge, one has only words. One can think about those words, and that can give one a sense of knowing. But it is unlikely that one will be able to use such knowledge in anywhere near as powerful and flexible a way, as knowledge gained through experience and informed reflection on it.

&

I might manage to bring out the implications of the above, if I next compare the way that a human being learns, with the way that a computer is said to learn. In doing so, I shall also continue to comment on the process of psychotherapy, for I believe that learning is fundamentally of a piece, no matter in what context it takes place.

A few years after computers first hove over the horizon, one writer typically claimed that 'duplicating the problem-solving and information-handling capacities of the brain is not far off; it would be surprising if it were not accomplished within the next decade'.[7] I am writing these words about fifty years after that claim was made, and 'duplicating the problem-solving capacities . . . of the brain' still seems an awful long way away. Those who have made such claims have usually based them on the fact that computers can sometimes do things that human beings can do. A favourite example is to play chess; another is to solve a mathematical problem; and on the strength of such successes, some of these people have claimed – claimed literally – that human beings are essentially machines.

I find such claims bizarre, in part because they are based on what I would consider trivial pursuits. However, there are people who take such claims seriously.

That is, they believe that computer programs can furnish a model of human learning; and, as the latter is the topic of this book, it would seem necessary to examine such a claim. However, instead of games and mathematics, I would have thought it more appropriate to consider something more characteristically human and mature, and I have in mind the simple fact of pain.

People sometimes suffer pain. They might have a broken leg or a broken heart, and they will want to be rid of their pain. Nature often does that for them, but sometimes a pain persists. When it does, it is a signal that action must be taken. That, after all, is the function of pain. But precisely what action?

Those who have examined this matter suggest that four steps are required. The person concerned must:

a) be aware of the pain
b) be prepared to deal with the pain
c) gain some understanding of the nature of the pain, and
d) be willing to take appropriate action after the pain has been treated.[8]

Quite often, it is not especially difficult to take these steps. But sometimes there are difficulties. For example, it is well known that some people will push awareness of a pain so far away that they are hardly aware of having it. Or, with regard to the third step, the need to have some understanding of the pain, we might know that we have a pain in our stomach, but, in the case of a persistent pain, such general knowledge is not enough. We have to go to someone who has been trained to understand such a symptom.

If the pain is due to something obviously physical, one goes to one kind of therapist. If it is due to something obviously emotional, one goes to another kind of therapist. In each case, a trained therapist should have some understanding of the factors causing the pain. In the case of unremitting emotional pain, all psychotherapists agree that such pain is often due to mis-learning. That is, the person concerned has learnt to respond to certain situations in an inappropriate manner. For example, a person might feel terrible each time he or she gets into a confined space like a lift. Lifts are not wonderful places to be in; but, feeling so bad about them that one is unable to get into one, is obviously inappropriate.

Another example might be a person who has had three divorces, with all the pain, loss of confidence, and mounting expenses that such experiences can cause. Such a person has also mislearnt. In this instance, how to find and remain with a spouse or partner, with whom life is better rather than worse.[9]

Matters are even more complicated when the problem is a more general one. Life being what it is, all of us at times experience pain and stress because these are features of being alive. One example is bereavement. Other pains are caused by destructive social forces, such as war, crime, prejudice, unemployment, and persecution. It is also soul-destroying to live in a culture in which it is possible to identify people as 'redundant'. Situations of this kind can be intensely painful, but a consideration of them is not a part of the remit of this book.

Feeling bad about lifts seems a simpler problem. One could deal with it, by never going inside one. However, if one lives on the seventh floor of a building, that might be difficult, and it might then be a good idea to try to deal with the problem. If the account of learning outlined so far in this book is roughly correct, the problem is likely to be related to some kind of mislearning in the past. Perhaps it was a matter of not having learnt to feel secure as a child, or perhaps one's parents come into it in some other way. Two thousand years ago, it was already known that, if the parents ate sour grapes, the children's teeth would be set on edge. Relatives, friends and society at large might also be implicated. The question now is: How have past experiences – encoded in the form of schemas – brought about a situation that causes an adult to feel pain when he or she gets into a lift?

The obvious answer is: Investigate the matter; and then help the person concerned to discover the cause in a sympathetic manner. That is, common sense suggests that, if a person is at a loss to understand why he or she feels bad inside a lift, he or she should be able to overcome such a fear if the reason is discovered and explained.

But, as is so often the case when it comes to a complex matter, common sense is as wrong here as when it shows us that the sun moves. Explaining will not usually help a person who is afraid of lifts, to get into one. And this, as has often been noted, is because explaining is verbal, and will therefore result in merely verbal learning.

As what I am noting here runs counter to common assumptions, readers might like to see what an experienced therapist had to say on this matter, and I quote:

'If we communicate to a patient some idea, that he has at one time repressed, but which we have discovered in him, our telling him makes at first no change in his mental condition. . . . On the contrary, all that we shall achieve at first will be a fresh rejection of the repressed idea. But now the patient has in actual fact the same idea in two forms, in different places in his mental apparatus: first he has the conscious memory . . . of the idea conveyed in what we told him; and secondly, he also has . . . the unconscious memory of his experience as it was in its earlier form. There is no lifting of the repression until the conscious idea . . . has entered into connection with the unconscious memory trace . . . .' A little further on this writer notes: 'To have heard something and to have experienced something are in their psychological nature two quite different things, even though the content of both is the same.'

Sigmund Freud wrote those lines about one hundred years ago, and I have still not got over my astonishment at such perceptiveness.[10] Notice that, if notions like 'repression' are removed, all the rest is given considerable support by empirical research on memory carried out seventy years later. That is surely remarkable. I had better add here that, for my part, I differentiate sharply between Freud's clinical insights, and his psychological explanations. That is, whereas I often find the former perceptive, I nearly always find the latter misguided. An example of the former might be the concept of 'the transference'; and an example of the latter might be 'the Oedipal complex'. But these are complex issues that take one far beyond the remit of this book; and I have quoted Freud here only to illustrate my contention that telling and explaining seldom result in a change of behaviour. Or, to put this in another way, that experiencing, and listening to an explanation, are very different things.

These comments lead naturally to a question, and it might be phrased like this. If someone finds it impossibly painful to get into a lift, and if explaining the probable causes of that difficulty to that person is unlikely to help him or her, what does one do? Before I attempt to answer that question, I pose another. It is: How can one simulate a computer to respond in this manner? As far as I know, this has never been attempted or even discussed; and I believe that the reason for these omissions is that such an attempt is *in principle* impossible. This is because, as I have already noted, whereas human beings have a sense of self, computers have silicon chips. In short, human beings experience, whereas computers record.

But now to return to my question about how a person who is fearful about lifts might be helped to get into one, and I begin indirectly like this. When psychotherapists discuss the progress a client of theirs is making, it is common to hear them say that their client is 'merely intellectualizing'. By this, they mean that their client is 'just thinking and talking'. That is similar to saying that a client finds it difficult to sense what he or she is *feeling*. This is an important matter because many psychotherapists believe that it is only when their clients are deeply engaged with what they are *feeling*, that they learn.[11] They take this position because they believe that it is only then, that a client might begin to gain some insight into the nature of the *experiences* – often coded in a non-verbal, unconscious form – that are responsible for the distress in which they now find themselves. Other psychotherapists take a different approach, and I shall come to that in a minute.

Before that, I should perhaps note that it sounds almost perverse to say that a person might not know what he or she is feeling. But we have all met people who seem much more 'in touch with themselves' than others. The trouble is, we tend to see this much more easily in others than in ourselves. But all this was known many years ago. Readers might here recall the words 'Know Thyself', engraved over the entrance to that famous cave at Delphi, the cave to which people went many centuries ago to consult an oracle about their future. Notice how that legend over the entrance turned people back upon themselves; and some people appear to find that difficult. Recall also that people who *talk* about their difficulties fluently are often the ones who find it hardest to *overcome* them.

Recall next that a change in behaviour can be difficult for a variety of reasons. First, early experiences might be difficult to access consciously. Second, they might be deeply painful.[12] And third, becoming consciously aware of them might result in seeing oneself in an unflattering light. The dilemma is acute. For, the more troubled one is, the less likely is one to see oneself objectively. But, unless one can muster the courage to take ownership of one's inmost feelings, one might continue to lead a troubled life.[13]

Considerations such as the above indicate that change towards a more appropriate response to life has little to do with explaining, and much more to do with becoming confident enough to become aware of what one has experienced. And when one has gained such confidence, one might begin to understand why one's life has taken the course it has. Given support, such understanding might generate attitudes that are more realistic. These, in turn, might encourage new behaviours, and these should bring about new experiences. Compare this account with accounts of people supposedly learning in psychotherapy, written by those who work in artificial intelligence. The latter sound like schizoid people talking.[14] For, in these accounts, people's feelings have gone dead, and everything is intellectualized. As is to be expected, they talk like computers.

The neurologist Oliver Sacks gave an apt illustration of this. He presented one of his patients with a flower and asked him what it is. The man answered, 'An object, six inches in length. A convoluted red form with linear green attachments.'[15] His response to people was the same. Sacks writes: 'no face was familiar to him, seen as a "thou"'. When we look at a face, we don't just see a *shape*. We see a *person* looking out. And this must be because we recognize something of our humanity in that person. However, this man: 'construed the world as a computer construes it, by means of key features and schematic relationships. The scheme might be identified, without the reality being grasped at all.'

I noted earlier that some psychotherapists have an orientation rather different from the one outlined so far. Some of these are so sure that talking about the possible cause of a problem would not help a client, they ignore all talking about causes. Instead, they go straight into new experiencing. Take again the case of a person who gets into a panic when in a lift. Very roughly speaking, with such a person, this kind of therapist might first discuss lifts in a supportive way. Next, therapist and client will look at a lift from a distance. Next, they will approach a lift together. Next, they will stand near a lift. Each time they do one of these things, the therapist will reassure the client. Eventually, when enough confidence has been gained, they will get into a lift together.

Notice again that, in this illustration, this client is learning because he or she is *experiencing*, not because somebody is *explaining*. The talk between client and therapist is merely one of the surface features of the learning process. Notice also that, when such an approach works, it is not enough to say that this is because this client has been 'reinforced'. It must also be because, first, in doing what the client is doing, he or she is *feeling*; and if the therapist is sensitive and intelligent, the client is probably feeling encouraged. And second, if this approach works, it is also because the client has had the *experience* of feeling better about lifts. At this point, readers might recall the comments made earlier about the human ability to think, and how it has been tacked onto the evolutionary-speaking earlier ability to experience, an ability that all living creatures possess.

The mode of therapy described above is called 'behaviour modification'. It affects behaviour only. The meaning of, or the underlying reason for, not being able to get into a lift is ignored. Although this approach appears to work with specific fears, like getting into a lift, it is much less likely to succeed when a problem is more complex, as, for example, when a person keeps falling out with a spouse. In such a case, psychotherapy usually begins with the client and the psychotherapist discussing the problem. And, after a few meetings, a client might say, 'Yes. Now that you have drawn my attention to it again, I can see how I let everyone dominate me. And instead of doing something about it, I tend to go away and sulk. But from now on, I'm going to tell people when I've had enough. I really am going to have it out with them!'

This client now seems to grasp that he or she unwittingly creates the very situations that cause him or her distress. But we have seen that being able to *talk* about something does not confirm that one has learnt how to *do* something. When people have really learnt something – when they have changed – they talk quite differently. In the case of psychotherapy, they find themselves engaged in consciously *re-experiencing* their previous non-conscious experiences, and seeing how these have helped to shape their lives.[16] Indeed, over the years, I have been dismayed to discover that quite a few people use psychotherapy as a defence. They become adept at learning the language of psychotherapy, and in this way, they achieve their underlying aim. This is to believe that they are doing something about their condition by coming for psychotherapy, while at the same time managing to remain exactly where they are. For, as I have repeatedly noted, in order to learn – i.e., change – one has to *experience*. And talking is a wonderful way to evade this often very difficult necessity. Clients of this kind are like those students who do well at exams, and nothing else. And their psychotherapist is sometimes like the teacher who teaches such students.

As this chapter is at the heart of what this book is about, I should like to rephrase the above with a seeming digression.

In discussing the difference between mediocre novels and great ones, E.M. Forster once made the following observation. He suggested that mediocre novels consist mainly of a plot, in which this and that happens; whereas great novels also have a plot – because a novel requires one – but in these, the plot is merely the vehicle which carries a certain message.[17] That is why, many years after we have read a great novel, we often have only the haziest recollection of its plot, but are left with a powerful impression of the attitude or message conveyed in it. I mention this because, while reflecting on my experience of being with clients, it came to me one day that the details that a client might relate, and the re-phrasing or interpretations which a psychotherapist might offer, are merely the plot that carries the 'message' of that which occasionally makes psychotherapy effective. And this 'message' consists largely of what the client and the therapist *experience* while they are sitting together.

I believe that the above conjecture is given support by two findings. One, that clients in psychotherapy do not make progress primarily because of their therapist's knowledge. And two, that the single most important factor contributing to success in psychotherapy is the quality of the relationship between client and therapist. I would further conjecture that the latter is important because it can powerfully affect the extent to which a client feels able to reflect on, and re-experience his or her past experiences. Here is the voice of a thoughtful person talking about her experience of psychotherapy.

'My analyst wasn't cold and remote. I felt his personality all the time, and he was a passionate human being . . . I knew when I was entertaining him. I knew when I made him angry. I knew when he thought, "stupid bitch, absolutely hopeless". It was projection, but also it was real. Yes, he was a real person. And I remember at the last session he asked me, "What do you think made the difference?" and I said "You. You came across as a real human being. And you were real enough to make me feel that it is worthwhile being real. That's all."'[18]

Readers might here agree that the kind of relationship described by this client is much more likely to generate a positive *experience* than anything a psychotherapist might *say*.[19] Compare the above description of a *relationship*, with how people who have led troubled lives often talk. They will frequently be heard to say that they are 'going to begin a new life'; and by this they mean that they intend to seek a new set of circumstances, or adopt a new attitude. But the only way to 'begin a new life' – if that is what one needs to do – is to discover why one is unwittingly structuring one's life in a manner that is making one unhappy; and that cannot be done on one's own. Trying to do that on one's own is like trying to measure a piece of cloth by using the same piece of cloth. In other words, we can only learn about ourselves in a relationship; and for this to happen, a person who has had some training in understanding relationships is sometimes required.[20]

It might now be helpful to summarize. Readers might have noticed that, in this section, I have often referred to psychotherapy and computers, and some readers might well have thought that these have little to do with learning and teaching. It has certainly not been my intention to encourage teachers to assume the role of a psychotherapist. It is rather that a client in psychotherapy is also a learner; and that some understanding of what helps this kind of person to learn might help one to understand something about all learning. As for computers, if the distinction I have tried to indicate between experiencing and explaining is apt, it is clear that it is impossible to simulate such a difference on a computer, because computers are dead.

I have also referred to computers because we live in an age that confers much prestige on these gadgets, so much so, that one often hears people say that humans are essentially machines. It seems to me that such claims can have very serious consequences. For clearly, if humans are essentially machines, it is perfectly proper to call them 'redundant' when they are sacked; to talk of 'body counts' when they are dead; and to refer to 'collateral damage' when they are slaughtered. Now, I get *worried* when I hear terms like these applied to human beings. Do computers?

At best, the attempt to show that a computer can simulate human thinking produces an important, but nevertheless a second-order phenomenon, for it produces a model that obscures what is most vital about being human. That isn't thinking. It is experiencing. That is why birds, hedgehogs and worms can learn, but not clouds, silicon rock or electronic computers.

&

Near the beginning of this book, I noted my surprise that some of the teachers I had had in my training college clearly knew a good deal about teaching, yet did not teach well; and later I suggested that this was because those teachers' knowledge had been verbal only. In other words, I am arguing that, to teach well, one must have repeated *experiences* of teaching well, in addition to reading and thinking about it. In short, I contend that, without the experience, the thinking remains only a potential. In the chapters that have followed since those observations were made, I have attempted to consider this matter in a variety of ways; and I have also cited a good deal of empirical evidence in support of my contention. In the last part of this chapter, I draw attention to some direct evidence on this matter, and I begin with a report by a researcher named Oliver.[21]

He first noted that, for many years, there has been broad agreement among many teachers about what constitutes effective teaching. He then described how he contacted 119 teachers, sent them a questionnaire about effective teaching, and asked them to express their agreement or disagreement with the statements in it. When he got the questionnaires back, he found that most of the teachers who had replied tended to agree with the statements. He then arranged to visit those teachers. He observed them teach, but he found that few of them taught in a way that tallied with their replies. Oliver concluded that his findings did not justify condemnation of those teachers, but condemnation of their training. They had not 'really' been enabled to learn.

Oliver conducted his research among primary school teachers. Combs and Soper conducted similar research among teachers at a university.[22] These researchers invited several hundred students to nominate 'the very best teacher', and 'the very worst teacher', they had had. When these researchers received those students' replies, they wrote to the teachers so designated (without of course telling them *how* they had been designated) and asked them if they would participate in some research. In contacting these 'very best' and 'very worst' teachers, these researchers hoped that the replies they received might throw some light on how one could distinguish between good and poor teachers. However, the people who had been nominated as the 'very worst teachers', sent in the same kind of replies as the people who had been nominated as the 'very best teachers'. Here again, an example of teachers who know, but do not 'really' know.

I turn next to a similar finding from research in medical education; and I do so for two reasons. One is in line with the belief I have argued in these pages, that a theory of learning requires evidence rather than opinion. The other is in line with my hope that teachers of any subject will find this book useful, – for I move here from research on primary school teachers, to research on teachers in a medical school. A researcher named Gonnella and his associates conducted the research I now report, and it involved 113 patients who were first screened by an experienced physician.[23] A patient care team then assumed responsibility for those patients (as is often the case in a hospital), and this team consisted of experienced physicians and senior students.

The initial screening had shown that 108 of the patients showed signs of urinary-tract infection. However, a review of those patients' clinic charts, during their stay in hospital, showed that the patient care team picked up such signs in only 68 of the patients; and in only 31 patients were further investigations undertaken. A test given to both the experienced physicians and the senior students in the patient care team showed negligible differences between them, and this suggested that such a test was not a good predictor of actual performance. These researchers therefore noted that it is:

'disturbing to learn that, in an examination, the students and physicians indicate that a history of catheterization, past treatment of urinary tract infection, hyper-tension, and diabetes mellitus are critical data, but in actual treatment situations they either fail to ask these questions, or fail to follow through once the information has been obtained.' And these researchers concluded: 'There are many instructional methods for correcting a deficiency in knowledge, but it seems that the same methods are less likely to be effective when the issue is that of translating knowledge into action.'

Poets knew all this many years ago. For example, in Shakespeare's plays, it is often the worst characters that have the best lines. Thus, many people know Polonius's words: 'Give every man thine ear, but few thy voice.' But what Polonius *does* in the play contradicts what he *tells* his son; and Hamlet also tells us that Polonius was a 'foolish, prating knave'. A few sentences later, Polonius tells his son, 'This above all, to thine own self be true, and it must follow, as the night the day, thou canst not then be false to any man.'[24] But it is clear from that play that Polonius was about as 'true' as the night is the day.

In another play, Shakespeare has one of his characters say, 'It is a good divine that follows his own instructions: I can easier teach twenty what were good to be done, than be one of the twenty to follow mine own teaching.'[25] Shakespeare has often been described as a keen observer of the human scene. He knew that the people who *don't* 'really' know are often the ones who are best at *talking* about it. I still remember how struck I was when I discovered, a few years after I had begun teaching, that the people who talked most eloquently about teaching were often the worst teachers. The second thing I noticed was that it was those talkers who tended to get promoted.

☙

Many years ago, Vygotsky began his classic work on thought and language by noting that he intended to examine the relationship between feeling and thinking. He first deplored the fact that these two topics tend to be studied separately. Then he noted that, separating them, 'makes the thought process appear as an autonomous flow of "thoughts thinking themselves", segregated from the fullness of life, from the personal needs and interests, the inclinations and impulses, of the thinker.'[26] And he continued, 'Such segregated thought must be viewed either as a meaningless epiphenomenon, incapable of changing anything in the life or conduct of a person, or else as some kind of primeval force exerting an influence on personal life in an inexplicable, mysterious way.'

I cannot think of a more apt description of much contemporary cognitive psychology. Because we have the words 'think' and 'feel', we tend to have the illusion that there are two quite separate entities, corresponding to those two words, in the real world.[27] Readers might like to try to find in themselves where one of their feelings ends, and a thought begins. Notice again how these comments relate to the observation made in a previous chapter, on how the human capacity to reflect is an evolutionary development tacked onto the existing capacity of all creatures to feel and hence experience.

The interplay between feeling and thinking greatly interested Vygotsky, but he only touched on this topic at the end of the book from which I am quoting. He then noted that the last step in his analysis is this. That thought, 'is engendered by motivation, by our desires and needs, our interests and emotions'. And finally: 'behind every thought there is an affective-volitional tendency, which holds the answer to the last "why" in the analysis of thinking'.

Bartlett came to much the same conclusion. He noted: 'Here is the significance of the fact, often reported in the preceding pages, that when a subject is being asked to remember, very often the first thing that emerges, is something of the nature of an attitude. The recall is then a construction, made largely on the basis of this attitude, and its general effect is that of a justification of the attitude.'[28]

Here is another finding that seems to corroborate the above. In reporting the work of the psycholinguist Slobin, Luria noted that Slobin had found that young children are often unable to repeat a word that they have just spontaneously said; and Slobin explains this inability as due to the fact that a child's spontaneous speech is organized by its motives. If those motives are absent, the child might be unable say what it knows.[29]

Notice how, in all the above observations, thinking follows on from a deeper feeling (or experiential) process.

At this point, readers might remember my description of an encounter with a tutor-librarian named Betty. There I attempted to illustrate that this woman began to 'really' learn, only when she discovered that she had a personal need to know this material; and further, only after she had made repeated attempts to *act* on what she had supposedly learnt. Cognition, of course, comes into all of this. But it is, I believe, in Vygotsky's words, 'an epiphenomenon', even though it is, of course, an important one.[30]

I note last and with pleasure that, although Vygotsky and Bartlett wrote more than 50 years ago, their work is still held in high esteem.

Chapter 10

A Theory of Learning

Living creatures are alive, and because they are alive, they can have experiences. When a creature has an experience, some kind of coding is laid down in its nervous system. This coding often has a non-verbal, abstract, tacit form, and it has been given the name 'schema'. As schemas become established, a creature 'learns'.

Human beings can go further. They can, in Frederic Bartlett's words, 'go back upon their schemata'. That is, human beings, unlike other creatures on this planet, can consider some of their experiences consciously. In short, they are able to reflect. With the help of language, people can also clarify some of their experiences, recombine them, evaluate them, plan ahead, communicate them, and store them in writing. Given the right conditions, people can sometimes also modify what they have learnt. However, this possession of language does not mean that one can bypass the need to have experiences if one wishes to 'really' learn. It is rather that the possession of language enables one to utilize one's experiences to maximum effect.

From the foregoing, it follows that the experience of listening to someone talk, will be of the talk, not necessarily of what the talk stands for. But here I recall a rider. It is that, if one already has a model of something in one's head, one might benefit from listening to someone talk about that something, – provided always that this talk is related to the model of that something that one already has in one's head.

Notice also that we do not have to do anything in order to have an experience. All we have to do, is to expose ourselves to it. In that sense, experiencing is the same as digesting. If an experience can be experienced, it will be experienced. One can interfere with this process, but one cannot make it happen. However, the way in which one exposes oneself to an experience, can make a difference. That is where teachers come in. They can help to arrange things so that their learners have experiences that suit them; and they can also foster a climate that facilitates learning.

The above is not always easy. When some learners are presented with a problem, they seem to see it as a threat. They then focus on the seeming threat, rather than the problem. Other learners seem less worried. They tackle a problem with interest, even pleasure.[1] They open themselves to it. In short, when the attitude is right, a good deal else is often right.[2]

It is also the case that we usually learn best when we feel personally engaged. The trouble here is that, what a learner might want, might not be what a community needs, and learners are always a part of a community. In former years, it was often a community's needs that were imposed on learners. With the increasing emphasis on self in developed countries, there has been a shift towards the learners' needs. The danger here is the creation of a 'Mississippi-Half-Baked-Chicken' kind of learning, hiding behind slogans like 'student-centred' and 'student-led'. Moreover, although the deepest kind of learning is usually personal learning, it does not follow that one can learn from only one's own experiences. One's own experiences are sure to be limited; and they can also be misleading, for we tend to experience that which we expect to experience. Consider the following illustration.

Freddy is twenty-eight, a chemical engineer, and married to Elizabeth. He is bright and conscientious, but much lacking in confidence. Liz is genuinely fond of him, but sometimes she gets exasperated by his willingness to work for an uncle who is grasping and essentially stupid. One day, she sees an advertisement for an engineer with exactly Freddy's qualifications. She points it out to him, and says, 'Freddy, I've found just the right job for you. You must apply! I bet you get it.' He looks at the newspaper, and says, 'Oh, I'll never get that.' But Liz urges him strongly, he reluctantly applies, and a few days later a letter arrives inviting him to an interview. He goes, and at the interview much impresses the director and chief production engineer. Only the head of marketing is doubtful. They talk to him for an hour, and then say they will let him know if he has the job. When he leaves, the three men say how nice and knowledgeable he is, but the head of marketing points out repeatedly how lacking in confidence Freddy is. The others have to agree, and they decide not to offer him the job. A few days later, their letter telling him that he hasn't got the job arrives. When Freddy has read it, he turns almost accusingly to Liz and says, 'I told you I wouldn't get it. What a waste of time.' This is a crude example, but it might illustrate how we tend to structure our experiences, rather than learn from them. Or how our experiences often corroborate for us what we already believe. Readers might here also recall the comments in an earlier chapter on how our thinking often functions to justify our beliefs and behaviour. It follows that, if we want to make progress, we would be wise to consider the experience of others as well as our own.

I would hope that most people would agree with much of the above. But teachers are engaged in teaching, and that tends to make them concerned with how they teach. However, the trouble with this understandable concern, is that it can have the effect of making teachers concerned with the wrong thing. For, if 'real' learning requires experiencing, it looks as if teachers need to shift the focus of their concern away from teaching and on to learning. This follows because learners won't have an experience of something, if they are simply told about it.

With didactic teaching, with the transmission style, with the teacher standing up front and 'teaching by telling', there will be a good deal of verbal learning. One guesses that, after repeated exposures to real-life situations, those learners will eventually find how to use some of this material practically. In the mean time, the learners are likely to feel that they are getting somewhere if they have a sheaf of notes after a lesson. Such an assurance is illusory, but, if those lesson notes are coupled with good examination pass rates, this illusion might maintain the confidence of some learners and most administrators. But the cost will be heavy, for the learners will have been given a false experience of learning, and their own capacity to 'really' learn might become undermined, perhaps forever. That would be a heavy price to pay, both individually and collectively, for no society can ever have too many real learners.

It might appear that helping learners to learn, as distinct from teaching them, is easy. Anyone who has tried to do such a thing will know it is very difficult. They will know that it isn't enough to tell learners to go to a library and read, or to sit in a wood and listen. To teach in a way that takes account of how people learn, requires systematic study, followed by a great many struggles to translate such study into effective practice.

The above could be summarized like this. Although the world is a complex place, we usually manage to respond to it pretty well; and, if we do, it cannot be because of any 'problem-solving strategies' that we bring to it. It must rather be because we are a *part* of life, and hence able to *experience* it.

The above might sound woolly, but it is difficult to be precise about learning. Many people much brighter than I am, have considered this matter, and they have found it difficult, too. To talk precisely about learning, one must be able to talk precisely about life, and, so far, no one has managed to do that.[3] I also fear that the current fashion to 'demystify' might make the foregoing sound a bit woolly. That would be a pity. Such 'demystifying' always trivializes, for our world is a complex place, and I have also found that there is much pleasure to be derived from contemplating that mystery, and trying to fathom it. I also fear that the outline of learning put forward in previous chapters is likely to be faulty. If the history of knowledge is anything to go by, it is *sure* to be faulty. I don't of course enjoy thinking about that, but such a state of affairs is both inevitable and useful. For it might spur someone to come along, explain what is wrong, and in that way, we might make some progress.

&

Near the beginning of this book, I noted that I would attempt to outline a theory of learning and teaching, and I added that I would do this, in the hope that it would provide teachers with a tool to help guide and amend their practice. If so, it might be helpful if I now more formally summarize the theory of learning outlined in the first half of this book. However, before that, it might be useful to recall the characteristics of a good theory. Roughly speaking, a good theory:

a) indicates connections between – often seemingly unrelated – data
b) suggests a concise explanation for this data
c) provides a guide to practice
d) is sure to exhibit anomalies in the course of practice
e) in view of the foregoing, will bring about a need to amend or scrap the theory
f) in view of the foregoing, will suggest further lines of research, and this is likely to
g) contribute to an improvement in knowledge and hence practice.

It might now be helpful to illustrate the above characteristics of a good theory, with the theory of gravity. (It will be recalled that, roughly speaking, this theory holds that bodies exert an attraction on each other in proportion to their mass and distance.) In line with points a) to g) above, the theory of gravity:

a) indicates that the fall of an apple and the movement of the tides (tugged as they both are by the sun, moon and earth) are connected
b) explains why apples fall towards the earth rather than drop off it
c) enables people to shoot arrows or rockets in a planned manner
d) made it possible for Einstein to come along and modify Newton's theory
e) suggests lines of further research that should eventually lead to an improvement in the theory and hence also in practice.

Shooting rockets and teaching students are obviously not the same. But, as this world of ours is an integrated whole, I believe that there is likely to be a lawful pattern in the way that people learn, just as there is a lawful pattern in the way that apples fall. The word 'lawful' is not fashionable at present, but that isn't important. What is, is that I shall state the theory of learning I am proposing as simply and clearly as I can. That should enable readers to evaluate it for themselves, and hence to amend it or discard it as they think fit.

The theory of learning I am proposing looks something this. Provided that people's natural capacity to learn has not been impaired, people learn when:

a) they discover that there is something that they do not know, and wish to learn
b) they are able to tackle this task reasonably directly
c) this task affords intrinsic rewards
d) the task is sensible and manageable
e) they are able to form hunches, test them, and see the results of their tests
f) they have access to suitable information
g) they are able to see patterns
h) they have a sense of making progress
i) they find themselves in a challenging but friendly and supportive environment.

I dare summarize the merits of this theory of learning like this.

First, a wide range of research findings support this theory. This does not of course ensure the soundness of this theory, nor does such evidence prove anything. There is no such thing as 'proof' in science, nor anywhere else except perhaps detective stories. What such evidence does do, is provide anchor points. It follows that it would not be enough simply to disagree with this evidence. One must rather show in what way this evidence is mistaken, and, better, provide better evidence. This again shows that there is no such thing as final evidence. There is only the best *available* evidence, so that seeking evidence always remains an unending quest. And that is how it must be, for the world is a complex place, and the human brain is only one little product of it.

Second, the evidence that has been cited in support of this theory, and the experiences that I have related, produce an integrated whole. That is, it suggests a pattern rather than a jumble of findings or opinions. Moreover, the approach is broad. It seeks to encompass all learners from about the age of eight to eighty-eight, of both sexes, learning anything from astrophysics to zoo maintenance.

Third, this theory is open to being tested. In this way, it is completely different from the expression of an opinion. If Jack states that pink is a lovely colour, he is expressing an opinion, and that's fine. But that statement cannot be tested. Opinions cannot be tested, and that, I think, is one of the things that makes them so popular. One can express opinions 'til the cows come home, and they can never be refuted. I mention these truisms because I think it is essential to try to distinguish between opinion and evidence when discussing important things like how people learn.

Fourth, the theory of learning put forward in this book, like all theories of learning, places learners in a certain position. This theory places learners on centre stage. That is, they do not learn because of something that is done *to* them, but because of what *they* do. This also places responsibility for their learning on them; and the teacher's role becomes that of facilitator. But this is *not* the same as being 'student centred'! In a so-called 'student-centred' situation, the students take charge of *what* they learn, and that is not the position described in this book. However, I would hope that the orientation towards learning taken here, might contribute to helping learners to become autonomous people.

Fifth, far from being something engraved in stone – as is often sadly believed – having a theory helps one to *amend* one's practice. This is because a theory is a clear statement, and this allows everyone to see both its strengths and its weaknesses. It follows that having a theory is the best way to ensure, as far as that is possible, an open and flexible approach.

Sixth, although the theory outlined in this book provides a framework, it allows for any amount of individual differences in learning. It also allows anyone who wishes to try out this theory in teaching, to employ a wide range of approaches.

And that brings us to the second Part of this book.

Part II

Teaching

Chapter 11

The Transmission Method and an Alternative Approach

This chapter contains descriptions of two lessons. The first is of a teacher in a school, the second of a teacher in an industrial training establishment. Having read them, readers might like to consider which approach relates more closely to the material on learning outlined in the first Part of this book.

&

The first lesson to be described is of a class of pupils being taught how to calculate the area of a parallelogram.[1] The teacher is up front, and begins by asking if anyone can remember how to calculate the area of a rectangle. A pupil puts up her hand, and says, 'Sir, the area of a rectangle is equal to the product of the two sides.' The teacher nods, turns, draws a rectangle on the blackboard, notes its dimensions, and asks the pupils to work out its area. A few minutes later, when it is clear that they all know how to do this, the teacher says, 'Now we are going to learn how to calculate the area of a parallelogram. A parallelogram looks like this.' He turns to the blackboard again, and draws a parallelogram.

He labels the corners of the parallelogram 'a', 'b', 'c' and 'd', and looks around to make sure that everyone is attending. He turns back to the blackboard, and says, 'I drop one perpendicular from the top left corner like this, and another perpendicular from the upper right corner like this.' Then he says, 'I extend the base line to the right, and I label the two new points "e" and "f".' He turns round again, and gives the proof that, 'The area of a parallelogram is equal to . . . .' He does some calculations neatly on the board, and explains each point as he goes along.

This is an experienced teacher. He speaks clearly, and he frequently looks around the class to make sure he is getting attention. He rubs the chalk dust off his hands, and says, 'You will find what I have been explaining to you on page 62. Read what the writer says, and then do the problems on the next page. You will have enough time to do about half the problems now. I want you to finish the rest at home. Are there any questions?' As there are none, he smiles and tells the pupils to get to work. They do, and it is soon clear that most of them know how to calculate the area of a parallelogram. Notice how many things this teacher does, which are generally considered things that a teacher should do. He:

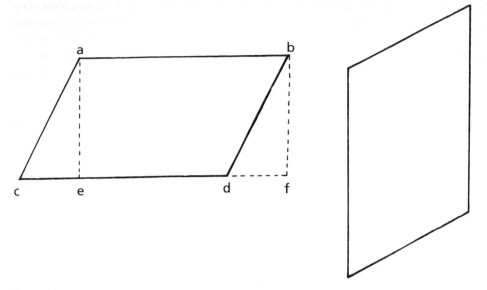

Figure 11.1

has a clear sense of aims
revises and checks on work previously done
begins from where the learners are at
speaks and illustrates clearly
states the appropriate rules correctly
elicits learner participation
checks on learning
refers the learners to a textbook
gets the learners to practise
knows his subject
is systematic
has a pleasant manner
manages the class well.

What more could anyone want?

But let us imagine that we are troubled, and that we invite ourselves to see this teacher's next lesson. This time, this teacher begins by asking if anyone can tell him how to calculate the area of a parallelogram. A hand shoots up, and a pupil gives the correct answer. The teacher nods, smiles, turns to the blackboard, and sets the class a problem. The pupils get to work, and soon it is clear that most have the answer right. But let us continue to be troubled, and imagine that one of us, say Jane, asks the teacher whether she might ask the pupils a question. The teacher readily agrees, Jane goes to the front of the class, and, on the blackboard, she draws a parallelogram standing on its beam-end. Then she turns around, and asks the pupils to calculate its area. Some of the pupils look puzzled. One of them says, 'Miss, we haven't had that yet.' But most are busy. They copy Jane's drawing, drop the usual auxiliary lines, – and then most are stuck. Why? I believe those pupils got stuck because, in their first lesson, they merely learnt the rote application of a rule.

Hence, when the conditions were changed, the pupils were lost. More exactly, they were stuck because they did not know the central principle that governs the way in which the area of a parallelogram can be calculated, and they were hence unable to transfer what knowledge they had. But recall that this teacher did everything that teachers are commonly expected to do. What else could this teacher have done?

Perhaps those pupils should have been given some paper and scissors, encouraged to cut up a parallelogram, and to fit the bits together again to see how it is similar to a rectangle. Such a suggestion is along the right lines, but it misses an essential point. The essential point is, I believe, that this teacher 'taught', instead of 'helped his learners to learn'. This teacher based his approach on telling, and the central argument of this book is that, to 'really' learn, one must experience. Too much telling gets in the way of experiencing.

At this point, readers might remember Gertrude Hendrix's finding, namely, that telling learners a mathematical rule before they have been helped to discover it for themselves, gets in the way of their being able to transfer their knowledge. This teacher told his pupils the rule for doing something before he enabled them to experience it. He thereby took that experience away from them. Had he helped them to find the rule for calculating the area of a parallelogram, they would have grasped the *meaning* of the rule.

This does not, of course, mean that this teacher should simply have told his pupils to find the rule for themselves. What he should have done, was to devise a carefully structured learning situation that would have helped his pupils to grasp the rule for themselves, and so experience it. He could have done that by posing a series of judicious questions, or setting a series of simple problems which hint at a solution.[2] Or he could have posed a number of problems of steadily increasing complexity, set some investigational work, or perhaps devised a game. Best of all, he could have introduced a combination of all of these, followed by practice to consolidate the learning. This teacher did ask questions, but notice that, when he did, he led his pupils by the nose. In short, he asked them to guess what was in his head. In other words, he never encouraged them to look for an answer inside their own heads. It might even be said that this man's teaching was damaging; and that the more successful it appeared to be, the more damaging it might have been.[3] That sounds severe, but notice that, not only was there no transfer of learning, those pupils were not given the tools or confidence to find their own answers. Readers might like to consider the kind of citizens that are likely to be produced by this kind of teaching.[4]

At the beginning of this chapter, I invited readers to consider to what extent the teaching just described tallies with the theory of learning outlined in the first Part of this book. It seems fair to say that it simply does not tally. These pupils were not encouraged to see a problem, nor were they able to form and test hunches. They were unable to discuss a problem in order to clarify it, and they were not able to derive much intrinsic reward from their work. Above all, notice that the mode of teaching that this teacher employed is widespread, but that it is not related to anything known about the way that human beings learn.

But there is nothing evil about this teacher! He merely practises what was practised on him, and he probably does a better job of it. Moreover, it seems somehow 'natural' to try to show others how a problem might be solved, especially when one is in the role of a 'teacher'. Isn't that what teaching is essentially about? Unfortunately, such a situation also provides an opportunity to shine, a temptation that good teachers intuitively resist.[5] A good teacher has the ability to clarify the nature of a problem, and then the generosity to give the learners an opportunity to discover the solution for themselves. Many years ago, Jane Abercrombie summarized beautifully what I am trying to convey. She suggested that a teacher's task is to tell the learners what to look for, without telling them what to see.[6]

"

I come now to the second lesson to be described in this chapter, and this one is on computer engineering. As this book is about fundamentals, it could be on space-capsule horticulture. The name of this teacher is Frank, and he works in the training establishment of a very large computer company. Here they run courses to train field engineers when the firm introduces new equipment, or to upgrade the knowledge of engineers in the maintenance of existing equipment. Lessons are usually divided into 'theory' and 'practice' sessions; and, in the practice sessions, the students work in 'labs', i.e., rooms that house examples of the various computers that this firm sells and maintains. These practice lessons usually go quite well, but the theory lessons can be problematic. In these, the students (all field engineers) sit behind rows of tables facing a teacher. The teacher stands up front, with several whiteboards behind him and an overhead projector next to him. There is no lack of equipment, and most of it is of the latest design. The teacher lectures according to a detailed course guide, and this includes a long list of objectives. He or she will also have literally hundreds of transparencies (or 'foils', as they are called here) to hand. As these teachers lecture, they project these transparencies onto an overhead screen, often at a rate of several a minute. These transparencies are all machine-made using the latest technology, and look perfect. From time to time, a teacher might refer the students to the thick manuals neatly stacked in front of them. At other times, he or she will draw diagrams on the many surfaces available. Anyone observing one of these lessons, is likely to be impressed by the expertise that these teachers clearly possess.

When I first visited this establishment, I was struck by the glazed look on the faces of many of the students attending these 'theory' lessons. The teachers noticed this, too, of course, and they frequently reassured the students that the topic would become clearer to them as soon as they had got to their 'practical' lesson; and even more so, when they were dealing with problems in the field. In the meantime, these teachers would say, they had to plough on, as there was 'such a lot of material to cover'.

It will be seen that the mode of instruction employed at this establishment rests on the belief that, if you can tell somebody something, then that person can learn it. Everything is then geared to making that 'telling' as efficient as possible. This is a prestigious organization with huge resources, and a very great deal of money is spent on training. It sounds positively in bad taste to suggest that what is being done here rests on a myth. In practice, what happens is that the students sit through these 'theory' lessons as best as they can, while most of what is said washes over them. When they come to their practical lessons, they pick up a few strands and weave them together into a shaky whole, but their real learning does not usually begin until they get into the field again. When I first observed Frank, he taught in the manner just described. (It was often called 'foil and toil' by these instructors.) On my fifth visit, this is what I saw.

The students, again all field engineers, came into the class and Frank welcomed them. He announced his name, and invited the learners to introduce themselves briefly. There were about twenty-five of them, so this only took a few minutes. Moreover, this time, the tables were so arranged that they formed a square in the middle of the room, and that made the introductions real. The students sat around the tables, and Frank sat at one of the tables next to a student. Everyone could see everyone else. When the introductions were over, Frank asked whether anyone present had had any experience of the new computer system that they had come to study. A few people nodded. Frank asked what they thought of it, and there were several replies ranging from laconic to amusing. Then Frank said that he would outline very briefly the way in which the new system differed from the previous one. He had a clear and simple way of talking, and he conveyed the impression that they were about to do a job of work together. At this point, readers might recall a case study called 'Simon Winch' noted near the beginning of this book.

Half way through a sentence, Frank asked one of the students, who has spoken previously, to continue describing the salient features of the earlier system. He said the others might like a change of voice. The student began, and when he stopped for a moment to get his bearings, Frank suggested he might find it easier to continue at the whiteboard. After a second of hesitation, the student, a man of about forty, went to the board, began to draw, and continued explaining. In this way, within fifteen minutes of the opening of the lesson, roles had been changed without any fuss. As the student out front continued to draw, Frank invited and got contributions from the other students. Throughout, Frank's manner was factual and easy. A few minutes later, he went to the front himself and sketched in some of the features of the new system. The while he talked in a conversational kind of way, asked questions, and invited comment. After about another fifteen minutes like this, Frank stretched his lanky frame and suggested a break. The students got up and went to the swish vending machines located just outside the classroom.

The break over, Frank gave out a sheet of paper with about ten questions on it. He announced that, instead of continuing to lecture, he was going to ask them to examine the new system directly. He added that he hoped that the questions on the sheet would provide a rough guide, and that they were intended to help them to determine in which way the new system differed from the system they already knew. He urged them to work in pairs, and said that he hoped the people who already knew something about the new system would help those who did not.

Frank led the students down a corridor, and five minutes later, they were busy with computer equipment. Frank sometimes moved around and exchanged a friendly word, but mostly he sat with me to one side. He had just read Jane Abercrombie's book, and was full of enthusiasm for it. Twice he said it felt odd not to be teaching. Now and again, one of the students came over to ask something. When Frank answered, he often rephrased the question, or asked another. When he explained something, it was always briefly and inofficiously. Then the student went back to lift covers, turn switches, or watch what looked to me like garbled Hungarian on screens.

All the time there was a hum of conversation in the room. This period of work lasted for about thirty minutes, and then Frank suggested another short break. When it was over, Frank invited the students to sit in a rough circle, and asked them how they had got on. From the nods and what was said, it was soon clear that the students had found the previous session instructive. Frank then said that it might be an idea to compare the answers that they had got. One of the women students read out her first answer, and there was general agreement with it. Then a man read out his next one. There were again murmurs of assent, although a couple of students suggested a rider. And so it went, with Frank seldom doing more than nod or smile in reply. Nor were these general agreements surprising for the students had been discussing their answers with each other all through the previous session. Then it was time for lunch.

In the afternoon, we met in the room in which the first session had been held. Frank exchanged a few comments with the students in his genial manner, and then gave out another worksheet. This contained a dozen questions relating to what they had been examining that morning. Frank said that a consideration of these questions should further develop what they had already discovered. He asked the students to reply to the questions in pairs, not to hesitate to go back to examine equipment, and to use the manuals on the tables in front of them when necessary.

Then Frank again sat to one side while the students worked. All the time there was the sound of students talking, turning pages, and scratching heads. Occasionally, one of them got up to consult someone on the other side of the room, and it was clear that they had got to know each other a little by then. Occasionally, one of the students consulted Frank, and then one would usually hear this person convey to others what he or she had just heard. At one point, Frank took me next door to show me some equipment. While doing so, he again said how odd it was not to be teaching all the time. Here I had better add that leaving school pupils like this is both inadvisable and unlawful.

Half an hour later, most of the students were finished, and Frank called for a short break. When we reassembled, Frank suggested that one of the students might like to invite somebody in the room to answer the first question. If everyone agreed that the answer was correct, the person who had answered should ask another person the next question. And so on, 'til all the questions had been answered. Frank said he intended to remain silent unless he was the only person to spot a mistake.

For a moment, there was silence. The learners, twenty men and four women, ranging in age from twenty-five to fifty-five, were obviously surprised by this approach. More silence. Then one of the men said something comical, pointed at a man opposite him, and read a question. The man addressed looked thoughtful, was clearly hesitant, but then began to answer. And for the next half-hour, I had the great pleasure of seeing human beings 'really' learn. Here is one incident out of a dozen.

A man began by saying that he was unsure if he and his partner had got that answer right, but he thought that 'so and so' might be the case. He paused and looked around. His partner and two other men nodded. One man shook his head. Prodded, the doubter said, if 'so and so', then things could not be quite like the first speaker had said. But he wasn't sure himself because . . . The first speaker and his partner exchanged a few words, looked at a manual, looked up, but did not say anything. Another man began to speak, but he was interrupted. A general hubbub ensued which continued for a minute. This was followed by an uneasy silence. Several students looked towards Frank, but he remained silent.

Then, quietly at first, the partner of the first man who had spoken began. He got to a certain point, and then asked a question. A woman who had not said anything so far spoke. A man took up where she left off. Then the man who had first answered the question said something in reply. He stopped, thought for a second, nodded hard, and went on. As he spoke, his eyes and face seemed to light up. He finished with a burst, and ended on a mock-triumphant note. There were nods all round. The learners looked at Frank, but he remained silent. However, his pleasure was evident.

Readers might notice how different this is from what goes on in many classrooms. In these, the learners usually sit and listen passively; or, when they are asked a question, they compete to provide the correct answer. As a result, learners in such a situation seldom make a mistake, and so are unable to learn from having made a mistake. In this class, the opposite was happening. Notice also how all this replicates life, and how experiential it is. And so this lesson continued. Four times Frank spoke. Once to give a clue when the students had thrashed around and got themselves into knots; twice to give a page reference; and once to suggest that the learners had gone too far in a certain direction.

At the end of that period, we all got up for a fifteen-minute break. It was striking that many of the learners continued talking about the topic of the lesson as they walked out. None had that glazed look I had noticed when they had listened to an instructor teaching by telling.

After the break, Frank summarised some of the points that had been made. He then asked for a volunteer to go to the whiteboard to draw the outlines of the new system. One man got up almost immediately. He began to draw against a background of humorous references to his cackhanded drawing abilities. For the next half-hour, never once moving from his seat, Frank made comments, asked questions, and invited people to go to the whiteboard to add other components to the system. Finally, he asked the students to respond to a quiz in one of the manuals. At the end of the afternoon, Frank put his hands behind his head and said he reckoned they'd done enough for one day. No one got up. Someone sighed, another person made a wry comment. Slowly people got their papers together, stood up, and left the room.

&

I believe that the approach to teaching described in the second lesson, will foster better learning than the teaching described in the first lesson. But a belief is only a belief. It does not provide evidence. One way to obtain some evidence on this matter would be to carry out an investigation. But, if this were done, it would not be enough to assess these learners' ability to write correct answers in an exam. The research would have to be so designed that it assessed whether the learners in the first and second lesson were able to apply their knowledge practically, and in situations that were only marginally similar to those they had experienced in their classroom.[7] In the absence of such research, it might be appropriate if I report the following. When Frank asked these learners (in my presence) which approach they preferred, the one common in that establishment or the one he was now using, most expressed a strong preference for his new approach. This response was corroborated by their written comments when they came to evaluate the course. As the above might sound like special pleading, I draw attention to four things.

1) The focus of the second lesson was on the learners' learning, not on Frank's 'skills' or 'competences'. Frank does have skills and competences. They are important, and required lots of practice. However, they are best seen as the unobtrusive and surface features of his understanding of learning.
2) Frank's teaching is closely based on the material on learning outlined in Part I of this book.
3) The learners in the second lesson are adults, but the approach illustrated there could be used with any learners.
4) In the second lesson, the frequent difference between 'theory' and 'practice' has disappeared.

Finally, readers might like to ask themselves in which lesson they would prefer to be a learner: the first, or the second?

Chapter 12

Research into Teaching

The previous chapter contained descriptions of two lessons; and, at the end of that chapter, I noted that the teaching in the second lesson was closely related to the material on learning outlined in the first Part of this book. I went on to say that the second lesson was therefore more likely to result in 'real' learning. A question that might now arise is as follows: Is there any research on teaching that would support such a claim?

Unfortunately, there is very little research evidence that indicates that one method of teaching is clearly better than any other. This unsatisfactory state of affairs exists in spite of over fifty years of research into teaching.[1] However, there is some research that indicates that teaching in a certain manner helps people to learn, but, before I report this, it might be helpful to note briefly some of the problems that can arise when such research is done.[2]

&

Should one wish to find out which kind of teaching helps people to learn, one could begin by observing as many lessons as possible. After all, most people believe that they can recognize good teaching when they see it. But there are at least two problems with such an approach. First, and as might have been noticed from the description of pupils learning how to calculate the area of a parallelogram given in the previous chapter, the conventional wisdom about what constitutes good teaching is questionable. Second, it is clear that relying on one's beliefs about what constitutes good teaching would not produce any objective evidence. This is because one cannot be reasonably sure that, what one believes to be good teaching really is good teaching. More exactly, one could not in that way feel with real confidence that such teaching helps people to learn. Here it might be recalled that it isn't easy to distinguish between a good performance, and teaching that results in 'real' learning.

One way to find objective evidence might be to consider exam results. If learners have passed an exam, it seems fair to assume that their teaching was good. But only a moment of reflection suggests that it is difficult to be sure, that learners have passed an exam because of something that their teacher did. After all, the learners might have passed their exam because they are bright, or because they had studied hard at home. It is also well known that learners sometimes pass an exam, not because of their teacher, but in spite of their teacher.

But perhaps one could begin with exam results. That is, one could look for a class that did consistently well at its exams, and carefully observe the behaviour of its teacher. Then, one could compare the teaching of that teacher with that of another teacher who had a similar class, but a class that did not do as well at exams. If that were done with several classes, a pattern might begin to emerge.

Another way to look for objective evidence might be to carry out an experiment. For example, one could first locate two comparable classes. To be reasonably sure that they really were comparable, one would have to give both classes a test in, say, mathematics. If the results were about the same, one could assume that the learners in the two classes were about equal in ability. Then a teacher would have to be found to teach both classes mathematics in exactly the same way, but with just one difference. That difference could be, for example, that in one class this teacher did revisions of material learnt, while in the other class she did not. At the end of the research period, say after a year, both classes would be given a second mathematics test. If it were then found that the class which had been given revisions did better than the other class, one could assume that doing revisions had helped them to learn more.

Of course, one such experiment would not be enough. Next year, the experiment would have to be repeated, with other classes and other teachers. The trouble however is that, when this has been done, inconclusive results have often been obtained. This is mainly because the variables in such research are complex. For example, even if one class initially scores (on average) the same as a comparable class in a mathematics test, that class might be very different in other respects; and it might be these other differences that are responsible for the higher scores at the end of the year, rather than the revisions that were done during the year.

Another factor that might be important in learning is a teacher's personality. Many researchers have found that effective teachers tend to be firm, kindly and demanding. But do all learners respond in the same way to such qualities? Here, too, a good deal of research has been done on this question, and here, too, the results are far from conclusive. In short, it is very difficult to isolate one factor in teaching, and to show clearly that it is that one factor that helps people to learn.

Another difficulty in doing classroom research is getting agreement between researchers on what they are seeing. Imagine two researchers called Lavan and Black. They have decided to investigate whether a teacher's clarity affects how well the learners learn, and in the course of a morning, they observe three different teachers. But what criteria are they to use to determine clarity? The two researchers might agree that one of the teachers is clearer than the others. But on exactly what grounds did they decide that?

A good deal of research on teaching is based on what is called 'meta-analysis'. In this, a researcher will try to find all the research on a certain topic that has been published in, say, the last twenty years. He or she will then apply certain statistical techniques to the data supplied by each researcher, and attempt to find whether, when that data is pooled, certain results obtain. I was nearly always disappointed when I read such work, and I even found much of it worthless. In brief, this was largely because all the details that were most likely to help one to understand an issue, were obscured by this blunderbuss approach, an approach that relies almost exclusively on numerical data. One concrete example of such a failing, is when a number of teachers are compared who ostensibly adopt two different approaches, say a 'traditional' compared with a 'progressive' one. These terms are so vague that they mean next to nothing; one is never told how well trained these teachers were in using such an approach; and the results obtained obscure rather than indicate anything worth knowing.[3]

Yet another problem lies in deciding what the aims of teaching are. Some people argue that the main aim is to help learners to pass exams. Others maintain that it is more important to help learners to become inquiring, independent, and responsible people. Which of these aims is the more desirable? Are they compatible? A good deal must obviously be considered before one is in a position to answer questions of this kind.

The above outlines a few of the problems involved in doing classroom research, and there are many others! But perhaps enough has been noted to suggest that one must be cautious when evaluating the findings of such research.

✎

What now follows, is based on the work of two researchers named Rosenshine and Furst.[4] These two researchers did not do their research in classrooms. Instead, they examined the published work of a large number of researchers who did do their research in classrooms, but they did not apply a 'meta-analysis'. They rather looked for what a large number of researchers had independently discovered. It is also important to note that Rosenshine and Furst:

a) selected only pieces of research that had been very carefully conducted, and
b) used only those pieces of research in which a *specific* behaviour of a teacher could be shown to relate to the *amount* that learners had learnt – as measured by exam results.

By the end of their investigations, Rosenshine and Furst came to two tentative conclusions:

a) that they had found fifty pieces of research that had been well conducted, and
b) that there are specific teaching behaviours that seem to help people to learn.

These researchers also emphasized that they consider tentative, both the findings that they had examined, and their own findings; and with those riders in mind, let us now examine their findings.

✎

Rosenshine and Furst found that the following teaching behaviours help learners to learn:

being clear
being enthusiastic
using a variety of approaches
good questioning
being task-orientated (remaining focused on the aims of the lesson)

being indirect (not giving straight information)

giving learners an opportunity to learn

making structuring comments (periodically summing up what has been done, and signposting the way ahead).

They found that one teaching behaviour inhibits learning. It is:

being critical.

Whenever I drew the attention of a class to the above list, I usually found that it did not generate much interest. The above items seemed to strike most people as self-evident, and I found that it takes time to see that this list is loaded with powerful implications. However, there was one item that nearly always elicited an immediate response; and it is the last one. In short, many people wanted to distinguish between destructive and constructive criticism.[5] In view of this interest, it might be an idea to begin with it.

☙

The distinction between destructive and constructive criticism seems obvious, but I was often struck to find that the people who most want to make this distinction, were often the ones who became most upset when I attempt to be constructively critical with their work. More exactly, I found that, when I tried to be constructively critical of their work, they felt hurt. This tended to make them defensive, and this very natural defensiveness then hindered their learning.

It might be important to remember here that this is a discussion about making mistakes in a classroom. It is not a discussion about, say, student nurses making a mistake when they plunge a needle into a patient. Educational establishments are educational establishments. They are not 'the real thing'. They prepare students for 'the real thing'. Student nurses can learn how to do their thing with needles on oranges. It is because classrooms are not the real thing that mistakes can be made in them. It follows that there is no contradiction between allowing learners to make mistakes inside a classroom, and ensuring safe practices outside them. Indeed, I found that the more mistakes learners feel able to make in a disciplined way inside a classroom, the fewer they tend to make outside them.

The above noted, one can return to consider what a teacher might do when a learner has made a mistake.

Imagine that a learner has just said something in a class, and, in doing so, he or she makes a mistake. Instead of saying that this learner has made a mistake, a teacher could ask that learner how he or she has got to that answer. If that teacher's attitude is a genuine one, the learner will explain the reasoning, and this will help to clarify the matter. At other times, a learner might respond by thinking, and then say something like, 'Ah, yes . . . what I meant was . . .'

Another thing a teacher might do when a mistake has been made or stated, is to acknowledge that learner's answer, say that other answers might be possible, turn to the other learners in the class, and ask them what they think. Seven times out of ten, someone will then give the more appropriate answer. But clearly, such an approach will only have a beneficial effect if it does not generate a competitive atmosphere, and if the process is handled lightly and sensitively. When that is the case, and where the friendly atmosphere I associate with good teaching exists, other learners will not wait for a teacher to correct mistakes. They will become accustomed to such exchanges, and will themselves object in a friendly manner when a mistake is expressed. What is important in all this is that, when a teacher acts in the manner I have just outlined, a teacher utilizes the inevitability that mistakes will be made, as a useful and integral part of the learning process. Notice also that, in the illustrations given here, there is an absence of either destructive or constructive criticism, yet incorrect responses have not been ignored. That is because the focus of attention has been on helping learners to learn, not on evaluating them. For, in good teaching, questions are not asked primarily in order to test understanding, but to foster it.

The above examples are of mistakes learners might make when they respond to a teacher's question. Mistakes are dealt with even better when lessons are so structured that the learners are able to discover and correct their mistakes themselves. For example, learners can be asked to design and build an electronic circuit from an outline plan and a set of incomplete instructions. When the task has been completed, they can be asked to test their work against a list of specifications. The same approach could be used with a text, photograph, graph, model or computer program; and sometimes it is a good idea for these things to be done in small groups.

Many years ago, when I taught English in a school, I sometimes asked my pupils to show their written work to a neighbour, and to ask that neighbour for comment. At first, some of the pupils didn't like that. Most had never been invited to do such a thing before. However, I found that, if I persisted, and if a relaxed but purposive atmosphere developed in a class, not only did the pupils get used to this approach, many of them also came to like it. Among other things, this made for more variety, and it tapped into social inclinations. We reached a stage when some of my lessons contained a period during which pupils showed each other their work. That way, also, they didn't always have to wait to get a response from me, and the response of a peer sometimes carries more weight with a learner than the response of a teacher. Recall also that, when people are at work, they often have to show each other what they have done.[6]

Making mistakes is obviously an inevitable and necessary part of all real learning. It simply isn't possible to learn anything without making some mistakes. In fact, it could be argued that, as we learn 'by consequence', we learn most of all from our mistakes. In an earlier chapter, I described people learning how to use a word processor, and from that description it was clear that, in such learning, one must test hunches; and when one does that, one will make more incorrect responses than correct ones. If so, it would surely help learning if a teacher could foster a climate in which learners feel able to make mistakes, can talk to each other about them, and hence learn from them.

Of course, there are occasions when it might be essential for a teacher to point out a mistake, as for example in a laboratory or a workshop. But, even in such a situation, it is a good idea to point out mistakes quietly and tactfully, for otherwise, an attempt to prevent an accident might precipitate one.

None of the above is intended to suggest that a teacher should not be demanding. There is no contradiction between being demanding, and being sensitive to the possible effect of being critical. If poor work has been done, I believe it should not be accepted. But, instead of criticizing it, it is surely much better to point out how it could be improved. I found that, when I did that, learners looked annoyed, upset, stimulated, sheepish or concerned. Their work then either improved, or they went off in a huff. I don't think such outcomes can be escaped. There is a bottom line to everything. Teachers have a duty to their community as well as to their learners.

One more detail might be worth mentioning. When I first corrected written work, I used a red pen. I was a teacher in a school then, and, as I was teaching English as a foreign language, I had to correct an awful lot of mistakes! After a year or two, the sight of all that red ink on a learner's work would bother me. I'd ask myself how I would feel if I saw all that red ink over a piece of work I had done. So, I switched to green ink. Before long, I came to dislike green, too. Over the next few years I experimented, and finally settled on any blue or black pen that was handy.

At first, I corrected all mistakes; but, after a year or two, I realized that most of my pupils hardly looked at my corrections. So it became obvious that doing all that correcting was a waste of time. It also eventually dawned on me that, what I was doing, was what my pupils should be doing! So, I corrected fewer errors, and told the pupils who made a lot of them that they would have to check their work more carefully if they hoped to improve. In short, I realized that people learn much more from disciplined practice than from being corrected. In line with that belief, I sometimes used a pencil for correcting, and invited my pupils to rub out anything that they did not like. Some of the younger ones rubbed out everything I had written! But their work often improved, too.

In later years, when I marked the work of adults, I kept to the approach outlined above, with this addition. If I thought a learner had gone off the track, or had not grasped what I thought should be grasped, I wrote a question. And when I thought I must point out a mistake, I tried to indicate the direction in which a better answer might be found. I also tried to find something to acknowledge.

So much for the last item, criticism, on Rosenshine and Furst's list. I turn next to their positive findings.

Chapter 13

Clarity, Enthusiasm and Variety

The first item on Rosenshine and Furst's list is: 'Being clear'. Not many people will be surprised to read that it is helpful if a teacher is clear; but it is sometimes difficult to know just what one must do in order to be clear. Four factors seem to come into the matter:

1) having a thorough knowledge of one's subject
2) the ability to see to the heart of a topic
3) the ability to see the matter from a learner's perspective, and
4) the ability to explain the matter simply.

The first item is obvious. The second and third items are probably related to one's personality. The fourth calls for a few practical suggestions.

Teachers who are clear use simple language. They use fresh, striking, and real-life analogies. They also often begin with a concrete example, better, a concrete problem. Where a technical term needs to be introduced, they will first use an everyday word with an equivalent meaning. This establishes a context. They will then use the technical term, and perhaps the everyday term immediately after. Next, they will define the technical term more closely. In this way, slowly, the appropriate schemas will become established in the listeners' minds.

Teachers who are clear also illustrate frequently. Having made a theoretical point, they will follow it with a practical example, for this has the effect of clarifying the matter. Such an approach will also help learners to remember it.[1] In illustrating like that, good teachers do not get lost in detail. They always come back to a central path, and frequently show us where we are on it. Now and then, they will briefly retrace their steps, remind us of the places we have visited, and recall where we are heading. In short, they keep the main point frequently in sight.

Teachers who are clear, are systematic. That is a most important point, for, to be systematic, one has to prepare. I might add here that I found that, no matter how often I had taught a given topic, I had to prepare it afresh each time I taught it if I wished the lesson to go well. Also, teachers who are clear, do not make their knowledge obtrusive. They do not flood their learners with a mass of knowledge. On the contrary, as they have no need to shine, they keep most of what they know in reserve.

Here, now, a few additional suggestions on how to be clear.[2]

> Think about the subject, not yourself.
> A short, well-known word is better than a fancy one.
> Better to use a concrete noun than an abstract one.
> Where possible, use a verb rather than a noun.
> Wherever possible, provide an illustration from life.
> Use everyday talk, not book talk.
> Talk in a personal, rather than an impersonal way.
> No matter how theoretical a topic, always attempt to tie it to a practical issue.
> Pause now and again in a relaxed manner to find the most suitable way to say something.
> Make spaces to allow the listeners and yourself to reflect.
> An occasional anecdote makes for variety.
> Have as few detailed notes as possible.
> Do not talk for more than four minutes at any one time.
> Enable (not just encourage) the learners to participate.

Readers might like to consider the following research with regard to that last item. Leavitt and Mueller arranged for an instructor to teach a class how to draw a geometric figure under four different conditions:[3]

1) When the instructor spoke while hidden behind a screen.
2) When the instructor spoke while visible.
3) When the learners were able to say 'yes' or 'no' in response to the instructor's questions.
4) When the instructor and learners were able to talk freely to each other.

Here are their main findings:

a) the learners were able to draw the figure most accurately under condition 4;
b) the learners felt most sure they had drawn the figure correctly under condition 4;
c) teaching under condition 4 initially took longer than teaching under condition 1; however,
d) as more lessons took place, less time was required to teach under condition 4, while condition 1 continued to take about the same amount of time;
e) the learners preferred condition 4;
f) when the instructor began by using condition 1, 2 or 3, and then changed to condition 4, the learners' comments were often aggressive. It looks as if the learners had been unable to express the hostility they had felt when they had had to learn under conditions 1, 2 or 3; however,
g) when the instructor began by using condition 4, the learners' comments tended to be friendly.

☍

The second item that Rosenshine and Furst noted was 'Being enthusiastic'. Again, few people are likely to be surprised by that finding. But a problem might arise here. Consider the following episode.

I was once chatting to some friends, and one of the people present was a girl of seventeen. A few days later, she passed me a note she had written during one of her lessons. Here is what she wrote:

'If only she would stop talking. She has such an excited voice. A sort of path with no end. It's unfair. She is learning all the time. Her eyes are shining with the pleasure of it. She is exploring, thinking, expressing herself, and hearing her own ideas. How lovely for her. She must enjoy teaching. Wow! She has just asked a question! I wonder what it was? Silence now. I expect everyone has, like me, kind of stopped listening. Everyone is so used to just sitting and listening that, when it's their turn to say something, they feel lost. She has just looked at me and is probably thinking: good girl, writing notes . . .'

A few lines further on, this girl continued, 'John is sitting next to me. He is bored, frustrated, breathing heavily. Playing with his pen. Rolling it from side to side. I wish I could write him a letter. God! She has just asked him to give an example of something! He probably never heard a word. He says, 'I don't know.' Dog eyes. She smiles at this and says, 'You're not doing enough background reading for my lessons, John.' I suppose that's the only way to really learn anything. I wish she would shut up. She is talking more slowly now. I suppose she thinks she was talking too fast before. Soon I'll be outside, won't have to listen to her voice.'

The first time I read those lines, I rather caught my breath. I could not help wondering whether those were the kind of things that my students thought during one of my lessons. My worries increased when I came across the following comment by a teacher called Simon Stuart:

'As a boy and master I have observed a kind of law whereby the teacher who speaks for long periods induces a corresponding deafness in the class; but the most painful aspect of it is that the deafness not only spreads with the duration of the lesson, but intensifies with the excitement, the self-preoccupation, the earnestness or even the brilliance of the teacher. . . .'And a few lines further on:

'. . . it will be found that in his enthusiasm, the teacher is making an assault upon the active principle of the class, ignoring their energy and giving no scope to their rivalry; instead, he induces an outward passivity (easily mistaken for interest and compliance) and an inner resistance (uneasily ignored). If he does not learn to amend this situation it can become a vicious circle in which the excessive activity of the master induces resentment in the pupil, while the resentment forces the master to close off his awareness of the pupils' feelings which have become too painful for him to observe.'[4]

When I first read those comments, it came to me that some people seem to be drawn to teaching because they have a need to talk. They seem to have a need to be out front, to be seen to displace air. And of course, I wondered whether this was also true of me. My worries increased when I came across the following comment by Winnicott, a man who had been a paediatrician:

'It is easy to picture a person with a great need to give, to fill people up, to get under their skin, really to prove to himself or herself that what he or she has to give is good. There is unconscious doubt, of course, about this very thing.'

Again, just like when we leaf through a medical dictionary and wonder whether we have some of the signs described, I wondered whether I was reading about myself. I felt a little better when I read Winnicott's next paragraph:

'No doubt the normal drive to teach is along these very lines. All of us to some extent need our work for our own mental health, the teacher no less than the doctor or nurse. The normality or abnormality in our drive is largely a matter of degree of anxiety. But, on the whole, I think pupils prefer to feel that teachers do not have this urgent need to teach, this need to keep at arm's length their own personal difficulties.'[5]

So far, three accounts of teaching: one by a pupil, one by a teacher, and one by a physician; and all three convey rather vividly that a teacher's enthusiasm can be damaging. So perhaps Rosenshine and Furst were wrong? It certainly is the case that it is commonly assumed that teaching is rather like giving a performance, and some people seem to be drawn to just this apparent requirement of the job. And if teaching is treated something like a performance, then the teacher will inevitably have the leading role. But, if learning requires active engagement, then the idea that teaching is like performing must be seriously misleading. Does all this then mean that teachers should not be enthusiastic? That simply cannot be the case. It would rather seem that enthusiasm is a subtle matter.

If I think about the best teachers I ever had, the first thing that comes to mind is that their enthusiasm was not for hearing their own voices. They seemed unconcerned about that. They came across as mature people who had other interests. They were not even especially enthusiastic about their subject. Their enthusiasm was more general, and it was often expressed indirectly, as when their eyes would light up when they mentioned a certain scholar, or when they outlined a certain line of thinking that illuminated a difficult question. In retrospect, I recall that they also conveyed a quiet sort of enthusiasm for commitment and integrity. And they seemed to have the confidence that, at the end of the day, what they were doing was worth doing, and worth trying to do well.

I think I am right to add that teachers of this kind convey an underlying sense of purpose. Most of them laugh easily, but one senses that, underlying this, they are serious about things. Administrative tasks bore them, and they get them done as quickly as possible so as to get back to the lesson. Nor do they ask their learners to do routine jobs to fill in time. When they ask their learners to do something, it is because they consider it of some consequence. And mostly, these teachers tend to be quietly energetic. But they can get excited; and when they do, it has the effect of switching learners on.

℞

The next item Rosenshine and Furst listed was: 'Using a variety of approaches'; and one of the researchers whom they cite, who did careful work on this matter, was called Kounin. Kounin initially set out to discover why some teachers have orderly classes while others have shambles.[6] Recall first that it is commonly believed that having an orderly class has something to do with a teacher's personality. But, even if that is correct, it would be helpful to know just what such teachers *do* to maintain order. It was with that question in mind that Kounin began.

However, after having observed a great many teachers teach, it finally dawned on Kounin that having an orderly class was not really a matter of a teacher doing anything in particular. Rather, it was a by-product of good teaching. It seems to me that this is a most interesting finding.

Having decided that an orderly class is a by-product of good teaching, Kounin of course realized that he now had a new question: just what is implied by the term 'good teaching'? It takes only a moment to realize that this question is far more difficult to answer than is immediately apparent. However, after much further research, Kounin and his colleagues came to the following tentative conclusions.

They found that teachers who had orderly classes were what they called 'withit'. That is, they knew just what was going on in their lessons, and they had the confidence to respond directly to it. For example, if two children were fighting and one was whispering, these kinds of teachers did not deal with the one who was whispering. They dealt with the ones who were fighting. And they did so in a thoughtful and direct manner.

Just as important, these teachers were good classroom managers. For example, they did not begin an activity without first ensuring that the class was ready for it. Nor did they initiate one activity and then go off on a tangent with another. Or, if they wanted a group to do something, they did not get bogged down dealing with an individual. And these teachers did not rely on what Kounin called 'prop-activities'; that is, they did not waste time worrying about things like collecting pencils in a certain order, or asking their pupils to sit straight. They focused on the learning task at hand.

A second set of Kounin's findings relate to the way these teachers taught. The first thing Kounin's data showed was that these teachers did not talk too much! Instead, they engaged their learners in a wide variety of activities; and this variety wasn't just in the content of the lesson. For example, they varied the challenges they posed: First one kind of task, then another. They also varied the social configurations in the class. That is, sometimes the learners worked individually, sometimes in groups, and sometimes the whole class worked together. Kounin also found that these teachers varied the teaching/learning methods they used: Sometimes the teacher talked; sometimes the learners talked to the teacher; sometimes the learners read; sometimes they wrote; sometimes they did practical things; and sometimes the learners discussed things in small groups. And all these things were organized in a purposeful manner.

It so happens that one third of my teaching career was spent teaching school pupils, and two thirds teaching adult students; I mention these details because, although Kounin did his research in schools, I found his findings very helpful no matter who I tried to teach. Thus, there wasn't one lesson when I did not remind myself that it was important to introduce some variety, and I don't mean just variety in my voice or the topic, but all the varieties that Kounin listed. I believe the following findings support such an orientation.

Research on very young babies shows that, when a new smell is presented to them, they turn to it with interest. But, after a time, they 'switch off'. To use more technical language, they become 'habituated'.[7] Then, when a new smell, even a weaker one, is presented to them, they show renewed interest. After a time, they pay no attention to that either. It is as if a stimulus is blocked from awareness after it has continued for some time, no matter how novel it first is. This happens in all the sense modalities, and it must be caused by an internal biological mechanism.

The above is also true of adults. For example, one might hear all kinds of noises around one; however, after a little while, one no longer notices them. Then, if there is a change, one will notice the change. But, if the new noise continues for some time, one will cease hearing that as well. This phenomenon might be related to the fact that, for many thousands of years, when our ancestors lived in the wilds, a steady input of noise (or movement) did not convey that anything of importance was happening. It was only when there was a change that we became alert. Perhaps we then said to ourselves, 'Food!' or 'Danger!' Whatever the case, it is clear that we become more alert when there is a change in our surroundings. In view of these considerations, it seems safe to assume that responding to change, but losing interest in what is the same, is functional and genetically driven. If so, it might well be the case that, when learners don't pay attention in a class, it is because they are getting too much of the same thing.[8]

It might be important to add that there is of course a limit to the amount of variety that there can be in any one lesson. I note this in part because I found that, once I had introduced variety into my lessons, some learners got restless when there wasn't more of it. Previously, when they had been taught didactically, they had not expected any; now, they wanted variety all the time. In response, a teacher might point out dryly that learning isn't the same as entertainment. In view of how the mass media has turned everything – news, nature, accidents, work, sports, catastrophes, the weather, you name it – into entertainment, such a comment might sometimes be necessary.

Chapter 14

Indirectness, Opportunities and Fit

The next item on Rosenshine and Furst's list is, 'Good questioning'. As this is such a large and important topic, I shall consider it in a separate chapter. I therefore move on to the next item in these researchers' list, 'Being task-orientated'.

By this is meant that they found that learners make progress when they have a teacher who uses the time available mainly for study purposes. Again, this finding is hardly surprising, for it is clear that, within reasonable limits, the more time one spends studying, the more is one likely to learn. This item is nevertheless worth noting, for many people will probably remember having had a teacher who spent a great deal of time announcing administrative matters, talking about their latest car, and collecting pencils in a certain order. The need to be task-oriented does not, of course, mean that a teacher should never crack a joke, or tell a story. We tend to welcome such diversions, but clearly, the bulk of the time in a good lesson is spent doing some work. This might also be the place to recall the truism that learners vary in the amount of time that they need in order to learn something. In other words, although some people can walk faster than others, it does not follow that the others are unable to get to the same destination a while later.

⍥

The next item on Rosenshine and Furst's list is, 'Being indirect'. At this point, I should perhaps admit that I used to find it difficult to describe this quality directly to my students. Eventually, I decided to describe what is involved by first standing up and going to the blackboard. As I almost never did that, I hoped that this might convey a change of direction. Then I'd tell the following story, drawing very roughly on the board from time to time.

I'd say, 'Imagine our topic for today is "The Nature of Responsibility". I could give you a talk on that topic, or I could introduce the topic to you indirectly via a story. I'd like to introduce the topic to you indirectly, so here is a story.

'Once upon a time, there was a village, and through its middle there flowed a swiftly moving river. At its narrowest point, about here [I'd point to my rough sketch], there is an old stone bridge. On the lower side of the river, near the bridge, about here, there is a house in which live a couple called Adam and Eve. One evening, Adam says, "They are showing a cowboy film in the village hall this evening. I think it's called *Midnight Cowboy*. Let's go and see it." Eve says, "No! Not another cowboy film!" Adam says, "What's the matter with cowboy films? I like cowboy films!" Eve says, "I know you do. But not another cowboy film. We saw . . ."

'And so the talk between the two continues. Until, at about 8.15, Adam stalks out of the house and heads unhappily towards the village hall. At 8.45, Eve walks out of the house feeling miserable. She goes to the bridge and sees the village idiot standing near the left-hand parapet, about here.[1] Eve has known this man for as long as she can remember. He is a part of the village landscape. He hangs about, drooling, vacant, and entirely harmless. Yet, that evening, Eve suddenly remembers what she has forgotten for years: that it has been said that this man will kill a woman one night. It is the kind of thing typically told in a small place to enliven a humdrum existence. But, that evening, when Eve catches sight of the man in the half-darkness, her heart misses a beat. She detours widely around him, and does not respond to his garbled greeting. Once across the bridge, she hurries up the hill on the other side of the river.

'Near the top, near the outskirts of the village, about here, lives Michael. He is an agent for a company. He is unmarried, and light of mind and foot. Eve has known him since they went to the village school together, and has always found him rather attractive. At nine o'clock, Eve is at his door. At 11.45, Eve suddenly realizes just how late it is. She leaves in a hurry and runs down the hill. Near the bridge, in the half-darkness, about here, she sees the village idiot. She could have sworn that he had been waiting for her all this time. When he sees her, he seems to lurch. Almost in a panic, Eve turns to her right and takes the path along the river. She rushes along, looks back, can hardly see a thing, but feels she is not being followed. In six minutes, she is at the ferryman's door.

'The ferryman lives in a shack, just outside the village, where the river broadens into a kind of lake, about here. He makes a living of sorts taking combine harvesters and other wide things across the river on his old barge. It takes Eve several minutes to get him out of bed. When he eventually opens his door, he scowls, and pretends he does not believe her story about the man on the bridge. When Eve persists, he asks for £20. When Eve says she has no money with her, he shuts the door in her face.

'Eve walks back to the village telling herself she is crazy. There is an occasional lap of water from the river. It is a sound she usually likes, but now it seems ominous. It is very dark. The trees along the path seem sinister. Feelings of regret, longings for home, snatches of conversation with her husband, alternate with thinking how unreal her present circumstances are. She feels deeply relieved when she enters the village, but the moment she approaches the bridge she catches sight of the village idiot. Mouth dry, she turns to the nearest door. David, the village schoolmaster, lives there. Eve has known him, too, since childhood. He is kindly and generous, and a bit ineffectual; and, because he is a little too fond of her, Eve tends to keep him more distant than she would really like. It is well past midnight when he opens his door, but he smiles with pleasure to see her standing there.

'The moment Eve is inside, she blurts out her story. David listens sympathetically. Then, one shoelace still undone, he looks up, red-faced, and says, "You spend the evening with Michael, and you come to me to take you home . . ." Something gives in Eve. She turns and rushes out.

'I cannot tell you what happened next. All I can tell you is that Eve is found the next morning, strangled, lying under the bridge. Actually, the exact details of her death do not concern us. If you remember, this lesson is on the nature of responsibility, and I would ask you to consider who, you believe, is responsible for Eve's death.'

I will have spoken for perhaps five minutes. As I'd come to the end of this story, I'd slide into my chair. I used to enjoy taking on the role of performer for a change, and also the way my students would look a mixture of amused and bemused. Then I'd usually turn to one of the students, and say, 'Well, Nick, what do you say? Please get us started.'

Quite often, once the learners had begun, it was difficult to stop them.

Who was responsible for Eve's death?!

At first, the speakers would tend to put the blame on Michael, Adam, David, the ferryman, – or men in general! Some would suggest Eve. Others the whole village. One or two would usually get caught up with deciding who is likely to have committed the murder, rather than who is responsible for it. Others would remain silent. Perhaps they sensed that, when we speak about things of this kind, we often say more about ourselves than the nature of the problem. Even so, if the discussion continued for long enough, almost everything – from a definition of sanity to the notion of free will – would be noted. Sometimes I found these discussions so interesting I'd almost forget to say that this was intended to be an illustration of 'indirectness' in teaching.

I believe that being indirect in teaching can be very important. This is because, in being indirect, a teacher is by definition not supplying an answer. Instead, a teacher is pointing in the direction in which an answer might be found. Or, to use Jane Abercrombie's marvellous phrase again, the teacher is telling the students where to look, without telling them what to see. In this way, when a learner comes upon an answer, that learner will experience it, not simply hear it. And, of course, it does not matter whether the topic is cooking or calculus. Perhaps I'll allow myself to anticipate at this point to note the pleasure I experienced when I discovered that there is here an instance where research into learning, and research into teaching, carried out completely separately, came in their very different ways to the same conclusion.

Recall here also that being indirect is an ancient teaching device. For example, it was practised thousands of years ago by the Prophets in biblical times. Consider the teaching: 'It is easier for a camel to go through the eye of a needle, than for a rich man to enter into the kingdom of God.' We have become used to that sentence. It no longer startles. If anything, it tends to slide through the mind. If we think about it at all, it tends to sound childish. But just what is the 'kingdom of God'? And why the implicit reference to *money*?[2]

If we can imagine ourselves hearing that sentence for the first time, and at a time when camels were the usual means of transport, it might begin to nag. And, if it does, that is likely to be because it is indirect. That is, it only hints at an answer, – better, it raises a question without directly asking one.

That sentence also invites us to compare things that, normally, we would not compare. Learning is often a matter of comparing. We compare that which we do not know, with that which we know. A child might ask, 'Why does an electric light go on when we flick a switch?' And a teacher might answer, 'It's like turning on a tap.' Of course, this analogy is incorrect, and answering like that immediately raises a question about taps. Nevertheless, answering like that can set the mind working. Hence, good teachers intuitively try to encourage their learners to compare things;

and, in that way, they go about things indirectly. Only later, will a good teacher draw an electric circuit, and note the difference between it and the way water flows along pipes 'til it reaches a tap. A comparison of this kind is called an 'analogy'.[3] Good teachers have a knack for thinking up clear and striking analogies. When a teacher uses an analogy, learners are not told what a thing is; they are encouraged to consider what they already know, and to expand on that.

When a teacher is indirect, the learners are also encouraged to imagine something, and thereby to view it from a variety of angles. That is, of course, what we always do when we have to decide on a course of action; and it is something that creative scientists and artists frequently do. And the more possibilities one can imagine, the more is one's course of action likely to lead to a positive outcome.[4] Notice that I have used the word 'imagine' here, not 'fantasize'. Imagination differs from fantasy in that, at its best, imagination is rooted in reality, whereas fantasy, in contrast, is an attempt to escape reality. Imagination is thus important in learning, for it helps one to consider possibilities that are not immediately apparent.

Readers might also have noticed the power of a story to convey a lesson.[5] Perhaps we take in a story containing facts, better than a bare string of facts, because a story usually has a human element. And it is certainly much easier to remember facts when they are embedded in a meaningful sentence, compared with trying to remember them on their own.[6] Notice also that, in a story that serves a serious purpose, the characters in it are lifelike, but they have the function of carrying a message that is more important than their individual destiny. But of course, one does not use indirectness in isolation. Indirectness is merely one item in a range of approaches that good teachers use.

୨⃛

The next item Rosenshine and Furst listed was: 'Giving learners an opportunity to learn'. At first blush, that item might well sound odd. Don't all teachers try to give their learners an opportunity to learn? If one is trying to teach as well as one can, one might be forgiven for thinking that one is trying to help others to learn! But perhaps teaching has to stop before learning can begin? Here is an illustration.

The teacher I shall now describe, teaches anatomy in a school of radiography. He could just as well be a teacher of underwater hairdressing in a school of mermaids. The first time I saw this young man teach, he stood in front of his class of twenty-eight learners. They sat behind their tables, and ranged in age from nineteen to thirty. They looked a pleasant enough bunch. The teacher, sandy haired, not much older than his students, announced the topic, and began to speak. He held up a bone, and noted that it was pointed here, and concave there. He explained why the shapes were as they were, and gave a name to each part. About fifteen names to one bone! On a table in front of him, he had his notes. This topic is highly factual and he did not want to leave anything out. His voice was pleasantly modulated, and he had a friendly manner. Occasionally he seemed a little unsure of himself, but that did not seem to matter. One sensed that his students liked him. While he spoke, the students sat and listened, took notes, fingered pens, sat and listened, looked at illustrations, looked at the teacher, looked at each other, looked out of windows, took notes, and sat and listened.

Occasionally this teacher went to a skeleton hanging in a corner and explained how the present topic fitted into the total anatomical structure of the human body. He made several sketches – one looked like the rigging on a sailing ship – and he wrote up lots of terms. It was like learning a new language. At several points, he passed bones around the class. Quite often, he repeated something, especially if he thought that there might be a question on it at the next exam. The while the students sat and listened, took notes, and looked at the teacher. Very occasionally, one of them asked a question. Sometimes they whispered. Once or twice, they teased the teacher, and, when they did, a ripple of good-natured laughter went around the room.

Mostly, though, these students looked rather vacant, and they clearly welcomed the occasional break, as when this teacher cleaned one of the whiteboards behind him. And so it went, – for an hour and a half. These were pleasant young people, and they sat and listened quite attentively. But, after the first half-hour, their attention often wandered. After all, they had been sitting in those seats for the past three hours, and how much information can anyone take in by sitting and listening for hours at a time? That was the first lesson I observed. On my sixth and last visit, this is what I saw.

In his previous lesson, this young teacher had asked his students to study half a dozen pages in preparation for today's lesson. He began by saying a few words of introduction, and then he divided the students into groups. One group he beckoned to the whiteboard, and he gave them a list of instructions. These required them to draw certain bone structures from memory and to label each significant part. The next two groups he took to the other side of the room, where he had prepared some fluorescent screens. Onto these, he now clipped X-ray photographs, and he asked the students to draw and describe in their notebooks what they were seeing.

Then he took one pair of students to a corner where there was a table. He told one student to lie on it and the other to palpate the recumbent one. He added that, as the former worked, he was to respond to some questions on a worksheet. He also gave them a checklist, and this required them to identify, on the other's body, the bones and muscles that constituted the topic of that lesson. In front of two other small groups, he placed a pile of numbered (plastic) bones, and he asked them to identify in writing which bones fitted the topic of today's lesson, and on what basis they had identified them.

Then this young tutor sat down. For the next thirty minutes, the room was a hive of purposeful activity.

After the students had settled to their various tasks, this teacher moved around. He checked that work was being done, he answered an occasional question, and he encouraged people to persist. On occasion, he expressed his displeasure when it became apparent that one of the learners had not prepared for this lesson. This young teacher did not do this very well. He clearly hadn't had much practice doing such a thing, for his previous teaching hadn't required it. But it was also clear, from the way the other learners were acting, that this teacher had, between that first lesson I have described, and this one, managed to encourage a new kind of attitude. At another point, he shared a laugh with a pair of learners who were palpating each other. Mostly he didn't say much. When a group of students had finished a task, they exchanged places with another group who had finished theirs. After about half an hour, all the students were finished.

This teacher then gave out a worksheet. The dozen questions on it required the students to respond with a combination of factual recall and analytical reasoning. The questions covered the work that had been done so far. The students answered the questions briefly in writing, again in small groups. Sometimes all the students in a group had the answer pat. Other times they discussed what they should put down. It took them about ten minutes to complete this work. The while, the teacher again sat to one side. When most students had finished, the teacher asked for their answers. These were read out quickly, compared, and in this way checked. The teacher commented only when necessary.

By then about an hour had passed, and this teacher had not done much that would conventionally be called teaching. However, it was obvious that a considerable amount of learning had taken place. Next, this teacher introduced a new topic, but that is of no concern here. What I can report is that, for the hour just described, I did not see any students look bored, and I believe that this must have been due, at least in part, to the fact that they had been given 'an opportunity to learn' rather than only taught.

Here, I would note the following more general point. Over many years of observing teachers and instructors at work, I noticed that a questioning approach is far more common in arts than science subjects. Among other things, this has the unfortunate effect of making many learners believe that science consists of a pile of often rather dry facts, rather than a series of exciting questions. Furthermore, I almost never saw any indication in those lessons, that progress in science depends on scientists being able to communicate with each other. Discussions are quite common in arts classes, but seldom in science ones. How vastly different this is from how science is actually conducted. Anyone who has been in a research laboratory, or has read an account of how they function, will know that scientists need to discuss things![7]

Arts subjects also tend to be more popular than science subjects, but this cannot be because the arts are intrinsically more interesting. I hazard the guess that this may be due to how, in arts subjects, fundamental questions about life are often raised, whereas this is seldom the case in science subjects. Only a moment of reflection is necessary to see how absurd this is. Perhaps arts subjects are also more popular because science subjects are usually taught in an impersonal manner. In the arts, it is common to come across strong feelings; but I am unable to recall having left one science lesson feeling strongly about anything. Yet, here is Kepler, one of the greatest scientists of them all: 'Having perceived the first glimmer of dawn eighteen months ago, the light of day three months ago, but only a few days ago the plain sun of a most wonderful vision, – nothing shall now hold me back. Yes, I give myself up to holy raving. I mockingly defy all mortals with this open confession: I have robbed the golden vessels of the Egyptians to make out of them a tabernacle for my God, far from the frontiers of Egypt. If you forgive me, I shall rejoice. If you are angry, I shall bear it. Behold, I have cast the dice, and I am writing a book for my contemporaries, or for posterity. It is all the same to me. It may wait a hundred years for a reader, since God has also waited six thousand years for a witness. . .'[8]

People often deplore the relative lack of interest shown by many learners in science subjects, but no expressions of regret will change the way a subject is seen. It is *how* a subject is taught that is most likely to affect the way that learners see it.[9]

The last item on Rosenshine and Furst's list was: 'making structuring comments'. That is, research into teaching suggests that learners are helped when a teacher periodically summarizes what has been done, and points the way ahead. For example, a teacher might have explained something, there might have been a discussion, or the learners might have completed a task. At such a point, a teacher might say something like, 'OK, we've had a look at how that circuit is put together, and that should give us a better idea about the kind of resistances that can be used. The next thing is to determine the overall . . .' But perhaps a word of caution is in place here.

First, in summarizing, a teacher might convey that a topic is now closed; that everything that needs to be said, has now been said. Of course, that is never the case. Also, something left a little unfinished – perhaps with a hint of what's to come – is often better remembered than something finished.

Second, when a teacher summarizes, he or she might inadvertently convey that a topic can be summarized in only that way. But of course, there are many ways of summarizing. Moreover, one way of grasping the nature of a topic, is to summarize it. If so, it might be helpful for teachers to encourage their learners to summarize themselves sometimes.

I might add here that I tried hard to remind myself to make structuring comments in my lessons from time to time. Most learners seem to find it helpful to be given these signposts as they push their way through the thickets of a new topic. I also tried to remind myself that a signpost is a signpost, not a guidebook.

☙

All of Rosenshine and Furst's findings – except good questioning – have now been reported, and some readers might have found the above moderately interesting, yet feel that these researchers' findings leave out several important factors in teaching. For example, their list does not include anything about the need for teachers to know their subject really well. But these researchers cannot be faulted here. They stated explicitly that their research was into the teaching *behaviours* that affect student progress. It might also have been noticed that these researchers did not refer to the personality of the teacher, and many people believe – I think rightly – that a teacher's personality is an important factor. But again, Rosenshine and Furst cannot be faulted here, because their research was into teaching behaviours.

There are other factors that are commonly thought to be important in teaching that Rosenshine and Furst did not mention. For example, it is often said that a teacher should not have 'distracting mannerisms'. By that is meant that teachers should not do things like jingle coins or stroke their hair. But there is no mention of this nugget in their findings. Nor is there anything about the need for teachers to motivate, reinforce, have clear objectives, use educational technology, or engage in task analysis. It is possible that these pearls aid learning, but there does not appear to be any clear evidence that such is the case.

Notice also that Rosenshine and Furst have nothing to say about classroom 'skills'. This omission might be due to the fact that this famous quality became the flavour of the times after their research had been published, or it might be the case that the behaviours I have described do not lend themselves to such a designation. Nor do these researchers have anything to say about being able to stand at a blackboard at a certain angle, and produce transparencies that are clear and colourful. But again, there does not appear to be any evidence that learners make progress when their teachers have such abilities. For my part, I suspect that the ability to do these things is useful because not being able to do them might be distracting. Whatever the case, these kinds of abilities are unlikely to be the ones that differentiate between mediocre teachers and good ones.

I believe the above also has implications for the appraisal of teachers. That is, I have seen many checklists of desirable teaching behaviours in which the items that are listed are not based on any evidence. But then, when it comes to discussions about teaching, we unfortunately still live in an age in which opinions are often preferred to evidence.

&

I came across the research on teaching presented in this and the previous chapter, several years after I had begun to form the understanding of learning outlined in Part I of this book. In other words, the research on learning, noted in Part I, and the research on teaching noted in this and the previous chapter, were done quite independently, and they came to my attention at different times. However, the two complement each other. For example, the finding that learners make progress when their teacher makes structuring comments appears to complement what was noted in a previous chapter about the importance of pattern. Or consider how the finding, that giving learners an opportunity to learn, complements the work of Carroll and Mack on the way people learn how to use a word processor. Notice also that giving learners an opportunity to learn, ties in with what was noted earlier about the need for learners to be actively engaged. Consider also how giving learners an opportunity to learn, recalls the effect of intrinsic rewards, the importance of experiential learning, that all knowledge begins with a question, and the need for personal involvement.

Or consider indirectness, and how this relates to the finding that telling learners an answer prevents them from experiencing it, and from being able to transfer their learning to a similar task. Or consider indirectness and the phenomenon of insight. Or how indirectness helps learners to make connections, and how this seeing of connections creates patterns and deepens one's understanding. Notice also that:

a) the material on learning, presented in the first half of this book, is coherent, that is, it hangs together
b) the material on teaching presented so far dovetails with the material presented in the first half of this book, and
c) the above two, discovered quite independently, make for an even larger pattern.

It took me several years to see these patterns, and I discovered more as the years passed. And whenever that happened, I felt a sense of pleasure. Readers might here recall some comments made in an earlier chapter on aesthetics.

More practically speaking, this sense of 'fit' that I seem to see, reminds me of cutting up some timber to build a porch, and finding not only that the roof fits, but that those dimensions are even right for a garage that is added later. It is quite possible that the 'fit' that I seem to see is no more than wishful thinking, and readers must evaluate these things for themselves. But whatever they decide, one thing remains the case. It is that, whatever teaching approach is advocated, it must square with a coherent description of learning that is based on some evidence. Anything else would be the equivalent of believing that an old woman is a witch because she does, or does not, float on water.

Lastly, I would hope that the outline of a theory is becoming distinct.

Chapter 15

Theory and Practice

Readers might have noticed that most of the lessons described so far have certain things in common, and this is of course because they are guided by a given theory. For example, the learners in most of these lessons are presented with a problem, and this is the case because the available evidence I have seen, has persuaded me that good teaching is often a matter of periodically turning that, which is to be learnt, into a tractable task or problem. (Another way of putting this is to say that the lesson is based on a question, not an answer.) It follows that one of the tasks of a teacher is to shape that task or problem into the appropriate size and complexity, so that the learners are intrigued by it, are able to cope with it, have access to suitable information about it, can derive intrinsic satisfaction from working on it, and obtain immediate feedback.[1] Readers might notice that this approach relates closely to the earlier chapters on what has been discovered about the nature of learning, and that it resembles what happens in real-life situations when one is learning.

Good teachers are, I believe, imbued with a problem-setting approach. This is perhaps due to their having a cast of mind that is endlessly curious, and the tendency to see puzzles where others see answers. Hence, to them, teaching becomes almost intuitively a matter of 'problematizing'. These kinds of teachers seem to feel uneasy when they are simply explaining, because they sense that no one really learns in that way. So, when talking, they often stop almost abruptly, and ask a question. For example, such a teacher might have been explaining the structure of certain muscles for a few minutes. He or she might have been saying something like, 'So you see that a muscle consists of a large number of fibres, and that each fibre is enclosed in a tissue called endomycium.' At that point, a fire alarm will go off in that teacher's head! He or she will then not say, 'And a bundle of these fibres is enclosed in what we call perimycium, and the whole muscle itself is enclosed in epimycium.' He or she will say, 'Now, if you look at that photograph, what else can you see about the way those fibres are organized?'

But this is not a rhetorical technique to gain attention. It is a reflection of how that teacher's mind works, and the learners will sense this. Moreover, a good teacher will not act like that occasionally. His or her whole lesson will be imbued with a questioning approach, and this will help to encourage an inquiring and participative orientation. But only a moment of reflection is required to see that one cannot be forever asking questions, hence this orientation is best encouraged by setting the learners tasks that provide them with 'an opportunity to learn'. Here I should perhaps note that giving learners a suitable task or problem through which to learn – rather than merely practise – seems easy enough, but anyone who has tried such an approach will know that it is far from easy. Not only must one prepare such tasks, one must know how to divide a class into pairs or groups, to generate an atmosphere in which work is done in a relaxed but purposeful way, and what to do when the work is completed.

Hence, such an approach requires considerable thought, lots of preparation, and reasonable resources. However, once the investment has been made, it can be used repeatedly. Such an approach also relieves a teacher from having to teach a whole class for the whole of each lesson, and that enables a teacher to help individuals as the need arises. My observations showed me that teachers seldom succeed with this approach when they first begin to use it. The first difficulty is to stop teaching; and the second is to see 'problematizing' as a way of teaching. Both require more imagination and sense of classroom management than 'teaching by telling'; and a certain kind of interaction with learners is also required; and that is very different compared with the one generated when one teaches by telling. I shall consider the latter matter in a later chapter. In the meantime, I can say that, when this approach is mastered, it affords most teachers and learners far more satisfaction than teaching by telling.

Here I had better add that I sometimes heard a teacher say that his or her learners don't like problems. I am sure that there is some truth to this, for I sometimes had the same experience. But I must also say that I usually found that the teachers who said this, tended not to like problems either. They liked answers; and, as that is what they liked, they insisted that that was what their learners liked. I put the matter like this because, when I observed these teachers, I usually found that, when they set a problem, they did so without much faith that it would work. That communicated itself to their learners, and then these teachers found that their learners didn't like problems!

Having written so much about setting problems, I had better emphasize that none of what I have written is intended to advocate 'learning by discovery'. The use of a catch phrase like that one, runs the risk of trivializing that which it names, for it often results in the application of a technique without any real understanding of the evidence on which that technique is based. What I am suggesting is something far more global, namely, that people learn best when they are encouraged to tackle that which they need to learn in a direct and structured manner. That isn't a technique or a method. It is an approach. It follows that setting learners a plain task can be just as useful as setting them a problem.[2]

An administrative matter arises here, and it is as follows. I sometimes heard the suggestion made that the teachers in a given institution could be encouraged to meet sometimes, with the aim of showing each other examples of the learning materials they had made. These materials could then be collected, stored, and made available to anyone who wished to use them. On the face of it, this suggestion seems to have much merit. However, I found, both from my own teaching and from having observed many other people teach, that it is best to produce one's own materials. I think there are several reasons for this. One is that such material is produced after one has developed an aim, and material produced in this way, will fit well into the overall scheme of one's lesson. On the other hand, when one looks first for teaching material, and then fits it into one's lesson, one's lesson will be a kind of afterthought set around that material. I cite in support of this position the finding that learners do best on courses that their teachers have themselves developed.[3]

Lastly, such material can consist of a text, a drawing, a simple diagram, an incomplete list, or two photocopied paragraphs, followed by a question that one has devised oneself. Such material should, of course, never consist of mere photocopied pages. Not only is that illegal, such material tends to be unwieldy, and to fit poorly into one's teaching.

In my classes, I used to set aside periods in which I asked student teachers and instructors to bring in learning materials that they had themselves devised. The following then often happened. A woman who taught computing would bring in a worksheet intended to help her students to learn how to organize a sub-directory. She would pass copies around, and tell us how she uses it. A man would then sometimes call out, 'That's interesting. I could use that idea for a worksheet on ways to classify types of handles in pottery . . .' I heard many surprising connections made in that way; and they reinforced my belief that the important thing is to understand principles. When one does, one can use them to suit one's circumstances. Those were some of my favourite lessons. This was because, in them, the learners themselves demonstrated and made concrete the way in which theoretical principles can be applied to varying circumstances. In closing, I will mention one such lesson that was particularly memorable.

We had come near the end of a term, and one student brought in a crate of wine. He said with feigned seriousness that he had discovered that people were pretty ignorant when it came to buying wine, and that he had devised a lesson that might remedy this appalling state of affairs. He said a few words about dry and sweet, red and white, designated areas, Pinot Noir and Chardonnay, Rhone and California; and then he gave out a worksheet, small plastic glasses, corkscrews, and the crate. I learnt quite a bit from that lesson, and it was most enjoyable!

Quite a few courses are based on a textbook. A textbook covers a certain field of knowledge, is intended for study purposes, and is often used to prepare for an exam. Many textbooks tend to be a rehash of other people's work, and are supposedly enlivened by photos, diagrams and summaries set in coloured inserts. I believe that a course based on a textbook runs the serious danger of fostering parrot learning. Like a dictionary, a textbook is occasionally useful for looking something up, but using it as one's main source of learning is like using a dictionary to learn a language. Compare using a textbook with a course that a teacher has devised, that is, a course in which the learners are encouraged to consider a variety of materials, including excerpts from original sources, discussion of real-life situations, and worksheets on a practical task. It's the difference between Omaha quick fried and some decent home cooking.

Lastly, there is the advent of educational technology, especially computer programs. As this is such a large topic, there will be a separate chapter on it shortly.

&

Some readers might have found the above comments moderately interesting, but consider that they do not really apply to the kind of teaching that they do. They might agree that things like indirectness, group work and worksheets have their uses in some lessons, but not with the kind of subject or learners that *they* teach. They might teach a factual subject, like mathematics, geography, pharmacology, accountancy or production engineering; and, in such a subject, they might maintain, the important thing is to convey information. These readers might also say that many learners could get almost as much out of reading a good textbook as from listening to a teacher, but many learners simply don't read textbooks. They come to a class expecting to be given information; and it is the primary job of a teacher to meet that expectation. In conclusion, these readers are likely to say that it is obviously important for learners to have practical experiences. But that comes later, in a lab, or when learners are out at work. It simply makes no sense to put learners to work *before* they know something about a topic.

I trust the above is a fair summary. If so, consider again the lesson on anatomy described in the previous chapter.

First, it is clear that Anatomy is a factual subject; and second, it would appear that learners cannot be expected to carry out a practical task in this subject before they have acquired some knowledge of it. And yet, the latter is exactly what was done. True, the teacher in that lesson required the students to read half a dozen pages before the lesson. However, such preparation is not always necessary. It is often possible to provide learners with one or two typed pages, a worksheet and a model, and to set them to work immediately.

It certainly is the case that, in many establishments, a teacher will first teach 'theory', and then give the learners an exercise so that they can get some 'practice'. But perhaps 'theory' and 'practice' are commonly taught separately, not because it has been established that such a separation aids learning, but because of administrative convenience and the dead hand of habit? In the anatomy lesson described above (or the computer lesson described in the first chapter of this Part of this book), the teacher announced the topic of the lesson, and then gave the learners a 'practice' lesson almost immediately. That is, he enabled the learners to tackle that which they needed to learn directly. Such an approach follows life. Perhaps I could use an illustration from repairing a car again.

Sometimes I had to carry out a repair I had never done. The evening before, I would get the manual out and begin to read. After about ten minutes of examining text and diagrams, I usually found I was unable to follow the directions. I would then feel I had to have the thing I must repair before me. So I would put the manual aside till the next morning. Next day, I would put on some old clothes, open the manual again, and soon I would be touching this and that on the car. And so it went: with references to the manual (i.e. the theory), followed by examination and manipulation of the faulty mechanism (i.e. the practice). Then back to the manual (theory), and then back again to the mechanism (practice), the two flowing in and out of each other. Anyone who has carried out a like task will have had a similar experience.

Here it might be objected that what I have just described is a relatively simple mechanical task, and nothing like learning literature, economics or law. If so, consider the following finding from medical education.

In most teaching hospitals, students are first taught basic medical science, then clinical practice. But in some medical schools, a training programme has been devised in which the two are integrated. When one such programme was evaluated, it was found, among other things, that, whereas students on a conventional programme tended to become increasingly cynical about the value of basic science studies, students on an integrated programme increasingly appreciated their value.[4] I might perhaps add here that the integrated programme noted above, was often based on a series of medical problems; and that these were so organized that, in order to solve them, the students had to acquire knowledge of basic medical science.

Here it might be helpful to add that, in preparing a worksheet, it is essential to choose a suitable text, or, as I suggested earlier, to write it oneself. A worksheet should contain clear directions, the relevant information, and a few questions. It should be written in a simple and direct way, that is, commonly used words, short sentences, and simple grammatical structures are best. The questions should be worded so that they require understanding as well as recall, and there should not be more than about four of them. Interestingly enough, research on this matter shows that a reader retains the information given in a text better, when the text is interspersed with questions; and when the answers to those questions are later supplied. In other words, here, too, we see that learning is helped when a reader is actively engaged.[5] Most important of all, all such tasks should be as lifelike as possible.

I found that it takes time to get these things right. I seldom got a worksheet right the first time I wrote it, and no matter how much time I had spent on preparing it. I often had to use such a thing several times in a class, and amend it in the light of the learners' responses before I was reasonably satisfied with it. And of course, worksheets are not the only kinds of aids that can be used in this way. A teacher can instead sometimes hand out a case study, place copies of books that contain relevant information on a table in a corner, and invite learners to get to work. But the principle remains the same. The material to be learnt or reconsidered, is given to the learners in the form of a problem – and they are invited to tackle the material to be learnt directly. In that way, theory and practice are integrated.

&

At this point, readers might like to see an example of a Case Study, and here is one that I sometimes used.

Case study: Sara Sassoon

Please read the following description, and then, after consultation with your neighbour, answer the questions at the end.

Your name is Sara Sassoon and you work in the School of Radiography at Drumnadrochit County Hospital. The School is a designated training centre, and has about fifty students and various members of staff. You are a Senior Tutor with special responsibility for Training, and have been in post for two months. The job is a new creation, established in response to many complaints about 'uninspired teaching'. You have a genuine interest in teaching, and an office on the fourth floor with a big window overlooking rooftops and trees. You also have a window ledge with one achimenes, one anthurium, two hibiscuses, three impatiens, two pelargonium, and one primula.

You were very pleased to get the job, but now, in your second month, you are troubled. It is a Monday, you have done a first teaching session, and you have not had time to water your flowers. They look droopy. Probably your colleague, Serge, forgot to water them while you were away last Friday on a training workshop. Like many men, he promises as easily as he forgets. Worse, you must now make your first visit to one of your colleagues, Miles Hewstone, and observe him teach.

When you get to his class, you place yourself unobtrusively in one of the back rows. There are eighteen students in the room. Miles is up front, laying out his notes. The lesson is on the anatomy of the pelvis, and Miles begins briskly. He is obviously knowledgeable, and soon the whiteboard is full of terms, and rough but accurate drawings. He also shows lots of transparencies, and manipulates them deftly. When he comments on one of them, he turns to the class and looks around the room. He is about forty and has been a radiographer tutor for much of his working life.

The students listen attentively. They also write notes, click pens, look at Miles, look at each other, click pens, look out of the window, murmur to each other, click pens, and take notes. After about half an hour, their attention often wanders. After all, how would you feel if you had just bought a kitchen gadget, and someone sat you down, and read the instruction booklet to you – for the next hour?

Very occasionally, Miles asks a question. It is always a factual one; and when he gets the usual two-word answer, he says, 'Good', repeats it, and continues speaking. His delivery is clear and logical, his voice is pleasantly modulated, his drawings are apt, and he gives the students lots of time to write their notes. An hour and twenty minutes after he began he says, 'Has anyone got any questions?' One of the girls asks something about a test, and Miles answers at some length. Then he asks, 'Are there any other questions?' As there are none, he announces the end of the lesson, and the students get up and file out.

You go up front and say, 'Thanks for having me in. You certainly covered a lot of ground this morning.' Miles says, 'Yes. There really is a lot to cover. It's ridiculous really. No matter what you do, there's never enough time to cover everything!' You say, 'I wonder if you would make it easier for yourself if you gave them some work to do sometimes?' Miles says, 'What do you mean? Don't you think they are working? They can hardly keep up with their notes as it is.' You say, 'No, I mean a little group work sometimes, using models and worksheets?' Miles says, 'But how can they do that with a new topic? They have never had anything on the pelvis!' You say, 'No, I don't mean a revision. I mean introduce the topic, and then ask them to work on material you have prepared beforehand.'

He says, 'But I haven't got enough time to cover what I'm supposed to be covering! And I've tried doing group work. The students don't like it. They consider it a waste of time. The other tutors have had exactly the same experience.'

You say, 'I mean . . . well . . . I wonder if you could give yourself a break once in a while by asking them to bring in their textbooks, clipping up some X-rays, giving them some questions, and asking them to respond in pairs? It wouldn't be difficult to set up half a dozen screens in this room. I'd be glad to give you a hand, and I'm sure Ted would be happy to do the necessary wiring.' Miles says, 'Catch the department letting me have some X-rays! I can hardly get a bit of chalk out of them without filling in a form in triplicate! Anyway, you must know yourself how difficult it is to get through the syllabus in the time available.'

You have both almost reached the door. You say, 'That girl, Cindy, seemed to be bothered about their next test, but I understand she has done very well so far?' Miles says, 'She'll be all right. It's some of the others I'm worried about. You saw how most of them participate very well, but there are a few who never say a thing. Not even when I ask them if they have a question!' You are both walking down the corridor now. At its end, Miles walks down the stairs and you go up to your room. It's almost 1 o'clock.

If you were Sara:

a)   would you water the flowers before or after lunch?
h)   what would you do about Miles?

Notice how a 'case study' is a life-like description that sets learners a problem, and the problem is often stated in the form: 'If you found yourself in this situation, what would you do?' A realistic and imaginatively stated case study helps learners to test and consolidate their existing knowledge, and it often also helps them to see how their knowledge might need extending. Case studies can be used to teach any subject from public administration to private plumbing. The section in which I discussed the importance of indirectness, and told a story about Adam and Eve, could very easily be presented in the form of a case study. If the subject is auto maintenance, and if the topic of 'braking' has recently been completed, a case study on that topic could read: 'What would you do if a customer brings in a car you serviced last month, and complains that one of the front wheels is squealing?'

The important thing is to give a case study to the learners, ensure that the necessary manuals or models are available, say as little as possible, and let the learners work on it in pairs or small groups. Few tasks generate a better discussion than a well thought-out case study, for this enables learners to test, clarify, modify and expand their knowledge. When the learners have finished, the teacher can ask for their answers. There is no need for a reporting-back stage. And on no account should a teacher stand at a flip chart and note the important points as they are called out! A case study is for the learners: The more teaching, the less learning.

&

Worksheets are common in teaching, but they tend to be used for revision purposes. That is, a teacher will first explain a topic (i.e. present the 'theory'), and then pass out a worksheet (i.e. give the learners some 'practice'). In the anatomy lesson described earlier, the worksheet is not used for 'practice'. It is used as a medium of instruction. As a result, the teacher did not dominate the lesson with explaining before or after the 'practice'.[6]

The same kind of thing can be said about demonstrations. Teachers usually demonstrate before they invite their learners to tackle that task. Occasionally that is helpful. Often it isn't. This is because such an approach often inhibits learners. That is, we seldom learn much when we merely observe someone, and it is also likely to inhibit us when we are asked to do something similar. It is much better to be allowed to tackle a practical task directly, and, if we don't manage it very well – as is likely to be the case – we will want to observe an expert doing it. That way round, we will have the beginnings of an idea of what is required, and that will make our observation of an expert far more searching. There are, of course, occasions when it might be necessary for a teacher to demonstrate first, as when not doing so might place someone in danger. But it is surely important not to stretch this requirement to cover situations when it would be perfectly safe to encourage learners to tackle a task directly themselves.[7]

If one takes this kind of an approach, classrooms become as much as possible like workrooms, for both theoretical and practical subjects. There is a tendency in that direction already in some educational establishments that have mathematics or language 'work-shops'. Learners can walk into one of these and practise, with or without the help of a tutor. The trouble with some of these workshops is that they are an adjunct to the 'real' lesson. A good lesson already is a workshop.

Where a practical task is being taught, it is best to outline what is to be done, provide the materials required to do it, and then let the learners get to work. They can be asked to work singly, in pairs, or in small groups. It is most important for a teacher not to elaborate. Doing that, takes the intrinsic reward of doing something well, and on one's own, away from the learners. The more teaching, the less intrinsic reward for the learners.

Occasionally, there will be a key element in a task at which learners tend to get stuck. One way to help a class in such circumstances is to tell just one of the learners about it. That element will then be conveyed from that one learner to all the others, but it is unlikely to be conveyed smoothly. At such moments, teachers tend to feel that they must 'make things clear'. If they can resist that urge, they will find that, as the bit of information is passed from one group to the next, a good deal of discussion is generated, and that helps to clarify it. A misunderstanding can, of course, sometimes arise, and then a teacher might have to speak. But it is helpful to give learners as many opportunities as possible to rectify their misunderstandings themselves.

I have heard some teachers say that the approach suggested here takes much longer than 'teaching by telling'. That magic phrase about the need to 'cover the syllabus' is also often used. Common sense suggests that teaching by telling should take less time than using a worksheet. But recall here that there tends to be a great deal of redundancy in all explaining. We never state one fact after another. There is always some embellishment. For example, it is common to hear a teacher say something like, 'You have all heard of Thorndike. He was one of the early experimental psychologists who made a significant contribution to educational thought, and he worked at about the same time as Pavlov, the famous Russian psychologist. But unlike Pavlov, he was one of those who . . .' These embellishments, especially the fatuous name-dropping kind, take up valuable time.

Consider next that, in any class of two or more learners, one learner will always know more than the other. Yet, to be clear, an explanation must be pitched so that all can understand. This means that, in explaining something to a group, a teacher will say a good deal that some of the learners already know. Consider also that the more factual a subject, the less does it lend itself to 'teaching by telling'. How boring it is to have to listen to something straightforwardly factual for an hour at a time! To the above, I can add a personal observation. In many years of observing teachers, it was my consistent experience that the approach described in this chapter usually takes less time than 'teaching by telling'.

But recall here that the learners in the above lesson were not simply told to go and find out. That really would take a long time. The very essence of the approach suggested here lies in this, that the teacher saves the learners a lot of time. This is because a good teacher will have contrived things so that the learners find out for themselves: efficiently, systematically, and with as few redundancies as possible.

Finally, it might again be worth remembering that, when teachers 'cover the syllabus' in class, they do exactly that. As learning requires active engagement, the learners then have to cover the syllabus at home. If so, it would surely be helpful to teach in a way that enables learners to cover at least some of the syllabus in class.

Chapter 16

Reflections on Educational Technology

Readers might have noticed that the aids mentioned in the previous chapters do not require any technology, and, except for the need to duplicate them, could have been produced 100 years ago. That might have struck some readers as backward, especially in an age when it is often said that education must keep up with the times. But then, when I was writing the first edition of this book some 20 years ago, there was a good deal of talk about teaching aids, but not much about educational technology. Today, educational technology is a buzzword; and, when I began work on a new edition of this book, it was clear that I would have to add a chapter on it.

I was rather apprehensive about such an undertaking, for I assumed that a consideration of educational technology would require an extensive revision of the first edition of this book. I was therefore more surprised than relieved to discover that I did not have to make any changes at all in that respect. On the contrary: the literature on educational technology that I read, indicated that the approach to learning and teaching outlined in the first edition of this book is in line with what has been discovered about the most effective use of educational technology. This discovery was gratifying for two reasons. One, because it indicated that the theory of learning I had originally outlined was on the right tack; and two, because one of the attributes of a promising theory is that it accounts for discoveries and applications made after it has been formulated.[1] I now outline a computer program to illustrate what I have in mind.

&

One computer program that has been unusually successful, is that which drives computer games; and one researcher, Malone, has investigated what makes some of these games exceptionally successful.[2]

He first draws attention to the difference between extrinsic and intrinsic motivation. He comes to about the same conclusions regarding their difference as I noted in a previous chapter, and he goes on to note that the most successful games provide a good deal of intrinsic motivation. He continues by noting two other features of these games. One is that they are challenging; and the other is that, although they have goals, the outcome remains uncertain until almost the end.

Here it is important to add that a player, in the best of these games, is able to adjust the level of challenge. This challenge, in turn, is characterized by novelty, complexity, surprise, and some incongruity; but a player is nevertheless able to identify the goal. Readers might here notice that this description is in line with much that was noted about learning in previous chapters.

Malone notes more generally that challenge is a captivating feature because it engages a person's self-esteem. However, it is important for players to be able to adjust the level of challenge, for it is only in this way that some success can be ensured, and thereby an increase in self-esteem. Another feature of these games is that they enable a player to explore freely, and thus to discover relationships of various kinds. Those relationships are initially hidden, and only become apparent when a player persists. Together with that, players obtain immediate feedback on the consequences of their actions; and, in this way, they learn about themselves as learners, and indirectly acquire a reflexive attitude towards learning. Here I would invite readers to recall what was noted in Part I about active engagement, and the many descriptions of learners given in previous chapters.

As noted, one of the features of the best of these games is that their level of complexity can be varied. Among other things, this prevents an approach that can become merely a routine. The most successful of these games also often contain elements of fantasy, and this also has the effect of nudging a player away from a mechanical approach. Together with these things, although a game might be complex, the tools used to explore this complexity work so effectively that these workings are almost hidden. Again, if one were to substitute the word 'imagination' for 'fantasy', this description is reminiscent of what happens when learners are given a well-designed worksheet and task.

I believe that the most significant feature of these games is that they simulate a problem-solving approach. The comments of this researcher also make clear that the attraction of problem-solving lies in the personal challenge that it poses to the learner to achieve a 'gestalt', that is, a picture of the situation in which all its facets fit together in a consistent and economic manner. Notice lastly that all of the above dovetails well with the theory of learning outlined in the first Part of this book.

The above noted, I feel I must next express my conviction that, if the wider implications of using educational technology are not carefully examined, such usage can be seriously damaging. As that might sound extravagant, I had better first outline what I have in mind, and only then go on to note how educational technology might be used to aid learning.

&

I begin with comments made by a man closely involved with the development of computers, Weizenbaum, a professor of computer science at the Massachusetts Institute of Technology. Among other things, he notes that the 'computer has long been a solution looking for problems – the ultimate technological fix which insulates us from having to look at problems'. As an example, Weizenbaum notes that, instead of trying to work out why many youngsters in English-speaking countries leave school with mediocre abilities to read, write and reason, some people appear to believe that sitting them in front of a computer will solve this distressing situation. He adds that some students sometimes become 'computer literate' in this way, but that this will not overcome the likelihood that many will leave school functionally illiterate. In short, the introduction of computers into educational settings can have the effect of obscuring problems rather than help overcome them.

It is also important to grasp some of the wider implications of becoming 'computer literate'. Weizenbaum gives as an example the fact that, upon graduation, many of the students who are most computer literate, will find themselves working for companies whose simple aim is to make as much money as possible at minimal cost; or for other companies whose aim is to find faster and more reliable ways to kill an ever-larger number of people.[3]

Recall also that, when a new technology is introduced, there is often considerable excitement about it, and little serious consideration of what some of its side effects might be. For example, when the motor car became readily available, there was considerable enthusiasm for it, and few people foresaw that, within a few years, cars would move more slowly in some cities than a horse-drawn cart. Nor did anyone foresee the way in which, through the building of roads, cars would change the shape and quality of life in many city areas, and sometimes cause terrible decay. There is of course also the problem of atmospheric pollution.

In the case of computers, because of business interests, there are often an ever-decreasing number of programs available for common tasks. Notice also that, when you buy one of these programs, and wish to ask a question about it, you are increasingly made to put your question in the form of an email. The answer you then often obtain will be automated, and hence often irrelevant to your needs. Notice also that subscribing to a service via the internet, is often made much easier than cancelling it! Recall also that we increasingly encounter electronic devices that prevent us from having contact with other human beings. One common example is the synthesized voice, that tells us what to do when we make a telephone call to a company.[4]

The last-mentioned development is also increasingly evident in educational technology, in that, with its help, it is often possible to sideline teachers. Examinations that are set via multiple-choice questions can be examined and graded with a computer; and publishing companies that specialize in producing textbooks, are keen to supply such multiple-choice questions to accompany their textbooks. These companies also supply computer programs, discussion questions, and DVDs/videotapes; and, in this way, teachers will soon be able to stop teaching altogether. Lest that sound extravagant, I note that this is already becoming the case in some sectors of higher education.

It might even soon be possible to remove the human element from teaching altogether, just as is increasingly the case with the human element in banking and many other service industries. The important thing in this scheme of things is to move the client along as fast as possible, by using a minimal number of pre-prepared materials, automating the system to a maximum extent, and getting the client to do as much of the work as possible. (Recall here that fast food chains thrive by strictly limiting what they provide, prefabricating and automating everything, and getting clients to serve themselves.[5]) At the same time, one throws in as many cheap thrills as possible, and one uses an utterly phoney language to convey friendliness. The focus is exclusively on efficiency, quantity and speed, for these make for more financial gain. I draw attention to these things because the unthinking application of educational technology can increase the tendency for education to become a part of the current sport, food, information, farming, tourist, newspaper, and health industries.

Recall also that the world of politics, i.e., the system that determines who gets what of the national cake, increasingly shows the same characteristics. That is, many events of a political nature that are 'reported' in the mass media are contrived, the facts stated in them are manufactured, speeches become sound-bites, and the debates carried out in them often provide opportunities for the stern articulation of platitudes.[6] Notice further that, with the help of this technology, the speeches of politicians or other leaders increasingly have the following characteristics. Nothing of any substance is said; only the seemingly most obvious enemies are ever mentioned; we are always told how good we are; the only kind of explanations ever given are trivial; promises of the most bland kind are given; sentences and speeches are made as short as possible; and all these trivialities are interspersed among pregnant silences.

Lest the above sound irrelevant or exaggerated, recall that educational technology is a part of a much larger enterprise. That enterprise is the development and use of technology to facilitate an economic order that is inherently exploitive, wasteful of human and natural resources, ultimately controlled by a very small number of people, and which has the aim of making as much money as possible for this small number of people. It follows that the education of citizens – in contrast to teaching them basic skills – is one of the last things that interests these people. The aim of these people is, in short, to push their products and services. They will also be in a far better position than any educational body to exert influence; and they are able to dress up their aims in the language best suited to convince consumers. It will therefore be these people who will gain increasing control of educational technology, and that in spite of the fact that their interest in education is minimal. And, as their main aim is to gain commercial advantage, they will bend their vast recourses in the direction of producing educational programs at minimal cost and hence minimal quality. Furthermore, just as consumers in general have increasingly little choice, so also will consumers of educational programs have little choice. Instead, they will be fobbed off with an increasing number of useless facilities, fashionable slogans and slick packaging.

The latter becomes apparent when one reads some of the current literature on the introduction of computers into educational settings. One then often comes across the notion that learners must be prepared to take their place in what is often called 'a computer-based society'. I trust I am not the only one whose heart sinks when a society is described in this way. Writers of this ilk will often begin by deploring the use of computers in educational settings for merely the learning of skills; and will go on to speak of higher aims. To these, they are prone to give fancy names like 'emancipatory', i.e., aims that allegedly enable learners to achieve 'higher things'. And what are those higher things? Well, they are usually vaguely called problem-solving abilities, and they are achieved, it is alleged, by doing projects on things like computers and personal privacy, skill obsolescence and retraining, and micro technology and unemployment. Notice that one effect of undertaking such projects, is to make the presence of such features in our society seem natural. Another is the application of prefabricated information. And there is no demand to really think.

It is certainly true that the use of computers in educational settings is likely to have the effect of increasing the ability of people to interact with computers. However, as interacting with computers is utterly different from interacting with other human beings, this facility with computers might also have the effect of inhibiting what abilities a person has for communicating with others. Recall here that all interactions with a computer are rule bound, and, although interactions with people are also to some extent rule bound, unlike the case with computers, those rules are often open ended.[7]

Consider next the people who are most engaged in promoting the use of educational technology. One group consists of the people who sell the stuff. A second group consists of people in big business and the military who use the stuff. And a third group consists of academics who make a living by writing about the stuff. The latter comment might sound uncharitable, but I make it nevertheless because, when I was preparing this chapter, I was very troubled to find that few of these people draw attention to the less happy implications of educational technology.

Some readers might be dismayed by what I have noted in this section so far. After all, the title of this book suggests that it is about learning and teaching, and the heading of this chapter suggests that it is on the use of technology in teaching. Yet, what I have written is largely critical. But I believe that that is as it should be, for teachers are more than technicians, and should be alert to the wider implications of what they do. Indeed, I intend to argue that the main task of teachers is not to teach Algebra or Zen, but to encourage an inquiring cast of mind. And I would have thought that one appropriate point at which to do this, is when educational technology is being introduced.

&

I begin now with one of the more modest technological aids used in teaching, the overhead projector. This aid is not used much in schools, but it is widely used in all kinds of training establishments. More exactly, I begin with any technology that enables a teacher to throw a brightly lit image onto a large screen, and this image can be produced in a variety of ways. One is by placing a transparent sheet – i.e., one on which a teacher can write and draw – in the appropriate place below the projector. This combination of projector and transparent sheet thus eliminates the need to write on a blackboard with messy chalk, and a teacher can face a class as he or she manipulates the projector. These transparencies are usually prepared before a lesson, and one can print on them, include diagrams and graphs, and add pictures in all the colours of a rainbow. Moreover, when an image is projected, it can first be covered with a blank sheet, the sheet can then be slowly moved, and, in this way, one section at a time can be exposed. And once such transparencies have been made, they can be re-used. In short, this relatively simple technology provides a teacher with a clean, handy, mobile, compact, flexible, permanent, multicoloured blackboard. The same effects and much more can be achieved by using a computer attached to a projector. This is because a computer can be loaded with programs that can produce a dazzling array of images, and these can then be stored on disk, and loaded into a computer with ease. What superb technology. But who is it for?

I trust that question sounds a little absurd. And yet, it is clear that this technology is an integral part of the transmission method of teaching. If so, this technology is intended to help a teacher. But, what if one believes that teaching has to stop before learning can begin? But surely, a reader might protest, learners are helped when they can see a drawing in the clear way that a projector can produce?

This might be true, but, if it is, it is an argument for giving the learners the picture. Thanks to even simpler technology, most teachers today have access to photo-copying equipment; and, with its aid, a teacher can make copies of drawings and give them to learners. Surely most people would prefer to look at a drawing in their hand, rather than one across a room?

Notice also that the use of any kind of projector has the effect of distancing a teacher. No matter how sophisticated such technology, it requires a certain amount of attention, and that tends to be at the expense of the learners. It also puts a teacher even more 'in charge' than is usually the case, and it thereby tends to inhibit a collaborative approach. It makes the learners more passive, and the use of this kind of technology makes it more difficult for them to ask a question, let alone to participate. Most interesting of all, I have yet to come across some evidence that indicates that using such technology aids learners. But then, evidence counts for little in comparison with the awe in which technology is often held.

&

Today, it is the computer that is most frequently mentioned in discussions about educational technology. However, the available evidence indicates that, although the number of computers in educational establishments is growing fast, few establishments have as yet enough of them, to enable learners to use them effectively. I would therefore guess that the teaching aid that is still most widely used in most teaching establishments is the DVD/video and TV set. Only two or three of these are sufficient to equip an establishment, so I shall consider these before coming to computers.

With the help of these two technologies, things that most learners would never see, they now can see: Mount Kilimanjaro and the Amazon Basin; peasants cultivating with bullocks, and the inside of bullocks; squirming bacteria and neat chains of chromosomes; the love life of locusts and the death throes of turtles. Learners can also be shown riots in Rio and riots in Romford, and thereby see instant history. As is well known, in the developed parts of the world, such programmes are shown nightly on tv, and yet, it is also well known that this has not increased the understanding of the many youngsters who watch them. I believe that the reason for this is that these programmes are fundamentally unreal, and I shall refer to the matter again later. But before that, a few virtues must be noted.

It is certainly true that, with a film and tv set, one is able to show learners, who are studying, for example, literature, a play that they might otherwise not see. Or, if one has a suitable film, one can show a certain chemical or cellular process. These are virtues, and should be appreciated. The trouble is that there is a tendency to believe that, if a certain technology is 'a good thing', more of it is a better thing. The best way to indicate what is at stake might be to provide an illustration.

I once watched a film on the topic 'inflation'. The film began by showing a group of well-dressed people walking up the steps of an aeroplane to attend a meeting of world financiers. Then one saw a big room with chandeliers hanging from an ornate ceiling. The next clip showed those people sitting around an enormous table. In front of each, there was a green, gilt-edged blotter, and that made them look even more imposing. Then the syrupy music stopped, and a velvety voice intoned the word 'inflation'. What is 'inflation'?

Imagine a desert island. It has some coconut trees, a few small animals, a scattering of huts in which live about 50 families, and lots of fish in the sea around it.

Most families produce what they need, but occasionally they exchange goods and services. For example, they might exchange 5 coconuts for 10 fish, or 25 coconuts for one day's help with repairing a hut. Now, imagine that, one day, a cask containing 100 coins is washed ashore, and that each family gets two coins. Imagine further that, in addition to the previous barter, families now use those coins to purchase things. For example, for one coin they can now obtain 50 coconuts or 100 fish. Of course, over time, what a coin will buy will vary depending on the state of supply; but, by and large, the rate of exchange will remain stable.

Imagine now that a second cask containing another 100 coins is washed ashore. Those coins also enter the system, but, as the supply of coconuts, fish and labour has not changed, the value of the coins will drop. In other words, after the advent of that second cask, one coin will now buy only 25 coconuts or 50 fish. This example should illustrate what happens if a government simply increases the amount of money in circulation by printing more of it.

A change in scene might further help to illustrate what is at stake. Imagine that, merely in order to achieve popularity, a government decides to raise state pensions. However, as this government does not have enough money from taxation to pay for this expenditure, it decides to print more money. In the meantime, though, the amount of goods in that country hasn't increased. Hence, when the money that this government has had printed comes into circulation, the previous balance between the amount of money available, and the amount of goods available, will be upset. In other words, more money will be available to buy the same number of goods. That is the same as saying that more money will be required to buy the same number of goods. That, roughly, is how inflation comes about.

Of course, the matter is more complicated than that. For example, nothing has been noted here about the value of savings in such a situation, or how loans can indirectly increase the amount of money in circulation. But the above illustration should convey the essence of the matter. What is that essence?

The essence is that one's understanding of the process called 'inflation' is abstract. But then, all understanding is abstract. In other words, inflation is not a matter of seeing coconuts and coins on a beach. That is, seeing pictures of these things can only marginally help to make clear that inflation is about the relationship between the amount of goods and the amount of money in circulation. Notice that it is impossible to show a picture of 'a relationship', and this is because the word 'relationship' is a concept or an idea, and there is no such thing as a picture of an idea. Can there be a picture of 'justice', 'corruption', 'intelligence' or 'equality'? Obviously not, and this is because an idea or a concept is something abstract. It exists in the head, not on the beach. Hence, no amount of looking will help anyone to understand the causes of inflation. Seeing people walking up the steps of an aeroplane, or marking up the price of beans in a supermarket, won't help anyone to understand inflation.[8]

All this is relevant to a consideration of the place of films in learning, and that includes many of the images used in computer programs, for a camera cannot show something abstract. A picture can only show an object. Notice here that a smiling face does not show 'contentment'. It only suggests the effect of contentment in a rather childish way. And, as static objects are boring to look at for any length of time, those who manufacture educational films and graphic images produce moving objects. But what have moving objects to do with understanding?

Notice also that, even when we study an object like a plant cell, looking at that object is only the beginning of the learning process. For what ultimately concerns a learner, is not the shape of a cell, but rather its chemical composition and how this contributes to how it works. True, films have been made that show a cell at work, but anyone who has seen such films will know that they are minor aids to learning. This is because pictures cannot remotely convey all the interactions that take place inside a cell; and more importantly, why they take place. If it were otherwise, all one would have to do to obtain a degree in biology would be to watch a few films of this kind. At this point, it might be argued that children, at least, learn better through a visual rather than an abstract medium. If the matter to be learnt is visual, then clearly it is better for learners to have a visual experience. But, if the matter is abstract, then learning is ultimately a matter of understanding, not looking. In any case, the thinking of children is far more abstract than is immediately apparent. Consider, for example, the ability of children to understand stories. These are often full of concepts like loyalty, deceit, friendship and bravery; and recall again that only the effect of such qualities can be shown in a picture, not the quality itself. In the books of a writer of children's fiction like Nina Bawden, all the most important episodes require a child to imagine – not picture – such concepts. If a creature from another planet were to examine most of the documentaries shown on tv, it would conclude that earthlings must be infantile because they are taught mainly by looking at pictures.

Unfortunately, in some schools, pupils are often *shown* things instead of being helped to *understand* things. One example is when pupils are taught about world religions by being shown the artefacts used, and the ceremonies common in them. Such 'things' lend themselves to being shown on film. But they are merely peripheral aspects of a religion. Such an approach trivializes.

Much the same is true of the so-called 'News' on tv. Consider first that those who produce these programmes find it difficult to report an event unless pictures of it are available. For, in the absence of pictures, all they can present is a picture of a person speaking. And second, when pictures are available, they contribute next to nothing to helping one to understand the *causes* that have produced them. This is because, unless an event is something like a natural disaster, the causes, leading to an event of some significance, are nearly always of an abstract nature. How can the *causes* of even a war be shown via a picture? It is for this reason that natural disasters are a godsend, in more ways than one, to the contrivers of these programmes. But then, 'The News' is increasingly a part of the entertainment industry, – as becomes obvious when one hears the music with which it begins. How reminiscent of an overture.

It is true that films are nearly always accompanied by a commentary. But these commentaries usually consist of just three to five sentences, and are therefore rightly called 'sound bites'. One can imagine how substantial these comments are, if one imagines a lesson on, say, the life of a tadpole consisting of five sentences. But that is not the most important limitation of these commentaries. Their most important limitation is that they are based on the *spoken* word, and I shall consider that very significant fact in another section.[9]

Recall here that many films are merely one aspect of a widespread culture, a culture which, at its worst, is largely a matter of gawking at endless, moving, flickering, coloured images, a kind of mental dummy for the fretful mind; or, as was once well expressed, 'chewing gum for the eyes'. That is, they are often an escape from reality, not an exposure to it, and some teachers with a difficult class understandably sometimes use them in just that way. Even when films are used with a serious intent, many are unfortunately no more than a glorified version of the transmission method of teaching. And, just as some learners like that method, so some learners like such films. They are even less demanding than picture books, for one does not have to turn any pages. As for the average learner, when films come on, blinds often come down, both in the room and in the mind. Some learners reward their teachers with silence for such legal glue sniffing.

As these comments might sound exaggerated, I recall here that, in previous chapters, I suggested that learning takes place when we discover that we don't know something (we consider worth knowing), form hunches about it, actively test those hunches, have access to suitable information, and obtain some feedback. If that is a roughly correct outline of real learning, then films, on their own, must be one of the worst teaching mediums ever devised.

One line of evidence for the above assertion comes from a consideration of the workings of the two sides of the brain, a topic considered in a previous chapter. In line with the comments then made, it has been found that printed material, or complex verbal or mathematical material, will tend to be processed primarily on the left side of the brain. Material presented via film, on the other hand, is primarily visual, so will be processed primarily by the right side. It would therefore seem reasonable to conjecture that, should the right side of the brain be stimulated far more frequently than the left, it might be the right side that will be strengthened and favoured for most uses.

It might be interesting to add here that this different functioning of the two sides of the brain is more marked in males than females, and that the verbal ability of girls tends to be better than boys. These two findings might help to explain why boys tend to watch more television than girls, and are more likely to have difficulties with reading.

It is important to recall here that even educational films are often made so as to require short spans of attention. If so, it seems reasonable to conjecture that repeated exposure to such material might interfere with the ability to concentrate for the relatively long periods required in order to understand complex materials. Notice also that one of the indirect effects of films might be to accustom the observer to watch, rather than to think and to evaluate. Moreover, the pace of most educational films or television documentaries is such that they do not allow a viewer time to work over, and hence properly assimilate the points made. Recall here that, when one reads, especially when one reads about factual matters, one must reconstruct that material mentally in order to make it meaningful.

I would summarize like this. Films convey primarily images, and images are concrete, not abstract. They are often also fast moving, and emotional in their impact. That is, an image is primarily a non-linguistic and hence a non-analytical medium, and when this medium is frequently used, it tends to undermine intellectual activity. An image is also always 'in the now'. Even a historical image is 'in the now'. If so, images do not foster a genuine sense of the past, of continuity, of development, or the future. Recall also that, even a person with a very limited education, is able to make reasonably good sense of most tv documentaries, but this same person might not be able to follow even an elementary lesson on a similar topic. If so, this again suggests that the intellectual demand of most films is far lower than that of even an elementary lesson.

But it would be a mistake to be overcritical, for films can serve some educational aims. For example, with their help, learners can be shown plays, planets, processes and provinces, things that they might otherwise not see; and sensible teachers utilize such a facility to show such things. In short, where knowing is primarily a visual matter, films can serve a useful purpose. And, as films can have a powerful emotional impact, they can be used to initiate a discussion on a controversial topic, but I emphasize the word 'initiate' here.

That is, with the help of a DVD/video machine, a teacher is able to show no more than one part of a film at a time. That is an important facility for, when the whole of a film is shown, it often has the same effect as a tv programme in a living room. It dominates, stifles discussion, and can turn even bright people into temporary zombies. After a part of a film has been shown, the film can be stopped and the learners invited to respond to it. Or a lesson might begin with learners being given a series of written questions to consider before a film is shown. Then, at certain points when the film is turned off, they can be invited to respond in writing to those questions in pairs. In this way, a film can become a useful adjunct to a main lesson, and turned from a passive into an interactive learning medium.

⁊

I come now to another matter allied to the above.

In school, one is taught about the different periods during which human beings have lived on this planet. For example, there is the period when people subsisted as hunters and gatherers, followed by the period when they subsisted primarily through agriculture. After that, came the period of industrialization, and with that the move to cities, and so on. Less emphasis tends to be placed on the period in which all communication was oral, and the period that followed during which the alphabet and writing was invented, and slowly came into use.[10]

I believe this latter difference is especially important in an educational context. For example, in a period that is primarily oral, many statements tend to be about certain people who act in a particular manner; and that gives such statements a personal and concrete nature. Statements of this kind also have a stronger impact, and are better remembered, than statements made in a more general manner. However, when statements are made in writing, it isn't necessary to make them personal and concrete for them to be remembered, for, if necessary, a reader can refer to a text several times until it becomes clear. What is important here is that, when one writes, one can more easily use abstract terminology. For example, instead of talking about a certain king, who treats all supplicants equally, one can write in the abstract about 'even-handed justice'. In short, the advent of writing led to a change from a centuries-long period, when people thought and spoke mostly in personal and concrete terms, to the more modern period when, due to the influence of writing, people often think and speak in the abstract.[11]

I trust that readers will see how these comments relate to what was noted in the previous section about the effect of films, and the brief spoken comments that accompany them. Recall here that, when images and the spoken word are deftly arranged, they can give great pleasure and generate strong feelings, hence few things can produce as much electricity in the atmosphere as a combination of vivid images and melodious lines. No wonder that some films can elicit more donations for a charitable cause than any number of facts or arguments. These effects can be contrasted with a culture of reading. In this, processes of the kind described above are less likely to occur. Instead, a culture of reading encourages one to evaluate, analyse, and reconsider.

I draw attention to these things because real learning does not come about when people are presented with images of heroes doing this and that, speaking lines that consist of no more than half a dozen words, against a background of melodious music. For example, no matter how ethically depicted are the actions of a certain hero in a film, one will only grasp the nature of ethics when one attempts to understand what is meant by ethics as such, – in short, when one grasps the nature of the concept that goes by the name of ethics. Indeed, a concept is most clearly understood in the absence of any action, for a concept is an abstraction. Readers might here recall the story about Adam and Eve related in a previous chapter, and that it was only when the concept of Responsibility was abstracted from the actions of the various participants, that some real understanding of this concept began to take place.

I also draw attention to these matters because, as is well known, people, and especially many youngsters, spend a great deal of time today watching tv, and are hence immersed in a culture of images and the spoken word. If so, they are increasingly likely to think in personal terms, for example, of heroes and leaders, rather than policies and ideas; and recent trends in voting suggest that this is increasingly happening. Some people even appear to vote for a person because of how he or she looks, rather than his or her approach to issues of the day. To put this in another way, a culture that is primarily visual and oral, runs the danger of generating the belief that things are the way they are because certain people have behaved in a given manner, rather than because certain underlying causes have certain effects.

Another possibility in such a culture is that the people in it, will come to believe that things, even quite technical things, like, say, unemployment, are a part of the natural order, rather than due to something abstract like an economic system. It is a kind of sleepwalking; and I would have thought that teachers who are serious about their work would wish to do their best to combat such a development.

Notice also that, when one stops thinking about complex matters in abstract terms, opinions tend to replace evidence. This is because an opinion, like an action, is usually associated with a person; whereas evidence does not need such a connection. That is, the value of an opinion is often determined by who utters it and how; whereas the value of evidence is determined by how it has been established and how rational it is.

It is also the case that, when one is induced to think in mainly concrete terms, observations tend to be tied to a given situation and to a given time. But two and two always make four, no matter what the circumstances or the time; and violent revolutions tend to produce violent ends, no matter where or when they occur. A concrete mode of thinking, in contrast, can cause people to believe that a violent revolution was due to the actions of certain people, carried out at a certain time. In this way, a culture that is primarily visual and oral generates the illusion that historical events consist of a chain of only vaguely related happenings brought about by certain people, rather than by causes generated by such abstract things as the values, structures and previous history of a given society.

Having written so much about the abstract, I had better add that none of this precludes attending to the practical. I would add that intelligence is often a matter of combining the two; and I would trust that what I have written in this book makes clear that I greatly favour a practical approach. It is nevertheless the case that, being only practical can lead to being bigoted and almost a fool. Notice, further, that people immersed in a predominantly visual and oral culture are prone to think in terms of effects rather than causes; and that, when they do mention a cause, it is often a banality. At worst, in such a culture, people might become blind to anything beyond obvious appearances. As noted, such a culture also favours opinions over evidence in even factual matters. This becomes apparent in the majority of tv programmes, as when one speaker states that unemployment is caused by the advent of new technology, another that it is caused by a fall in demand, another that it is due to laziness, and another that it is due to globalization. Speakers seldom refer to any evidence, except of the most superficial kind, and such trivialization is partly due to the fact that the medium employed – images and the spoken word – does not favour the consideration of evidence.[12]

I believe that the above comments on the effect of a certain culture are very important in any discussion of educational technology, and I might manage to convey what I have in mind like this. For centuries, the centre of many large towns was dominated by a place of worship. That might have been a temple, a mosque, or a church; and it was often a most imposing building. Once inside, the lofty arches made people feel small, the glittering decor would dazzle them, and the air of solemnity would remind them of their mortality. All over the world, this situation has increasingly changed, and today, the centre of a town is usually dominated by a Shopping Centre. If there is a place of worship in the town, it often looks deserted, and in comparison with the splendours of the shopping centre, it often looks drab.

On Saturdays, especially, a shopping centre reflects much that is characteristic of our age. Motor traffic will have been excluded so as not to disturb the secular worship that takes place there; and it can make a powerful impression to stand still in such a place for a moment and to listen. There is a kind of hush, interspersed with heels clicking on pavements, as many thousands of people file past holding the Plastic Bags that have so clearly uplifted their spirits.

And people do not always go to a shopping centre merely to buy something. 'Shopping' is rather an integral part of modern life, like 'Worship' used to be; and the two have a good deal in common. Just as in past centuries, life used to be played out against a background of chants and bells, so now it is played out against the sounds of a new kind of advertising. And, just as people used to go to a place of worship in part to ease a troubled mind, so now they go to a shopping centre when they feel empty.[13]

For there are few things in life as therapeutic as 'Buying Something'. Buying Something seems to ease an inner ache. Even just looking at Things seems to make people feel better. And shops are full of Things! They come in a thousand colours and a million shapes, and with them, one can cover one's vulnerable body and look lovely, or perform functions that would have been thought miraculous until quite recently. At the press of a button, food can be cooked, clothes washed, and homes cleaned. Other Things can cool or heat us, flush away our excrement, produce light when it is dark, and conjure up music out of thin air. With the help of Things, one can also draw money out of walls, send one's voice across miles of space, and fly like Ali Baba through the empty sky. Nor is any specialist knowledge, or contact with the powerful of the land, required to enjoy these Things. All one has to do is to pass another Thing called money into a person's hand.

I would not want to be misunderstood here. For many years, as boy and man, I often found gadgets attractive; and to this day, I get much pleasure when I have managed to mend something. I also get as big a kick out of going into a tool shop as a bookshop. But what has all this to do with learning and teaching? It is that modern technology, and the culture of the consumer society, have radically changed our lives, and tend to make us believe that we must try to use this technology in learning and teaching. And yet, when one does, one might lose sight of a far older technology: print. I also draw attention to these matters because they obviously have a very considerable import for what teaching is essentially about.

As that last comment might sound merely nostalgic, it might be helpful to add a few more words on how reading a passage is different from seeing an image and hearing a brief accompanying comment. When we read a written passage, we process symbols; and symbols of course stand for something that is not present. For example, when we read the word 'dog', the letters that make up that word do not remotely resemble a dog. We might imagine a dog as we read that word, but the word itself is something quite abstract. Moreover, if we imagine a dog, it will not usually be any specific dog; it will rather be a vague amalgam of all the dogs we have ever seen. In other words, when we process symbols, we move away from concrete experiences in the present, to a timeless world of concepts in the mind.

Compare the above with how film works. Here, the form of communication is primarily in the form of pictures and brief comments. It follows that, with such a medium, we remain largely in the world of specific experiences. A picture of a dog is always a picture of a specific dog. There is no such thing as a picture of the concept 'dog'. Nor is there a picture of 'mankind'; or 'happiness', 'work', 'justice', 'unemployment' or the thousands of other abstract concepts we use in order to understand our world. It follows that a medium that consists primarily of pictures and a few spoken words, has severe limitations, for, in such a world, the sun moves, the earth is flat, and questions about these things never arise.

Many teachers will also have noticed that an increasingly large number of learners seem unable to concentrate for long on any one topic, and this might be due in part to the fact that a topic in a television programme is seldom considered for more than a few minutes. Notice that radio programmes, with their 'sound effects' and frequent movement from one topic or speaker to another, increasingly produce the same infantile effects. But then, everything in the mass media, even death, is turned into entertainment, as when a report of a shooting is accompanied by the sound of shots and music. This is very different from when one must attend to a text, especially a text that contains a consideration of an issue of some substance. Sustained attention, and some power of analysis are then required.

Recall also that there is nothing attractive about a written passage. The words don't move around, and there are no lighting effects. There isn't even any music! In a television programme, on the other hand, it is precisely these things that have an effect, and often at the expense of the content. And further, unlike the case with a provocatively written passage, a film tends to leave no holes in our understanding. A picture is a picture, and, unless it is contrived, it is unlikely to have implications beyond itself. But even a single written word can have more than one implication, and hence raise questions and make one think.[14]

&

The technological aid that carries the greatest aura of potency at present is the computer. More than any other Thing, it promises education a 'breakthrough', and few buzzwords are more favoured today than that!

Before I continue, it is obviously important to distinguish between helping people to learn how to use a computer, as compared with using a computer as an aid to learning. As computers have many useful functions, it makes sense to help people to learn how to use them. But here it might be worth recalling that computers also carry a considerable mystique. For example, merchandise is sometimes advertised as being 'computer designed', as if that were an advantage to the buyer rather than the seller! But anyone who knows anything about computers will know that, although they can be very useful tools, they are no more than that. One more rider is, I think, in place. As one reads the literature on educational technology, one soon begins to suspect that one reason for the introduction of computers into educational institutions is financial rather than educational. That is, it is often due to an increase in student numbers, without an increase in teaching hours. A reading of this literature also suggests that failures in the educational use of computers are seldom reported, and one suspects that this is because those who write about educational technology do not want to undermine the source of their income.

I believe that the most valuable feature of computers in an educational setting is that, when they are loaded with a well-designed program, learners are able to use them to work out something for themselves, and at their own pace. A computer can also be programmed to interact. That is, it can prompt a learner, provide alternatives, and indicate errors. In short, a computer can help a teacher to assume the role of a facilitator.

Unfortunately, many educational programs are almost infantile, and, after the novelty of working with them has worn off, most learners get bored with them. It is also the case that some programs do not facilitate more than mere drill and practice. In short, it isn't something unique to a given program that often helps learning, but rather the fact that a computer enables learners to be actively engaged, and provides practice. These things being so, it is important for a teacher to recall that computers are an addition to a lesson, not a substitute for it. In other words, computers are useful to the extent that they are integrated into a carefully structured scheme of work, rather than something used to fill up a Friday afternoon.

Notice that, when computers are used in the way described so far, they dovetail well with the theory of learning outlined in previous chapters. That is, in using a good program, learners can find out what they don't know, form hunches, obtain information, test hunches, and in that way work their way towards an accurate conclusion. I should perhaps add here the truism that all this is much easier to describe than achieve. For, even when computers and good programs are readily available in an institution, and teachers are conversant with their use, it can take learners much time and effort to learn how to use them, and teachers are likely to be concerned that time so spent is at the expense of doing more substantial things. However, in time, those problems are likely to be overcome, for computers are becoming more readily available, and an increasing number of people learn how to use them on their own.

When people have learnt how to use a computer, some become fascinated, for computers are powerful machines, and it is exciting to manipulate powerful things. For example, when a computer is loaded with the most common program in use, a word processor, the technical aspects of writing become far easier than is the case with pen and paper. This is because the letters, on which one taps on a keyboard, appear on a screen, not a sheet of paper; and, by tapping on certain other keys, one is able to delete words, substitute words, and move sentences around on the screen. That is, as all these things happen on a screen, there is no need to keep re-writing on sheets of paper. And further, when one is reasonably satisfied with what one has produced, a few more taps on certain keys will save what one has written onto a disk located inside the computer. Or, a few taps on yet other keys, will get the computer to print one's work on a sheet of paper. Then, after one has re-read what one has written, and if one finds that one would like to make some alterations, one can press a few other keys. This will bring what one has written back to the screen, and one can then make whatever additional changes one wishes. And after that, a few more taps on keys will get the computer to print the amended text.

Even though many readers will know these details, I have risked noting them, in order to highlight the fact that a salient feature of all technology is that it enables one to do what one could anyway do, but far more conveniently and easily. Compare boiling water with the aid of an electric kettle, with boiling water over a campfire.

Another example of the above is the correcting of spelling. A modern word processor has a spelling checker, and a poor speller will find that a great help. This is because a spelling checker does not automatically provide the correct spelling of every word one writes. That is anyway impossible. It is rather that, if one misspells a word as one types, a spelling checker will signal this by placing a wavy line under that word when it appears on the screen. Now, in ordinary writing, if one is unsure about how to spell a word, one must wade through a dictionary, and a poor speller finds that very frustrating and time consuming. However, when one is using a computer and spell checker, a tap on a key will bring up on the screen, several correct spellings of the word that has been underlined. For example, one might have typed the word 'wrait', and that is what therefore appears on the screen. If so, the spelling checker will underline that word, and present the words 'write', 'right', or 'rite' as alternatives on the screen. One must then select the appropriate word, and, as this process is repeated, one's writing will not only be corrected, one is also likely to learn a good deal.

Notice also that, in using a computer like this, one is likely to feel a good deal less inept than when a teacher points out one's mistakes. Moreover, the focus is on the learning, not on the need for correction. One is also saved from the tedium of re-writing, and can concentrate on the task at hand. These things are likely to make the act of writing far more pleasant than when one uses pen and paper.

But a word processor can help in a more substantial way. This becomes apparent when one learns that there is good evidence that indicates that a combination of reading and writing can contribute to one's ability to think in a judicious and critical manner. This is because, in order to think in a judicious and critical manner, it is necessary to reflect, and there is more of a chance to do that when one is writing, than when one is speaking. It may be that this is why some people find writing in a sustained manner difficult. This kind of thinking is further developed when learners are encouraged to produce improved drafts of what they have written; and it is here that word processors again become very useful, for they do away with the need to reproduce what one has already written once.

Furthermore, when a new draft is produced, further reflection will take place; and, when that happens, a learner, like anyone else doing such writing, comes to see the strengths and weaknesses of an argument, and how it is possible to express the same point in various ways. And if appropriate reading has preceded such writing, the writer will have a model, with both strengths and weaknesses, in the mind. At this point, readers might recall a previous chapter in which I described some of my experiences while writing this book.

I have again risked describing in some detail, because the above highlights how a computer can, first, help one to do more easily what one could anyway do; and, second, serve as a powerful aid to learning. But again, it is nevertheless still no more than a tool. One still has to do the actual writing! I mention this because, as computer programs become increasingly sophisticated, the latter is sometimes forgotten. For, again with the example of writing in mind, one can spend a long time choosing a certain kind of print, a certain kind of layout, and a dozen other embellishments; and I have seen students spend far more time and effort on things like that, than on expressing what they want to say in an appropriate manner.

The above noted, I might have managed to indicate why I believe that the most important characteristic of a computer, when used as an aid to learning, is that it enables learners to be actively engaged. This is in contrast to how learners are often passive listeners in most educational settings. The second merit of using a computer, is that learners are themselves able to control the level and the pace of the learning process. A third merit is that learners are able to interact with a computer in an individual manner. And a fourth merit is that, if a mistake has been made, a good computer program will indicate this in a non-judgemental way.

When a teacher has prepared a lesson in which the above kind of activity takes place, he or she is also freed from the illusionary need to teach didactically. Instead, having introduced a lesson, a teacher can encourage students to get to work. He or she is then free to move from student to student, or from group to group, encouraging, questioning, praising, helping weaker students, drawing attention to previous work, initiating discussions to clarify a point, signposting, and giving students an opportunity to learn. In this way, learning becomes collaboration, not imposition.

In the above, in order to illustrate the use of educational technology in general, I have referred to using a computer and word processor; and I did this because a reasonably straightforward program like this enables one most easily to identify what is valuable in this technology. Other, more specifically educational programs are also available. For example, there are programs that enable learners to carry out experiments. As these are not real experiments, they are said to take place in 'virtual reality', and I have seen a few that I have thought useful in subjects like biology and geography.

However, I have also often had doubts about them. This is because virtual reality isn't the same as reality; and, in line with the emphasis placed in previous chapters on the need to experience, I believe that one will learn a great deal better from any experiment carried out in reality, than one carried out in a pseudo world. As also noted in a previous chapter, a word is not the same as the thing for which it stands. In the same way, an image is not the same as the thing it represents. It follows that, if such simulations are not followed by real experiences, they will generate a false sense of learning. In short, a pseudo world is likely to produce pseudo knowledge.

I draw attention to the above because it has been found that some teachers use educational technology in just that way; and one assumes that they do this in order to escape from the arduous task of designing suitable lessons. Others use educational technology as a kind of adjunct to their customary didactic teaching, and here one assumes that they do this out of habit or ignorance. What is for sure, is that using educational technology in the productive way I have described, requires a shift in roles, and that does not come easily.[15]

℞

Another aspect of computers, often discussed in an educational context, is that, with their help, one can connect to the internet. As is well known, the internet, among other things, enables one to access a vast store of information that is held at a great number of electronic sites. Information can of course also be found in a good library, but not everyone has access to a good library, and it can be far easier to find the information one needs by using a computer.

But, as is so often the case, an advantage can carry a cost. For example, the information available on the internet varies greatly in value, for, unlike the case with books and journals, it hasn't been edited. It follows that only people able to evaluate such a source will be able to make judicious use of it; and most learners do not have such ability. Having very easy access to information can also lead to plagiarism. There are even sites that enable learners to download ready-made essays on dozens of topics.

Moreover, because such a huge amount of information is available on the internet, selecting that which one needs becomes a problem, especially for a learner. Many learners overcome this problem by writing the name of the topic on which they seek information, into a so-called search engine, and then accepting the first or second option on offer. This process might sound authoritative; but it is likely to be superficial, for what is supplied is intended to be read by anyone, no matter what that person's education might be. The worst aspect of such a process is that it prevents a learner from undergoing the arduous experience of learning how to distinguish trash from that which is valuable.

But there is an even more important issue at stake here. When one reads about educational technology, one soon notices that there is a recurrent focus on information. But education is clearly not merely a matter of acquiring information. This becomes obvious when one recalls that knowing facts is not the same as understanding them; for, as noted in a previous chapter, in order to understand a fact, one must have some knowledge of the context into which it fits. The popularity of quiz shows obscures this. In these inanities is it is possible to win a staggering sum of money because one is able to answer a question like, 'What is the longest river in the world?' One answers, 'The Amazon', but one might have no idea what makes this river so long, or the way in which it affects the lives of the people who live near it.

It is also important to recall that market forces largely determine the kind of information that is available on the internet. Moreover, after production, this information is treated as a commodity, that is, it is increasingly made available on condition that it is saleable. Furthermore, like many commodities, extremely large corporations increasingly control its manufacture and sale; and from this it follows that this information is intended to benefit business, rather than public or private interests. Recall here also that the design, manufacture, distribution, and sale of many products, would be impossible without the extensive use of information technology. And only a brief examination shows that a very large proportion of information available today is on the sale of goods, stock market prices, currency movements, commodity values, shipping transactions, international insurance, oil stocks and the like.

Another aspect of this manufacture and distribution of information, is that it ensures the dominance of Western business interests. This is often subtly conveyed through what is called 'The News'. Probably few people know that the great bulk of international news comes from just four Western news agencies, two of which are American, one British, and one French. And these often convey that 'the West is best'. Recall here also that the rest of the world is often portrayed on 'The News' as consisting of 'trouble spots'.[16]

There is another very important aspect to information technology. It is that, as human beings still live in nation states, there is often enmity between them; and, quite often, this enmity is necessary to enhance the cohesiveness of the nation state. (Who were the good ones and who the bad, in the several hundred years of war among the Dutch, French and British?) These features, in turn, generate a powerful impulse to identify internal enemies; and, in developed countries especially, this spawns a vast technology for searching for, and storing information on, millions of people.[17]

But there is an even larger issue that one must surely consider with regard to this focus on 'information', and it is that the vast bulk of this information is of a factual nature. It is about the cost of goods, the movement of money, the state of the weather, the drugs available for certain diseases, and how to get from Honolulu to Honduras. And true, from time to time, one might want information on these things. But we are awash with this information, and tend to take this state of affairs for granted, for the bulk of our schooling has accustomed us to see things in this way. But it takes only one moment of reflection to recall that much of our more serious thinking is not bent on acquiring information, but has more to do with attempts to seek an understanding of basic questions. Questions like: How should one relate to one's children? To what extent is it sensible to trust others? In what way are women and men the same and yet different? What makes life worth living? The focus on mere 'information' has the effect of obscuring such issues.

Another application of computer technology is for the transmission of messages via the internet, messages that are called 'e-mail'. I note this because it is often claimed that using this technology with school pupils will enhance their learning. For example, it is claimed that, unlike the case when a pupil is asked to write an essay, when a pupil is asked to write an e-mail to a distant pen friend, a context for writing is provided, and it is well known that learning is always best when done in a realistic context. The difficulty here is to separate the effect of mere novelty from context, for, unless such a context develops into a personal interest, research into this matter indicates that learners either tire of merely exchanging e-mails, or those e-mails become increasingly superficial. Nor is it true, as is sometimes said, that a learner's horizons are dimmed when he or she writes only for a teacher, for, if that teacher is even partly admired, a pupil will endeavour to obtain the esteem of that teacher by giving of his or her best.

Recall also that learning to write requires more than mere repetition, and that a judicious response can help a great deal to improve one's writing. However, when one writes to another learner, the latter is unlikely to query anything of any substance that one has written. There is also a danger that, when exchanging e-mails reaches a certain pitch, a teacher will become so occupied with organizing this activity, that the aim of learning is likely to become submerged. In short, and as is so often the case with technology, it often itself becomes the focus of attention, rather than that which it is supposed to support.

It is also sometimes claimed that, in using e-mails, learners are able to communicate with other learners over vast distances, and that there is much to be gained by this. At least four things must be considered here. One is the way in which such communication furthers the aims of globalization. A second is the interest that large corporations have in having available a workforce that is familiar with the use of e-mails. A third is the manner in which interacting with others five thousand miles away, might deflect attention from others who are five miles away. And a fourth is to consider what precisely is the educational value of exchanging e-mails with learners across the globe. On the face of it, it looks as if such exchanges might further the diminution of racial and national prejudices. But only a moment of reflection reminds one that, until very recently, most wars were fought between neighbours, and that there is no evidence that prejudice is reduced merely through contact.[18]

When faced with the admonishments of those who favour the introduction of educational technology, it might also be sensible to recall that, when many youngsters sit in front of a computer, much of what they do is trivial. For example, youngsters will often use a sophisticated computer to chat about nothing in particular to another youngster who lives two streets away.

Another example of computer technology is the so-called 'hypertext'. I could write much on this technology, but, as doing so would make this chapter unwieldly, I must summarize like this. When new technology is introduced, the hype about it usually greatly exceeds the amount of substantial research that has been done on it, and that is also the case with hypertext. In an authoritative review of the matter, several researchers conclude that hypertext is, above all, a mechanism that allows speedy access to information, and where that is the primary aim, hypertext is likely to be a useful tool. Notice that no claim is made here for the educational value of hypertext, and scepticism as to this aspect of the matter is a consistent characteristic of the work of these researchers.[19]

№

We have come to the end of this chapter, and I would summarize like this. First, the use of educational technology is helpful to the extent that it is based on a coherent and testable theory of learning. That statement is almost a platitude, but I make it nevertheless, for I was dismayed to discover that the great bulk of works extolling the use of educational technology, that I read in preparation for this chapter, did not contain a reference to any theory of learning. Compare this with works on growing apple trees that contain no references to soil conditions. Anyone who advocates the use of educational technology, and who doesn't base it on a coherent theory of learning, is like a quack who prescribes antibiotics without any knowledge of medicine. I would go further and note that much of the literature on educational technology is most strongly marked by the absence of any coherent theoretical base. Studies are often of merely individual cases, and one senses that the writers not only know next to nothing about learning, but that they consider this irrelevant. Many of these works also seem based on the belief that, if one accumulates sufficient facts, then knowledge will grow.[20]

Second, in many years of observing teachers at work, I noticed that the best aids are often simple, and that teachers have made them themselves. Effective examples I have seen include a coloured poster, a knitted bag to illustrate how a womb contracts, or a balloon pushed through a hole in a piece of cardboard, inflated, and skimmed across a floor to illustrate the laws that govern how a hovercraft works. Good teachers use such things peripherally. They also know that there are Teaching Aids and there are Learning Aids; and if teaching has to stop before learning can begin, it is clear which are the more valuable.

Third, none of the above is intended to suggest that whiteboards, DVDs/ videos, tapes, slides, projectors and computers have no value in an education setting. That would be absurd. If I have been critical, it is in reaction to the tendency to see in modern technology some kind of 'breakthrough'. Learning is a biological process that must take its course. Just as there are no 'breakthroughs' in breathing, there are no 'breakthroughs' in learning. Good teachers know these things intuitively. They are neither for nor against modern technology. They use it as an aid – no more.

That latter comment is, I believe, very important. We are immersed in an age that is infused by technology and consumerism, and there is serious risk that we might become blind to the implications that flow from such a state of affairs. In one of his books, Werner Heisenberg draws attention to what I have in mind by referring to Chuang-Tzu. Heisenberg noted that, some two and a half thousand years ago, this man wrote: 'whoever uses machines, comes to work like a machine; whoever works like a machine, tends to grow a heart like a machine; whoever has a heart like a machine, loses simplicity; and whoever loses simplicity, becomes unsure of the strivings of the soul.'[21]

Heisenberg was one of the leading physicists of the previous century, but we live in an age in which many people find talk of this kind childish, even stupid. 'Simplicity? The strivings of the soul? Don't make me laugh!' For my part, I believe that we sorely lack such simplicity, and with it the strivings that go with it.[22] But talk of this kind might sound contrived, and what I have in mind might be better expressed by quoting Arthur Koestler. In one of his books, he wrote that he used to go skiing as a young man. He went on to say that, when he and his companions reached a mountain, they sometimes had the choice of using a ski lift, or climbing up. He noted that both ways got you to the top; but those who used the lift got a view, while those who climbed up got a vision.

Koestler was denigrating the use of drugs. He argued that imbibing these things produces pseudo, not real sensations. But it seems to me that his comments serve equally well to draw attention to how the use of technology can not only lift burdens from us, but also distance us from nature and thereby our inmost selves.

Am I the only one who has sometimes elected to chop wood in preference to using an electric saw? And am I the only one who has sometimes got out of a car with relief and begun to walk? Of course not. Most everyone not bowed down by an oppressively low standard of living, enjoys the experience of using their hands and being close to nature. But I am writing in an age when people, especially young-sters, spend increasing hours hooked onto machines. Hence, I write as I do; and I hope that, in doing so, I remind teachers that, when they introduce educational technology into their classes, they introduce more than machines. They introduce a way of life. The important thing is surely to use technology, but to remember that we can drift into allowing it to use us.

Chapter 17

Planning

As far as I know, there are no research findings that indicate that learners are helped when their teacher prepares for a lesson. However, in many years of teaching, I found that I had to prepare for a lesson, no matter how many times I had taught a given topic. It is, of course, important to keep abreast of ever-growing knowledge, but, in addition to that, I used to find that I always had to ensure that I had a reasonably clear idea of what I hoped to achieve in a lesson, and for that a plan was necessary. In line with these admissions, in this chapter I shall be unable to cite much evidence in support of what I say, and must therefore hope that readers will find what follows nevertheless cogent. I can also note in support of such a position the well-known fact that preparation is important in many tasks, and that, in some cases, the preparation can take longer than the actual task. Repainting a wooden window frame is one example, and sowing seeds another.

Teachers must also often prepare for more than a single lesson, for they usually teach a whole syllabus, and that must be divided into the available lessons. Beginner teachers usually find doing that far from easy. This is because beginners seldom know how much can be achieved in any one lesson, and that is not something that can be learnt by reading a book. It can only be learnt through practice. However, I found that the instructors and tutors with whom I worked all concluded that having a 'Teaching Programme' is very helpful, and indeed essential.

Such a programme consists of broadly three elements:

1) a set of lesson plans
2) one or more assessments to help determine what the learners have learnt
3) an evaluation to help find out what went well and what needs improving in the programme.

First, lesson plans

Lesson plans come in all shapes and sizes, and I use one that looks like the example provided below. (I have completed the spaces in italics to illustrate how the plan works.) This format is, of course, based on the theory of learning outlined in the first Part of this book; and it is for that reason that the focus is not on what a *teacher* does, but on what the *learners* do.

Lesson plan
1) Aim: *To explain the use of 'objectives' in teaching.*
2) Objectives: *By the end of this lesson the learners will be able to: a) state the origins of the idea of objectives; b) given a simple topic, write five behavioural objectives for it, using appropriate wording; c) list three advantages and three difficulties with this approach; and d) write two expressive objectives correctly.*
3) How will learning be assessed? *By listening to how the learners frame their objectives.*

Timing	Learner activity	Teacher activity	Resources
9 a.m.	*listening*	*introduce topic*	*blackboard*
9.05	*listening and responding*	*describe objectives*	*handout*
9.10	*discussing and writing*	*observing*	*worksheet*
9.25	*examine work of others in class*		
9.30	*listening*	*note advantages and limitations*	
9.40	*general discussion*	*observing*	
9.45	*listening*	*describe expressive objectives*	
9.50	*writing expressive objectives in groups*		
9.55	*hearing what others have written*		
10 a.m.	End of lesson		

Readers will notice that the plan printed above begins with an aim. A beginner teacher, especially, will find it helpful to spend a few minutes jotting down the aims of a lesson, for that helps to focus one's attention. It is then easier to do the necessary reading, calculating, practising or whatever, in preparation for that lesson.

After that comes writing a list of objectives. An 'objective' – as that word is used in education – refers to what a teacher has decided that the *learners* will be able to *do* by the end of a lesson. That is, an objective refers, first, to the learners' activity (not the teacher's); and it refers, second, to what they will be able to do (not, for example, 'understand'). It takes much practice before one is able to write clear objectives, but long experience showed me that, when teachers list objectives in the way just indicated, they are able to clarify what they hope their learners will achieve during a lesson.

Notice again that an objective refers to a practical action. It follows that words like 'listen', 'understand', 'grasp', 'appreciate', or 'know' cannot be used. One has to phrase objectives like this: 'Given a pile of different bones, the students will be able to *select* and correctly *name* those that are a part of the wrist.' Or, 'Presented with two texts, the students will be able *explain* why one text is cogent while the other is windy.' From these two examples, readers will see, first, that writing objectives requires some imagination and practice; second, that the more abstract the topic being learnt, the more difficult, and eventually impossible, writing objectives becomes; and third, that this approach has nothing to do with behaviourism but is prompted by a belief in the importance of being actively engaged.

The form then shows a number of columns. The first should help a teacher to time a lesson. The second draws attention to what the learners will be doing. I found that, when teachers use this form, it has the effect of directing their attention towards their learners. This is important because teaching is such a demanding activity. Hence, teachers tend to be both very aware of their learners, yet also liable to forget them. Readers might also have noticed that, in several places in the above form, the teacher appears not to be doing anything in particular. This is natural if one believes that teaching must often stop before learning can begin. The converse is surely true: it does not follow that anybody is learning because somebody is teaching, even teaching well. The third column is self-explanatory.

The fourth column should remind a teacher what materials will be required for a lesson. In the case of a teaching aid, it is essential to check that it works before a lesson. It is very frustrating to discover that a bulb has burnt out just as one is about to use an overhead projector. One tends to become flustered, a great deal of time can be lost, and learners can be very critical about such a lapse. One dud bulb can spoil a whole lesson!

The third item, at the top of the form, asks how one knows that learning has taken place. That question is intended to remind a teacher of the truism that a lesson is useful to the extent that the learners have learnt how to do something, – that is, that they have 'changed' in some way. Of course, it isn't always easy to determine what learners have learnt without properly testing them, but that cannot mean there is no point in asking oneself *how* one knows that learners have learnt something in the course of a single lesson.

Here I would emphasize that a lesson plan is not something that one should slavishly follow. On the contrary: a lesson plan is useful because it enables one to rehearse a lesson. That can help one to see it as a coherent whole; and that, in turn, can help one to be more flexible. For example, it so happens that I once used the lesson plan outlined above, and found that it is far too ambitious. The next time I taught that topic, I cut the content by about half, and having the lesson plan helped me to do this. It is also far easier to go in all kinds of directions during a lesson when one has a clear plan before one – compared with when one has only a general idea in the back of one's head – because a plan provides points of reference to which one can always return. I also found that I was seldom able to stick to a plan, especially when the learners became interested in a particular point. However, having a plan enabled me to recall what had not been considered in a lesson, and to draw attention to it in a subsequent one. Lastly, and as already noted, I taught for many years, and, when I had not prepared for a lesson in roughly the way just described, I tended to be flustered. That can make for a lack of focus, and that is unfair to both the learners and the teacher.

&

Next, assessments

By assessment is of course meant how a teacher, and the learners, can find out whether the learners have learnt what they are supposed to have learnt. A well-prepared teaching programme will contain two or three assessments, based on the objectives stated in one's lesson plans; and such assessments can take various forms. Common ones are: a set of questions, an essay, an assignment, a multiple-choice test, or a project.

Assessment is a large topic. For my part, I often felt that some writers exaggerate its importance, perhaps because, unlike many topics in education, assessment lends itself to a reasonably clear exposition. But assessment is obviously an important topic, and for several reasons. One is that every society needs competent practitioners, and an assessment is one tool for establishing the presence or absence of competence. Another is that students would rightly consider themselves grossly abused if they were asked to do an assessment that is poorly designed, and that was responded to in an obviously subjective manner. Assessments also provide a goal and end point in learning, and these can be helpful when learning has to be assessed formally. But assessment is not strictly speaking one of the topics of this book, so I shall confine myself to making just a few comments as follows.

1) I believe that any good assessment has two characteristics. One is that it assesses as unambiguously as possible whether learners have learnt what they are supposed to have learnt. The other is that learners learn more about the topic being examined while doing that assessment. In short, good assessments are also learning aids.

2) A great many assessments require learners to reproduce what they have been told or have read. Some assessments are designed to enable learners to go beyond that, but it is often enough merely to reproduce material to gain a pass. Such assessments are the antithesis of what real learning is about. They are responsible for producing parrot learning, and to some extent also for cheating and plagiarism. One can add the truism here that the form taken by assessments on a given course, indicates the kind of orientation to learning possessed by those who organized the course.

3) Among other things, a well-designed assessment will require learners to apply what they have learnt, if possible to their own circumstances, or to real-life situations. These situations will vary from one assessment to the next, and will therefore prevent the ills noted in the previous item.

4) For a variety of reasons, the use of multiple-choice assessments has increased; and when they are used primarily in order to assess knowledge of facts, that can be appropriate. Unfortunately, with the growth of student numbers, and the reluctance of some teachers (especially in higher education) to concern themselves with teaching, these tests are increasingly used to assess wider aims. They then often become tools to assess peripheral things, like accuracy in reading.

5) I favour the use of assignments for assessing. These lend themselves to asking learners to apply knowledge and understanding to a specific situation, and in a personal context. Such an approach makes it difficult to rely

on parrot learning, or to lift material from an external source and fob it off as one's own.

⊗

Evaluation

The third item in a good teaching programme is evaluation. By this is meant a tool to help a teacher to find out how well the total teaching programme has worked. Here is an example.

Evaluation
You have just completed a course on tents. The course team would find it very helpful if you would respond to the following questions, for we are keen to try to make this course as good as possible for future students.

1. You studied the following topics. Please give a mark, out of five, to show how useful you found each one, by putting a circle around the appropriate number. (1 = low, 5 = high.)
Tent construction and design: 1 2 3 4 5
Site selection: 1 2 3 4 5
Erecting tents: 1 2 3 4 5
Weather conditions: 1 2 3 4 5

2. A variety of teaching methods was used. Please give your reactions to them by jotting down a few comments.
a) lecturing
b) group work
c) practicals

3. You were asked to do three assessments. Please note your reactions to each one.
a) a multiple-choice test
b) a written assignment
c) a practical task

4. You were asked to do the following reading. Please give a mark out of five to show how useful you found each one.
A.G. Nobble, *Tent Use Through the Ages.*   1 2 3 4 5
G.A. Cobble, *Tent Construction: Materials, Techniques and Marketing*   1 2 3 4 5

5. Please note your overall reaction to the course below. Thank you.

I would not want to argue that the above is the best kind of evaluation possible. I would rather hope that it might serve as a kind of model for teachers to amend and adapt to their circumstances. I would also hope that readers will see that this approach to lesson planning is in line with the theory of learning outlined in the first Part of this book.

Chapter 18

Communicating and Participating

Most people would probably agree that good teachers communicate well, but it isn't easy to determine what makes for good communicating. Is this a matter of having a certain kind of skill, or is it also a matter of having a certain kind of personality? Both are likely to be important. If so, it would be helpful to know what kind of technique, and what kind of personality help to encourage good communicating. I shall come to the matter of technique in a moment, but the matter of personality seems rather elusive. For example, how people communicate might depend, in part, on how interested they really are in others, and that cannot be easy to determine. So, it might be an idea to consider the work of somebody who spent a great deal of time studying this matter.

I turn here again to the work of Carl Rogers even though it was published some years ago, for this aspect of his work has largely stood the test of time. Thus, the most recent research, on the factors that determine whether progress is, or is not made in psychotherapy, continues to show that such progress depends to a very considerable extent on the nature of the relationship that develops between a client and a therapist. In this respect, Rogers found that clients make progress in counselling when their counsellor has, among other things, what he called 'unconditional and genuine regard' for them. By this he did not, of course, mean that a counsellor has to show a client such regard. That is impossible and hence absurd. He meant that, *when* a counsellor has such regard, a client might be helped to make progress. It follows that, when a counsellor does not have such regard – as is inevitably sometimes the case – a client is best advised to go elsewhere.[1] In more recent research, the focus is on somewhat different details, but the general thrust of the findings remains the same.

I draw attention to the above because, at some centres, when people come for training to become counsellors, they are given instruction on how to show unconditional and genuine regard. This is clearly absurd because whether I show or do not show genuine regard cannot depend merely on what I do, for what I do, ultimately, depends on who I am. Hence, another central concept in Rogerian therapy was 'congruence'. That is, that counsellors are able to help a client to the extent that their behaviour accurately reflects the way they actually feel. If Rogers was even broadly correct, it follows that, to become an effective counsellor, one must first learn what one really feels. At first blush, that might sound obvious, but, as noted in a previous chapter, that can be difficult. Nevertheless, some counselling centres even offer a course on 'The Advanced Empathic Response'!

But perhaps such a trend is not surprising, and for two reasons. One is the prevailing myth that, if one has the right technique, all can be achieved. The other is an increasing sense of unease when it comes to the personal. The personal is often fraught with risk, and perhaps the growing use of that word 'skill' in our culture is an attempt to objectify, and hence depersonalize, that which is very personal. For my part, I do not believe that it is helpful to compare communicating in a classroom with the 'skill' required to mill a crankshaft. To communicate is to relate. Learners are people. Learners are not bits of metal that can be placed in a lathe and 'skilfully' turned. If they are normal, they won't respond for very long to anyone's 'skills'. They will respond to who one is. If those comments sound sharp, it is because they are written in opposition to the increasingly instrumental values of our society. I am fortunately able to add that I found it was possible to help the teachers and instructors with whom I worked to improve their ability to communicate. But this was not a matter of inculcating skills, but of increasing sensitivity. For example, when the time came to consider this topic, I asked my learners to find a partner in the class, and then to listen to that partner speak about a personal event of some significance that had occurred in the last few months. The event should not take more than about five minutes to relate, should not be about a confidential matter, and should not be interrupted. When the speaker had finished, the listener was to summarize the story, and ask the speaker whether the summary was accurate. The partners would then change roles. I found that participants would find doing this relatively simple exercise most enlightening, and some would later say that it had affected their interactions with other people, and not only their learners. Quite clearly, more than a skill or a technique was involved here.

I believe that these matters are important, for the manner in which teachers communicate conveys their underlying attitude towards learning and teaching. And, if that is roughly correct, it follows that how well people teach will be determined in part by how well they communicate. It also follows from such a view that it might be helpful to consider 'communicating' as the outward manifestation of much that goes on in a lesson.

&

It seems safe to assume that the majority of teachers are pleased when their learners participate. Among other things, when learners participate, teachers feel that they are showing an interest. And more generally speaking, if being actively engaged is important in learning, then learner participation must be desirable. However, although schoolteachers sometimes complain that their pupils talk too much, those who teach older learners often say that they do not get as much participation as they would like. The odd thing is that, the moment those learners leave a classroom, many talk a good deal. That last observation suggests that it might be a mistake to begin the topic of 'learner participation' by considering how to encourage it. It might be better to begin by asking what inhibits participation. Readers might remember that I adopted the same approach when considering motivation. What follows is, then, a partial list of factors that I believe inhibit or encourage participation.

1) The first constraint on participation must be the transmission method of teaching. There is surely a contradiction between, on the one hand, believing that it is a teacher's primary job to transmit information, and, on the other, to expect participation. Years of observing teachers at work suggested to me that, although many would like their learners to participate, they do not really listen to them when they do. This is not because they are insensitive, but because they believe that their primary job is to 'cover the syllabus'. Learners sense this and respond accordingly.

2) Even when a teacher would welcome participation, it is obviously not something that can be forced. It can only be invited; and that invitation will be accepted to the extent that the recipients feel that the invitation is sincere and made for a good reason. But the problem goes further. For example, a teacher might be perfectly sincere in his or her wish for participation, yet undermine that wish by an equally strong need to shine.

3) Learners feel encouraged to participate when they sense that their teacher will not evaluate them each time they speak. I am not, of course, suggesting that teachers should always agree with learners. Only that learners will be encouraged to participate if they feel they are not going to be evaluated each time they open their mouth.

4) Learners will feel encouraged to participate when they sense that their teacher does not need to be talking all the time. Unfortunately, some teachers are so convinced that their primary job is to convey information that, in spite of themselves, they are like a coach who never passes the ball.

5) Learners will feel encouraged to participate if they sense that, at bottom, their teacher feels that everyone is of equal worth in the general scheme of things. Such a teacher will seek to treat all learners, of whatever age or kind, with a dignity that is theirs by right. None of this is to suggest that teachers should jettison their ultimate responsibility for what goes on in a classroom. Only that, having established essential boundaries, learners will feel able to participate when their teacher encourages as much freedom as possible within those boundaries.

6) A teacher who values participation will also try to make each lesson a collaborative venture. Such a teacher will try to be an authority, not an Authority; and will be pleased, at times, to become a participant in the learners' activities.

7) Lastly, I believe that learners will feel encouraged to participate if they sense that their teacher is genuine, more warm-hearted than cold, and more genial than dour.[2]

Before I continue, I would hope that readers might have noticed that all of the above is in line with the theory of learning outlined in the first Part of this book. I turn next to a few concrete descriptions.

✂

In many years of observing teachers, the most common exchange between teacher and taught that I heard took this form:

a) Teacher: *asks question*
b) Taught: *gives two-word answer*

   c) Teacher: *evaluates the answer* ('right', 'yes', 'good', 'no')
   d) Teacher: *repeats learner's answer*
   e) Teacher: *elaborates, and continues speaking.*

I do not know what readers will make of this exchange. It is certainly very common; but I found that, whatever else it does, it kills real participation stone, cold dead.

I noted earlier that we speak most readily to a person when we sense that this person will not evaluate us. That must be especially the case when we speak in a classroom, for a classroom usually contains a teacher, and most people feel uncomfortable when they are asked a question by someone who is in a position of some authority, as teachers are. And of course, classrooms also contain other learners, and many learners are understandably more worried about *their* reaction than that of a teacher.

In short, when teachers generate the sequence:

1) teacher's question
2) learner's two-word answer
3) teacher's evaluation of the learner's answer,

that is, when teachers do that which is most characteristic of many teachers, it is precisely then that they most inhibit their learners' participation. Whenever I made that suggestion to practising instructors and tutors, some always protested. They would say that, unless they indicated whether a learner's answer is correct or incorrect, neither the learner who had spoken, nor the other learners in the class, would be able to tell whether an answer is correct or incorrect. How true is this?

Consider first that the majority of questions teachers ask tend to be relatively simple. Consider second that, when learners answer a question, they must feel reasonably secure that their answer is correct. If so, what is gained by stating that an answer is correct? Participation is surely more likely if an answer is simply courteously acknowledged. At this point, readers might recall a previous section on intrinsic and extrinsic rewards.

But what if a learner's answer is incorrect? Where a participative atmosphere exists in a class, another learner is more than likely to correct a mistake. And, if that does not happen, a teacher can unostentatiously ask the learner who has made a mistake how he or she had got to that answer. In responding to that second question, a learner who has made a mistake is likely to discover, not only that he or she has made a mistake, but also why it was made.

So far, I have drawn attention to the first three steps in the five-step sequence noted above. What of the fourth step, repeating an answer? Whenever I suggested that this, too, inhibits participation, some practising teachers protested. They would say that repeating a learner's answer 'reinforces' it. Even if that is correct, surely such 'reinforcing' inhibits participation? Imagine that you and I are talking. How would you feel if, every time you said something I considered correct, I repeated it? You would think me either condescending or an imbecile. I believe you would also very soon stop talking to me.

Notice next that the five-step sequence begins with a question. Many teachers would probably say that they ask a question, either to test knowledge, or to encourage participation. First, I think it is safe to assume that if a question is asked to test knowledge it is unlikely to encourage much genuine participation. Second, what of questions intended to encourage participation? My observations indicated that most teachers genuinely believe that they ask some of their questions for that reason; but many years of observing teachers also suggested to me that it would be more correct to say that quite a few teachers ask questions in an indirect attempt to retain their learners' attention.

That would not be surprising. Whenever we talk for more than a few minutes at any one time, we tend to fear that our listener might have switched off. If so, it would hardly be surprising if a teacher, who has talked for more than five minutes, asked an occasional question in the hope of encouraging continued attention. But such a question must be a poor way to encourage genuine participation.

Most teachers probably do not analyse their asking of questions in the way just described. Most probably ask questions in the way they do, because that is how they were asked questions when they were learners. I feel reasonably sure that this analysis is correct because, over the years, I heard the five-step sequence described above repeated hundreds of times, – by teachers who had become convinced that it inhibits participation. In discussing their teaching after a lesson, some of these teachers would say, 'I know I'm still repeating their answers. I can hear myself doing it! It's ridiculous. But it's very hard to get out of the habit.'

And because teachers often ask questions and repeat answers as a kind of reflex action, learners find themselves having to play a game that might be called: 'Guess the Answer the Teacher Wants'. As it is often difficult to guess the answer that another person wants, one is forced to produce short, vague and childish answers. And of course, quite often, these answers will not be the ones a teacher wants. When teachers ask a question, they usually know what answer they want. When they get it, they are pleased. When they do not get it, they go on asking, 'til they get it. A learner's contribution is seldom seriously explored because, as I have repeatedly noted, many teachers are concerned with 'covering the syllabus'. It follows that, if teachers are concerned in this way, they are not able to listen to their learners' answers properly. Furthermore, if their questions are also intended to retain their learners' attention, then the answers they get will be less important to them than the mere fact that a learner has answered. Learners are of course affected by all these things, and answer – or do not answer – accordingly.

In the case of pupils in a school, when a teacher asks a question, many children wave their arms whether they know the answer or not. If they are picked, and know the answer, they give the usual two-word reply. If they do not know the answer, they mumble, – or pretend they have forgotten it.[3] They act like this because they sense it is their attention, not their answer, that many teachers primarily seek. Older learners are even more clearly aware of these things, and stop responding altogether. If there is some truth in all this, there is reason to fear that younger learners especially might come to see the act of responding to a teacher's question primarily as a matter of gaining that teacher's approval. Responding to a question in that frame of mind might then have the added effect of destroying rather than fostering considered reflection and hence real learning.

Unfortunately, the patterns of behaviour noted above tend, in time, to be reinforced by the learners, for they have also become conditioned. In this way, a style of interaction develops that neither teachers nor learners really want.

Having drawn attention to some constraints on participation, I come now to a few suggestions on how participation might be encouraged.

Classrooms are usually arranged so that the learners sit in rows and face in one direction, and there might be anything from 5 to 500 learners sitting in this way in any one class. In some institutions, smaller classes might be common, and in these, the learners might sit in a semicircle behind movable seats. Whatever the details, when a teacher faces a class, and learners sit in rows and face a teacher, three basic results obtain:

1) it is emphasized that it is the teacher who is responsible for what goes on in a class
2) the teacher will do most of the work
3) the lines of communication go mainly from the teacher to the taught.

These effects are even stronger when a teacher stands. When a teacher stands, he or she:

a) conveys the idea that he or she is in charge
b) confirms the common expectation that it is the teacher who is the active one (especially if they move about)
c) suggests that the learners have a subordinate and passive role
d) creates expectations of a performance, and will hence make learners feel like spectators and often bored
e) undermines the idea that learning is best seen as a collaborative enterprise
f) might frustrate the development of a sense of social cohesion in a class.

Perhaps the worst aspect of the above is this: when teacher and taught face each other in two parts of a room, a sense of opposition might be created; and I would have thought that few things could undermine participation more than that. Lastly, when a teacher faces learners in the way described above, he or she encourages the absurd belief that, in order to learn, one needs a teacher.

When I met a class for the first time, I would sometimes begin by asking the learners what they would do if I just sat there and did nothing. After a slightly uneasy pause, somebody would usually say that he or she would talk to a neighbour. Another might say that he would doodle or read. Another might say that she would wonder what I was up to. If I asked what would happen after that, some of those present would say that they would ask me what I intended to do, or that they would leave the room, or that they would complain. And when I asked how they would feel while these things were going on, someone was likely to say that he or she would feel surprised or annoyed. My aim in asking those questions was, of course, to try to illustrate the extent to which we tend to believe that learning is something that follows from being taught.

Very young learners, say those below the age of 12, do need a teacher in order to learn many things (clearly not everything). However, I often found that mature people, who had clearly learnt a great deal on their own, did not always consider that this constituted a case of real learning. Hence, it is common to hear people complain about not having been sent on a course; and they presumably complain like this in the belief that it is necessary to be on a course in order to learn. Most classrooms help generate this myth by the way they are laid out.

Lest it be thought that I place too much emphasis on mere topography, I had better note the following. It so happens that I once embarked on a course of study at the Institute of Education at the University of London. There were about 25 other students on this course, and the classroom we used contained a number of tables set in squares. During a lesson, about five of us would sit around each one of those squares, and the lecturer would stand in front of the class, – and lecture. In short, the topography of the room had no effect whatsoever on the mode of instruction employed in it.

Compare this with another course that I attended at that same institution a number of years earlier. On that occasion, there were about 160 students on the course, and we sat in serried rows in a huge lecture hall. One of the subjects we had to study was taught by a man who would come into the hall, say hello, and spend about five minutes introducing the topic for that session. Then he would report either two conflicting points of view, or one controversial one. Then he would cite the source or evidence on which those comments were based, stop talking, and ask, 'What do you think?'

He would smile, and quietly wait for a response. And soon, somebody would say something; for this man somehow managed to convey that he would be genuinely interested to hear what someone might like to say. Having listened to a response, this man would nod his head as if to say he understood, smile his appreciation, look round the hall, wait, and then another student would say something. When half a dozen people had spoken in this way, this lecturer would nod his head thoughtfully, thank the last speaker, and say that the next point he felt he ought to bring to our attention was . . . He would then continue speaking for another 20 minutes, stop, and invite a comment as before. And get it. From a crowd of 160 learners, very few of whom knew each other!

Three weeks after that course had begun, I found myself saying something in response to one of this man's questions. When I had finished, he nodded, smiled his thanks, and said, 'Yes, Eric. Incidentally, you may know that Weber made much the same objection long ago. But what do you think has been said in response to that?' And he again looked around the hall expectantly. I sat there flabbergasted. How on earth had that lecturer known my name? Never, but never, had he and I ever met. And that was only the third time I had sat in that hall! During the next break, I mentioned the matter to some fellow students, and we agreed that this man must have gone through the 160 application forms my fellow students and I had sent to that institution, and matched and memorized the photograph and name on at least some of those applications. I mention this man for two reasons. One, to indicate that it is possible to encourage participation in a lecture hall with 160 learners sitting in rows in front of you. And two, to suggest that such an ability requires a certain kind of teacher. That is, a teacher who teaches people, and only then a subject. That is like those rare doctors who treat a person rather than a disease. Or, as I noted at the beginning of this chapter, the way we communicate might have more to do with who we are, than any technique we might possess.

❧

In the lesson described above, there was participation. However, even this teacher was unable to encourage interaction among his learners. How could he, when what the learners saw was either him, or the back of a score of heads? That is, in a lecture hall, the lines of communication go only from a teacher to the taught and back again. However, it is a simple fact that discussions can aid, and are sometimes essential, in learning.[4] Imagine again a research establishment in which no discussions are possible. With these things in mind, it requires only a moment of reflection to see that a genuine discussion can take place only if a classroom is arranged so that:

a) the teacher does not occupy a prominent position
b) the learners are able to see each other's faces.

For my part, I found that it is most apt to arrange the tables or desks in a block in the centre of a room, for the learners to sit in a circle around the tables, and for me to sit among the learners. Where small desks (or chairs with a writing-arm) are in use, they can be placed in a circle. However, such an arrangement creates an empty space in the middle, and I have heard some learners say that they find talking across a large, empty space inhibiting. Where the numbers are too great for sitting in a circle, as is often the case, learners can be invited to sit in groups of three to five around a room. Most discussions will then be in small groups. I also found that it is possible to encourage a whole class to take part in a general discussion using such an arrangement, because learners will spontaneously turn their chairs to gain the most suitable position at any given time. Recall here the man with 160 students whose lessons I described earlier.

To the above I can add that I often found myself working with instructors and tutors who began to adopt the approach to teaching outlined in the first Part of this book, but who hesitated to rearrange the seating in their classroom. Sometimes this was because they shared a classroom with colleagues who had not been exposed to the kind of approach suggested in Part I. Whatever the reason, I would see such teachers labour in vain to raise the level of learner participation. Then some of them would make a break. They would rearrange the room in which they taught along the lines suggested above, and the results were often remarkable. It was as if their learners had been liberated to participate. I also had the good fortune to work with some teachers who reached a stage when they felt that fixed fittings (like lab benches or electric sockets) had to be moved, to allow desks to be rearranged. Making such a change can be very difficult. An electric socket can be as stubborn as an administrator. But once such fittings were removed, and the seating arranged as described above, the change in their classes was again often remarkable.

A square room is best because it is difficult to create a circular seating arrangement in an oblong room. With a big class, say over 30 learners, having a big room is most helpful, for this enables a teacher to encourage groups to form in the corners and in the middle. Unfortunately, not every establishment has decent-sized rooms, but a great deal can be done with whatever accommodation is available. The biggest problem is habit, not accommodation.

It is also unfortunate that some classes consist of hundreds of learners, and when that is the case, it is almost impossible to encourage interaction between learners.

Such classes often meet in so-called 'lecture theatres', places that were commissioned by people who know nothing about learning, and base their ideas of teaching on what took place in medieval times. Recall here that lecture theatres generate theatre-like expectations. One expects a Performance in them. They force a teacher to take on the role of an entertainer; and they encourage learners to believe that learning has something to do with being entertained. So learners sit back and expect the equivalent of a tv programme, with beautiful images, resonant commentary, subtle music, reassuring expertise, slick superficiality and an illusion of learning. As most teachers are unable to reproduce the phenol-barbiturate world of tv, many learners soon switch off. Most teachers sense this, and become either cynical or resigned. A few have a flair for showmanship, and manage to evoke enthusiasm. That is probably better than resignation. But neither kind of teaching will generate much 'real' learning.

Many teaching establishments already have lecture theatres; so scrapping them raises questions of cost. So did scrapping slavery. But lecture theatres can serve useful purposes. I refer here to what I noted earlier when I stated that, when one already has a model of something in one's head, listening to someone knowledgeable talking about it can be valuable and enlightening. It can also be very interesting to listen to someone who has made a significant contribution to a field of study, especially a field of study with which one is acquainted. After all, ideas have to come from people. Only people can dream up the bizarre idea that humans are essentially machines.

Chapter 19

Interacting

I come now to some further comments on interactions in a classroom. It might be an idea to do this by describing one of my lessons, for that might enable readers to see my mistakes, and where I have managed to get things right. As I no longer teach much, what follows should be in the past tense; however, I use the present tense as that might help to keep what I note realistic.

I try to get into a classroom a few minutes before a lesson. If there are about fifteen of us, I arrange the seating in a rough circle. If there are two dozen of us, I arrange the seating in a square with all the tables in the middle. If there are more of us, I arrange the tables and chairs in clusters so that the learners are able to get into small groups. I also try to ensure that the room is reasonably tidy.

I begin a lesson by sitting down, usually in a different place each time. I do this to convey that I am not going to put on a Performance; that I might be the teacher, but the lines of communication can go in any direction. Then I say hello and smile. After that, I say something original, like something about the weather, or how nice it is that the end of a week is coming. I begin like that to try to convey that, although I might consider the lesson to come very important, I am aware that the learners might think otherwise. A few pleasantries before a lesson can also allow the learners to get settled, and act as a bridge between the classroom and the outside world. If such a beginning does not help to focus attention, I look around and try to sense the mood of the class. There might be a concern that needs to be dealt with. Occasionally, I try something a little unusual. I bring out an odd object, or pass out a gumdrop. At other times I say something mildly provocative. The last thing to do is to launch straight into details.

Then I invite comment. Sometimes there are comments, and sometimes there are no comments. Sometimes somebody will mention a recent experience that has illuminated something we examined in a previous lesson. At other times somebody will say that they found a book or an assignment boring or interesting. Somebody might suggest that we consider a different topic, or tackle our present topic in a different way. At yet other times somebody might ask a question. Occasionally, one of the learners will launch into something. Of course, the value of these comments varies greatly. Some people make them to sabotage a lesson, others to move things along. Either way, I believe it is helpful to make a space at the beginning of a lesson to enable learners to say anything they might have on their minds.

Next, I might make an administrative announcement, or ask whether the learners would like a 'free group discussion period', that is, a period during which they can discuss anything they like, with me absent or present. As I am usually asked to leave at such times, it is hard to say what then takes place, but I have heard that, among other things, learners use them for discussing things like assignments. I had better emphasize here that a teacher can act like this only with mature students. It is against the law, and could be dangerous, to act in this way with schoolchildren.

Next, we tend to do one of two things: either we do a revision of the previous lesson, or I introduce a new topic. We do a revision for these reasons: no matter how thoroughly a topic might have been examined in a previous lesson, some learners might not have understood it very well; a revision helps to build bridges between a previous lesson and the coming one; and it is likely to aid someone who has missed the previous lesson.[1] A revision goes like this. Very briefly, I remind the learners of the topic of the previous lesson. Then I give out a worksheet with a few questions on it. In choosing questions, I try to remember that theory is most useful to the extent that it helps intelligent practice. I ask the learners to answer the questions briefly, in writing, after discussing them with a neighbour, or in a small group. I make it clear that this is a revision, not a test, and that I shall not ask to see any answers.

As the learners work, I sit to one side. When people are learning, it is best for others to keep quiet. When the learners have finished, I ask if anyone has got stuck. Sometimes a learner will say something, and a brief discussion might then develop. At other times, I might chip in to clarify a point. Quite often, no one wants to say anything. I am usually happy to leave it at that, for the learners had a chance to check their answers with each other, or to ask me. The question-sheet will show them what they know, or do not know, and it is now up to them to act accordingly. This part of the lesson takes from five to ten minutes.

Next, I outline the topic we are going to consider in today's lesson. Readers might remember my comments in a previous chapter about how things get their meaning from the way in which they fit into a pattern. In introducing a topic, I try to convey that pattern. I do that sitting, and it usually takes from three to five minutes.

Then I draw attention to a few of the most salient facts of today's topic, or I report briefly what various researchers have claimed. I happen to enjoy a radical approach, and often mention one. In reporting a matter, I try not to be too personal, for I do not want to get in the way of the topic. That is, I believe that one should try to be objective, but also that a good teacher will sometimes convey feelings or attitudes. The kind of things I have especially in mind include: an awareness that seemingly simple things are often the most mysterious; that genuine scholarship is something to be esteemed; that there is an excitement in discovery; and that much pleasure can be derived from understanding something.

I also think it best to introduce a controversial position in the name of the person who first made it. Insights and discoveries are made by people, usually in a specific context, and often allied to personal needs. Learners are people, too, and I have found that they are more likely to make such insights their own when they are introduced to them in this way.

If one of the learners objects to a position I have outlined, and no one speaks for it, I try to defend it in the originator's name. I also try to remember that a position is most likely to gain consideration, if opposing ones are also mentioned. In doing these things, I try not to make my knowledge obtrusive, for, if I do, I risk swamping the learners. It is important to know one's subject really well, but I think most of what a teacher knows should be kept in reserve. I have found that learners are more switched on by empathy than expertise. This part of a lesson takes from five to fifteen minutes.

Then I give out brief reading material on the topic. This might consist of an article I have shortened, or two paragraphs I have photocopied from a book. Sometimes the material is in the form of a list or diagram. Whatever the form, I always add one or two questions. But I don't just pass this material out. I try to 'sell' it. I say something like, 'I think you will find this material interesting. I came across it by chance when . . .'. And I mean these things sincerely, for I believe that personal allusions in such matters are helpful. There is often a kind of residual resistance in every class, and a little wooing, or a little good humour, can help to counterbalance such a tendency. Then I ask the learners to respond to the questions briefly, in writing, after consulting a neighbour, or having a discussion in a small group. I make such requests because, as I have frequently noted, such exchanges help learners to clarify their understanding. This also makes for variety in a lesson, and readers might recall some comments on that matter in an earlier chapter. Such discussions also provide scope for social inclinations.

At other times, having introduced a topic, I dictate a one-sentence question, and invite the learners to jot down an answer after discussing it with a neighbour. Of course, I don't ask to see these written answers. I act like this because I believe that inviting learners to jot down an answer sometimes, is more likely to generate thought than always asking a question that requires merely a verbal response. Also, in that way, all the learners will be engaged, not just the usual vocal few.

Readers might have noticed that, in acting as I have described, I try to 'problematize' the topic we are studying. That is, rather than give learners information, I ask them to answer a question on it, either on the basis of their experiences, or on the basis of descriptive or research material that they have just examined. I trust that readers will immediately see how this approach rests on the materials on learning outlined in the first Part of this book.

Of course, instead of handing out a text, a teacher could hand out a set of calculations, a series of slides, or a piece of equipment, each followed by a question. Or, if access to a computer and a suitable program is available, these can be used. The essential thing is for the students to be actively engaged in answering a question, and the material should be intrinsically interesting. After that, the important thing is for the teacher to sit back and let the learners get on with the task.

Many years of experience showed me that many teachers find this way of going about things difficult. For a teacher to sit in a class and apparently do nothing, for periods ranging from five to twenty minutes, seems almost a dereliction of duty. Should one not be teaching? Isn't that what one is paid for? It takes time for teachers to learn to resist the urge to get in there and do something. In my case, it got easier from year to year, as my conviction grew that the only way of really learning something is to grapple actively with it.

To return to the class being described: when the learners have finished, I suggest we consider answers, and I remain seated. I ask one learner to get us started, she gives her answer, and a discussion might then develop. If it doesn't, I might invite a learner by name to comment on the answer we have just heard. As that learner speaks, I try to listen as well as I can. When he or she has finished, I don't comment (or evaluate or repeat), and I don't say 'Yes' or 'Aha'. All these will draw attention back to me. Instead, I try to show that I appreciate that contribution. Then I look around to try to convey that I'd be pleased if someone else spoke.

In most discussions, the teacher is the centre of attention. That is the case even if he or she does not want that. Most learners are conditioned to seeing a teacher in that way. They tend to see a teacher as a figure of Authority, and they tend to want confirmation for what they have said. Obtaining confirmation can be important. We all need what might be called 'authentication'. The trouble is, when a teacher keeps confirming, the learners tend, unconsciously, to see the topic of the lesson as somehow 'belonging' to the teacher. They are then likely to view it as something 'out there', something that has little to do with them personally. When that happens, the material of the lesson seldom becomes real. At this point, readers might recall a lesson by a tutor librarian called Betty described in an earlier chapter.

So, usually, I don't comment after a learner has spoken. I acknowledge the contribution with a friendly nod, and then look around expectantly. If no one speaks, I invite another learner by name to speak. Quite often, when that person speaks, and especially when the learners and I are new to each other, that comment will be directed at me, or spoken quietly. In reply, I say that I fear not everyone has heard. That is usually enough to encourage the learner who spoke to address the whole class. I then nod again, and look around expectantly. I try again to convey that I would be pleased if someone else spoke. I often have to wait quite a while like that, because many learners find such behaviour on the part of a teacher unusual. The more outspoken ones sometimes say that they don't understand what I am up to. Some call it a 'laid-back' approach. Others suggest I am playing a game, and wonder when I am going to come clean. A few say they find me manipulative. Others say my silences disturb them, or that they find me discouraging. Some say that they want me to tell them if they are right or wrong.

I am always troubled by such comments. I say I am not playing any game; and I add that I am behaving in the only way that now makes sense to me. I say that I'd prefer to hear another learner's reaction to my own, and that the lesson is as much theirs as mine. I urge the learners to read some of the material that has influenced me, and I give names and titles. In the following weeks, I sometimes have the impression that a few of the learners have looked at this material, for some of them now smile in class, and participate more. Some even argue with the ones who want me to be more directive. Readers might here recall the comments made in an earlier chapter on how answers are best sought inside one's own head.

Very slowly, after I have used this approach for a few weeks, most learners get used to my not commenting after a learner has spoken, and increasingly they themselves comment on what someone has just said. Increasingly, too, they don't wait for me to say anything. They bring up points themselves. I find I can sometimes encourage such learner-to-learner exchanges when I turn my head, or simply sit back and let things take their natural course.[2]

I have just noted that, when I ask a question, quite often I do not get an imme-diate response; and that, when this happens, there is silence. I believe most teach-ers find such silences troubling, especially if they continue for a while. I certainly felt that way when I began to adopt the approach outlined above. In observing other teachers, I also found that many say something to break such a silence, for, not doing so, and allowing a silence to continue, seems to be experienced as stress-ful. The odd thing is that learners hardly notice such silences. They are usually too busy trying to work out a possible answer, and are seldom given enough time to do that.[3]

Research into this matter has produced some interesting findings.[4] For example, it has been found that the majority of teachers do not wait for more than one second after they have asked a question; and, if they do not get a response within that time, they tend to do one or all of the following things:

a) repeat the question
b) rephrase it
c) ask another question
d) call on another student for an answer.

Then, if the usual two-word answer is offered, they repeat it, and ask their next question, – all in less than one second. To anyone who has had an opportunity to observe this process, the main impression conveyed is of a teacher incessantly talking. Research into this matter indicates two other things:

1) that teachers tend not to be aware of this pattern; but that
2) when they do become aware of it, and wait for three or more seconds after they have asked a question, their learners tend to be affected in the fol-lowing ways:
   a) the length of their responses increases
   b) the number of their spontaneous and pertinent comments increases
   c) their confidence when responding increases
   d) they comment more frequently on each other's responses
   e) the usually quiet ones respond more frequently
   f) they ask more questions.

So, when there is a silence after I have asked a question, or one of the learners has given an incomplete reply, I try not to say anything. I lean back and wait. More often than not, if I am patient, the same learner will continue speaking, or another will offer a contribution. Again, I try to listen as carefully as I can, and, when that speaker has finished, I express my appreciation through look or gesture, and look around expectantly again.

If no one says anything, and I feel that some encouragement might be helpful, I turn to a learner and ask her by name what she thinks. Using names is important. It conveys that a teacher is interested in what a particular learner might be think-ing. In this way, I try to involve as many people as possible, but, of course, I never press anyone to reply.

Another thing I occasionally do, when there is a silence after a learner has spoken, is to laugh, and say to the last speaker, 'It's disappointing, isn't it? You say something real bright, and no one says a thing! It happens to me all the time.' As noted, when learners get used to this approach, they increasingly speak to each other. And when I think it is appropriate, I come in, too. Sometimes I come in because I can't help myself! That usually happens when somebody has said something I consider outrageous. And, if I am not too vehement, that might spark off more comment. And so it goes, until I feel no more will be usefully said.

Notice that the process outlined above frequently takes place in everyday life. For example, when two people are speaking, and the first one says, 'Let's meet at the entrance to the supermarket', the second one is likely to say, 'Do you mean the main entrance, or the entrance in the car park?' Even in a situation as straightforward as that, a discussion is often necessary to get something clear.

At this point, I enjoin readers to notice that the approach being outlined above is far removed from the one called 'question-and-answer'. In this, the teacher stands out front, and, by a process of judicious questioning, attempts to elicit answers from learners. The most obvious characteristic of this approach is that it is teacher led. The learners remain essentially passive; there tend to be few learner-to-learner exchanges; and the learners tend to be hazy about where they are going. If there are more than three of them, they will spend most of the time listening to comments directed to another person. This tends to create frustration and boredom.

But I had better add that I quite often find that the approach I have outlined above does not always encourage participation. Sometimes I do all the things I have outlined, and yet, the class remains glum. I worry about this, and sometimes mention it to the learners. They then usually shake their heads and urge me not to worry so much.

જી

A few more words on asking questions might be helpful.

I found that I managed to encourage participation best when I asked a question that conveyed that I hoped it might help to clarify things. For example, instead of saying, 'How much is two and two, Ben?' I would say, 'Ben, considering so and so, what would you say makes two and two?' In asking questions in that way, I also hoped I might manage to convey that I did not wish to test, gain attention, or assert authority. It was rather that I favoured an enquiring approach. I should perhaps add that print does not convey the tone in which something is asked, but readers will know that tone is an important matter here. What is for sure, is that genuine learning is not the same as playing quiz games. That's for tv. And questions should surely not be seen as opportunities to show who is the brightest of them all.

With young learners, teachers might first ask a question that requires the recall of information, but good teachers will follow that with a question that seeks a reasoned reply. Many research findings lend support to such a view, for it has been found that the kinds of questions learners are asked, helps to determine the kind of learning that ensues. For example, if learners are asked only factual questions, they tend to process the material to be learnt in a superficial manner. But if they are asked questions that require some 'thinking', they tend to process the material more deeply.[5]

A word on what is meant by 'thinking' might be helpful here. A question that stimulates thinking is one that helps learners to see links between facts. That helps them to grasp a pattern, and readers might recall a previous chapter in which the importance of pattern was noted. Another kind of question that promotes thinking is one that helps learners to see the difference between a symptom and a cause. For example, in teaching history, one might ask students to consider whether Hitler caused the Second World War, or whether he was the kind of leader likely to be produced by the conditions prevalent in Germany after the First World War. Or, in teaching child development, one might ask students to consider whether a child's stealing reflects something about the child, or its environment. Another kind of question that promotes thinking is one that helps learners to see why an inference might (or might not) be justified. And perhaps nothing encourages thinking more than a practical project, especially one that is of an experimental or observational nature, and which comes at the beginning, rather than at the end, of a course.

The above indicates that good questions probe below the surface, and help learners to discern an underlying structure. That is important because most structures are hidden from casual view. Recall, for example, that it is quite impossible to see or feel the force called gravity; or to grasp via common sense the process called photosynthesis that makes leaves green. Indeed, one of the most important results of being educated is that it alerts us to the need to look beyond surface features if we wish to understand many things. Consider ice-floes.

Beginner teachers sometimes find it difficult to frame questions that require learners to think, especially in the middle of a lesson. If so, they might find it helpful to jot down before a lesson the questions they could ask. Eventually, with practice, one gets used to framing higher-level questions. One then feels embarrassed about asking the childish kind that can be answered with two words.

It has also been found that good teachers seldom need to:

a) rephrase their question, or
b) answer their own question.

There are probably two reasons that cause teachers to do these things. One, that they have not managed to make themselves clear. And a second that is more important. Recall here that, when a teacher asks a question, it usually follows on from what was said before; and the link between the two will be clear to a teacher. But it might not be clear to the learners. So, they sit there, looking interested, vacant or bored. Teachers are then tempted to rephrase their question, or to answer it themselves; but, if they do, they are unlikely to help their learners. Teachers then often repeat their question; and in that way, they are sometimes able to wring an answer out of one of the learners. However, it will then often be incomplete or wrong.

Earlier I suggested that, when that happens, it is a good idea to ask a learner how he or she has got to that answer. If this is done in a friendly way, the learner will explain. A teacher will then usually be able to see what point that learner has reached; and he or she can then go there, and help that learner to extricate him or herself from the thicket. In other words, an answer to a question can help a teacher to enter a learner's frame of reference, and that can provide a teacher with opportunities for clarification. And if a teacher is consistent in going about things like that, learners are likely to see that such a practice serves a useful purpose, and might be more willing to participate.

When teachers are about to introduce a new topic to a class, some sometimes ask whether one of the learners knows anything about it. But I found that, when I encouraged a learner to introduce a new topic, that learner seldom knew the topic thoroughly enough to do this well. And when the latter occurred, I had to do some correcting. The learner who had spoken then sometimes felt put down, and the other learners gained a confused view. Those experiences convinced me that it is better to introduce a new topic myself, and only then to ask for reactions to it.

One more detail before this chapter ends, and with it, a return to its beginning. No matter what the seating arrangements in a class, many learners tend to choose the same seat each lesson. They have a right to do that, of course, but, if they always sit in the same place, they usually find themselves in the same group in each lesson, and that can limit their experiences. So, I mention this, in the hope that it might encourage them to take a different seat now and again. Many hesitate, but some take my point and move around.

Chapter 20

Discussing

Like most teachers, I was sometimes asked a question in a lesson. When I was, I usually asked the learner who had asked the question what she thought might be the answer. I acted like that because, the moment a learner has asked a question, that learner has, I think, indicated an awareness of at least the nature of the answer. I also learnt that, when I returned a question like that, many learners were able to answer their own question; or they conveyed that they knew how they could find an answer. These things suggested to me that learners often ask a question to get corroboration for an answer they already have, or almost have in their head. I would have thought that being given a chance to state one's own answer, and finding that it is correct, or finding that one is heading in the right direction, is the best kind of corroboration.

Of course, learners do not always know the answer to a question they have asked. When that happened, I would turn to the others in the class and ask what they think. Nine times out of ten, somebody would suggest an acceptable answer; and, when no one was able to answer a question, and I was able to, I answered it myself. Occasionally, I wasn't able to answer a question, and when that happened, I (usually) said I couldn't. I would then ask the learner who had asked the question to find the answer for us. After all, it was her question. In short, I seldom answered a question. Instead, I usually returned it to the class; and I did that for primarily three reasons. One, in the belief that questions, not answers, must be kept in mind; two, to encourage the belief that answers are best found in one's own head; and three, in an attempt to encourage a spirit of cooperative enquiry.

For many years, 'brainstorming' was a much-favoured approach. As is well known, this term is applied to a process in which participants are invited to get into small groups, and to suggest any and every solution to a question that comes to mind. The important thing in this approach is to accept every suggestion made, no matter how absurd it might initially seem. For my part, I seldom found that the answers obtained in this way were better than what a single student might have found. This experience suggested to me that it is very important not to use brainstorming to avoid the need for serious study.

I noted earlier that some teachers sometimes say that their learners don't ask any questions, even when they ask them whether they have any. If one is using the transmission method of teaching, that is hardly surprising. Participation does not depend on whether a teacher invites it at a particular moment, but on whether it has been encouraged throughout a lesson. That comment might illustrate what I meant when I earlier suggested that 'communications' is best seen as a manifestation of everything that goes on in a lesson.

My experience also showed me that there is one question that is least likely to elicit a response, and it is the question, 'Are there any questions?' It is usually asked when a didactic teacher has finally ceased talking, and, if we have had to listen to somebody talk for an hour, we are usually relieved when he or she has finally stopped.

❧

It is usually the teacher who asks most of the questions in a lesson; but it might be an idea to consider that custom for a moment. After all, the answers we most appreciate tend to be the ones that we have ourselves elicited. If so, it looks as if teachers would help learners if they could encourage learners to ask more of the questions. Consider at this point findings from research, in which the way young children behave at home was compared with the way they behave at nursery school. Many customs are, after all, established in the early years. In this research, it was found that: 'teachers were in no position to satisfy the children's curiosity because the children hardly ever asked them any questions. The girls asked their mothers on average twenty-six questions an hour, but they only asked two questions an hour of their teachers. Nearly half the children (fourteen) asked five questions or less during two mornings at school, and a further three children asked no questions at all.'[1]

These researchers went on to report: 'of those questions that were asked at school, a much smaller proportion were "curiosity" questions and "why" questions, and a much larger proportion were "business" questions, of the "Where is the glue?" type.' The researchers also noted that challenging questions, or questions that suggested a child was trying to understand something, were entirely absent at school. Why do young children ask many intelligent questions at home, but hardly any at school? The researchers suggested two answers. One: that teachers consider it their job to ask questions and do so; and that, in doing so, they unintentionally convey that it is the teacher who asks the questions. And two: that the kinds of question teachers ask tend to be about what is going on in school; but children's questions at home tend to be about life in general; and it is, of course, the latter that naturally interests them the most. I draw attention to those findings because most people, of whatever age, try to find out what is going on around them. If so, it again looks as if it would be wise if teachers could contrive things so that it is the learners who ask more of the questions. But I do not have in mind here the factual questions that learners usually ask, but higher-order questions; and teachers can encourage these by inviting learners to elaborate on what they are asking.

Recall here also that creative scientists and artists often begin their work with a question. They ask: 'Why is this the way it is?' Or: 'How can I express that idea in a fresh and striking way?' The most creative among them are then sometimes able to answer their question. In other words, the most eminent scientists and artists are not people who know a lot. They often do know a lot. But, much more important than that, they are people who see questions where most people see only the prevailing answers. In short, being creative is first a matter of discovering a question!

One problem about encouraging learners to ask more questions is that much of our schooling obscures the obvious fact that there must be a question before there can be an answer; and this can cause learners to believe that answers are somehow 'out there', inside a textbook or in a teacher's head, waiting to be learnt. Perhaps that explains why some learners find classrooms rather unreal, for they are often places in which you are expected to learn an answer without first knowing what is the question.

How, then, can learners be encouraged to see and ask questions? Not the ones that ask for clarification about something a teacher has said, but the kind that children ask their mothers at home. Questions like: 'Why is water wet?' Or, 'Why does a cut hurt?' Again, readers might notice from these examples that powerful thinking depends, to a considerable extent, on seeing that it is often the most obvious things that are the most mysterious.

Recall here that, when people are told about new information, they often ask a few questions about it. The same is true of students, except that the questions students ask tend to be nearly always of a factual kind. That is, they seldom ask questions about any unstated assumptions, or any possible flaws in that information; and this propensity is probably generated by teachers, because many teachers tend to stress *knowing* information, rather than knowing and also evaluating it. If these things are roughly so, it would be beneficial if teachers could contrive things so that their learners ask more of the latter kind of questions.

⅄

For my part, I always tried to convey that knowledge usually comes about because somebody has asked or discovered a question; and I did this in one of two ways. Either I introduced a topic by drawing attention to the questions that had led researchers and scholars to give the answers that now constitute the 'subject' we were studying; or I invited the learners to say what they found problematic about a certain matter.[2]

Second, when I felt that the learners had begun to see the complexities involved in either of the above two cases, I outlined some of the answers that had been suggested; and I did so either with a short talk or by handing out brief material for examination. I have already described the kind of worksheets I used, and how the learners were invited to tackle them. Once I had handed out such material, I did as little explaining as possible, and encouraged the learners to tackle this material. I found that, if the material is of the right size and complexity, aside from eliciting answers it often raised further questions in the learners' minds, and I usually left things at that for the time being. Moreover, I never dictated anything, and I never talked with the expectation that notes would be taken.

Possibly as a result of going about things like that, a few learners in each class of mine would tell me, in the first few weeks after we had begun a course, that, although they had sometimes enjoyed a lesson, they did not feel they were learning very much. Others would say that they had very few notes, and could hardly remember what we did from one lesson to the next. Some of these learners were angry or upset when they said these things, and that made me feel upset as well. In response, I'd try to reassure. I'd say that our work in class was only an introduction, and that whatever real learning was going to take place, would do so when they got to work on their assignments. Most learners seemed reassured by this answer, but I fear that this was sometimes for the wrong reason, for many learners see assignments as tasks in which you reproduce information; and they tended to see assignments in this way because they had indirectly learnt at a young age that learning is the same as remembering.

But of course, learning is much more than remembering; and I have tried to show that this is the case throughout this book. I come now to this matter again more concretely, by describing what I consider is the essential place of assignments in learning and teaching. In a nutshell, I came to see that assignments should be seen as an essential part of the learning – not testing – process; and that assignments become a part of the learning process when learners are required to do two things:

1) learn something that has been carefully specified; and
2) *apply* what they have learnt to their personal or professional circumstances.

I found that, when these two things were done, learners often produced assignments that suggested they had, at least to some extent, 'really' learnt. I say 'to some extent', because learning never reaches an optimal level until learners use their learning practically in the real world. But work done for the kind of assignment outlined above appeared to lay a good foundation for doing work in the real world. Those assignments often conveyed a sense of immediacy, of 'felt experience', sometimes even of personal urgency. But it took quite some time before learners warmed to this approach; and there were often a few who seemed to find this approach confusing, for, as noted, previous experience had led them to believe that learning is a matter of remembering. Hence, they became upset when they were asked to *apply* their knowledge, rather than merely reproduce it.

The approach described above became self-evidently appropriate to me, even though, as noted, a number of learners usually found it difficult, and complained. This happened every year, and every year I was as surprised and dismayed as when it had happened the year before. The criticism most often made was that I am not 'clear'; and it took me some time to understand that, by 'clear', those learners meant a teacher who 'tells', rather than asks learners to consider a question. So, halfway through every course I taught, I felt that the approach I used must be somehow wrong, but also that I was unable to go back to teaching in a didactic manner even when I wanted to. So I would continue teaching as I had learnt to do, often feeling bad, often feeling clumsy, and sometimes feeling so bad I wanted to give up teaching altogether. But I continued, and, as a course wound on, I'd sometimes feel cheered by a word of approbation from a learner.[3] Then, as a course continued, a few learners began to smile in class. Later, as a course drew to an end, a few learners sometimes told me that they had never learnt so much. It was at times like these that I thought that teaching had perhaps become learning; and that, if it had, that was because the focus had been on questions, not answers. I very much hope that readers will see how such an approach is in line with what was noted about learning in the first Part of this book.

☙

Readers might have noticed that there was a considerable amount of talk in the lessons described above, and that some of this talk took the form of discussion. Such activities take time, and must be justified. But before I mention my justification, I had better note that it has nothing to do with such notions as 'progressive' teaching. I have no time for terms of this kind, for using them often bypasses the need to understand. My justification for encouraging discussion is related to what was noted in an earlier chapter on how we see. Readers might remember that I noted then that our brain never records anything as it is, but always processes experiences in terms of the schemas already in it. Teachers have repeated evidence of this. For, whenever they read or see work that their learners have done, they will see almost as many versions of that topic as there are learners. If so, it follows that, in any one class, there will be several different understandings, and misunderstandings, of a given topic. It also follows from what was noted about the process of perception, that it is not enough to state a fact loud and clear to ensure that it is understood. In short, the justification for encouraging discussion in a lesson is that it enables learners to find out whether they have understood something, or to clarify something.

People who teach a factual subject sometimes told me that they can see the point of having a discussion in a subject where it is possible to have a difference of opinion, but not in a subject where facts have to be learnt. I have already tried to show why such an objection misses the point. This is because the main reason for encouraging discussion is not so that opinions can be exchanged, but to enable learners to clarify their understanding.

It is also well known that, when people are faced by a problem, they tend to form a hunch (or hypothesis) about what the solution might be. They also tend to seek things that confirm their initial hunch, and ignore things that contradict it; and it can take a good deal of time, and a considerable amount of information, before people drop a mistaken hunch. These things being so, having a discussion can help to clarify a hunch, or persuade learners to consider forming a new one. In an attempt to encourage such discussions, I sometimes invited one of the learners to chair the discussion. To signal the switch, I got up and exchanged places with that learner. I found that most learners, even young ones, do well as a chairperson. Even unlikely seeming ones, often rise to the occasion and show qualities I had not noticed before. I also found that, when I acted in this way, usually quiet learners tended to participate more. Such an approach also gives learners more responsibility for what goes on in a lesson; and, with young ones, might contribute to preparing them to take their place in the world of work that is to come.

With mature students, I sometimes excused myself and left the room once a discussion had begun. I did that partly in an attempt to signal that it is the learners' lesson, and partly because I heard that more people participated when I left than when I remained. This might be because, when a teacher is present at a discussion, learners feel that having such a discussion is a rather contrived business, for there isn't much point in discussing anything if there is a teacher around who knows all the answers anyway.

I also found that one way to encourage a discussion was to set a problem, and then to ask learners to frame their hunches or hypotheses out loud. When that was done, another learner was likely to respond, and, in that way, a hypothesis would be tested. As we continued like this lesson after lesson, learners began to question their own hunches out loud; and, again in this way, they seemed to absorb a mode of thinking without realizing that it was happening. At this point, readers might recall an earlier chapter in which I described a lesson by a man called Frank who taught in a large computer company.

Most teachers would probably agree that it is important to have some evidence for believing whatever it is that one believes; and it is, after all, in part the ability to differentiate between evidence and opinion, which marks off intelligent discussion from hot air. It might be possible to remember facts by listening to a teacher, but it is impossible to learn how to come to a valid conclusion in that way. To come to a valid conclusion, one must have the repeated experience of weighing up the available evidence. But what, exactly, constitutes 'a valid conclusion'? I don't think it is easy to answer that question. A start might be to say that a valid conclusion is a conclusion that is consistent with what has gone before, is based on the best available evidence, and is open to rational debate.

I should perhaps add here that, by 'rational', is meant, among other things, an approach that always allows further sensible questions to be asked. For example, it is of course perfectly in order to believe in God. But it is not 'rational' for a believer to give as a reason: 'Because of faith', and this is so because no further questions are then possible. I had better emphasize here that none of the foregoing is intended as a criticism of faith; it is only intended as an illustration of what is meant by 'rational'.[4]

As I consider this matter of evidence very important, during a discussion in class I often found myself asking, 'What is the evidence for that statement?' After a time, this phrase became a sort of in-joke. For example, when a learner made a largish claim, another learner would sometimes grin sarcastically and say, 'Ah, but what's the evidence for that?!' I didn't like that sort of grin, but was secretly delighted at the question.

Here is an illustration of this process. One learner might say, 'Too much salt causes heart disease.' Another might respond with, 'How do you know?' The first speaker might say, 'Everyone knows that!' The second speaker might reply, 'Yes, but is that evidence?' It seems to me that requiring at least tentative evidence for any assertion made is one of the most important things that anyone can learn. Notice how this illustration suggests that having a dialogue can be very important in learning. In the course of a dialogue, learners often discover that things are seldom the way they first appear; in other words, that learning is often a matter of having to discard first assumptions, and grope for new ones. That can make learning and teaching quite an anxiety-provoking business.

Another feature of a good discussion is that it can sometimes enable learners to relate the facts under discussion to their own experiences. One will typically hear a learner say, 'Yes, but I couldn't do it that way because . . . ' and another learner might then say, 'But how about if you . . .?' When such an exchange takes place, a topic stops being merely a classroom exercise, and begins to take on possibilities in the real world.

Occasionally, I found it helpful to be more personal during a discussion. The subject I used to teach was learning and teaching, and the topic being considered in a given lesson might have been 'motivation'; and if a discussion on this had continued for some time, and become rather nebulous, I might have said, 'Here we are, talking about motivation in the abstract. But how do you, Susan, feel at present? Do you feel motivated right now?' Such an intervention can revitalize a discussion. Learners might say how frustrated, bored or involved they feel, and such comments can lead to an examination of the circumstances that cause such feelings. And of course, this can happen in a discussion on any topic.

Occasionally, a teacher might divide the learners into groups, and invite each group to consider a different question. When the groups have finished, a spokesperson in each group announces the conclusions of that group. As this is being done, the teacher notes the main points on a flip chart. The whole class then discusses these points in 'a plenary session'. I believe that this approach has merit in subjects like management training, in which the aim is often not so much to acquire new knowledge, as to refine and extend the knowledge one already has. But I doubt whether this approach generates much learning in most classrooms. Worse, when this approach is used in some classrooms, opinions tend to become confused with evidence, and the balance between studying something and discussing it tends to be weighed towards mere discussing. Most of the ideas thrown out will be put on a flip chart, and, in the nature of things, some will be half-baked. Teachers will hesitate to point this out, partly in order not to offend the speaker, partly in deference to the present fashion that holds that, as long as learners are encouraged to express ideas freely, learning will take place, and partly in line with the current culture of bogus democracy.

But anyone who knows anything about learning, will know that learning isn't a matter of exchanging opinions. It is a matter of demanding evidence, of being able to think critically, of seeing relationships, and of trying to state things accurately. To learn these things, is to learn a discipline. This awareness – that a subject is also a discipline – tends to be obscured in flip chart led discussions. Such discussions can also be very time consuming because many points tend to get discussed twice, once inside one's own group, and then by the whole class. Further, if each group has considered different questions, the learners never seriously consider more than a fraction of the material to be studied. And if the teacher does the flip chart act, he or she will tend to dominate the lesson. I would add that group work and discussions have been fashionable in some educational circles for many years, and I believe that they can easily be misused and overused. I would argue rather that discussions are useful after learners have studied new material, and as an aid to its clarification and consolidation.

Group work and discussions can easily go wrong. The same speakers might do most of the talking, and important points might arise and not be given the attention they deserve. Sensitive learners might hold back for fear of being considered pushy, and thoughtful ones might become irritated by the trivialities that are sometimes stated. Among younger learners, a discussion can become rowdy; and among older ones, there is sure to be someone who will bury a topic under a rubble of irrelevance. These things are not easy to deal with. Too much intervention on the part of a teacher might inhibit participation; and too little might cause some learners to feel that they are wasting their time. Rowdiness I'll deal with later. With the learners who talk too much, I found it best to suggest in a friendly way that others be given a chance to speak. When a discussion has continued for some time, it is often apparent that the attention of the learners has wandered, and I believe that a teacher must then intervene. At such times, I used to gather strands together, and restore a sense of purpose by introducing a new activity. Readers might here recall comments made in an earlier chapter on the importance of variety and good classroom management.

☙

Many teachers will have had the experience of preparing a lesson really well, intending to have a discussion at one point, and finding that a discussion either does not begin, or fizzles out quickly. Perhaps the teacher has been too keen to have a discussion, – after all, a discussion cannot be forced. Or perhaps the learners had had a test in a previous lesson, or perhaps something else happened that day. But a silent class can be deceptive. Provided that the learners had some direct access to the material to be learnt, a good deal of learning can take place without anyone saying anything. Sometimes, weeks after a seemingly unsuccessful lesson, a learner might say something that indicates that things of some importance were, after all, learnt in that lesson. When learners have had direct access to suitable lesson material, it will register somewhere. When that happens, the learners are just as likely to consider it outside a lesson as in it. We consolidate our learning best when we reflect on it, or are able to use it practically, and these things often happen long after a topic has been considered in a lesson.[5] But sometimes, discussions don't seem to develop in a certain class at all. When that continued for some time, I used to feel uneasy. In response, I would try to be friendly but not too personal. I would say, 'Our discussions haven't got off the ground lately. I wonder why?' Then I would sit back and wait. Obviously, the last thing to do is to make a speech about the need for participation. When I managed to put the matter fairly, and was patient, I usually got a reply. One of the more outspoken learners would usually say something. It might not have been complimentary, but it usually cleared the air. Discussions then sometimes got under way again.

The above was with adults. With schoolchildren, I sometimes took the same tack, and sometimes it worked and sometimes it did not. When the latter happened, I'd ask if something was wrong. That is a more personal kind of thing to do, but participation is a personal matter. When learners participate, they signal that they are willing to collaborate. So, I'd ask what is the matter. In reply, a more outspoken learner would sometimes say that they were bored. Or that they could not see the point of what we were doing, or that they were fed up. Sometimes a learner would say something critical about my teaching; and sometimes these comments were more than simply critical. I'd then sometimes feel so bad I wanted to give up teaching altogether. But, as time passed, I came to see that occasional attacks like these are inescapable. Genuine participation will only develop in a class when a teacher is reasonably open, and that involves taking some risk.[6] Not being too serious about these things, and some humour also help!

So, I would listen to these comments, and I'd say I'd think about them. I did think about them, and occasionally I felt I had learnt something from them. But quite often, I'd sense that these comments were not really about what they seemed to be about. Instead, they often struck me as being expressions of the resentment, anxiety or frustration sometimes inherent in being a learner. At other times, I had the impression they were intended to test a teacher, and I'll say a little more on that later.

Sometimes there is good participation in a class, but not by all the learners. Some sit there and hardly say a word. These quiet learners seem to be of two kinds.

One kind consists of those who prefer not to speak, but do not dislike discussions as such. The second kind dislikes discussions. The first kind also tends to be shy, or prefers to work alone. These learners can produce both good and poor work. The same holds for those who participate. In short, I learnt that the extent of a learner's participation in a lesson indicates little about the kind of work he or she otherwise does.

I used to try to speak privately and informally with every learner in my classes. To those who did not speak much in class, I'd say I had noticed that they don't say much, and I'd add that I would value any contribution they might care to make. Some replied that they had always been shy about speaking in public, and others would say that, by the time they were ready to say something, someone else had already said it. The thing that these learners most frequently said, was that the ones who participated seemed much more intelligent and articulate than they were. In reply, I'd say that I had often heard learners say this, and that I had often felt that way myself. Later, in class, I'd sometimes smile and call on one of these learners by name if I sensed that he or she might like to say something.

Such an approach sometimes helped. At other times it did not. Some people have a dread of self-disclosure. Others find it difficult to assert themselves enough to take part in a discussion. Others have a poor self-image, and stay silent for fear of saying something that might lower their self-esteem even more. Others stay silent to indicate their aloofness. Some learners only speak when certain other learners are absent. It is difficult to know what to do in such circumstances. A teacher must certainly try to encourage learners to participate. If one does not do this, and certain learners continue to remain silent, they can begin to assume the role of being 'a silent one'; and that role is then reinforced with each passing lesson. And if that continues for long enough, it becomes almost impossible for such learners ever to say a word.[7] But, if a teacher has been sympathetic, and done the best that he or she can, there comes a time when one must let such things rest. There is only so much any teacher can do. It is also true that some people gain just as much from listening as from talking. And learners of whatever age have just as much right not to participate as to participate.

So much for the first group. As was noted, the second group consists of learners who positively dislike discussions. When I asked learners in this group about this, I learnt that they want an unambiguous delivery of lesson material, and appear to believe that this would help them to pass their next exam. Their approach is strictly instrumental. They come to study in order to obtain a qualification. Notions like 'personal development', or 'self-expression' irritate them; and, if you say that simply listening to a teacher is unlikely to generate much learning, you irritate them even more. They don't like discussing things! These experiences of mine are corroborated by the work of several researchers. For example, one of the earlier and best I came across was Lauren Wispé, and she reported the following findings.[8]

She found that learners tend to fall into three groups: 23 per cent who like discussions; 51 per cent who do not; and 26 per cent who tend to be satisfied with whatever kind of teaching they get. These proportions probably vary, and are likely to be affected by the climate of the times, but I found that those proportions held largely for my classes. Wispé also found that learners held these preferences very strongly; so that those who like direction want more of it, even when they are getting a great deal of it; and learners who like discussions tend to want more of them, even when they are getting a great many of them.

Wispé also investigated the personality of these learners. She found that the ones who like discussions tend to be academically able, and fairly secure and independent individuals. Those who dislike discussions, and prefer a more didactic approach, tend to be academically weaker, and appear less secure. She also found that the latter kind of learners tend to be 'very critical, of lessons, instructors and fellow-learners'. They even expressed 'hatred of an open approach'. On the other hand, the learners who prefer a more open approach, including lots of discussions, tend to express themselves as 'moderately favourable' towards lessons in general. I draw attention to these findings because they suggest that, no matter what a teacher might do, some learners will be unhappy with the approach taken. In response to this situation, Wispé suggested that it might be an idea to match learners with teachers. That is, let the learners who prefer a didactic approach have teachers who prefer that; and let the learners who prefer a more open approach have teachers who prefer that. On the face of it, this seems a sensible proposal, but it raises many questions. For example, is the aim of teaching no more than helping learners to acquire knowledge? Shouldn't a teacher also try to encourage learners to evaluate knowledge? And if the latter, can that be done by 'telling'? Furthermore, the material on learning outlined in the first Part of this book indicates that the transmission method of teaching does not rest on anything known about how human beings best learn.

For my part, I found such findings helpful. However, rather than accommodate my teaching to the possible inclination of some of my learners, I persisted in encouraging discussions when I thought they would help the learning process; and I found that some of the learners who had initially expressed resentment at time 'lost' in discussions, increasingly took part in them. Interestingly enough, I found that this development was helped when I drew attention to the findings noted above. I also found that the attitude of some of these learners – all tutors in their own right – then became ambivalent. On the one hand, they participated more in my classes, and encouraged participation in their own; many even became proficient at encouraging participation in their classes. But, in discussing my teaching, and that of others who encourage participation, they continued to be critical about things like 'time lost', and the absence of 'clear objectives'.

The above findings and observations indicate that participation is not just a technical matter, but is probably also related to personality.[9] It is as if some people who are critical of discussions can see their educational value; but, as they have an authoritarian personality, they feel uncomfortable when someone in a position of some authority, like a teacher, is not authoritarian. But then, it is a truism that human beings are complex creatures. And if that is so, it is hardly surprising that teachers sometimes become aware of ambivalent feelings in their class. Coal miners have to put up with dirty and dangerous conditions, bus drivers with obnoxious drivers and traffic jams, and teachers with the vagaries of human nature. It could be worse.

৶

It might appear from the above that I am suggesting that an absence of participation in a class must be due to something inside a teacher, or inside a learner. But there is another possibility. Most teachers teach because they want to; and the majority probably feel that the material they teach is worth teaching. But their learners might not think so. They might be there because they have to be there. This is because, in developed countries, pupils must attend school because that is what the law requires, and older learners often attend classes because they have been sent. Many others attend, not because they are particularly interested in a subject, but because they wish to obtain a qualification that will enable them to earn a living. Furthermore, a good deal of schooling is not simply a matter of acquiring useful knowledge. It is also about winning a kind of hurdle race that determines who gets what of the national cake.[10] Many learners are prepared to put up with course material they consider irrelevant, and with teachers whom they consider boring, in order to take part in that race. But, in view of the circumstances just outlined, it would not be surprising if some learners felt reluctant to partici-pate. In short, teachers work inside a system that is to a considerable extent coer-cive, and coercion does not encourage participation. It is also the case that the main interest of many learners is social. That is, they are often most concerned with who they will be sitting next to in a lesson, and who they hope to meet during the next break; and, in such a system of values, lesson material tends to be seen as a secondary matter. However, I found that, once inside a classroom, and provided that the teacher has some insight into how participation might be encouraged, many learners will be prepared to participate. Perhaps that is due to the social interests I have just noted, and because participating is usually more interesting than not participating.

I also found that the extent to which learners participate varies from country to country. I have no empirical evidence for that assertion, but it has certainly been my experience that, in some countries, learners participate more readily than in others. After all, you can travel for hours by public transport in England, and people sitting close to each other might not exchange a single word. If so, it is hardly surprising if that also sometimes happens in an English classroom. Go back far enough, and child-rearing practices will probably come into it.[11]

Chapter 21

Difficult Lessons

We don't usually discuss our failures except with close friends, and perhaps that explains why I have not come across many books on teaching in which the author describes what it feels like to have a bad lesson. One book in which there are such descriptions is by Wittenberg, and it did me good to read what she wrote. I had many poor lessons, and this writer helped me to understand why some of them made me feel so bad.[1]

When I began to teach, I used to think it was my fault when I had a bad lesson, but there came a time when I felt less guilty. This came about when I grasped that not every learner is a paragon of virtue; and, if we think about the world around us – from how some people drive a car, to how the people of one race sometimes act towards the people of another race – we remember that human beings can treat each other dreadfully. Unfortunately, the irrational nature of much human behaviour is seldom discussed in the current literature on teaching, especially the teaching of adults.[2] In my own years of teaching, I often noticed how full of quirks and difficulties a great many learners are. Especially adult learners. And of course, teachers, too. And classrooms are not neutral places like parks. They can generate a considerable amount of stress. But it is probably best to begin with simple difficulties.

One sometimes has a bad lesson because one has not prepared for it, and, life being what it is, one then pays. But anyone who has taught knows that to teach well is very difficult, so it isn't possible to get it right each time; and always, one is dealing with the most complicated things on earth: other people! These things being so, it is hardly surprising that some lessons go wrong; and it would therefore seem best not to blame oneself too much, but to try to use the occasion to learn something from it.

A more subtle difficulty can arise when one teaches an examinable subject, for a teacher is then sometimes tugged in opposite directions. Teachers are in the business of trying to help their learners, but they must also try to safeguard the needs of their community. It does not matter if they are teaching children or electricians. Always teachers must try to reconcile their wish to help their learners to achieve individual competence, with the need of their community to have competent practitioners. An effective teacher manages to achieve both aims most of the time, but that can be difficult, especially in today's climate when so much emphasis is placed on meeting the needs of 'the individual'.

Another difficulty teachers sometimes have is that the more they offer, the more some of their learners seem to want. Provide variety in lessons, and some learners will want more variety. Pass around lots of handouts, but ask to have the longer ones back, and one learner is sure to complain that they are not allowed to keep handouts, while others complain that they are given too many. Give out a guide for doing assignments that is into its seventh rewrite, and someone is sure to say that it isn't clear. Such reactions are especially common among learners who are used to a didactic approach. When a more open approach is introduced, some learners respond in the same way that some people respond when they get their first taste of democracy. Their demands run beyond the bounds of the possible. I remember here an occasion when the college in which I then worked carried out a market survey. One of the questions in the survey asked students what they thought of the building. The range of responses was amazing. What to some people was 'pleasant', to others was 'smelly, tatty, dirty'.

Another problem teachers have is that they personify a figure of some authority. That is the case no matter how old the learners, or how much a teacher tries to foster a spirit of independence. Learners bring their prevailing attitude into every classroom, and some people's attitude to any kind of 'authority' can be very negative. But that is hardly surprising, for not everyone has had the good fortune to have had decent parents. The foregoing is most easily seen when it comes to assessments. If a course is examinable, a teacher must indicate whether the learners have reached a satisfactory level of competence (even when the teacher is not responsible for the final grade given). This inevitably makes some learners feel vulnerable, and that can make some of them aggressive.

Some learners turn their disappointment with their difficulties inward; others, the extra-punitive kind, take it out on a teacher. They will complain bitterly about not having been given enough time, about things not having been explained clearly, about how boring they have found lessons, how irrelevant most of the material has been, and how only the teacher's word seems to count. They will be biting, even savage in their criticism. That can hurt! One way of dealing with such difficulties is to teach with another teacher. Unlike most other professions, teaching is usually an individual activity. When two teachers can work together in a class, the kinds of difficulties just noted are sometimes easier to deal with. However, team-teaching can also cause difficulties. If two teachers are to work effectively together, they must collaborate closely beforehand, and that can take a lot of time. They will also have to have similar orientations and enjoy each other's company, and it isn't easy to find someone with whom one can work that closely.

At other times it might be appropriate to call bluffs. Many years ago, when I was working in a school, I had a pupil in one class who caused many problems. One day, I found myself saying to him, in a friendly way, that I believed he was causing difficulties because he was scared he couldn't cope with the lesson material, and that playing up was his way of taking the easy way out. I added that I believed he could cope, – if he were prepared to take the risk. He laughed and played up some more. But to my surprise, a subtle, and then a marked change occurred. He began to work, and both his behaviour and his learning improved.

When I felt that things had become difficult in a certain class, I sometimes suggested that some learners might like to work on their own. I have of course adult learners in mind here. I used to say this in a friendly way, and did not mention any names. I'd add that it was not in my power to excuse anyone from class, but that any learner who so wished should feel free to work in the library during my lessons, and that I'd be glad to offer suggestions about reading material. I'd also say that I would not be offended if anyone left in this way. On the rare occasions I took that tack, a learner sometimes chose to work on his or her own. Mostly he or she later asked to come back, and I of course always agreed. Perhaps that learner had missed the company of the other learners. Whatever the case, I found that the main effect of suggesting that learners might like to work on their own was to clear the air. And if certain learners would prefer to work in this way, why not? Some people do best on their own.

Another difficulty that teachers sometimes have is that they can pose a threat to their learners. This is because all real learning implies change, and change, as is well known, can be very difficult. That can be a serious problem in some subjects. For example, in the subject I taught, teaching, one is unlikely to evoke much hostility if one suggests that a teacher must remember not to talk to a blackboard when addressing a class. The obvious usually goes down quite well. But consider the likely effect if you suggest that teaching has to stop before learning can begin. The non-obvious tends to cause some hesitation, disbelief, even resentment. At the very least, we are seldom indifferent to the new. Over the years, I learnt that quite a few learners seem to resent anything that probes, or that challenges the accepted view; but teaching is often a matter of suggesting that the obvious is not so obvious after all. Hence, the more probing the teaching, the greater the possible threat. No wonder Socrates and Jesus died in the way they did.

Another difficulty arises when one teaches a subject about which people have had some experience. One such subject is teaching; and students will have had at least ten years' experience of it! So a common response to subtle research regarding teaching can be: 'So what?' or 'Fancy that!' In Haste's memorable phrase, such responses suggest a case of 'assimilating new material into existing schemata with the minimum of cognitive disturbance'.[3] The same reactions occur in classes on subjects like child development or politics. I recall to this day the amazement of some students in a course on politics I attended many years ago, as they slowly discovered that almost everything that they had believed turned out to be false. In nearly every class I taught, there were one or two learners whose faces fell whenever I tried to go beyond the obvious. As long as we were talking about something relatively straightforward, most learners seemed content. But the moment I struggled to get past the obvious, a grimace of boredom was sure to appear.[4] Whenever I caught sight of such a look, I felt a sense of despair. I wondered whether my understanding was cockeyed, or whether I was simply a poor teacher. Next day I wasn't so sure. I'd ask myself if everyone is generous enough to acknowledge a contribution, or if everyone really is interested in the new. And if learning implies change, does it follow that every person will want to learn, even if responsibility for the learning is passed to him or her?

The term 'creative' carries much kudos today. But even a little reading soon indicates that the most truly creative people have often been considered misguided or fools by their contemporaries. Consider an example taken from the world of painting. As is well known, the group of painters commonly called Impressionists have had a powerful effect. Not only were many later painters greatly influenced by them, they also influenced all the decorative arts. And, as these painters taught us to see in a new way, it seems fair to say that they were 'teachers' of a kind. Here, now, some comments on these 'teachers' by a contemporary of theirs. The first is a critic writing in an influential newspaper: 'The impression made by the impressionists is that of a cat walking over the keyboard of a piano, or of a monkey that has laid hands on a paint box.' Another critic wrote: 'Cézanne can only be a bit of a madman, afflicted while painting with delirium tremens. . . . In truth, it is only one of the weird shapes generated by hashish, borrowed from a swarm of absurd dreams. . . . No audacity can surprise us. But when it comes to landscapes, M. Cézanne will allow us to pass in silence; we confess that they are more than we can swallow.'[5] Are people less bigoted today?

It might be objected here that the response I outlined above is quite common in the arts, but not in factual subjects, so here is one of the foremost scientists of the previous century, Max Planck. He wrote, 'It is one of the most painful experiences of my entire scientific life that I have but seldom – in fact, I might say, never – succeeded in gaining universal recognition for a new result, the truth of which I could demonstrate by a conclusive, albeit only theoretical proof. This is what happened this time, too. All my sound arguments fell on deaf ears. It was simply impossible to be heard against the authority of men like Ostwald, Helm, and Mach. . . . The universal acceptance of my thesis was ultimately brought about by considerations of an altogether different sort, unrelated to the arguments which I had produced in support of it – namely, by the atomic theory, as represented by Boltzmann.' And Planck concluded: 'This experience gave me an opportunity to learn a fact – a remarkable one, in my opinion: a new scientific truth does not triumph by convincing its opponents and making them see the light, but rather because its opponents eventually die, and a new generation grows up that is familiar with it.'[6] I read comments such as these by a man who was truly creative, and ask whether people really are keen to expand their understanding. Does everyone strive to be self-aware?

Here is another difficulty I sometimes encountered while teaching. In a previous chapter, I noted that I did not usually comment on what a learner had just said, and that, instead, I tried to convey my interest and appreciation by listening carefully; and further, that I did my best to encourage other learners to comment. In response to such behaviour, a few learners would tell me that they felt I did not really value their contributions. They even maintained this after I had assured them that I did value their contributions. At such times, I would find myself wondering, yet again, to what extent I was responsible for what happened in a class. For one thing was clear: there were always a few learners who believed that I have attitudes that I do not have. I learnt from this that teachers sometimes serve as a kind of screen, onto which learners project some of their hopes and fears. But none of this is surprising. For, as indicated in the chapter on schemas, we do not simply react to the events around us. It is rather that the events around us trigger reactions already inside us.

Occasionally, when I felt that I had got into a rut with a class, I remembered that, when some actors sense they have got into a rut after playing a certain part for a long time, they try to imagine their role in a new light. I believe it is a serious mistake to equate teaching with performing, but I sometimes found it helpful to try to imagine what it might be like to take a new approach with a class.

ℒ

It has often been noticed that, when people are in a group, they sometimes act in a way different from how they act when they are on their own. An early analysis of this difference can be found in Freud's comments on the work of LeBon.[7] This work is now a hundred years old, but I believe it can still help to explain why learners sometimes behave in a class in the way they do. When shorn of the psychoanalytic sub-structure, the points made in the above work might be summarized like this:

1) As a group consists of a number of people, those in it are likely to feel stronger than when they are on their own. If so, being in a group might make people feel more able to express and act on certain wishes. Wishes, for their part, can be conscious or unconscious; and an important difference between the two is that unconscious wishes are sometimes unconscious in part because some would be considered anti-social.
2) People in a group seem inclined to fall in with a common aim. That is, people in a group are often inclined to adopt the sentiments of a few members.
3) When the above occurs, some members of a group can perform at a level far beyond their usual capacity; and such performances can be moral or immoral, brave or cowardly, sublime or bestial.

In short, when people are in a group, they sometimes behave in an unusual manner, and experienced teachers will have noticed this more than once. Most will also know that the most effective way of responding to such behaviour is to listen, not to take the matter too seriously, and to be as cheerfully accommodating as possible. However, if that behaviour is potentially destructive, and if the responses just noted do not work, one must act with unobtrusive and quiet firmness. Moreover, teachers who practise an open approach are more likely to encounter destructive behaviour than teachers who practise a didactic one. The former are also more likely to become aware of various undercurrents in a class. For example, in every class there is likely to be some approval, some hostility, some indifference, and lots more that is difficult to fathom.

A consideration of group dynamics might help to shed additional light on these matters. For example, in observing groups, Bion found that a group might consist of a bunch of children determining an outcome, a committee trying to decide a course of action, a dozen managers conferring about policy, or a class of students discussing a topic. In such situations, the surface features of the situation seem clear, but, when people are in a group, all kinds of undercurrents are often generated.[8] One kind of current is generated when certain people in a group want a charismatic leader, and an example of this is when a few learners in a class want a teacher to clear up all ambiguities. If they get such a leader, they are pleased; if not, they are disappointed, and show this. But most teachers are not charismatic, and the best have no wish to be. They are mature people who do not have an itch to shine. They prefer their learners to shine. Nor do they want to clear up all ambiguities. On the contrary, they deliberately create manageable ambiguities that will enable their learners to 'really' learn.

Another kind of current is generated when, in a stressful situation, certain people in a group 'attack' or 'run away'. Most classes contain a few learners who are inclined to help things along; but there are also likely to be a few who prefer to find fault. A third kind of current is generated when certain people jettison the group, and pair off. One manifestation of this in a class is when two learners work together to undermine a teacher. A teacher might have said something quite reasonable, and one of the learners might then say, 'But as Rachel was saying before: it isn't always like that. You have to take a broader view. It's simplistic to say . . .' The teacher who had spoken had probably not remotely suggested that things are always any kind of way. He had probably stated a generality because the whole of science, and even common sense, is based on being able to generalize. And the last thing he or she had done was to make things 'simplistic'. But when learners repeat the kind of criticism quoted above, the effect is to sabotage a lesson or to undermine the credibility of a teacher, and a teacher must then brush off such interventions, or object in no uncertain terms.

The important thing to remember about the kind of currents noted above is that they are often prompted by factors below conscious awareness. But it is unwise to suggest such a thing, for that is likely to antagonize the participants even more. In any case, classes are not encounter groups, and teachers are not psychotherapists. I would have thought it enough if a teacher is simply aware of such things, for he or she might then be in a better position to deal with them.

At this point, I must confess to an embarrassment, and it has two sources. One stems from the fact that, in noting Freud and Bion, I have referred to a psychoanalytic source; and, to my mind, this source rests at best on clinical evidence, and this is suspect because clinicians – like most of us – tend to see what their theory predisposes them to see. The other source of this embarrassment stems from the fact that, at several places in this book, I have emphasized the importance of having some evidence for what one asserts, and I have just confessed that I consider suspect the evidence I have used.[9] I have nevertheless decided to retain the above comments on the nature of groups, for many years of experience suggested to me that they have some validity. Perhaps I might next relate a rather personal but factual episode to indicate what I have in mind.

One year, I had a class with which I felt I was getting on reasonably well. One day, as I was returning assignments, I said that several students had done less well with that particular assignment than might have been expected, and that I had tried to indicate in my comments how those assignments could be improved. I added that I hoped that a certain student, whom I then named, would not mind if I said that, in her assignment, she had dealt with the topic well, and that, if she agreed, the other students might like to look at her assignment. There was no response to that comment, and I thought no more of it. I was therefore very surprised soon after to hear, from my then head of department, that my students were very angry, and wished to have a meeting with her and me. I should perhaps list here the people on that course whom I best remember. They included: three weak students, one of whom derided the approach taken in this book; two police officers of different age and rank; a highly intelligent, attractive and destructive young woman; the woman whose work I had commended and who seemed silently angry with me; a man who taught law about whom I noticed mostly a kind of blandness; one black student of quiet integrity who unobtrusively distanced herself from the others; and a dozen who took the usual uncommitted stance. The meeting began pleasantly enough, but, very soon, I found myself attacked in a manner that seemed so critical and irrational I was often at a loss for words when I tried to respond. I also found it very painful that what I had thought had been some of my best efforts were sharply criticized, and by people whom I had thought favourably inclined towards what I was trying to do. Throughout, the head remained silent, as did another member of staff who was also present.

In retrospect, I felt that what had happened was a kind of lynching; and, as is common when a lynching takes place, I never did manage to understand clearly by what it was motivated. However, the material on groups I outlined above suggested to me that what I had experienced was common enough; and readers might recall my mentioning near the beginning of this book that a tutor in my training college underwent a similar experience while I was there. In conclusion, I found the above experience very distressing, but what has remained with me years after, is its irrational nature. This is perhaps especially so because, after that course had ended, one of the police officers who had been highly critical of me at that meeting sought me out, and told me that he had not intended any animosity. And in the evaluation sheets of the course handed in at its end, the comments made were largely favourable, and there was no mention whatsoever of anything said at that meeting.

Episodes of the above kind are fortunately rare, but some frictions in teaching are common. When the latter occurs, and when I meet that class again, I try saying something wry, or mildly amusing; and, in general, I found that, if one lets things blow over, they blow over. Learners who have never spoken sometimes chip in, and one can usually continue working. But it remains a fact that an open approach elicits all kinds of responses, and not all of them will be positive.

There is one sure way of having problems, and that is to expect them. If one goes into a classroom expecting to have problems, one's manner will tend to be seen as antagonistic, and that is likely to elicit a like response. If one walks into a classroom cheerfully, responses are more likely to be cheerful. I speak from experience![10] The alternative is to go back to didactic teaching. That way one is safe. The angry learners then hide their hostility and express it elsewhere.

Unlike anything I have read in the books on teaching that have come my way, I sometimes had a learner in a class who seemed bent on destroying lessons. With school pupils, there are usually accepted sanctions a teacher can use in such a situation. With older learners, things can be more complicated, and I was sometimes at a loss as to what course to take. Sometimes I felt like walking out, but that is clearly the last thing one should do. In such a situation, I half-expected the other learners in a class to help me, but none ever did. No matter how badly a certain student behaved, the others seemed most unwilling to intervene. Occasionally, I even felt that the other students enjoyed my discomfort. It was as if they had a need to see me in the hot seat for a change. Perhaps this is because there can be some anxiety and resentment in being a learner, and there is often one person in a group who will express such feelings for the others. If there is some truth to that conjecture, it follows that a teacher should sometimes consider responding to the group, not to the student who has expressed what the group might be feeling. Otherwise, that one learner will be turned into a scapegoat for the rest.

From situations like the above, I learnt that students expect a teacher to cope; and I would have thought that students could learn a lot from such examples of coping. After all, whether they like it or not, teachers serve to some extent as role models. I also learnt that, no matter how hostile a situation might become, one must never get into a slanging match with a learner. True, teachers are people, but they also have a professional role to play. But, as I see it, a role isn't something behind which one hides. It is rather something that helps one to avoid contaminating the professional enterprise with the merely personal. In this way, it signals that there is a common task at hand that is more important than the wishes or inclinations of certain individuals.

Sometimes, when faced by the kind of difficulties outlined above, I wondered whether I shouldn't perhaps be more open. Perhaps I should confess that I feel hurt and inept; and perhaps, if I said such things, my students would sympathize and respond constructively. Although I sometimes had such thoughts, I never acted on them; and I did not, because I believe that learners have a right to expect to have some faith in a teacher. In that respect, I think that being a teacher is a little like being a physician. That is, it is generally agreed that the extent to which physicians are able to help us does not depend only on how much they know, but also on how much faith we have in them. Hence, a physician who confesses ineptitude – rather than occasional ignorance – is unlikely to help us much. In short, I believe that the extent to which a teacher should disclose personal feelings, should be governed by the extent to which he or she believes that such disclosures will aid the learning enterprise, not him or her.[11] So, in a difficult situation, I would count to five, try not to take the matter too personally, and get on with the task at hand. Humour can be a great help at such moments, but it is easier to write this than to act on it!

With an especially difficult learner, I used to try a friendly approach first. I'd ask him or her to come for a chat, and I'd try to be quietly myself, not some authority figure. And when I did that, some learners opened up, and all kinds of difficulties were sometimes aired. When I began to teach, I used to find such an experience encouraging, even flattering, and I tried my best to help. But I discovered in time that it is best not to go too far in that direction. Not only can this process become very time consuming, it can also become highly complex. This is because the aims of counselling and the aims of teaching can differ in certain important respects. For example, whereas counselling is often a matter of being primarily supportive, a teacher must sometimes be primarily demanding, as, for example, when work is not handed in. And sometimes it is difficult to reconcile such aims. For reasons such as this and many others, when a serious difficulty arose with a learner, I often found it best to refer him or her to a superior or to a counsellor.

Very occasionally, one might have an especially aggressive learner in one's class. With that kind of learner, it is obviously best to try to avoid situations that are likely to generate aggression. This kind of learner seems to respond best to a calm and professional manner. All one can do is to play things by the book. In such circumstances, I tried to convey the following in a straightforward manner. I'd say that it was my job to get certain things done; that this is a part of an organizational endeavour; that there is a limit to the amount of difficulty any organization is able to tolerate; and that, if that learner pushed too hard, I and the organization would have to act in order to protect this endeavour. In short, in a non-threatening way, I'd try to persuade that learner to be more realistic.

Occasionally I had a class – more exactly, a few individuals in a class – whom I found an ordeal no matter what I tried to do. Such a situation was always made worse when I knew I could not count on support from higher up. In fact, I cannot remember a single instance when the two problems were not present together. When I knew I had the support of colleagues and managers, I had the confidence to tackle difficulties with a mixture of consultation, good humour, steadiness and self-reflection. When I knew I did not have such backing, I was unsure; and that always made things worse. In the field of education, superiors can be negative or positive, the same as anywhere else; but many in this field moved into administration because they do not like teaching, and some, I discovered, then have ambivalent feelings about teachers, especially teachers who take an unconventional approach. Nor do administrators have much real contact with learners except when one of the latter complains, and then some administrators use such opportunities to show how 'responsive' they are. I will only add that, in the case of a serious conflict, it is essential to keep written notes of dates and events; and it is also essential to adopt a professional approach – rather than a personal one – and to be cheerful, remain calm, and not be too ready to accept the other person's agenda.

&

There are writers who would maintain that my calling certain classroom behaviour 'aggressive' is merely self-indulgent, even destructive, and that such labelling obscures the real issue.[12] The real issue, they would argue, is that all systems of knowledge are social constructs; that the main function of all such systems is to serve the needs of those in power; and that the behaviour I have called 'aggressive' is a justified reaction against a fundamentally coercive social system that uses what passes for 'knowledge' to keep wealth and power in the hands of those who already have them. These writers would add that I have understandably been made a target of aggression, because I am the unwitting agent of that unjust social system.

Such writers might also maintain that, in labelling someone 'aggressive', rather than 'dissenting', I have devalued, even degraded a person whose behaviour is functional. For, instead of attempting to examine what such behaviour might tell us about the society in which we live, I try to silence it because it threatens my own power. Moreover, I am aided in this by an army of administrators, psychologists and policemen, all of whom unwittingly act with me as agents of social control. Such alienated behaviour on our part enables those in power to retain their power.

In response to the above, I would say, first, that I believe there is some truth to such a view, and I stress that word 'some', for there are levels of injustice. Without question, there are profoundly unjust social systems in many parts of the world, and that includes some Western countries. However, in this chapter, I have in mind countries in which the social system is at least halfway reasonable.

Second, even when a so-called democratic country has an unjust social system – as I believe is often the case – it does not follow that aggressive behaviour towards an individual is caused by an unjust social system. I suspect that, when a learner acts aggressively towards an individual teacher, that aggression is more likely to be caused by unjust personal rather than social circumstances. The way that people behave is, of course, always embedded in, and related to, a given social system. But that does not imply a direct causal relationship between a social system and an individual act.

Third, the above writers do not make clear what an individual teacher might do to combat an unjust social system. Until they do, I can see no reason why a teacher should not use an existing system to draw attention to the unjust social system in which it is embedded. And fourth, I consider the belief, that 'all systems of knowledge are social constructs' has more the attributes of a fashionable slogan than a scholarly hypothesis – a topic to which I shall return. Lastly, I believe that, although teachers must be sensitive to such issues, in going about their daily work, both they, and their learners, have the right to expect that the people around them will behave in a way that makes personal life tolerable.

&

I would summarize like this. When I began to teach, I used to feel that it was my fault if a lesson did not go well. That made me feel bad; but, as time passed, I grasped that teachers do not carry all the responsibility for what goes on in a lesson. On the contrary, I realized that parents and society at large often contribute more than teachers to the unfortunate events that sometimes occur in a lesson; and I also realized that teachers are often made the scapegoat for these events. In short, there is only so much any one teacher can do; and, if one has done that, that's that. If the worst comes to the worst, the end of a course will always come. Then one can go one's separate ways. In the meantime, one can cheer oneself up by remembering classes in which things went better. Teaching has its difficult times, just like any other profession.

Chapter 22

Learning a New Approach

This chapter is on the difficulties and rewards that the tutors and instructors with whom I worked experienced when they tried to adopt the kind of approach to teaching described in this book. I begin by recalling a lesson I described in an earlier chapter, namely, the lesson that I and 160 other learners attended, and in which there was considerable participation. While I was on that same course, there was an elective on cognition, and I decided to take it. There were about 15 of us in that class, and the man who taught it – also a specialist in teacher education – began his first lesson by saying that he did not think anyone would learn much if he lectured. He added that he soon got tired of hearing his own voice; that he proposed to run his classes in the form of seminars; and that he thought we would all learn more if we discussed things. For the rest of the term we heard mainly his voice.

That experience strengthened my conviction that we tend to speak most about what we would like, rather than what is the case. Perhaps that is why so much love poetry is about the lady who wouldn't say yes. I begin like this to draw attention to a fact about which I wrote in an earlier chapter. That fact is that, if one wants to know something, it isn't enough to want to know it, one must also *act* on it; and readers might recall that I drew attention to this fact when I described the difference between verbal knowledge and experiential knowledge.

I am sure that the teacher who I described above would have liked to have had more participation in his class, but, as noted, such wanting isn't enough. Many books on teaching make it appear that this is enough, but that is childish. Many years of experience showed me that facilitating participation isn't easy, and that it took the tutors and instructors with whom I worked several months of supervised prACTice before most of them managed it. But before I continue, I must emphasize that facilitating a discussion is merely one example of the difficulties that people experience when they seek to adopt a new approach to teaching; and there are several reasons for this.

One is that, before one is able to practise a new approach, one must un-learn a good deal first, especially many things that one learnt from being a learner. But such un-learning is difficult. In the chapter on the way in which schemas become established, I noted that, when we experience something, that experience is coded in our brain, and in that way it becomes a physical part of ourselves. Such a process has a distinct advantage, for it enables us to act automatically on the basis of our past experiences; and what we can do automatically, also usually feels 'right'. However, and as is often the case, there is a cost to such automaticity; and the cost, in this instance, is that such actions can be very difficult to override. In a previous chapter, I attempted to illustrate what is at stake when playing a game, that is, tennis.

A second reason a change to a new teaching approach is difficult, is because one is unable to acquire it by listening to a teacher, watching tv, or reading a book. Doing such things results in merely verbal knowledge, and is therefore not available for practical use. For knowledge to be usable, it must be experienced.

A third reason that makes adopting a new approach to teaching difficult is the fact that more than merely developing a new skill is involved. This is because one has to change as a person to some extent. For example, one has to become less directive, yet remain reasonably confident that one's lessons won't fall apart. To put this in another way, many people find it very difficult to practise a way of teaching that is different from the way they were taught, especially a way that requires a focus on the learners rather than on the teacher. This is because, when one teaches, one indirectly strives to remain in control, and it is difficult to do this and at the same time to focus on the learners.

A fourth reason is related to the fact that teaching is a two-way process, that is, learners are also involved. It follows that, unless the learners are very young children, they will have had masses of experience that will predispose them to seeing teaching in a certain way; and if a new way is seriously different from what they are used to, they will not know quite how to respond.

And a fifth reason that adopting a new approach to teaching can be difficult is due to the fact that teaching always takes place in a certain culture, that is, in the culture of an establishment, a curriculum, and indeed a whole society. And it isn't easy to work in a manner that is foreign to the culture in which it takes place.

&

Above, I outlined some of the difficulties one can encounter when one wishes to adopt a new approach to teaching. Next, I note what my experiences over many years taught me about how these difficulties are sometimes overcome. Here are some of the factors:

1) knowing one's subject really well
2) discovering a new approach to teaching that is backed by considerable evidence, that works in practice, and which one finds attractive
3) having doubts about the approach one is presently using
4) having a strong desire to try a new approach
5) feeling reasonably confident that, if one adopts a new approach, one's learners will not tear one's lesson apart
6) observing a teacher who uses the new approach, and seeing that he or she feels reasonably comfortable with it
7) being prepared to try that new approach many times even though one fails to master it immediately
8) the presence of someone who is knowledgeable and supportive while one is trying out this new approach, and who gives one judicious and friendly feedback.

Here, now, are a few comments on the above.

Teachers must obviously know their subject well. But, in addition to the obvious reasons for this, if one is unsure about the material one is supposed to be teaching, one will be nervous about anything that might show up one's deficiencies. As a result, one will want to keep tight control of a lesson; and the best way of doing that is to talk non-stop.

The second factor is obvious, but not so obvious, for it implies a certain attitude to others and to life. The same is true of the third and fourth factor. I would add that, having the confidence that learners won't tear one's lesson apart isn't so much a matter of being able to do anything in particular, but of not being too afraid of anything in particular. Many student teachers told me that, until they had actually tried a more open approach, and accepted the possible risk, they were unable to deal with that risk. However, once they had taken that risk, they found their fear had been greatly exaggerated. In fact, it was difficult to remember it afterwards.

The sixth factor is important for we are all helped to carry out a task when we have a role model for that task. Having such a role model provides one with a picture of a person in action, and a yardstick with which one can compare oneself. The importance of this point might be gauged from the following. It has been found that simply viewing oneself teach on a film, in the absence of having a model of what one considers good teaching in one's head, does not result in much improvement in one's teaching.[1]

The seventh factor is again obvious, and perhaps again related to one's personality. And the last factor is most important because, as repeatedly noted, we learn best when we act, and get supportive feedback on our actions.

At this point, I would urge readers to recall a tutor-librarian I called Betty, one of whose lessons I described in an earlier chapter. I then noted that, when I had observed one of my tutors or instructors teach, I almost always initially found that attending my lessons had not had much of a practical effect on their teaching, even when that person had expressed enthusiasm for the approach to teaching suggested in this book. The observations offered in this chapter might further help to clarify why the above is the case; and, as this matter comes to the heart of what this book is about, I will risk repeating it like this. In short, I found that, no matter how I taught, on their own, my lessons had almost no practical effect. And as a result of this experience I came to see that, unless I worked together with student teachers – that is, unless I observed them teach and discussed their teaching with them afterwards – my lessons were largely a waste of time. But no, perhaps I exaggerate. For my lessons might have served a purpose after all; but, if they did, it was not a self-evident one. That is, I conjecture their main effect might have been to offer my students an experience, – the experience of seeing and hearing a person struggle to teach in a certain way.

I write the above even though I risk inflating my importance thereby, for the above is what is to be expected if the theory of learning presented in the first Part of this book is broadly correct. Of course, the above account of my tutees might merely indicate that I was an ineffective teacher. But the following observation, by another teacher from a very different discipline, suggests that it might not have been my ineptitude that was responsible for the fact that my lessons had little practical effect. This man, Alexander, once famous in his field, noted: 'The belief is very generally held that, if only we are told what to do in order to correct a wrong way of doing something, we can do it, and that if we feel we are doing it, all is well. All my experience, however, goes to show that this belief is a delusion.'[2]

That comment might sound provocative. It is not intended to be. It is, I believe, rather the case that, the moment one says something that flies in the face of widespread belief and practice, one sounds provocative. I quote this man here, in part, to remind readers of the material on learning presented in the first half of this book. In a nutshell, this is that the words that stand for something are not the same as the thing itself. I would urge readers to consider the references I cite here.

As the above might sound too abstract, here is a concrete illustration. When I visited my tutees, I always looked at their lesson plan before I observed them teach. (As was noted in an earlier chapter a lesson plan, among other things, indicates what a teacher hopes to achieve, and what the learners and the teacher will be doing at various times during a lesson.) I then had the following repeated experience. Here I again refer to discussions, but only because it was in that activity that what I have to say was most striking. From the lesson plan I had been given, I would see that a given teacher intended the learners to discuss something at a certain point in the lesson. However, on my first visits to that teacher, I usually found that no real discussion had taken place in that lesson (usually because the teacher had dominated the lesson). After the lesson, the teacher and I would chat, and it then often became painfully obvious that this teacher actually believed that a discussion had taken place in that lesson. In short, I found that teachers often genuinely believed that something had taken place that had not taken place! As this might sound counter-intuitive, even absurd, I invite readers to recall the comment by Alexander quoted above. I would also again draw attention to how this example illustrates something striking about the difference between verbal and experiential knowledge.

I note further that, when I was faced by the above situation, I would as sympathetically as possible draw the attention of that tutor or instructor to what I had observed, and most of them would then react in a defensive, sometimes hurt, and quite often an angry manner. In time, I learnt that it was then extremely important not to insist. If our relationship until that point had been one of mutual respect and some affection, it was enough that this matter had been lightly mentioned. I also found that much could be achieved when a student of mine agreed to allow a good video camera into his or her lesson. For, when we viewed that film after a lesson, I would often hear a teacher say things like: 'My, did you see . . . ?! I didn't really give that student a chance to answer . . .'. Or, 'I shouldn't have said anything at that point . . . It's amazing, I didn't even notice it at the time . . . .' Unfortunately, I am unable to reproduce the tones in which these words were spoken. The mixture of astonishment, interest and recognition were often astonishing. I will only add that I also found that I helped most, when I listened sympathetically, corroborated in an unobtrusive way, and otherwise remained silent.

That silence is especially important, for I learnt that, what such tutees most need after the above experience is time to assimilate (new schemas) and reflect. Later, that teacher would need further opportunities to practise in a supportive environment. (Notice the parallel here with those people learning how to use a word processor, described in an earlier chapter.) And as the years passed, I learnt that student teachers only made substantial progress if they had repeated experiences of the kind noted above.[3] But then, if the thesis outlined in this book is even partly correct, that is exactly as is to be expected.

I noted earlier that, if progress is to be made in acquiring a new approach, a relationship of mutual respect and some affection between student and teacher is required; and I made that statement because I occasionally found myself working with a tutor with whom such a relationship had not developed. When that happened, the kinds of exchanges described above fell flat, and I felt unable to make a useful contribution. Fortunately, I was then usually able to call on a colleague to work with this student teacher, and I withdrew.

I should perhaps also note that I sometimes found myself working with a tutor or instructor with whom a cordial relationship had developed, but whose teaching remained essentially didactic no matter what I tried to do. Most often, such a teacher would tell me that the approach to teaching suggested in this book 'does not suit my subject or my learners'. He or she would say that the learners were too old or too young, too inexperienced or too sophisticated, or too traditional or too unruly. At other times, these people would say that the subject they taught was too factual or too unstructured to allow for the application of 'my' approach. Whatever the exact details, the problem always lay in either the subject or the learners. And as a result of the experiences related in this and the previous paragraph, I came to think that the single most important quality a person requires in order to master a new approach is the ability to consider and reconsider one's teaching honestly. I found that when this quality is absent, nothing much can be done.[4]

But it would be quite wrong to end on this note. For I found that a remarkable change would take place in the teaching of the majority of the tutors and instructors with whom I worked. Instead of them talking for most of a lesson, a participative atmosphere would develop in their classes. Their learners ceased spending most of a lesson listening or writing notes. Instead, they would frequently grapple with materials directly, testing hunches, seeking information and discussing what they thought they now understood. Occasionally, a learner would express some frustration, but such episodes usually passed quickly. The majority of the learners seemed much more cheerful, and there would be an engaged and thoughtful atmosphere in the class. In short, this change brought a lightness to these lessons; and it was then a keen pleasure to see these tutors and instructors beam at this development.

At this point, some readers might well want to object that what I have written seems plausible, but, quite contrary to what I have repeatedly written about the need to offer some evidence for what one asserts, I have not offered any evidence in support of the comments I made above. And it certainly is the case that the only evidence I have offered in this chapter is my observations, and these might well be governed by my wish to justify my thesis. I must of course accept this objection, but I would want to add the following. To have offered some objective evidence in support of what I have noted about the changes that took place in the teaching of some of the instructors and tutors with whom I worked, another teacher would have had to be found who taught another kind of training programme. And, at the end of, say, a year, any changes in his or her tutees would have had to be compared with the tutees I taught, and by someone knowledgeable but unbiased in the matter. I trust that it will be seen that I was simply not in a position to carry out such or similar research; and in the absence of such research I must hope that my descriptions are cogent enough to suggest that they might be accurate.

To the above I would add the following. The shift I have described did not appear to result only in more effective teaching, or even more powerful and enjoyable learning. Quite a few of the tutors and instructors with whom I worked, also told me that some of their attitudes towards life in general seemed to have changed. With a touch of self-consciousness, some of them would say that they felt they had become a mite more open and generous; and, although they now quite often felt dissatisfied, they also seemed to feel less anxious.

Chapter 23

Variations on a Theme

It might now be an idea to present a series of vignettes to illustrate the approach to teaching outlined in the previous chapters. All are from lessons that I observed.

The teacher in the first lesson I describe is a young woman named Sara. She is a dietician in a large hospital, and one of her many duties is to give a talk on diet in pregnancy to mothers who come to this hospital for a weekly antenatal class. When I first observed Sara teach, she gave the kind of talk that is common on such occasions. She began at 2 p.m. and finished at 3.15 p.m., and, near the end of her talk, she asked if there were any questions. She was asked one or two, she answered them, and then she smiled and thanked the mothers for their attendance. As these women left, I thought Sara had put on a good performance. But I wondered how much her learners had really learnt. Here is how Sara taught the same topic on one of my later visits.

It is a Thursday afternoon, and we are in a pleasant enough room in a hospital. Sara enters the class a few minutes before the lesson and arranges the seats in a circle. As people come in, she greets them, asks their names, jots these down, introduces herself, and invites people to sit in the circle. As more people come in, she exchanges comments about the weather, where they live, and how they reached the hospital. Aside from twelve expectant mothers, there are three husbands, two student nurses, and I. The nurses and I are introduced as interested in the topic, and for the rest of the lesson we are treated the same as everyone else. Three of the mothers are of Asian origin, two are of West Indian origin, and one of the Asian women appears not to understand English very well. Sara also sits in the circle, and, when we are all settled, she announces the topic of the lesson: 'Diet in Pregnancy'. She says that many of us will know a good deal about healthy eating, and that she hopes we will contribute our knowledge to the class. Then she asks if anyone would like to ask something.

There is silence. Sara smiles and waits. After about a minute, one of the women says she still suffers from morning sickness. Sara nods, does not say anything, but her face shows she is listening. Several women nod their heads. One woman nods emphatically. Sara asks her if she has the same problem. The woman describes her symptoms, and goes on to say how she has found some relief. Another woman adds a comment. Sara nods, turns to another woman and asks her whether what had been said so far tallies with her experience. The woman says something quietly. Sara says she fears the others might not have heard. The woman raises her voice and addresses the whole class. Another woman comes in with a few more comments. Finally, Sara briefly reports a few additional things that are recommended in such a situation.

Then Sara says it might be an idea to consider what kind of diet is best for a pregnant woman. She says it has been found that a healthy diet consists of a balanced intake of four kinds of food: calcium foods, protein foods, vitamin foods and energy foods. Sara has a set of colourful posters on the floor next to her chair. She has made them herself. They have pictures of foods, and, under them, Sara has written in bold letters to which group they belong. She holds the posters up, and points to the foods. She talks in a cheery manner, without in the least putting on a show. She sounds more like a person chatting than a teacher giving a talk. Her introduction takes about five minutes.

Next, she hands out sheets of paper that contain three case studies. The first reads: 'Mrs Patel is a strict vegetarian and has a part-time job. She is a bit underweight and has some problems with morning sickness. Suggest a healthy diet for her to cover three days.' Sara asks the women to get into groups of three, and to note their recommendations for each case. She places the posters in a line against a wall. She has a few pencils handy for those who might need one.

At first no one moves. The people in the room smile, look a little uneasy, and move their chairs about an inch. But, with a little encouragement, a few smiles, a quietly assured manner, and herself helping to move chairs, Sara soon gets her 'students' to sit in groups of three. What happens next might surprise anyone who has not witnessed such a thing before. After a minute or two of silence, most of the people present begin to chat. And within about three minutes, the talk in some groups is animated. Several things soon become apparent. The Asian woman, the one who seemed to find English difficult, actually speaks it quite well; one of the groups contains a health visitor who is knowledgeable and adds her expertise; and the woman who had spoken quietly in the full class is happy to chat in a small group. While the 'students' work, Sara sits to one side.

It takes the learners about six minutes to complete the case studies. Then Sara invites comment. There is no 'reporting back' stage, and no use of a flip chart to summarize. When one person says something, Sara does not repeat or evaluate it, and she seldom elaborates herself. All through she remains seated in the circle. Now and again, Sara asks a question. When she does, it does not require merely factual recall. Her questions always come after she has reported some information, or after someone has made a statement, and she then asks people for their reaction. When someone replies, she uses that contribution for further discussion by asking what someone else thinks. Sometimes she makes a point herself. Often there is enough collective knowledge in the room to supply information and correct misconceptions without her having to say much.

Next Sara begins another talk. She reminds the class that it is considered inadvisable to eat large quantities of certain foods. She mentions over-refined foods, animal fats, salt, sugar and alcohol. She notes that there are good reasons to suspect that large quantities of these are implicated in certain maladies. She cites one or two pieces of research by name and gives their date. She is obviously well read, but her expertise is unobtrusive. Her talk lasts about five minutes. She frequently stops, invites comment, and in this way encourages the active participation of the learners. Next, Sara gives out a worksheet. It contains two 'diets'. Sara asks the learners to examine them and suggest improvements. Here they are:

DIET ONE

Breakfast: toast (white), butter, marmalade, fried bacon and eggs, tea and sugar. Mid-morning snack: coffee (with milk and sugar), chocolate biscuit. Lunch: egg sandwich, potato crisps, ice cream, Coca-Cola. Tea: tea (with milk and sugar), jam tart with cream, chocolate cake. Evening meal: fried fish or ham, chips. Late evening tv snack: beer, peanuts (salted).

DIET TWO

Breakfast: toast (wholemeal), butter, orange juice, tea (without sugar). Mid-morning snack: coffee (black with sweetener). Lunch: tinned low-calorie tomato soup, bread roll, butter, banana, Diet Coke. Tea: coffee (black with sweetener). Evening meal: baked potato, butter, coleslaw salad, coffee (black with sweetener).

Again, Sara's request that the participants get into groups is met with silence. But, this time, she has to do much less encouraging, and discussions are soon under way while Sara sits to one side. When the tasks have been completed, Sara invites the people present to form a circle, and to relate the improvements they have recommended. And again, at first, no one says a word. Sara makes a humorous reference to her own diet; another woman mentions hers and laughs; Sara turns to the one husband present and asks him what he has recommended; and soon a new discussion is under way. When it falters, Sara turns to one of the people in the circle and asks her by name what she thinks. (She takes the name from the list that she quickly compiled at the beginning of the lesson.) She sounds as if she is extending an invitation to participate rather than asking a question.

In the last quarter-hour, Sara gives out a question-sheet containing twenty short items. They cover a good deal of the material discussed so far. One question asks whether skimmed milk contains less calcium than whole milk; another whether a baby is harmed by cigarette smoke in a room; and another whether a breast-fed infant can get drunk if its mother drinks a gin and tonic. Sara invites the learners to answer the questions in pairs, and with a smile promises those who get all the answers right two gold stars. When they have finished, Sara encourages the more outspoken ones to give their answers. The others protest or agree. Five minutes before the end, Sara gives out a crossword puzzle she has herself devised. The clues and answers summarize the objectives of the lesson. She suggests that the women might like to try it on their husbands when they get home. One clue reads: 'plenty of fibre helps'. The answer is: 'constipation'. There are smiles all round as people leave.

The above is a threadbare description. It does not convey the quality of the many comments these women exchanged, Sara's deft responses, her touches of humour, and especially her thoughtful, encouraging and pleasant manner.

Even so, I hope I have managed to indicate how incomparably better a lesson this was, compared with her first one, and I believe it was better for at least the following reasons.

If we agree that nobody is likely to remember more than a fraction of the information that can be conveyed in one hour, twenty-four hours after they have heard it, it is clear that attempting to convey a great deal of information in such a lesson is a waste of time. In any case, the main aim in such a lesson is not so much to convey information as to encourage a certain attitude, and that is far more likely to occur if the clients are able to participate. Furthermore, people tend to get bored when they have to listen to one person speak for more than ten or fifteen minutes at a time. Some teachers are born entertainers, but most are not. Anyway, why should anyone who does not have the gift of the gab assume a role that has no educational value anyway?

Next, unless a learner is given repeated opportunities to speak, there will be no way to check whether any learning has taken place. And, as was noted in the chapter on Perception, nor will there be any opportunities to correct misconceptions. It is also very easy to assume that learners know less than they actually do. In Sara's lesson, one of the learners (the Asian lady) knew more than might have been expected, and the health visitor who was present was likely to be knowledgeable. Most groups of people have considerable collective knowledge, and unless people are given opportunities to speak, this source of knowledge remains untapped.

But readers might have noticed that this lesson was not based on 'having a discussion'. Most such lessons are fatuous. Sara introduced topics briefly with unobtrusive expertise. She had also prepared excellent learning materials that were simple yet professional, and she invited her learners to consider them in small groups. In this way, scholarship and sociability were combined. As a result, opportunities were created for people to learn new information actively, and to check on whether they understood that information. It had taken Sara time and effort to prepare her learning materials. But, having made them, she could now use them repeatedly. And not only had they helped her learners to learn, they would also serve as useful summaries when the women got home.

Sara might even have managed to help some of the women to become acquainted, and that would have been a notable achievement. For, in the Western world especially, many mothers can feel isolated when they first have a baby. It would be a great bonus to come to such a class, and perhaps become acquainted with another woman in similar circumstances who lives locally. In teaching in the way she did, it was far more likely that Sara might have managed to encourage such possible contacts than if she had taught didactically. Last, I would draw attention to the fact that Sara used no technology; and achieved what she did with total strangers, and in a single encounter.

To the above, I would add the following. There is a tendency in some training circles to believe that content determines method; i.e., that the way one teaches depends on the subject taught. A symptom of this tendency can be seen when training programmes are put on for specific occupational groups. The implications of such a position are serious. One is that no general teaching principles are possible except at the simplest level. All through this book, I have argued the exact opposite. The lesson described above was on 'Diet in Pregnancy'. In an earlier chapter, there was a description of a lesson on 'Computer Engineering'. No two subjects could be more different. Yet, the approach to teaching in both is funda-mentally the same; and it is the same because it is based on what I believe is a viable theory of learning and teaching. In short, there is nothing as practical as a good theory.

Readers might have noticed that most of the lessons described in this book have been with adult learners. I described such lessons because I believe that I must provide descriptions of lessons I actually observed. However, I hope it will be agreed that the approach to teaching illustrated here lends itself not only to any subject, but also to most learners.[1]

&

People are sometimes asked to give a talk on a certain topic to a group of strangers, and that can be difficult, in part because it can be hard to know at what level to pitch one's talk. In such circumstances, I have found it helpful to begin by asking the participants what they hope to gain from the talk. When I have con-sulted people like that, I have sometimes discovered what is wanted and what is already known. That way, the participants also seem more interested in what is to come. But I have found that I have to be patient if I begin in this way. Not every-one is used to being consulted by an invited speaker, and many are probably expecting a Performance. Some might also feel uncomfortable about speaking in front of others. So one has to ask one's question, sit back, – and wait. However, I have found that, if I act like that, someone is sure to speak eventually; and, when that happens, I don't repeat or evaluate what has been said, and I don't elabo-rate either. Instead, I acknowledge the comment with a thoughtful smile, look around, and hope for further comment. When I feel enough has been said, I try to summarize very briefly what I think has been said. Then I ask if I have got the matter right.

More discussion might then develop, and this might continue for some time. I then have to weigh up whether I should encourage the discussion to continue, or begin my talk. After all, the people present might find a discussion more useful than anything I could say, for it might help them to clarify what they find problematic about a topic or a situation. At other times, I have found that such a discussion is getting us nowhere. Some of the participants seem to want to use the occasion to attract attention, others to air a pet idea. When this kind of thing happens it is obviously best to thank the contributors and to begin one's talk.

After I have spoken for a little while, I pause and invite comment. If I begin in the manner just described, somebody usually comments; and these comments often help to clear up a misunderstanding, or add something that has been left out. It seems to me that such comments are more valuable than using that time to convey more information, for, after all, the participants will forget most of this information a day after they have heard it. Many participants also appear to like such an approach, perhaps in part because it helps them to get to know each other a little better.

&

There is always a day when learners and a teacher meet for the first time. This can generate a rather odd situation, for the people present might not know each other at all, and learning and teaching often require personal interactions. Quite often, the learners might know each other, but the teacher knows no one at all, and, if one thinks about it, this is also a rather odd situation. These things being so, it would be helpful if a way could be found that would enable the people present to get to know each other a little. Doing such a thing would ease any tensions that might be present, encourage the social bent in most of us, help to facilitate communication, and lay a basis toward a collaborative approach to learning. Provided that there are not more than about twenty-five participants, I found the following two activities helpful at such times.

1) Invite the learners to get into pairs, and to interview each other briefly. Then ask each person to introduce the person they have interviewed to the whole group. The teacher should be one of the participants.
2) Invite the learners to approach someone in the class to whom they have never spoken, and to exchange a few pleasantries with that person.

At one time, I feared that, if I suggested such an activity, some people might think it artificial. But I soon lost that fear because I found that people participate readily in such an activity. Such activities can help to relieve the sense of awkwardness many of us feel when we first find ourselves with strangers, and most people are pleased when a teacher attempts to do something about this very natural feeling. These activities should have about them the air of a game, and they should not be too lengthy, too personal, or too serious. It is obviously important not to force anyone to speak, and the teacher's contributions should be brief, light and unobtrusive.

Having 'broken the ice', I sometimes decide it would be best to go a little further. One way of doing that is to write two or three questions – that can be answered in a few words – on a board. Examples of questions are: 'What would you most like to gain from this course/meeting/workshop?' 'How would you like people to respond during discussions?' 'Is anything likely to annoy you?' 'Have you any anxieties?' The participants can be asked to write their responses briefly on a sheet of paper, and to stick it up somewhere in the room. Then everyone walks around for ten minutes to see what people have written. Learners often worry about whether they will be able to cope; whether the other learners will be brighter than they are; and whether the course will be useful. Many welcome an opportunity to air such thoughts in an informal way.

&

Teaching is usually a matter of helping learners to acquire new information, or to learn how to carry out a task. But teaching sometimes also aims to encourage a certain attitude. And if 'real' learning requires experiencing, it follows that people will learn a new attitude best if they can experience it. Role-play is an approach that can help learners to experience a new attitude. Here is a concrete example.

Many people are now employed (in more affluent countries) to care for the disabled, and one of their duties might be to feed their most disabled clients. On the face of it, such a task does not appear to require much training. However, it isn't easy to imagine what it might feel like to be an adult, yet require feeding. Instead of talking about how a person with such a disability might feel in such circumstances, one of my past students (a tutor in a school of nursing) went about the matter like this.

His name is Grant, and this is what I observed him do in one of his lessons. He began by giving a short talk, and during it stopped repeatedly to ask for comments in the way frequently described in this book. Then he said that there was no better way of learning something than to experience it, and cheerfully asked the participants to get into pairs. Then the hands of one of the pair were tied behind his or her back; and then the one who had been tied up, was blindfolded. Grant then handed out dishes with some cornflakes in them, and asked the other person in the pair to feed the bound and blindfolded one. When the feeding had been completed, roles were reversed. All this took about twenty minutes, and then cords and blindfolds were removed, and Grant asked the participants – there were about fifteen of them – to sit in a circle again.

I was forcibly struck by the lively air in the room as the participants settled into their seats. There was not one glazed look as is frequently the case after people have listened to someone give a talk. Grant seemed in no hurry to start anything, and waited good-humouredly while people chatted. Then he asked the participants for their reactions. Very soon, one young woman said how struck she was by how powerful the experience had been. Another mentioned feelings of rage, frustration, resentment, appreciation, helplessness and relief; and the expressions on the faces of many of the others seemed to reflect just such feelings. As I sat there and observed, it was obvious that none of those feelings could have been conveyed remotely as well by a teacher 'telling'. It was also obvious that an awareness of such feelings would help a person to take better care of someone who is severely disabled.[2]

To the above, I would add the following. In addition to increasing a learner's sense of empathy, role-play can also help people to learn how to follow certain procedures based on knowledge of important facts. Examples might include preparing a patient for an operation, or approaching a person with a view to making an arrest. As it isn't easy to do these kinds of things well when one is new to them, it would be very helpful if one could have lots of practice at them in simulated circumstances. Role-play provides such circumstances.

All the examples given so far have been taken from work with adults. But role-play can also be used with children. It so happens that my maternal grandfather was a scholar and teacher. Among other things, he taught religion, and he did so in part via role-play. For example, instead of always teaching didactically, he sometimes encouraged children to act parts out of the Bible.[3] That must have generated some powerful learning!

Like most things, role-play works best under certain conditions. The following suggestions might be helpful.

1) Teachers sometimes worry that some of their learners might not be happy to take part in a role-play. I had such worries myself, but soon learnt that most people are happy, even eager to take part in a role-play. Overcoming such hesitations is important, for role-play works best when a teacher feels confident about it.

2) It is probably best to introduce role-play when learners have begun to feel comfortable with each other. However, in some classes, it might be a good idea to introduce role-play early in order to help learners to feel more comfortable with each other. As is so often the case in teaching, tact and good judgement are necessary here.

3) In certain circumstances, it might be important to consider the advantages and disadvantages of casting before one begins a role-play. For example, it is often a shy person who might best be cast in the role of a dominant one.

4) Participants should be prepared for a role-play. Preparation can take the form of some reading or a short talk, followed by a discussion. It can also take the form of prompt cards that a teacher has devised. A prompt card is given to each participant, and on it is written a very brief description of the situation that the role-play will simulate. Each card will also include a few words on the character that the holder of that card will enact. As so often in teaching, here, too, careful preparation is necessary if aims are to be achieved.

5) A teacher should aim to involve all the participants, and as actively as possible. If the class consists of more than twelve learners, and there is enough space, the class can be divided into groups. All the groups can then enact a role-play in various parts of a room. Furthermore, those who do not participate in the role-play should be given a list of written questions to answer while observing the role-play.

6) It is helpful to spend a little time organizing the room. This helps to 'set the stage'. In the theatre, this is sometimes called 'the suspension of disbelief', and it is generated by things like lights going down and a curtain going up.

7) A teacher's main job is to help organize the role-play; and, as in most of the lessons I have described, a teacher should do as much of the work as possible before the lesson. Once a role-play is under way, a teacher should remain to one side and interfere as little as possible.

8) Participants often stereotype situations and people in a role-play. Teachers can draw attention to this tendency beforehand, or they can allow stereotyping to occur, and invite the participants to consider what it implies afterwards.

9) A role-play can generate strong feelings. It is therefore most important for the participants to be able to leave their roles behind them when a class moves on to other things. Teachers can help to create a demarcation between a role-play and the rest of a lesson by clearly announcing the end of the role-play. One of my past students managed this neatly by having his police cadets put on hats when a role-play began, and take them off when the role-play ended.

10) At the end of a role-play, a teacher must thoughtfully thank the participants. They have collaborated to make a success of a lesson, and taking part in a role-play is a little like taking part in a play. Unless there is some applause at the end, one might feel deflated, and consider what has been done a waste of time.

11) A role-play is a part of a learning process, and should hence be followed by a discussion. The participants should be encouraged to say what they believe that they have learnt, and how they felt during the role-play. If a teacher encourages such expressions tactfully, and allows for lots of silences, the participants will be able to verbalize their new understanding and feelings, and thereby clarify and assimilate them.

12) The greatest benefit from role-play comes when the insights so gained are practised in real-life situations; and even more gains are made when one can

practise them in the presence of a supportive, unobtrusive and knowledge-able person with whom one can discuss one's progress. Many people teach subjects that do not appear to lend themselves to role-play. Role-play serves certain aims, and it is obviously important to match the methods used with the aims of a lesson. However, a little reflection will often show that a certain topic does lend itself to role-play. Role-play increases the range of things done in a class, and thereby provides variety; and readers might recall what was noted about this factor in a previous chapter. Role-play also enables learners to express certain facets of themselves that might other-wise remain quite unnoticed.

There are variants of role-play like simulation and gaming. These also enable learn-ers to gain some experience of a situation in a simulated environment. Though these, and role-play, serve limited purposes, such methods are often neglected because of the predominance of the transmission method of teaching. It was my consistent experience that, when teachers and learners tried these activities, they often found them valuable. Interested readers will find numerous books on them.[4] Lastly, notice that role-play fits in well with the theory of learning outlined in pre-vious chapters.

☙

The last vignette is of a young woman named Jill who is a tutor in a college of hor-ticulture. She has a variety of duties, and one of them is to teach head park keepers about new regulations, as they come in from Brussels, on the storage and use of horticultural tools and implements, fertilizers, and the chemicals used for such things as pest and weed control. These regulations are complex, often written in terse language, and cover many pages. The 'students' in the lesson I am about to describe, are park keepers of every age and educational background imaginable, and many are much older than Jill. They come to this college one day a week for three weeks, and then they sit an exam. How is one to teach such a subject, to such a bunch of people? Give a lecture? Here is a brief account of how Jill taught for half of one morning.

The college is housed in a scatter of large buildings, perhaps once a country estate, set in a half-acre of rambling parkland. The buildings are old, and we assemble in a room with a vaulted ceiling and huge windows. Dusty specimens of ancient lineage are arranged along the walls, and the fittings suggest that the room was once used as a laboratory. In spite of the huge windows, the room is rather gloomy, and I feel sorry that Jill has to teach in such a place. The 'students' amble in, and collect in groups to chat. On the whole, they look a sceptical but good-humoured lot. The majority are men of various ages, but there are also a few young women. They are obviously used to such periodic demands on their time, away from the parks for which they are responsible.

When Jill walks in promptly at 9 a.m., she joins one of the groups, and chats for a few minutes. Then she goes to the head of the class. She looks not much more than a slip of a girl of about 26. She smiles, and says that the participants must be pleased to have a day off work. This is greeted by a murmur of ironic comment. Then Jill says that she doesn't envy the participants. She holds up a thick volume, and says that the regulations that they must master are contained in that book. A mock groan goes around the class, and the word 'Brussels' is used as if it were an expletive. Jill says that today they will look at the topics of Storage and Record Keeping, that the next meeting would be on Checking and Applications, and that the third and last meeting would be on preparing for the exam, with the actual Examination in the afternoon. Someone asks a question, and Jill answers briefly. Then she smiles again and says that she recognizes someone in the room. She points at a young man and calls out, 'Aren't you Charles Keene?' The man also smiles and agrees he is. Jill tells us that they had been in college together, and that if she doesn't know something, she will call on this Charles to answer. Charles says something I can't hear, and when he is prompted to speak up, he says, 'Don't let her fool you. She was doing research when I was training, and has a PhD. She's just here to pass the time of the day.' Mild laughter ripples across the room.

Jill begins by sympathizing with the participants' need to deal with an increasing workload of administrative duties, but adds that what they had come to consider that morning boils down to the need for safe practices, possibly even to safeguard lives. She says that she has spent a lot of time studying the regulations, that they consist of a formidable array of facts, and that she reckons that the important thing is to understand the underlying principles because that would enable one to find the necessary facts easily and quickly. She holds up a sheaf of papers, and says that she has summarized the relevant facts in these six-page booklets, and that the only thing that the participants must now do is to learn those six pages off by heart. She laughs, and I have the impression that the man sitting next to me looks relieved.

Next Jill says, 'What I suggest we do is get down to business right away. I've prepared a worksheet for you, and I'd like you to find a partner, and answer the questions on the sheet. We are now going to an outhouse where I've arranged a large store of equipment, and I want you to do the following. Look at the questions on the worksheet, examine what you see in the outhouse closely, if necessary consult my summary of the regulations, and answer the questions on the worksheet in writing. I think you'll find some ambiguities here and there, and you'll then have to discuss the matter with your partner and decide on the best answer. Any questions?' As there are none, Jill hands out the materials she has prepared, and then we follow her out of the building, and along a winding path till we reach an outhouse. Jill unlocks the door, and inside there is a huge array of equipment. Some of it is on the floor, and the rest on dozens of shelves ranged along the walls. The equipment and materials are arranged in every kind of manner, from the neat to the downright careless, and as the participants walk in, there are murmurs ranging from surprise to disgust.

Jill says, 'Well folks, I reckon you have about an hour of work ahead of you. I'm going to make myself comfortable under that tree just outside, and if anyone wants a chat, I'll be happy to see you. OK?' I look at the participants, who seem a little bemused, and at Jill who is walking out of the door. For a few minutes, the participants stand around, but soon, in various ways, they set about the task ahead. I attach myself to one pair. They begin by reading a few of the questions on the worksheet, then return to the first one. They shuffle the summary that Jill gave them, and then examine the labels on some sacks. One of them says that the answer to the first question seems clear enough, and suggests a wording. The other says it might be an idea to consult the regulations before they write anything. I go outside and see Jill sitting under a tree. I go over to her and say, 'You call this teaching?' Jill says, 'You told us that teaching is a waste of time, and I've acted on that. What do you want?' I didn't know how to reply. This girl understood better than me what I had been trying to say.

Chapter 24

Overview

___

In this book, I have attempted to outline a theory of learning and teaching, and it might now be helpful if I first summarize the theory of learning. This theory holds that people learn when they discover that they don't know something they consider worth knowing, form hunches about a possible answer, seek information, apply that information to test those hunches, and get feedback on what they are doing. When these things happen, they have experiences, and in that way, they learn.

The theory of teaching, in turn, holds that a teacher's task is to help learners discover that they don't know something worth knowing, and then to help them find information so that they can learn that something in a reasonably orderly and satisfying way. It has also been my argument that, for teachers to be able to do these things effectively, they must study a considerable body of knowledge, and have lots of supervised practice in applying it.

※

Quite a few practitioners might agree with the above, but they might want to say that one does not need to have a theory of learning and teaching in order to teach in the way just outlined. Indeed, I know from first-hand experience that some of the principles advocated on many training courses, are similar to the ones suggested in this book. However, on those courses, no theory of any kind is ever mentioned. I believe that such an approach is flawed in a fundamental kind of way, and on at least two counts.

First, when a person applies a principle without first having made a sustained endeavour to understand on what evidence it is based, that person's practice tends to be unimaginative and superficial. Second, a person who applies a principle without first having made a sustained endeavour to understand on what evidence it is based, is unable to criticize that principle except in a trivial kind of way. It follows that such a person is unable to develop the principle intelligently, and is therefore in a similar situation to that of a robot.

I wrote the first edition of this book at a time when it had become fashionable to assess knowledge via 'competences'. In this approach, what people are able to do – rather than what they appear to know – was the focus of attention, and readers of this book might assume that, what I have advocated in this book appears to be in line with such an approach. Unfortunately, when an old approach is replaced with a new one, a new fallacy often replaces a previous one; and I believe that that is what happened when the competency-based approach was introduced. For an examination of what a person is able to do, seldom indicates how well that person also understands the justification for what he or she is doing; nor is it easy to assess such understanding on the basis of further 'competences'. In other words, instead of trying to tackle the thorny problem of the relationship between theory and practice, the competency-based approach tried to sidestep this problem, and in doing that, it created a new problem.

I could put the disadvantage of the competency-based approach in another way. It seems to me that the single most important competency that anyone could possess, is the ability to question the validity of any competence. But it is precisely that competence, that the competency-based approach undermines. This is because all the competences that one must learn in this approach, are 'givens'. It is also because all competences are givens, that the competency-based approach is rather authoritarian, especially as it appears to be transparent and egalitarian. I believe that the application of this approach might also affect people's general inclination to question, and some governments would clearly favour this.

☙

In an earlier chapter, I drew attention to the nature of theories, and why I believe that having them in certain situations is essential. In short, whenever we must carry out a complex task, like build a house or relieve a persistent pain, we need knowledge; but the kind of knowledge required in such circumstances isn't simply a matter of knowing a number of facts. If that were all that was required, everyone could be their own builder or dentist. When we have something complicated to do, we need a deep and integrated understanding of it. That is, we need to be able to see how all the facts of a topic hang together, and produce a pattern. And for that, we usually have to go to somebody who has spent a considerable amount of time studying the matter, and who has had extensive experience of it. In short, to have that kind of knowledge, is to have a 'theory' of it.[1]

My argument all through this book has been that teaching is a complex matter. If so, the knowledge required to do it well, can be compared with the knowledge required to build a house or deal with a persistent pain; and, if that is the case, it follows that experience is not enough. In short, the foregoing suggests that we need a theory to guide us in classroom practice. However, it is also the case that even a brief reading of a history of the various branches of knowledge, soon shows that we never gain a complete understanding of anything. Nor could it be otherwise, for the human brain is merely one product of nature, and it would be very strange indeed if this one small product could comprehend the whole of that which produced it. But a reading of the history of the various branches of knowledge also indicates that we do make progress, for we know a little more about medicine, astronomy, engineering and human development than we knew even a hundred years ago.

Notice here that those who debunk such modest claims, always do so in an abstract way. For example: they never compare the concrete results of the medical practice of an aborigine, with that of a family physician in the west; they never compare the efficacy of applying the system of navigation of those intrepid Polynesians, with the system of navigation we use today; and they never compare the outcome of Amazonian sanitary practices, with those in present-day Amsterdam.

As noted in a previous chapter, another great advantage of having a theory is that it makes criticism easier, and in that way progress more likely. This is because a theory consists of an integrated series of statements based on some evidence; and, if someone can show that one of those statements is based on evidence that is faulty, then that statement is probably wrong. And when that happens, the theory might have to be modified, or abandoned altogether. On the other hand, when we have a series of integrated statements based on some evidence, more evidence is often found that complements the existing evidence, and that will make the theory stronger. A thoughtful practitioner will also recall that all theories are partly the product of a given culture, and will attempt to take account of that.[2]

The above makes clear that there is no such thing as foolproof theory. All theories are provisional statements that must be evaluated in the light of practice; and, in this way, all theories are repeatedly refined, modified, extended or scrapped. It seems to me obvious, that the kind of knowledge that can be acquired in this way, is likely to be far more powerful – and far less prone to changes in fashion – than only personal experience, reflections on personal experience, and doing one's own thing.

&

As with all theories, many criticisms could be made about the one I have put forward in this book. I can think of several myself, and take this opportunity to mention the following.

1) There is nothing about the social make-up of the teacher and the taught here. Many people believe that these can have a strong effect on learning and teaching, and I believe that, too. For example, a teacher who genuinely believes that learners can often do better than they themselves believe, and who conveys that belief, is likely to encourage more learning than a teacher who does not have such beliefs. Likewise, learners who feel that they will be able to cope with a task, are much more likely to cope with it than learners who do not. Nor is there enough here on the social relations between teacher and taught, or among the learners themselves. These are serious omissions, but I have not included anything on these topics because they are such big ones. They need consideration in a separate book.

2) Another topic not considered here is the context in which learning takes place. That includes things like the economic, political, cultural and social system of a country, as well as the nature of the relationship between the individual and the state. These factors have a very powerful effect on learning and teaching, and if I have not included anything on those topics here, it is again because they are such large ones, and require consideration in a separate book.

3) A third topic hardly touched on here, is the nature of the material to be learnt, and how it is best organized. Yet again, this is a big topic; and, although I have referred to it here and there, I have not done it anywhere near the justice it deserves, and this is because I have feared that doing so

would make this book unwieldly. Fortunately, there is a considerable literature on this topic, and readers interested in it will find it easy to locate.

4) Another topic not considered in this book is creativity. Creativity is a quality
most of us believe we understand, but it is difficult to separate it out from
things like imagination, innovation, artistry and doing one's own thing. As
most people value creativity, and as every society needs creative people, it
would be advantageous if teachers knew how to foster it. Here again a large
topic, and, with any luck, I shall write a book on it one day. But I had better
stop now, for otherwise I might be tempted to begin that book right now,
and readers must be getting impatient to reach the end of this one.

Even after the above admissions have been made, I fear that the theory of learning and teaching put forward here is likely to have many additional faults. A great
deal of work has been done on the topic of learning and teaching, and I have not
managed to consider anywhere near all of it. Nor have I managed to understand
all the contributions that I have considered. Learning is a mysterious business,
almost as mysterious as life itself. There are also sure to be contradictions and
weaknesses in what I have written; and there are sure to be many people around
who will understand these things very differently from me.

But there is only so much any one person can do. One does the best one can, but
eventually, one has to stop and accept one's limitations. But in this, there is also a
virtue, for it might spur someone to come along and suggest improvements. In the
meantime, there might be enough here to give a teacher something to begin with.
I write 'to begin with', because a consideration of the materials presented here
would obviously constitute only a small part of what is required to become an
effective teacher. However, I do know that, when the tutors and instructors with
whom I worked considered the materials presented here, they usually came to see
that it is not enough to go into a classroom with a set of objectives, lesson notes
and a computer. They came to see that effective teaching is much more a matter
of trying to understand how people learn.

Such a view has many effects. One is to stop one from thinking about teaching
primarily in terms of the content of the lesson. Content is important. But, when
one begins to think about teaching in terms of learning, it becomes obvious that
content is only half the matter. The other half is what the learners *do* in a lesson.
Another thing that happens, when one begins to focus on learning, is that one
often feels disappointed after a lesson. But then, that is common in any creative
enterprise. There cannot be many architects or chefs around who are pleased with
every one of their endeavours.

It follows that teachers will not improve because they have perfected a skill.
Shall we say that Einstein was a 'skilled' mathematician, and Cézanne a 'skilled'
painter? A person who sees teaching primarily in terms of learning, will know that
acquiring a skill is a way of playing safe, and hence a path to mediocrity.

Being creative is an arduous undertaking. It is a matter of developing a sensitivity based on systematic study, endless practice, and deep reflection. And it is in
this way that teaching can become a creative endeavour. And, like any creative
endeavour, when it succeeds, it does not result in simply helping people to acquire
more knowledge, or even a lifelong interest in a particular subject. It can alter the
way they see things.

Chapter 25

Why Teach?

At the end of the previous chapter, I noted that good teaching sometimes changes the way that people see things. But what things? One answer might be, 'One's view of the world.' That might be so, but that sentence sounds a little pretentious and it is unclear. Still, one often hears that good teachers do more than help people to acquire knowledge; and most teachers would probably feel pleased if they were able to help learners to become, for example, more confident or thoughtful.

The trouble of course is that helping learners to acquire qualities of the above kind is far from easy. A learner will not become more thoughtful because a teacher says that that is important. This is because, if real learning requires experiencing, learners will only acquire qualities of that kind if they have repeated experiences of them. It follows that learners are more likely to acquire such qualities as a result of *how* a teacher teaches, rather than *what* a teacher teaches.

The above alerts one to the fact that teaching is seldom a value-free activity. If a teacher says that trees take up moisture through their roots, he or she is not making a value judgement; and we do not consider such a statement good or bad, but accurate or inaccurate. The same holds for when a person teaches other physical processes, like the movement of electricity or the falling of stones. These things are all value free, although it could be argued that they reflect a certain world outlook. From this it seems to follow that being value free in teaching, depends on the subject that one teaches, for in teaching a subject like government, literature or biology, a teacher might well convey certain values.

However, as already noted, how people teach, rather than what they teach, can indirectly but strongly convey an attitude, and hence a set of values. From this it follows that values can be conveyed no matter what subject a person teaches. And further, values will be conveyed no matter what teaching approach is adopted; and this is the case even if a teacher is unconscious of this fact, or has no wish to convey any values. From such observations, it further follows that it is impossible to talk intelligently about teaching without considering the wider implications of teaching.

But before I continue, I had better consider a very common assumption. It is that one of the aims of teaching is to help produce an educated workforce, for it is often said that such a workforce is necessary to ensure a high standard of living for a country. It is also often argued that the better one is educated, the more likely it is that one will get a well-paying job. The latter is possible, though I suspect that many a market trader earns more than a lawyer who deals mainly in the transfer of home ownerships. In short, it seems to me that this coupling of education with the standard of living in a whole country is misleading, and this becomes obvious the moment one recalls two things. One, that multinational companies do not invest millions to build factories where there is an educated labour force. On the contrary, they often build their factories where the labour force is uneducated. And two, the rise in employment in developed countries is due less to a demand for graduates, and more for people who do relatively unskilled work, people like shop assistants, fork-lift truck operators, hotel receptionists, car cleaners, building workers and so on. Furthermore, there is no evidence to show that levels of education have a direct impact on national production levels, for there are many countries with thousands of graduates and a poor standard of living. In short, whether a country has a high or low standard of living depends on many factors, and talk of the importance of education in this respect might be prompted by a wish to keep educational practices safely instrumental.[1]

To come back to more adult concerns, readers might recall that, in an earlier chapter, I noted that any approach to teaching that does not rest on a systematic study of how people learn, is childish. It is the equivalent of forecasting the kind of weather one can expect tomorrow, by examining tea leaves today. If one accepts that a sensible approach to teaching must begin with a study of how people learn, it follows that the account of learning that one accepts as valid, will affect how one teaches. It also follows that this account of learning will suggest an image of what human beings are like. Eisner expressed this well when he somewhere wrote, '. . . under the rug of technique lies an image of man'. It might be further recalled that, in this book, I suggested that people learn, 'when they discover that they don't know something worth learning, form hunches about it, test those hunches, get feedback, seek information, and practise'. The image of learners that this account suggests, is of people who are capable of learning on their own, find being led irksome, and who appreciate being given some cheerful support. If one considers the wider implications of such an image, it isn't difficult to grasp why right-wing death squads in Latin America often kill village teachers no matter what subject they teach.

But the above is still not enough, and I might manage to convey what I have in mind if I relate the following. It so happens that I once heard the principal of an institute of technology make a speech on a graduation day. He began by congratulating the graduates on their achievement. Then he smiled, and somewhat surprisingly went on to say that he had no doubt that, if the graduates in that auditorium were asked to design a pipeline to pump blood from Aberdeen to Aberystwyth, they would do a fine job. He added thoughtfully that this would be no mean achievement, for blood is a fragile liquid, and much thought would have to be devoted to the design of such a project. His face then puckered, and he added that he also hoped that the graduates he was congratulating today would consider why they had been asked to carry out such a task.

I believe that the above account comes to the heart of the matter. This is that teaching, at its best, can be about much more than helping people to acquire knowledge, and even the kind of qualities noted so far. In short, I believe that good teaching can convey that it is important to open one's eyes, and thereby

escape the shackles of common sense, conventional wisdom, and the garbage purveyed by the mass media. That might sound an extravagant, even a melodramatic
claim, but it is an ancient one; and there is a famous example of it in Plato's writings on education.[2]

Many readers will know that, in Book 7 of his *The Republic*, Plato relates a story
that has become well known. This is a story about a group of human beings who
have lived all their lives in an underground cave. Their legs and necks are also so
chained, that they have to stay where they are, and can look only at the wall of
the cave immediately in front of them. Behind those people's backs, there is a low
embankment, and behind that embankment, there is a big fire. Or, to put this in
reverse order, there is first a big fire, then an embankment, and then those people
(really prisoners) facing the wall of the cave before them. Imagine further that, on
that embankment, behind those prisoners' backs, there are creatures hidden
behind a screen; and that those creatures hold up puppets just above the screen.
It follows from such an arrangement that, with a big fire behind the puppets, and
those puppets manipulated behind and above the prisoners' backs, the shadow of
those puppets will be thrown on the wall of the cave that those prisoners are
forced to face.

Plato went on to note that we might find the situation just described very
strange; and yet, if that situation were the only one that those people had ever
experienced, they would not find it strange. On the contrary, as they had never
experienced anything else, what has just been described would constitute their
reality; and it would also follow that, even if those people were able to discuss the
shadows on the wall in front of them, they would do so as if those shadows were
reality, and hence the truth.

As one continues reading, it becomes clear that Plato wished to convey that all
of us human beings are like those prisoners. More exactly, that, just like those prisoners, what we take to be reality, or the truth, is merely shadows. He went on to
note that reality actually consists of what he called Forms, but a consideration of
what he meant thereby would take us beyond the aims of this chapter. For this
chapter, it is enough if I have managed to suggest that, although Plato's story is
more than 2,000 years old, and on first encounter seems a bit weird, I think it still
serves as a good illustration of what I believe should be one of the chief aims of
any teacher. It is, in short, to help learners to become aware that appearances are
often deceptive. Recall ice-floes instead.

As noted, at first blush, Plato's claim might sound far-fetched, even absurd. If so,
sceptical readers might like to recall that, appearances to the contrary, this book is
made out of tiny particles; the spaces between those particles is far larger than the
particles; and the force that holds those particles together can create a flash
brighter than a thousand suns.[3]

But this awareness, that appearances are deceptive, is not only important in the
learning of physics or biology; for never before has such an awareness been so
important in our daily lives. This is because, with the advent of mass communications, huge accumulations of wealth by a small number of people, the purchased
brains of slick speechwriters, and the dope of television, it is clear that a great
many people can be persuaded that spaghetti grows on trees.

I imagine that, at this point, some readers might be feeling an increasing sense
of doubt, for, among other things, I earlier used the word 'truth', and many people

believe today that there is no such thing as 'the' truth. In short, it is commonly believed that the truth is relative, – that is, that we all construe the truth in line with our personal predilections, and the culture in which we happened to grow up. Now, if this view is correct, it clearly has some very important implications for teaching.[4]

☙

Imagine that a certain teacher teaches geography, and that, at one point, he or she corrects a pupil. That pupil might then say, 'Ah yes, that's the way you see things. But the people actually living along the banks of the Irrawaddy River see things very differently. You just impose your western outlook on us, and you even imply that that is the only valid one. But then, what really motivates you is your need to impose your will on this class and to retain your job!' If one takes seriously the notion that everything is relative – not a notion that one uses when it is personally convenient to do so – it isn't easy to refute such an objection. Or consider a lesson in contemporary history in which the Holocaust is being examined.[5] The tutor might be endeavouring to examine the causes for this event, and a student might say, 'Hey, wait a minute. Although you don't say so, you obviously believe that this extermination of people was a terrible thing. But the records show that a very large number of selfless, idealistic, dedicated, highly educated German and Austrian officials genuinely believed that they were serving the whole of humanity by carrying out this programme. If the truth is relative, how can you maintain that this was a terrible event?'

At this point, some readers might want to object that teachers are primarily engaged in teaching facts, and that the belief that the truth is relative, does not apply to facts. But such an objection is quite mistaken. This becomes clear when one recalls that facts are not isolated entities, but gain their meaning from how they fit into a pattern. Imagine telling a person who has had no contact with western science, that malaria is caused by a certain kind of mosquito and not by spirits. Having no conception of parasites, blood stream, corpuscles, and so on, this person's eyebrows are likely to rise in polite incredulity. He or she might then say, 'Tiny mosquitoes can cause a grown man such suffering?' This example might illustrate that what we call 'a fact' is 'a fact' because it is embedded in a world outlook composed of thousands of interlocking postulates. Change the outlook, and the notion that something is 'a fact' disappears.[6]

Notice further that, if everything really is relative, no one theory can be more valid than any other. All one can do is to examine how consistent is a theory, and compare it with a similar theory; and in the absence of any agreed criteria of 'truth', it is impossible to say which theory is more valid. Or consider some guy who writes a book like this one, and believes that he is telling it like it is. As everything is relative, this guy is a dumb-bell, for tomorrow somebody will come along, write the opposite, and, as there is no such thing as the truth, that book will be just as good as this one provided that it is coherent and does not lead to contradictions.

Of course, some people teach subjects that do not raise considerations of the above kind. If you teach computer maintenance, you don't have to worry about the truth of what you teach. You have to worry about the accuracy of what you teach, and that's a different matter. Still, you would be in trouble if you believe that the truth is relative, and if what you teach is also examinable. For you might catch one of your learners passing a note during an exam; and, if you then disqualified that learner, you would be hard pressed to answer if he or she turned on you and said, 'As I see it, the main aim of this exam is to limit the number of people who practise this trade. It is also a part of a competitive system that I consider abominable. I believe in free and open access to all occupations, in allowing customers to choose the person they want for a job, and in encouraging cooperation between learners. And if you genuinely believe that everything is relative, you should apologize, not reprimand me!'

I trust I have said enough to persuade anyone who teaches anything, and who sincerely believes that the truth is relative, to consider handing in their notice.

&

But of course, the above is not the end of the matter. In several places in this book, I argued that it is important to consider the available evidence if one wishes to come to a sensible decision about a factual matter. But if everything is relative, there is no way of determining the ultimate worth of any evidence. From this it would seem to follow that it is impossible to decide whether the sun goes around the earth, or the earth around the sun; all depends on what a given society holds to be 'true'.

Fortunately, there is a way out of such absurdities, and it is by using what is called a rational approach; that is, an approach by which one attempts to seek evidence that is, as far as that is possible, open to objective investigation and refutation. This is not to say that the collection of evidence is what a rational approach is essentially about. Evidence is a secondary matter. Its purpose is to support an argument; nevertheless, evidence is important, for, if it runs counter to the argument, the argument must be amended or scrapped.

Other important attributes of being rational include the following. It requires that one consciously chooses what to believe, that one attempts to lay bare the reasons for those choices, and that one endeavours to express those beliefs in a clear, brief and coherent manner. Notice that such a process requires some self-reflection, and from this it follows that being rational is not a matter of applying a certain approach mechanically, for, in thinking rationally, one will be aware of one's own thought processes, and what assumptions might not be warranted in that process. One might also become aware of the moral and aesthetic implications of what one is doing. Notice, further, that all these processes take place before and while one acts, and are hence not a matter of justifying one's actions after they have taken place. In short, rational behaviour is not the same as rationalizing one's behaviour.

It is of course perfectly possible that people in another society might adopt a different way of going about things, and that's fine by me. I nevertheless insist on my wish to adopt what I consider a rational approach; and if, on examination, I decide that the approach of another people is not rational, I reserve the right to ignore it, – which is not the same as deriding it.

At this point, it might be helpful to pause for a moment and recall that this is not a discussion about tastes. If Jack says that blue is a nice colour, and Joan says she prefers lilac, it is taste, not truth, that is being debated. Likewise, there is a place for opinions, as, for example, when one is discussing the merit of a guided tour as compared with going off on one's own. Again, this is not a matter of truth or reality; it is a matter of opinion. In short, this section is about the truth (or the construction of truth), in situations in which it makes sense to speak in this way.

Notice further that, if one continues to insist that everything is relative, and that there is no such thing as reasonably objective evidence, it becomes impossible to distinguish between evidence and opinion. Notice also that those who possess power would be delighted at such an outcome. For, if all statements are ultimately no more than opinions, then it is impossible seriously to question, for example, the idea that large disparities of wealth have serious implications for the physical health of a society.[7] In fact, it becomes impossible seriously to question anything; for, as noted, if everything is relative, all statements are ultimately no more than opinions and are equally valid. This is a very important matter, and for the following reason.

The relativist position became fashionable, in part, because many people rightly wished to object to much that went unquestioned in the conventional wisdom. For example, conventional wisdom held that a woman's place is in the kitchen; that intelligence is inherited, fixed, and measured by the IQ test; and that, as the natives of Africa are primitive, colonialism is justified. A relativistic position undermines all such self-serving beliefs. The trouble is that relativism also undermined the concept of truth, and this has tremendous implications.

First, recall that those who have great wealth, and hence great power, want one thing above all, and it is to retain those things. Recall, second, that these people constitute never more than about 20 percent of a population – often far less – and that they control the main levers of power – i.e., huge manufacturing and service corporations, enormous banking and insurance conglomerates, and political decision making. Together with these, they also own the mass media, and they thereby control the information that comes to us.[8] And what do we get from the mass media? Surprise, surprise, an ever increasing load of opinions! And as one opinion is ultimately as valid as any other, nothing can ever be seriously questioned. In such a situation, those in power are able to sleep quietly; and in this way, the advent of relativism has strengthened the very forces that many of its adherents sought to question.

☙

One should perhaps next consider the implications of certain aspects of physical theory, for those who speak in favour of relativism, often cite people like Einstein and Heisenberg in support of their position. Isn't the theory of relativity one of the most famous ever stated? Or consider the implication of the uncertainty principle! First Einstein; and, as is well known, among other things he showed that every physical description of something, like a body moving through space, is only explicable when seen relative to the things around it. For example, if everything in the universe, including light, were moving at the same speed, it would be impossible to measure the speed of anything. In short, it is how things appear at a certain point that is relative; and Einstein did not hold that 'everything is relative', but that appearances are relative. Indeed, for a long time he called his theory the 'invariant' theory. Furthermore, Einstein's non-scientific writings show an unquestioning belief in an ultimate truth; and he even took pains to point out that his work in physics has no relevance to life in general. He flatly stated: 'The present fashion of applying the axioms of physical science to human life is not only entirely mistaken, but also has something reprehensible in it.'[9] As this is such an important matter, it might be best to quote Einstein again. On Max Planck's 60th birthday in 1918, Einstein delivered a celebratory address in which he made the following statement: 'The development of physics has shown that at any given moment, out of all conceivable constructions, a single one has always proved itself decidedly superior to all the rest. No one who has really gone deeply into the matter will deny that in practice, the world of phenomena uniquely determines our theoretical constructs, and this in spite of the fact that there is no logical bridge between phenomena and theoretical principles. This is what Leibnitz described so happily as a pre-established harmony.'[10]

As for Planck, the originator of quantum physics, he wrote like this about Kepler, one of the key figures in our understanding of astronomy: '. . . one can realize that, in studying his life, that which renders him so energetic and tireless and productive, was the profound faith he had in his own science, not the belief that he could eventually arrive at an arithmetic synthesis of his astronomical observations, but rather the profound faith in the existence of a definite plan behind the whole of creation.'[11] One can now ask bluntly: Is Kepler's work, work that helped to establish that the earth goes around the sun, and not the other way around, a contribution to our understanding of reality, or is it a social construct, no more and no less valid than any other?

Notice that, in the foregoing, Einstein maintained two things. One, that of all possible theories advanced to explain natural phenomena at a given time, i.e., in view of the available evidence, there is always one that is better than the others. And two, it is the natural world that determines the theories that we invent to explain the natural world, and not the other way around, as a relativist would maintain. Notice also that it also follows from Einstein's comments that he believed that there is an intimate link between the world and our minds, a matter to which I shall return.

Readers now have a choice: To go with the Keplers and the Einsteins of this world, people who attempted to explain this world, and, in practical terms, succeed in this endeavour to some extent; or to go with the relativists who maintain that such attempts are ultimately no more than social constructs, and who themselves explain nothing.

I come next to Heisenberg; and again, the same orientation is to be found in his occasional writings.[12] True, in his work in physics, he advanced the notion of indeterminacy, the uncertainty principle, and the experimenter effect. Yet, if one reads what he had to say on, say, atomic weapons, he did not even pause to consider that his comments were no more than mere opinions. He obviously intended that what he said on such a topic, was to be judged on an absolute conception of what is true or false; and he wrote in this way because he also maintained that his writings on physics were only applicable to physics.

It is surely remarkable that people who are not themselves physicists see social and philosophical inferences in the work of physicists, that are the opposite from the inferences that practising physicists make. And this seems to go unnoticed! I imagine that such a situation has come about because the belief in 'the social construction of reality' has so permeated thinking since the early years of the last century, that this belief has achieved the status of a self-evident truth. Moreover, to question it, risks getting oneself bracketed with the reactionary, blind, dogmatic, insecure and illiberal. In spite of such risks, I note my belief that this position is logically untenable, and pernicious to serious inquiry. And for reasons I shall give in a moment, I believe it can also destroy human relationships.

At this point, I should perhaps mention what is commonly called the 'Constructivist' position. This holds that we all construe the world about us, and that what is important is to understand people's constructions, rather than what might be the case. In view of what I have written about schemas, it might be thought that I would find such a position congenial. I do not, and this is because, in the constructivist position, 'what might be the case' tends to be lost by default. People who favour this position often refer to the work of George Kelly in support of it, so it seems appropriate to quote this man as well. He typically wrote, 'We have long since committed ourselves to a point of view from which we see the world as being real, and man's psychological processes as being based upon personal versions of that reality.'[13]

⅋

Consider next some of the everyday implications of believing that everything is relative. For example, how could parents honestly decide whether a child of theirs had lied in a certain situation, or did not share their outlook? Or how is one to differentiate between a genuine and a fake emotion? In short, notice how qualities like sincerity, honesty, genuineness or integrity become blurred if one seriously adheres to the notion that everything is relative or construed.

As the above might sound too abstract, consider the following scenario. I sadly tell you that my wife, Jane, keeps insisting that I am selfish. I add that I am very worried about this because I fear it might lead to a breakdown in our relationship. You now have two options. You could point out that Jane and I construe things differently, and suggest that we must find a way to negotiate these differences so that they can be settled amicably. Or you could attempt to help me discover the extent to which Joan's complaint is true. The trouble with the first option is obvious, and it is that I don't have a relationship with only my wife. I also have a relationship with my children, parents, cousins, friends and colleagues; and, if I really am selfish, I am likely to have problems with these people as well. Do I then start negotiating with all these people? And what if Joan and I part, I take up with another woman, and the same problem arises? Do I then engage in more negotiating?[14] But notice how convenient it would be for me to argue in such a situation that everything is relative!

The above leads to a wider question. Recall here that two things are especially characteristic of severe mental distress like paranoia, schizophrenia or black depression. One is that the person concerned suffers terribly; and the other is that the sufferer's view of reality is impaired. If so, how does one decide that a person is up a gum tree, as compared with construing things differently? And how can one of the main characteristics of severe emotional distress be that it is out of joint with reality, if reality is something that we all construe?

Consider another scenario. After much effort, my wife and I manage to get a house built for our family. We gain much pleasure from this, and we are careful to insure it properly. One day a fire breaks out, and the house is gutted. My wife and I feel terrible, but console ourselves by thinking that none of the members of our family were hurt, and that we have insurance and will build again. But the insurance company raises all sorts of objections, and we are forced to go to court. As the company has vastly more resources than we do, it wins the case, and my wife and I are left with about one quarter of what the house was worth. We are devastated; and not only by the huge financial loss, but also by what we perceive to be an abominable absence of justice. But where is justice in a scheme that holds that the truth is relative?

I write as I do in an attempt to indicate that this matter of truth is not an armchair matter, but pervades the whole of our lives; and having a viable life, depends to a considerable extent on there being a shared conception of 'truth', and how one might agree about it. But if there ain't no 'truth', then the latter becomes impossible, and the qualities noted above reduce to hot air. In other words, if the relativists are right, notions like 'true', 'false', 'genuine' and 'fake' are social constructs, and hence ultimately illusory. One wonders how relativists would cope if they found themselves in real-life situations that are exactly as they describe. For there are lots of societies in which the people in them will agree to complete a job in three days when they know that it will take twelve; who will tell you that certain materials will be necessary that they have no intention of using; and who will quote you a price that they will then treble as if nothing whatsoever had earlier been said about the price.

Or consider how one might square the belief that the truth is relative with the fact that we are deeply moved by the struggles of King Oedipus and King Lear to understand the position in which they find themselves. If what is at stake is merely the construction of *their* truth, what is the big deal? Or consider Othello. He murders his wife before our eyes, but we cry with him only when he discovers 'the' truth about her. But again, if there is no such thing as 'the' truth, what is the big deal? With such a thought in mind, one can now make a choice: Go with Hamlet – and look how he ended up! – or take the relativist tack.

Recall here the expression 'The truth will out'. In a relativistic world, this is nonsense. But the *world* is not relativistic; and that expression points to the fact that the truth is not something in our head, or some sort of moral notion, but reflects the fact that reality is real! *People's* notions can be untrue or unreal (and they always pay for that in one way or another), but that has nothing to do with reality. The implication of what I am stating here might become clearer if I note that there is accumulating evidence that people's physical health depends in part on the extent to which they acknowledge, at least to themselves, the extent to which they are in pain. There is even mounting evidence that our immune system is affected by the extent to which we acknowledge when something is wrong with us! I cannot even begin to see how such evidence can be squared with the notion that the truth is relative.[15]

Notice here that those who argue in favour of relativism are unable to explain why they favour this position. And this is because the only sensible explanation anyone can give for holding a certain belief, is to say that one thinks that it is true. But that is precisely what a relativist cannot do. If so, one might want nevertheless to ask *why* anyone should hold that all truths are relative. Unless relativists are quite unlike the rest of us, the answer must be that they have a personal inclination for this; but why they have such an inclination, is a question I leave open.

But I can note the following. One of most striking characteristics of the relativist position is that it is impregnable, and for this reason. Recall first that one of the characteristics of a rational approach is that no discussion about a factual matter can ever be closed. For example, if I maintain that the industrial revolution began in Britain, someone might ask, 'Why in Britain?' I'd answer, 'Because it was easy to find coal and iron near the surface in that country.' The questioner might then ask, 'But that's also true of other countries, so that can't be the reason.' And so on, and the topic always remains open to further questions. But a relativist can always fall back on saying that something is an opinion, and, as one opinion is as good as any other, the discussion ends. The interesting thing here is that this is also the most prominent characteristic of a dogma. If you question a dogma, the defender will tell you that it is the word of some deity, and with that statement, the discussion is closed. In short, at bottom, relativism is a dogma. But it is perhaps even more striking that relativism undermines its own position, for, if everything is ultimately an opinion, relativism is also an opinion, and hence no more valid than any other.

Notice further that, in the relativistic scheme of things, even the notion of reality becomes illusory. There would only be different constructions of reality. If so, how is one to determine whether what one is feeling or thinking has some link with reality, or is a fantasy? In a world where everything is relative, a cloud could be a cuckoo. That comment might sound fanciful, but we are often already in this position; for that is precisely what happens when certain politicians talk about an event in the way that they want us to see it. In that way, an event becomes what they say it is. But then, if reality really is construed, what they say is as valid as what anyone else might say. The end result of such an approach is the destruction of meaning, and that is of course precisely what a good many leaders want.

Notice that, as brute force is no longer fashionable, and costly, it is difficult for those in power to gain what they want unless current myths support them. And current myths do, for it is fashionable today to speak of 'deconstruction'. And what does this boil down to? Briefly, for it goes against the grain to spend much time on claptrap, the notion of 'deconstruction' is based on the observation that words always have an indeterminate meaning, that they refer more to other words than reality, and that it is therefore impossible to pin down the meaning of anything. And of course, there is a grain of truth in this; and in previous chapters, I often noted that the words that stand for something, are not the same as that thing itself. But it is only people like academics, who spend their time primarily with words, who would, from these observations, go on to claim the need to 'deconstruct' everything, and in this way, to destroy meaning. I wonder whether they would come to the same conclusion if they had to milk six cows by hand, on a hot, flyblown day, in a muddy yard.

Compare this view of things with the one advanced in previous chapters. In one of them, I noted that, in the course of having experiences, schemas are formed in our brain, and that we respond to the subsequent events around us on the basis of those schemas. It follows that, as everyone will have somewhat different schemas in their brain, people's reaction to the things around them will tend to differ. For example, if four people are present at the site of a traffic accident, their accounts of it are likely to differ. Or one could say that they construe the accident differently. But from this it does not follow that the accident cannot in *principle* – if not in actuality – be described accurately. It also follows from the latter view that one account of that accident might be more accurate than another.

I would briefly summarize the two conflicting views outlined above like this.

a) One could say that, because our responses to the world around us are based on the schemas in our brain, and as these schemas are based on our personal experiences, we often find it difficult and sometimes impossible to state the truth of any matter. It is also the case that, as the human brain is just one small product of nature, it is often far too weak to encompass nature, and is hence only able to produce partial and often inaccurate accounts of nature. However, if the human brain perseveres, it is often able to improve on its accounts of nature. From the foregoing, it follows that the truth of any matter might be difficult or even impossible to discover, but that it nevertheless exists *in principle*.

b) Or one could say that, as it is impossible to apprehend the world around us directly, all statements about the world are constructions, depending on our biological inheritance, personal predilections and the culture in which we live, and are hence relative. It further follows that no one construction can be more valid than any other, and that there is therefore no such thing as 'the truth'.

The first account seems to me to be far more plausible than the second. However, it is impossible to prove this. But then, it is impossible to prove anything. For example, for several hundred years, everyone in the western world – not just ignorant peasants – believed that witches exist. Moreover, people accused of being witches were brought to trial, and many were burnt to death (especially in German- and French-speaking Europe). Today, this is no longer done, but that change did not come about because it was proved that witches don't exist. That's impossible. What happened is that the circumstances that led to this belief changed, and the available evidence made it clear that it is unlikely that such creatures could exist. In the same way, one could now ask what led to the belief that the truth is relative. I earlier suggested one possible answer. It was roughly that, not so long ago, many people wished to reject some of the beliefs that were current in the conventional wisdom; and they did this in part by drawing attention to the fact that these beliefs were self-justifications. But a more important reason is, I think, as follows.

❧

It seems to me that, at bottom, the relativist position is a manifestation of a western divorce from nature. In short, it seems to me that many people in developed countries now stand so far outside of nature, that they see it as construed by them. Such a view goes hand in hand with an individualism that is turning increasingly into alienation. Interestingly enough, the idea that everything is relative – if you think about it for a minute, a very simple idea – became widespread only in the last hundred years, that is, together with an increasing focus on the individual. This has sometimes become an individualism in which the only thing that really counts is 'me', and hence what 'I' think.

As I have made a number of critical comments about individualism, it might be appropriate to recall here that a culture in which there is a focus on the individual has many blessings. At its best, such a focus ensures that human beings are treated with dignity. However, such a view is like a two-edged sword. For example, when a crisis arises in a country, a focus on 'the individual' can lead to the appearance of a dictator, and with that, the destruction of national institutions. This is because, in such a culture, people might come to believe that only a certain individual can bring order to the country. To some extent, that is how Hitler came to power in Germany, and how, together with the assumption of power by him, there came about a destruction of civil institutions in that country.[16]

A consideration of what is at stake, when there is an endless focus on the individual, is perhaps best seen when one considers what is most commonly seen on television, especially American television. Television presents people as if they were largely concerned with one thing: personal ambition. From the way that the camera focuses on these people, at one moment from this angle and then another, a picture is conveyed of glamorous individuals, almost isolated from society at large. Even when the aim of these people is to improve something of a social nature, the reward sought is individualistic. These people expect nothing from society, and, except for superficial corruptions, do not question the values of their society, for they share and express those values. Moreover, the sumptuous settings in which many of the people depicted on tv lead their lives, amounts to an endless advertisement for the consumer society; and this in turn conveys the idea that consumption is essential if one is to have a sense of fulfilment.

In an earlier chapter, I noted that tv is best at conveying images and feelings, and poor at conveying abstract ideas. Hence, its producers attempt to generate a succession of sensations. The result is that one sensation is experienced as being as good as any other, and all sensations are then ultimately experienced as being equally significant. With a press of a button, one moves from a quiz show to a police drama, and from these to a family comedy, and then a documentary about melting ice caps. At the end of such viewing, one is left mainly with a series of impressions or sensations. And further, both in dramas and documentaries, and even within one programme, discontinuity is the norm. Episodes become increasingly shorter, and the connection between them increasingly tenuous. Even within a single episode, the camera moves around relentlessly. Dialogues consist of clipped sentences, quite often no more than three words long; but they often seem pregnant with meaning, for the speakers are shown in close-up, and the words made significant by evocative music. No one talks for long enough to express anything of any substance; and depth of feeling, if it exists at all, is expressed in no more than a single word or glance. In any case, in television, the underlying focus is on how people feel rather than on what they think. Hence, both in dramas and documentaries, the relationships depicted are as brittle and shifting as the movement of the camera. Except for a few stereotyped individuals in whom no one believes, a high proportion of characters on tv turn out to be unreliable. In such a world, suspicion and mistrust are signs that one is streetwise, even intelligent. Any commitment expressed, is usually to another individual, or to an abstract symbol like a flag, and almost never to a community or a substantial idea. Aside from this focus on self, nearly everyone in this tv world works almost only to attain material rewards. The trouble of course is that, if one is engaged primarily in trying to gain material rewards, one is often engaged in trying to outwit others, either by producing goods that are ephemeral to human needs, or stealing from them, and in this way the personality becomes destroyed. Notice how the comments in this chapter echo much that was noted when some of the negative aspects of educational technology were being considered.

A world outlook such as the above generates alienation and disintegration, and signs that that is so lie in the increasing number of volunteer societies in which people seek to join others in achieving non-material gains, and in the growing number of people who suffer from depression. The irony is of course that individuality and dignity, freedom from want, and access to the essentials of life, can only be achieved when there is a basic sense of solidarity with others, and a wish to transcend one's own needs sometimes.[17]

☙

I must return now to a consideration of the relationship between human beings and the rest of nature, and I trust that readers will soon see how this relates to the enterprise of teaching.

Most people today accept the likelihood that human beings did not arrive on this planet by some magical means, but rather, slowly evolved as they were shaped by evolutionary forces. The available evidence certainly indicates that this is the case with all other creatures. It follows that the nervous system of a creature on this planet must develop in a manner that will enable it to interact with what is around it. That is, our nervous system and brain are produced by nature to fit into nature. In other words, just as evolutionary forces shaped our lungs and eyes so that they can make life on this planet possible, so must the same forces have shaped our brain. And if that is so, one would expect that, just as our lungs and eyes serve us reasonably effectively, so is our brain also likely to serve us reasonable effectively, – that is, that it is able to register nature reasonably accurately.[18]

One could put the above crudely like this. Creatures that live under water, do not develop wings. I would argue in the same way that a brain, that was produced via the process called natural selection, must be a brain that is able to comprehend nature. As this matter is so important, I risk repeating the foregoing by noting that there must be an intimate link between our brain and the rest of nature; and readers might recall that I quoted Einstein to that effect in an earlier section. As relativists are fond of quoting physicists, here is Schrödinger, with Einstein and Heisenberg one of those scientists most responsible for advances in modern physics. I quoted the following in an earlier chapter, but it bears repeating: 'The same elements compose my mind and the world. This situation is the same for every mind and its world. . . . The world is given only once, not one existing and one perceived. Subject and object are only one.'[19] The following three illustrations might help to explain the implication of Schrödinger's comment.

Imagine a tomato plant when it has reached the stage of producing a few small green tomatoes. Day after day, the tomatoes get larger; and then they begin to redden. Although I have written that the tomatoes 'redden' – i.e., that they 'do' something – they obviously don't 'do' anything; and this notion of 'doing' is conveyed because this is the way that language works. It would be more accurate to say that it is the sun, or the light, or the chemical reactions in the plant that 'do' things. But that would not be accurate either, for 'reddening' is a process, not an action. Hence, about the nearest one can get to accurately describing those tomatoes, would be to say that a 'reddening process occurs' in them.

Consider as a second illustration a bee taking pollen from a flower. First, we know that bees do not approach flowers to obtain pollen. If they can be said to have an intention, it is to obtain nectar. So the taking of pollen by bees is a by-product of them settling on a flower. As for the nectar, bees obviously don't have 'intentions', so one cannot accurately say that bees 'take' nectar either. Again, it is more accurate to speak of a process taking place.

Consider as a third illustration a boy or a girl picking an apple off a tree. In this instance, they certainly appear to be 'doing' something. But perhaps this notion is also an illusion, buttressed by the way that language works? Perhaps what really happens in such a situation is that the sight of an apple triggers off an almost automatic response, which is interpreted by our mind as our intending to do something? As that comment might sound highly implausible to some readers, I would urge them to consult the references I cite.[20] What I am trying to convey with these illustrations is that, because of the way our language works, we tend to divide the world into, on the one hand, the environment, and, on the other, living creatures. But, as Schrödinger suggested, it might be more accurate to consider the environment and living creatures as an integral whole.[21]

This position might become more intelligible when we recall what happens when we have an experience. That is, if we pause for a moment and reflect, it becomes very difficult to grasp exactly who is this 'we' that have an experience. We tend to say that it is our 'ego', or our 'I' that experiences. But exactly who or what are those things? And if one continues ruminating in this way, one might find oneself sliding into the odd supposition that that, which has an experience, and that which is experienced, seem to run into each other. Recall here that, when you see a tree, you don't have the experience of 'you' seeing a tree. The tree is simply there. It is only if you think about the matter, that the notion of 'you' creeps in. In the vast bulk of situations, an experience simply takes place; and it is only as an afterthought, that we believe it is 'we' who 'have' that experience. To put this another way, for most of the time 'we' and the world seem to merge into each other.[22]

&

In a previous section, I tried to show that the relativist position is not just some notional idea, but has very important practical implications. I should now like to illustrate this most important matter further, and I take the writing of this book as an example for it is something practical and to hand. In this book, I have put forward a theory of learning, but I do not present it as my opinion. Nor do I hedge my bets by saying, for example, that it might be found useful in developed countries. (I do hedge my bets by saying that it only holds for people in whom the wish to understand has not been destroyed.) I go way out on a limb. I say that, to the best of my understanding, this theory holds for all learners, between the ages of 8 and 88, studying anything, in any place between New York and Yokohama. Now, at the back of my head, I of course know that, if someone were to examine my theory, he or she would probably be able to show that I've got this or that wrong, perhaps even seriously wrong. And I know this because the history of all knowledge shows that this always happens; and furthermore, it is precisely in this way that we make progress. But, in the meantime, I make my suggestion, and hope for the best. I also insist that, if you would like to criticize this theory, so be it, but it wouldn't be enough to fob me off with talk of constructivism, modernism, positivism, postmodernism, relativism and other mumbo-jumbo. I use this kind of derisive language because one of the main characteristics of these approaches is to obscure understanding, not encourage it. I further insist that this criticism is practical, and is supported by some sort of evidence; and better, that the criticizer suggests a better theory. I also argue that this is the only responsible way to act. Relativists, on the other hand, see 'merit everywhere and validity nowhere', and in this way avoid taking any responsibility.

Of course, I have no guarantee that the theory of learning and teaching that I have outlined in this book is valid, for the simple reason that there are no such guarantees. All I can do is my best. To say that this is not good enough, for I can never get at the final truth, is to abandon the quest and to sit back. I don't accept this. I don't want to go back to the caves. I want to take part in the quest out of Plato's cave, even if I crack my head on some rocks in the process. Relativists, in contrast, seek to evade the need for responsible inquiry, and are hence at bottom selfish. Actually, they are worse. As I have repeatedly noted, because the world is a complicated place, and as we human beings are just one of its tiny products, no amount of mere thinking, or the application of any technique will ever make the world completely intelligible to us. But I am happy to accept this, for this is the price one must pay for being free to explore, and I want to explore. I relish my ability to cast about in search of the truth even though I know that I shall only catch glimpses of it. The relativists do the opposite.[23] They sit back and tell me it can't be done; and their position irritates me.

I say that it irritates me, because I have never come across work, by any of those who argue in favour of the relativist position, that has helped me to do something a mite more effectively. The only thing that these people seem able to do is to criticize. Perhaps these people irritate me because of my early years in farming. When you wake up in the morning wondering how to grow, mend or build something, people who merely criticize, irritate you. I mention these mundane things because I believe that the shoddiness of the relativist position is best revealed when one considers the fact that all our theories have the ultimate aim of helping us to cope with the practical aspects of living on this planet, and relativism offers no such help. It is ultimately destructive.[24]

Consider the effect on a creative scientist of arguing that everything is relative. If everything is relative, research becomes pointless, for all it could produce is subjective descriptions. That might be entertaining, but most scientists would consider the ardour of research pointless if all it produces is a subjective opinion. For centuries, it was unclear whether the blood circulates, or does not circulate. It was a matter of opinion. Fortunately, practising scientists like Harvey carried on with their work, unaware that their eventual discovery, that the blood circulates, is merely a social construct. Serious researchers persist in their endeavours because they believe that there is an elusive but absolute truth out there somewhere. And they are intrigued by this endeavour, wish to make a contribution, and gain the esteem of friends. Say this in some circles today, and you are told you are naive, but it is precisely because of this 'naive' belief that those speakers are unlikely to die of smallpox.

The relativist position is selfish in another way. As previously noted, I believe it arose together with, or perhaps as a consequence of, a preoccupation with self. I have in mind current notions about the right we all have to live our own lives, to be true to our inmost nature, to achieve our potential, to make the best of ourselves, and to decide for ourselves what is right and wrong. Such a view of things is a lot better than being cowed by the despotic religious and social norms that once prevailed. However, in the justified move away from such iniquities, I think we have landed ourselves with a new despotism, – that of 'the self'. I put it like that because, in this focus on self, large and important issues tend to be obscured. These include how we see our family, our neighbours, our community, and our society in all its aspects from taxation policies to health care.[25] This new despotism is also as unquestioned as the former used to be. This becomes clear when one considers a famous song in which the main words are 'I Did It My Way'. These words express well the extent to which 'doing it my way' is actually nothing more than doing it in the way that my culture has bent my mind to doing things. Furthermore, this focus on the self is incapable of producing what it is alleged to produce, namely, satisfaction and happiness, for these are by-products, not ends that can be achieved directly. Recall also that one of the most characteristic attributes of depressed people is a preoccupation with self. No wonder that depression, especially in young people, is on the rise in our self-obsessed culture.

☙

By now, some readers might well be wondering what all this has to do with teaching! Here is just one concrete example. In the culture of relativism that now prevails, talk in educational circles is increasingly about 'information', and this is in part the case because the acquisition of information sidesteps the thorny issue of evaluation, and hence the truth. (Hence also the rise in the interest of some educators in the internet.) Information is also increasingly seen as a kind of ready-made product, like sliced bread, easily digested even if one must chew a little. In this way, education increasingly becomes a part of the consumer society, with all the superficialities that this implies. In other words, I am suggesting that the wide acceptance of the bizarre notion that the truth is relative, helps to explain why the acquisition of information has replaced the development of understanding. Again, I would invite readers to recall the chapter, on educational technology, and how this book is an attempt to describe a seamless web.

Recall here that, when a teacher aims to foster understanding, he or she must ask learners to grapple with the difference between evidence and opinion, accuracy and inaccuracy, the genuine and the phoney, and the perceptive as compared with the trite. But, if everything is relative, these distinctions become blurred, and all you are left with is the acquisition of knowledge, for example, that the Amazon is a long river and that crocodiles live in parts of it. In such a culture, those who do well in quiz programmes are considered intelligent, and those who control the mass media can tell us that green is blue, and a population, taught to admire mere information, remains too stupid to notice.

None of this is new. Many years ago, Whitehead noted that, from a real education, one learns that certain ideas have great power, a coherent structure, and an intrinsic beauty. He added that such ideas do not, of course, exist in a vacuum, and that, to be valid, they must be based on the painstaking acquisition of information. But this information is not valuable in itself, but is valuable to the extent that it furnishes material out of which powerful ideas might develop.[26] Notice also that an emphasis on the acquisition of mere information, goes hand in hand with the notion that one of the chief aims of teaching is to prepare people for the workplace. After all, what increasingly counts today is to be able to sell a microwave oven 2 percent cheaper than your competitor, and the more that you merely know, the better your chances are of achieving such an aim. In such a culture, all educational activities, even those of an artistic nature, end up serving the interests of consumerism, and remaining dumb as to the intentions of those who have power. Consider, for example, that, although there is good evidence that violence on tv is related to violent behaviour, those who control the mass media systematically obscure this evidence.[27] There is also very little mention in the mass media about how television stifles conversation, deflects attention from the expression of decent manners, obstructs reflection, replaces imagination with fantasy, interferes with sharing meals, displaces reading, deregulates the ability to concentrate, impedes social interaction, turns us into passive spectators, undermines the inclination to learn to play an instrument, and causes us to neglect to have some exercise.

Even the notion of democracy is corrupted in such a culture. If one believes that everything is relative, the opinion of someone who merely has the gift of the gab, becomes equivalent to the evidence that someone might have worked years to collect. This is apparent in chat shows, where mere opinions, no matter how trivial, are aired. Tv documentaries are another illustration of this subversion of democracy, for even a feeble-minded person is able to understand one of these, and in this way everyone is made equal, and what could be more democratic than that?![28]

&

To what does the above bring one? Before I attempt to answer that question, please notice, first, that I have not suggested that teachers should advocate any specific belief. Teachers could advocate all kind of beliefs. They could advocate Anarchism, Atheism, Bolshevism, Capitalism, Catholicism, Communism, Conservatism, Determinism, Druidism, Ecumenism, Egoism, Fanaticism, Fascism, Globalism, Hedonism, Hinduism, Humanism, Individualism, Isolationism, Jansenism, Judaism, Liberalism, Libertarianism, Messianism, Militarism, Mohammedanism, Monarchism, Mysticism, Nationalism, Nihilism, Nudism, Opportunism, Organicism, Pacifism, Pantheism, Patriotism, Quakerism, Reformism, Romanticism, Secularism, Shintoism, Socialism, Stoicism, Taoism, Traditionalism, Unitarianism, Vegetarianism, Wholism or Zen Buddhism! And of course, there are all the ones that end with a 'y' like Astrology, Christianity, Democracy, Meritocracy, Necromancy, Papacy, Sociology, Usury and Zealotry. So many beliefs! But notice that many have one thing in common: many confer a sense of identity to their adherents, and that is probably why some people have clung tenaciously to them.[29] But I believe that teachers would usurp whatever authority they have if they were to advocate any of those beliefs. Furthermore, these beliefs provide answers, and I have been arguing that teachers are in the business of asking questions.

Here I had better add a rider. I have just suggested that teachers have no right to advocate any belief. I should have written any 'specific' belief (e.g., like those just listed). For, as I noted earlier, teachers will convey their beliefs whether they wish to or not, through *how* they teach. If so, teachers would probably be well advised to express clearly whatever general beliefs they have, for, otherwise, their learners will be left in the quandary of sensing what their teacher's general beliefs are, but without being sure about it. However, when a teacher states a belief, the learners are able to question that belief, at least in their minds, and thereby come to some evaluation of it. But I emphasize that I am speaking here about *general* beliefs, like a belief in egalitarianism or elitism, not a belief in a specific religion or political ideology.[30]

Second, I would have wasted a great deal of time and paper if I were now to answer the question that heads this chapter by suggesting that teachers should try to encourage attributes like responsibility and thoughtfulness. This is not because attributes like these are unimportant – they and many like them are obviously very important – but because everyone already agrees that they are important. But before I come to my point, two seeming digressions are called for, and the first is contained in a paper by another Nobel laureate, George Wald.[31]

Wald began by noting the simple fact that there is a universe. From this seemingly trite observation, something much less trite follows, and it is that there could just as well not be a universe. If so, one might want to ask why there is a universe. Wald then noted that the existence of our universe depends on a number of physical factors, like, for example, the subtle forces of attraction between sub-atomic particles. If these were even minutely different, there would be no universe. If so, how explain why those forces are just as they are? Wald next noted that there is life on this planet; and, just as is the case with the physical universe, the conditions supporting life in this universe are very subtle. Hence, if there were even slight deviations in them, life would not be possible. If so, the question again arises: Why are there conditions that support life in this universe, when there could just as easily not be such conditions?

Wald then turned to the existence of consciousness; and here he noted that, unlike anything else in the universe, its existence cannot be ascertained by any of our senses, so it cannot be measured or even located. We can only say that we experience consciousness; and, as this is a totally subjective state of affairs, it is not amenable to scientific investigation. We thus find ourselves in a paradoxical situation. This is that consciousness is necessary in order to conduct science – that is, to attempt to understand the universe – but it is impossible to use science to understand consciousness.

Wald then brought these two facts together. First, the plain fact that life exists; second, the plain fact that consciousness exists. If so, it seems plausible to conjecture that the function of consciousness is to enable life to know itself. In other words, the development of human beings on this planet – who possess the faculty we call consciousness – enables the world to know itself. From this it does not seem far-fetched to conjecture further that a world, which made consciousness possible, is likely to be a world that, from its very inception, must be in some sense a world able to know itself. It also follows from such a view that being and understanding are likely to be connected. Here I whistle: Being and understanding are connected?!

The second seeming digression derives from the work of the writer Barrett, and I paraphrase some of his observations like this.[32] If one examines one's nose, one becomes aware of all kinds of details; but, if one examines one's consciousness, one becomes aware that one is unable to describe it at all. The only things, with regard to consciousness, that one can describe, are the things *about* which one is conscious. In other words, it is as if consciousness is a sort of medium that has neither shape nor form. It is like looking into an enormous tank, in which there are moving, fish-like entities that we call thoughts, that are not suspended in anything whatsoever. In other words, our consciousness is invisible, and what appears to be in it, always refers to something outside it.

Now, if one keeps the above in mind, and examines the word 'truth', one might well decide that this word does not really stand for anything inside our mind either. This is because what we call the truth again refers to something in the outside world. But precisely to what does it refer in the outside world? We get a clue to a possible answer when we recall that, when we say that we see the truth of something, we mean that we see something in a way that is now different from how we previously saw it.

I was greatly helped to understand this matter a trifle better when I learnt from Barrett that the ancient Greek word that is translated into English by the word 'true' is *alethes*; and that this word means, first, 'un-hidden'; and then 'evident', 'manifest', 'open', or 'present'. Even so, I found that it takes quite a wrench to break away from the idea that 'the truth' is not a matter of there being a correspondence between a statement and a fact, or some sort of judgement, or any 'thing' inside one's head. It is rather that something in the *outside* world, that had been previously hidden, has now become evident.

I trust that readers will notice that these two digressions tie in with my earlier comments on relativism, and on how our thinking must have been produced by evolutionary forces in order to help us make our way on this planet. And I like to think that all of the above also ties in with the dozens of comments made throughout this book on the process of learning, and especially with how real learning is often a matter of discovering things that were previously unknown, or hidden, but had always been there. If so, I believe I can now attempt to answer the question that heads this chapter. My answer would be that teachers would do well if they were able, first, to encourage their learners to grasp that few things are as they appear to be; and, second, that much can be gained by trying to understand what they are really like. In short, in view of the mystery of life, and the state of our planet, and the garbage put out by the mass media, teachers would achieve a great deal if they were able to foster a wish to seek the truth.

As the above might sound rather highfalutin, I had better offer a few practical suggestions. But, before that, I must recall a creature from outer space that I introduced in a previous chapter. I then noted that it stands 35 cm high, that its upper part looks like a dish of blackcurrant jelly floating on spun sugar, that it has several antennae sticking out of it; and that, having been suitably radiated, it can speak some English. I did not then give its name.[33] It is $\sqrt{x1ay2bz3c}.44$; however, as some earthlings find this difficult to pronounce, it tells you to call it 'Square Root'. (I should perhaps divulge that some earthlings have abbreviated this to 'Screwy'.) Now, it so happens that I chanced to meet 'Square Root' because he/she had been sent to earth in order to bring back a report to its fellow creatures on the star KT7777789123, about life on this planet; and I found that, when Square Root and I met, it was asking the kind of questions that I thought teachers might like to ask. Here are the first half-dozen questions on Square Root's list. I had better mention that it so happened that Square Root and I met in the UK; and that the wording I use here is taken directly from this creature's list.

1) In my travels, I have noticed many statues in your capital cities of men on horseback with a sword at their side, and it eventually became clear to me

that these statues are there because you earthlings consider that these men were heroes. Furthermore, I learnt that these men had gained that status because they had defended their country. It then did not take me long to work out that someone must have attacked their country. However, although I have sought far and wide, I am unable to find a mention of an attacker that has come from one's country. Could you please explain to me why I come across only defenders and never attackers?

2) I have noticed in my investigations that, in your detective films or newspaper reports, one particular man or woman will be repeatedly depicted as having fought not only criminals, but also his or her organization. For example, in what I think you call 'cowboy' films, a stranger rides into town, finds certain nasty men terrorizing the place, discovers that the people who are supposed to defend the citizens are either corrupt or inept, becomes embroiled in this state of affairs in spite of himself, never speaks about himself, kills the nasty people at great danger to himself, and then leaves town. Or a certain teacher or doctor will be singled out as particularly commendable, especially as their school or hospital has obstructed them. Always the focus is on a particular individual. For example, in your elections, you earthlings increasingly vote for a certain person rather than for people who clearly articulate an approach. How do you explain this way of seeing things?

3) The data I have collected shows that, in your country, about 10 small children are killed by their parents every week, and that scores of other children are otherwise severely ill-treated by their parents.[34] However, in your newspapers, it is always evil strangers called, I think, paedophiles, who molest children, almost never parents; and on the tv machines that you earthlings spend much time watching, this topic is never shown or mentioned, whereas the buying of homes and cars frequently is. Does that mean that the earthlings in your country are more interested in cars than in the welfare of their children?

4) Last week, I was sitting in one of your courts of law, and I heard about a man who had killed 13 people he did not know, and had not even met before. One group of officials was arguing that, as this man had not planned those murders, he was insane; but another group was arguing that, as he had planned those murders, he was sane. I think the word 'premeditated' was used. From this I understand that you earthlings believe that, if a man *plans* to kill 13 people he does not know, he is sane. Could you please explain this to me?

5) I have learnt that, among you earthlings, the number of divorces in recent years has risen steeply, but that the number of marriages has also increased. I found especially interesting that the incidence of divorce is about 40 percent in first marriages, about 55 percent in second marriages, and over 75 percent in third marriages. If, as you earthlings say, people learn from experience, how do you explain this rise in percentage of second and third divorces – and all the pain and loss of money involved – in the case of people who do not, I also understand, need to get married in order to live together?[35]

6) When you earthlings see something, you say it is as if you had 'a picture' of it. I have also learnt that the process you call seeing takes place in your brain, not in your eyes, for your eyes act merely as receivers. But if one of your

surgeons were to open your skull, he or she would find that your brain is a lump of meat, in which there are chemical and electrical activities, but no kind of picture. If so, where is the picture you say you see when you look at a tree?[36]

Having taught for many years, I am of course aware that teachers do not usually ask questions of this kind. But then, as I noted, learners do not learn from *what* teachers say, but from *how* teachers teach; and, if teachers adopt a way of teaching that is characterized by asking questions, and especially questions of the above kind, learners might come to internalize a habit of considering the above kind of questions where others see nothing.

Notice that the above kind of outlook entails making attempts to analyse and to evaluate; and such an outlook is likely to have an underlying emotional component. This is because, in order to be engaged in this way, a person must possess an inner alertness that such a process is necessary in a world that is both complex and full of garbage. One must also be willing to persist in such an endeavour, and often at the risk of being thought a fool. Even so, when one meets people of this kind, one often notices that they seem to have a cheerful scepticism about common assumptions, and a strong desire to reach the truth of a matter.[37]

The above observations remind one that not everyone has such a cast of mind. Consider the following comment by a thoughtful woman: 'I've been accused at times of being a bit of a masochist, because I always wanted to know. . . . But always I would rather know, whatever it costs. But, then, in my family, not knowing went as far as madness.'[38]

Or consider the following description by a well-known writer of fiction, John Fowles. True, fiction is not life, but some writers of fiction manage to illuminate life pretty well. One of the characters in one of this writer's short stories says the following: 'Look. All right. Maybe you don't know the kind of world I was brought up in. But its leading principle is never, never, never to show what you really feel. I think my mother and father were happy together. But I don't really know . . . that's the world they lived in, and I have to live in when I'm with them. You pretend, right? You don't actually show the truth till the world splits in half under your feet.'[39]

As noted, descriptions such as these suggest that 'wanting to know' is not primarily a matter of the intellect, but more one of emotion; because, in asking questions, one might end up discovering things about oneself that might be painful. This, in turn, suggests that asking questions will only have a beneficial effect if it is accompanied by some love. In short, encouraging an inquiring approach can be difficult.[40]

But, in view of what ails us on this planet, and the satisfactions to be gained from getting a mite closer to the truth of anything, I would have thought it a task well worth attempting.[41] Moreover, in so acting, teachers would be professing something of some significance; and in this way become a part of a profession as well as an occupation.

Further Reading

As the notes that follow are often detailed, readers might like to have a reading list in which are noted works that I believe are especially helpful for a better understanding of learning and teaching. As it is obviously important to be aware of wider issues when engaged in either of these tasks, I have added a few books on further horizons. All are highly readable, and many are, I think, fascinating. As some of the works listed were published some years ago, I should perhaps recall that good books are more like wine than cars. No books on teaching specific subjects or age groups are noted, and that is not an oversight.

Works that should, I think, be read in any serious study of learning and teaching are marked:** Works that are otherwise strongly recommended are marked:*

Abercrombie, M.L.J., *The Anatomy of Judgement*. Free Association Books, 1989.** If I had to choose just one book on learning, it would be this one.

Bartlett, F., *Remembering*. Cambridge University Press, 1932.*

Bartley, III, W.W., *The Retreat to Commitment*. Open Court, 1984. On what is involved in being rational.*

Bettelheim, B., *The Informed Heart*. Free Press, 1960, especially Chapter 4. Often reprinted. The writer spent time in a concentration camp and describes his attempts to understand racialism rather than condemn it.

Bowlby, J., *The Making and Breaking of Affectional Bonds*. Tavistock, 1979.*

Brewer, I.M., *Learning More and Teaching Less*. SRHE and NFER-Nelson, 1985.

Carroll, J.M. and Mack, R.L., Actively learning to use a word processor. In *Cognitive Aspects of Skilled Typewriting*. Cooper, W.E. (ed.) Springer-Verlag, 1983. Excellent on how people learn.*

Eiseley, L., *The Immense Journey*. Vintage Books, 1946. Often reprinted. The writer lifts the eyes beyond the furthest horizon by writing science like a poet.*

Havelock, E.A., *Preface to Plato*. Basil Blackwell, 1963. And Havelock, E.A., The coming of literate communication to western culture. *Journal of Communication*, 1980, 30, 90–7.**

Hebb, D.O., Drives and the CNS. *Psychological Review*, 1955, 62, 243–54. Reprinted in *Personality Growth and Learning*. Open University Press, 1971.*

Holt, J., *How Children Fail*. Penguin, 1969, rev. edn 1987. Especially helpful for teaching adults.**

Katona, G., *Organising and Memorising*. Hafner, 1967. On how we learn.

Kelly, G., *A Theory of Personality*. W.W. Norton, 1955. Also Kelly, G., Man's construction of his alternatives. In *Assessment of Human Motivation*. Lindzey, G. (ed.) Rinehart, 1958.*

Klapper, P., The professional preparation of the college teacher. *Journal of General Education*, 1959, 3, 228–44. Contains brief descriptions of lessons, and early but perceptive comments on them.

Koestler, A., *The Sleepwalkers*. Penguin, 1964. Often reprinted. The subtitle is *A History of Man's Changing Vision of the Universe*.*

Köhler, W., *The Mentality of Apes*. Vintage Books, 1956. First published in English 1925. Often reprinted. The best single source I know for a better understanding of understanding.**

Kounin, J.S., An analysis of teachers' managerial techniques. In *The Social Psychology of Teaching*. Morrison, A. and McIntyre, D. (eds) Penguin, 1972.

Krishnamurti, J., *The First and Last Freedom*. Gollancz, 1969. Often reprinted. I don't accept this writer's ultimate aim, but I believe that he often conveys a way of looking at things that is exceptionally enlightening.**

LeDoux, J.E., Brain, mind and language. In *Brain and Mind*. Oakley, D.A. (ed.) Methuen, 1985.*

Lynch, J.J., *The Broken Heart*. Harper & Row, 1977. About how people are ultimately social creatures.*

Mann, R.D., *The College Classroom*. Wiley, 1970. Contains helpful comments on human dynamics in a classroom.

Marton, F. and Saljo, R., On qualitative differences in learning: 1, outcome and process; and Symposium: learning process and strategies: 2, outcome as a function of the learner's conception of the task. *British Journal of Educational Psychology*, 1976, 46, 4–11 and 115–27.*

Miller, G.E., The contribution of research in the learning process. *Medical Education*, 1978, 13, 28–33. The writer takes a very close look at conventional approaches to teaching.

Muir, J. and Gregg, J., *How to Keep Your Volkswagen Alive*. Santa Fe, NM: John Muir, 1969. Many times reprinted. The best example I know of how to write and illustrate learning material.*

Nisbett, R.E. and Wilson, T.D., Telling more than we can know: verbal reports on mental processes. *Psychological Review*, 1977, 84, 231–59.*

Oliver, W.A., Teachers' educational beliefs versus their classroom practice. *Journal of Educational Research*, 1953, 47, 47–55. An early paper that still sheds light on the nature of that famous gap between theory and practice.

Peddiwell, J.A., *The Sabre-Toothed Curriculum*. McGraw-Hill, 1937. The first chapter amusingly describes how all knowledge eventually becomes fossilized.*

Phillips, D.C., *Philosophy, Science, and Social Inquiry*. Pergamon Press, 1987. Clear comments on the fundamental issues that arise when examining learning and teaching.

Piattelli-Palmarini, M. (ed.) *Language and Learning*. Routledge & Kegan Paul, 1983.

Polanyi, M., *Personal Knowledge*. Routledge, 1958. Often reprinted. Shows how much knowledge is personal, universal, and often tacit.*

Popper, K.R., *The Logic of Scientific Discovery*. Hutchinson, 1959. Often reprinted. A great help for deciding what makes sense and what doesn't.**

Postman, N. and Weingartner, C., *Teaching as a Subversive Activity*. Penguin, 1971. I believe the writers made mistakes, but they demonstrated that how one teaches has a greater final effect than what one teaches.*

Rogers, C.R., *On Becoming a Person*. Constable, 1967, especially Chapter 13. Often reprinted.**

Salzberger-Wittenberg, I., *The Emotional Experience of Learning and Teaching*. Routledge, 1983.

Sherrington, C., *Man on His Nature*. Cambridge University Press, 1940. Often reprinted.**

Slobin, D.I., *Psycholinguistics*, 2nd edn. Scott, Foresman, 1979. A beautifully written introduction to the relationship between thinking and language.*

Squire, L.R., et al., The structure and organisation of memory. *Annual Review of Psychology*, 1993, 44, 453–95.

Turnbull, C., *The Mountain People*. Paladin, 1984. This illustrates that, just as when we were children and didn't really know our own home till we went into another one, so we don't really know our own society till we have lived in another one for some time.*

Vogt, E.Z. and Hyman, R., *Water Witching USA*, 2nd edn. University of Chicago Press, 1979. Illustrates in a lively way the difference between having an opinion and having some tentative evidence, and what follows from that extremely important difference.**

Vygotsky, L.S., *Thought and Language*. MIT Press, 1962. Often reprinted. For more recent comment on the relationship between thought and language, see Donald, M., *Origins of the Modern Mind*. Harvard University Press, 1991, especially Chapter 3.

Watson, J.D., *The Double Helix*. Penguin, 1970. The author describes how he and others made a discovery, and thereby gives us many clues on how real learning takes place.*

Watts, A., *Nature, Man and Woman*. Wildwood House, 1958. A Zen way of looking which helps to make clearer how we usually see things. Also Needham, J., *Science and Civilisation in China*, Vol. 2. Cambridge University Press, 1956.*

Weizenbaum, J., *Computer Power and Human Reason*. Penguin, 1984. On what computers can and cannot do. For a more recent and lively comment on the practical limitations of computers, see Landauer, T.K., *The Trouble with Computers*. MIT Press, 1995.*

West, K.M., The case against teaching. *Journal of Medical Education*, 1966, 41(8), 766–71. An early, short, clear, and penetrating look at 'common sense' about teaching.*

Whorf, B.L., *Language, Thought and Reality*. Carroll, J. B. (ed.) MIT Press, 1956. Often reprinted. See especially the last four chapters that hint at what might lie behind language.*

Wilber, K. (ed.), *Quantum Questions*. Shambhala, 1984. A collection that indicates how creative scientists see the world.**

Notes and References

Introduction (pages 4–5)

1. Those were the days when class, codes and control were in their heyday.
2. I have often found that the works I have considered most valuable are written in a relatively simple style; and I was gratified to discover that other readers have the same reaction. It is as if, when people have something worth saying, they take pains to make themselves understood. Or perhaps writers vary in the extent to which they take account of being read. See Hartley, J., *et al.*, Style and substance in psychology. *Social Studies of Science*, 2002, 32(2), 321–34. And Hartley, J., *et al.*, Clarity across the disciplines. *Science Communication*, 2004, 26(2), 188–210. In line with this approach, works are cited in these Notes and References in a style intended to help a busy reader to find them in a library.
3. I would go further today and say that it seems to me that some academic writing is parasitic on practice. This may also be the place to note that many of the works I cite were published some time ago, and that there are several reasons for this. One is that, as noted in the new Preface, all books are of their time and place, and producing a new edition cannot completely avoid this. Second, an examination of the various citation indexes shows that the great bulk of works published in even refereed journals sink without trace, to some extent because many are produced to further a career rather than knowledge, and that only about 10 per cent have much of an impact. It follows that substantial works are rare. And third, as human understanding is limited, only a very small percentage of books are seriously valuable, so it is hardly surprising that many were published years ago. Indeed, some of the works that have most influenced me in the writing of this book, for example Bartlett's *Remembering*, Havelock's *Preface to Plato*, Köhler's *Mentality of Apes*, Krishnamurti's *First and Last Freedom*, Popper's *The Logic of Scientific Discovery*, Sherrington's *Man on His Nature*, and Whorf's *Language, Thought and Reality* were published fifty and more years ago.
4. An example of the former is John Holt. An example of the latter is Jane Abercrombie. See Holt, J., *How Children Fail*. Penguin, 1969, rev. edn 1987. And Abercrombie, M.L.J., *The Anatomy of Judgement*. Free Association Books, 1989. First published 1960.

Preliminaries (pages 7–18)

1. For a discussion of the 'transmission' method of teaching see Perkinson, H.J., *Learning from Our Mistakes*. Greenwood Press, 1984. For a description of various approaches to teaching and their implications see Fox, D., Personal theories of teaching. *Studies in Higher*

Education, 1983, 8(2), 151–63. For penetrating comments on the conventional wisdom regarding teaching see Miller, G.E., The contribution of research in the learning process. *Medical Education*, 1978, 12(3), 28–33. Also West, K.M., The case against teaching. *Journal of Medical Education*, 1966, 41(8), 766–71.

2. *Fifteen Thousand Hours: Secondary Schools and Their Effects on Children*. Rutter, M., *et al.* (eds) Open Books, 1979. As the writers have no theory to give meaning to their 'facts', I do not believe that teachers will find much else of use in this book.

3. Anning, A., 'Curriculum in Action' in action. In *Action Research in Classrooms and Schools*. Hustler, D., *et al.* (eds) Allen & Unwin, 1986. Also Mitchell, P., A teacher's view of educational research. In *Educational Research: Principles, Policies and Practices*. Shipman, M. (ed.) Falmer Press, 1985. A recent publication on research on teaching, *Handbook of Research on Teaching*. Wittrock, M.C. (ed.) Macmillan, 1986, measures 28 × 22 × 5.5 cm, contains 1,037 double-column pages, and weighs 2.75 kilos! It is difficult to imagine a practising teacher reading it. No matter how conscientious the work of the editor and contributors, such a work raises fundamental questions about the relationship between practising teachers and the academic fraternity. It might be worth adding that, while writing this book, I read several hundred journal papers and many scores of books on learning and teaching and, to my initial surprise, found the majority unhelpful. (Some, however, provided useful references.) For further comment, see Bolster, A.S., Jr., Toward a more effective model of research on teaching. *Harvard Educational Review*, 1983, 55(3), 294–308. The writer's introductory comments are helpful.

4. I am greatly indebted to J. Krishnamurti for helping me to understand this matter a little better. A good entry into his work is through his *The First and Last Freedom*. Gollancz, 1969. Often reprinted.

5. For an amusing illustration see Casey, D., The awful nature of change: motivation in hostile conditions. *Management Education and Development*, 1985, 16(1), 14–16.

6. I believe there is a tendency to underestimate what is involved in fruitful reflection. The work of those who advocate this in teacher training is obviously based on extensive reading, and the habit of reflection derived from systematic study. Yet, these writers often disparage systematic reading and study. This kind of contradiction, based as it is on a one-sided emphasis on the personal and the practical, leads to a new kind of obscurantism, highly destructive of the educational enterprise. For an example of this trend see the introduction to *Educating Teachers*. Smyth, J. (ed.) Falmer Press, 1987.

7. Hora, T., Tao, Zen and existential psychotherapy. *Psychological Bulletin*, 1959, 2, 236–42.

8. The 'skills' approach gained prominence as an understandable reaction against merely theoretical knowledge. However, I believe the wholesale application of the skills or 'competence' approach to education has been pernicious, a case of throwing out the baby with the bathwater. In short, I believe that giving students a list of competencies to master tends to: make for doers rather than reflective practitioners; undermine the critical faculty; create an illusion of clarity; foster an atomistic approach; stress product over process; trivialize theoretical underpinnings; give students an answer before they understand the question; nurture an authoritarian impulse (because it stresses the given rather than the discovered); discourage a creative inclination. See Hart, W.A., Against skills. *Oxford Review of Education*, 1978, 4(2), 205–16. For a scholarly and sustained critique of the notion of 'competence' see Barnett, R., *The Limits of Competence*. Open University Press, 1994. Also Hyland, T., *Competence, Education and NVQs*. Cassell, 1994.

9. Many of those engaged in training teachers seem to accept a great many teaching 'competencies' on no more evidence than that there is some consensus about them. Anyone who believes that consensus makes for good practice should read Trevor-Roper, H.R., *The European Witch Craze of the Sixteenth and Seventeenth Centuries*. Penguin, 1988. As I mention witches several times in this book, I also cite Macfarlane, A., *Witchcraft in Tudor and Stuart England*. Routledge & Kegan Paul, 1970.

10. The political left and right in the UK often seem more similar than different, with the left emphasizing *individual* social needs, and the right *individual* economic needs, the two sides existing in a kind of symbiosis, with one stressing the distribution of wealth, and the other its making.

11. Downie, R.S., Professions and professionalism. *Journal of Philosophy of Education*, 1990, 24(2), 147–59. This is a clear exposition of the issue, and a relief after the aridity of most philosophical writing.

12. James J. Gibson attributes this lovely sentence to K. Lewin. See Gibson's fascinating contribution in *A History of Psychology in Autobiography*, Vol. 5. Boring, E.G., *et al.* (eds) Appleton-Century-Crofts, 1967. For further comment on how teaching is often seen as a self-evident activity, see Sotto, E., The self-evident nature of teaching. *Innovations in Education and Training International*, 1996, 33(3), 203–9.

13. Popper, K.R., *The Logic of Scientific Discovery*. Hutchinson, 1983. First published in English 1959. The quotation comes at the end of the book. This work has powerfully affected my understanding. As some readers might suspect a determinist orientation in my text, note also Bartley, W.W. III, The philosophy of Karl Popper. Part II. Consciousness and physics. *Philosophia*, 1977, 7, 675–716. For a scholarly, brief and readable review of the history of the notion that progress in science begins with the formation of a hypothesis, see Medawar, P.B., Hypothesis and imagination. In Medawar, P.B., *The Art of the Soluble*. Penguin Books, 1972. Holton notes that the most creative scientists 'do not build their constructs patiently by assembling blocks that have been pre-cast by others and certified as sound. On the contrary, they melt down the ready-made materials of science and recast them in a way that their contemporaries tend to think is outrageous'. Holton, G., *Einstein, History, and Other Passions*. American Institute of Physics, 1995, 13. See also Kukla, A., Nonempirical issues in psychology. *American Psychologist*, 1989, 44(5), 785–94. This writer notes, 'Data do not yield up theories of themselves, nor will theories emerge by adding more data to the lot. There is no alternative but to invent a theory.' For excellent real-life illustrations of the above process that led to a Nobel Prize see Watson, J.D., *The Double Helix*. Penguin, 1970.

14. This is how one scholar described past attempts to construct a theory of learning: 'Consider the hundreds of theoretical formulations, rational equations and mathematical models of the learning process that have accrued; the thousands of research studies. And *now* consider that there is still no wide agreement, even at the crassest descriptive level, on the empirical conditions under which learning takes place, or even on the definition of learning or its empirical and rational relations to other psychological processes or phenomena. Consider also that after all this scientistic effort our actual *insight* into the learning process – as reflected in every humanly important context to which learning is relevant – has not improved one jot.' Koch, S., Reflections on the state of psychology. *Social Research*, 1971, 38, 669–709.

15. Huberman, M., Teacher development and instructional mastery. In *Understanding Teacher Development*. Hargreaves, A., *et al.* (eds) Cassell, 1992. I have a view rather different from the one mostly expressed in this work, but found Huberman's paper helpful.

16. In addition to Popper's work noted earlier, see also *Criticism and the Growth of Knowledge*. Lakatos, I., *et al.* (eds) Cambridge University Press, 1970. For an application to education see Gibbs, J.C., The meaning of ecologically oriented inquiry in contemporary psychology. *American Psychologist*, 1979, 34(2), 127–40. The Introduction in Brown, B.B., *The Experimental Mind in Education*, Harper & Row, 1968, has comments on the need for a theory to guide intelligent educational practice. A brief, clear and engaging introduction to the philosophy of science is Chalmers, A.F., *What Is This Thing Called Science?*, 2nd edn. Oxford University Press, 1982. For a good introduction to scientific method see Beveridge, W.I.B., *The Art of Scientific Investigation*. Heinemann, 1979. An older but interesting account is George, W.H., *The Scientist in Action: A Scientific Study of His Methods*.

Williams & Norgate, 1936. For a brief, clear and elegant exposition of these matters see Medawar, P.B., *Induction and Intuition in Scientific Thought*. Methuen, 1969. See also Cohen, I.B., *The Birth of a New Physics*. W. W. Norton, 1985. This is a most important topic, and I must resist the temptation to add further references.

Part I Learning

Chapter 1 Motivation (pages 21–31)

1. I am greatly indebted to George Kelly for the orientation taken in this chapter and for much that follows. See his Man's construction of his alternatives. In *Assessment of Human Motivation*. Lindzey, G. (ed.) Rinehart, 1958. Also in *Clinical Psychology and Personality: The Selected Papers of George Kelly*. Maher, B. (ed.) Wiley, 1969. See also Kelly's paper The autobiography of a theory. Also in the latter publication. For criticism of Kelly's position – though not of the position taken in my text – see Foulds, G.A., Has anybody here seen Kelly? *British Journal of Medical Psychology*, 1973, 46, 221–5.
2. The phrase is Kelly's.
3. For an examination of what is implied by viewing learning as a biological process see Chomsky, N., *Rules and Representations*. Basil Blackwell, 1980.
4. It appears that people are more likely to engage in a task positively, especially when change is required, when they are able to decide how best to tackle it. See Coch, L., *et al.*, Overcoming resistance to change. *Human Relations*, 1948, 512–32. Also Levine, J., Lecture versus group decision in changing behaviour. *Journal of Applied Psychology*, 1952, 36, 29–33. I first came across this idea as a teenager when reading the work of A.S. Neill. See his *Summerhill*. Gollancz, 1962, or Penguin, 1968. Many times reprinted. See also Percy, K. and Ramsden, P., *Independent Study*. SRHE, 1980.
5. Vygotsky, L.S., *Mind in Society*. Cole, M., *et al.* (eds) Harvard University Press, 1978.
6. Postman, N. and Weingartner, C., *Teaching as a Subversive Activity*. Penguin, 1971. I believe these writers made mistakes, but I found many of their observations valuable.
7. For a succinct review of the relevant research, see Sirotnik, K.A., What you see is what you get: consistency, persistency and mediocrity in classrooms. *Harvard Educational Review*, 1983, 53(1), 16–31.
8. For much in this section I am indebted to Hebb, D.O., Drives and the CNS. *Psychological Review*, 1955, 62; reprinted in *Personality Growth and Learning*. Open University Press, 1971. See also the paper in the same publication by Hunt, J. McV., Using intrinsic motivation to teach young children.
9. Heron, W., *et al.*, Cognitive effects of a decreased variation to the sensory environment. *American Psychologist*, 1953, 8, 366–74. For a more recent overview of such studies see Reed, G.F., Sensory deprivation. In *Aspects of Consciousness*. Vol 1. Underwood, G., *et al.* (eds) Academic Press, 1976. For some critical comments on the notion of 'stimulus barrier' from a psychoanalytic perspective see Stern, D.N., *The Interpersonal World of the Infant*. Basic Books, 1985, 232.
10. I believe experiments on animals should be humane because I believe violence is indivisible. That is, I don't believe a society can have humane relationships among its people and at the same time be inhumane to animals.
11. I was introduced to the work of Papousek by Margaret Donaldson. See her *Children's Minds*. Fontana, 1978. For Papousek, see his rather technical paper, Individual variability in learned responses in human infants. In *Brain and Early Behaviour*. Robinson, R. J. (ed.) Academic Press, 1969. See also Kagan, J., On the need for relativism. *American Psychologist*, 1967, 22, 131–47; reprinted in *The Ecology of Human Intelligence*. Hudson, L. (ed.) Penguin, 1970. Kagan refers to the interesting work of Charlesworth. For further

comment see Bower, T.G.R., *The Rational Infant*. W.H. Freeman, 1989. For further comment see Marler, P., The instinct to learn. In *The Epigenesis of Mind*. Carey, S., *et al*. (eds) Lawrence Erlbaum, 1991.

12. This is not to suggest a one-to-one correspondence between things in the outside world and things in the brain. For a review showing how models of the world become established in our brain see Oakley, D.A., Cognition and imagery in animals. In *Brain and Mind*. Oakley, D.A. (ed.) Methuen, 1985. The evidence Oakley cites questions the belief that knowledge is built up through stimulus-response associations. For further comment see *Perception: An Approach to Personality*. Blake, R.R., *et al*. (eds) Ronald Press, 1951.

13. Tizard, B. and Hughes, M., *Young Children Learning*. Fontana, 1984.

14. I am indebted to Jerome Bruner for that sentence. See his *The Relevance of Education*. Penguin, 1974.

15. See Covington, M.V. and Omelich, C.L., As failures mount: affective and cognitive consequences of ability demotion in the classroom. *Journal of Educational Psychology*, 1981, 73(6), 796–808.

16. The figures are to be found in the relevant material published by the Department of Education and Science in the UK.

17. See Handy, C., *Organising for Capability*. Occasional Paper No. 2. Royal Society of Arts, London, October 1984. Also Raven, J., An abuse of psychology for political purposes? *Bulletin of the British Psychological Society*, 1979, 32, 173–7.

18. Spuhler, J.N., Somatic paths to culture. In *The Evolution of Man's Capacity for Culture*. Spuhler, J.N. (ed.) Wayne State University Press, 1965.

19. I again draw on the paper by Kelly noted above.

Chapter 2 Two Accounts of Learning (pages 33–54)

1. A very good introduction to the behaviourist position on learning is Lefrançoise, G., *Psychological Theories and Human Learning: Kongor's Report*. Brooks/Cole, 1972. It's even funny! For a brief introduction to Behaviourism see Rachlin, H., *Introduction to Behaviourism*. W.H. Freeman, 1976.

2. For an early paper that questions the usefulness of the notion of drives see Diamond, S., A neglected aspect of motivation. *Sociometry*, 1939, 2, 77–85. For a searching review of the concept of drives see White, R.W., Motivation reconsidered: the concept of competence. *Psychological Review*, 1959, 66(5), 297–333. White shows how the concept of drives had to be expanded to accommodate more and more data 'til it fell apart under the weight of its own contradictions. See also Segal, E.M. and Lachman, R., Complex behaviour or higher mental process. *American Psychologist*, 1972, I, 46–55.

3. See Skinner, B.F., *The Technology of Teaching*. Prentice-Hall, 1968. Notice the wording of this title. Readers who have not actually read Skinner should read this, not so much for the content, but for the machine-like style and hence underlying attitude. Readers might like to compare this with the prose and attitude characteristic of many eminent scientists, as in *Quantum Questions*. Wilber, K. (ed.) Shambhala, 1984.

4. See Skinner's chapter, The science of learning and the art of teaching. In *The Technology of Teaching*. For further comment see McKeachie, W.J., The decline and fall of the laws of learning. *Educational Researcher*, 1974, 3, 7–11.

5. For a devastating critique of the behaviourist position see Chomsky, N., Review of Skinner's *Verbal Behaviour*. *Language*, 1959, 35, 26–58; reprinted in *The Psychology of Language, Thought, and Instruction*. De Cecco, J.P. (ed.) Holt, Rinehart & Winston, 1969. See also Koch, S., Psychology and emerging conceptions of knowledge as unitary. In *Behaviorism and Phenomenology*. Koch, S. (ed.) University of Chicago Press, 1964. Also Rogers, C.R., The place of the individual in the new world of the behavioural sciences. In that writer's *On Becoming a Person*. Constable, 1967. And Weimer, W.B.,

Psycholinguistics and Plato's paradoxes of the *Meno. American Psychologist*, 1973, 28, 15–33.

6. See White, S.E., The active organism in theoretical behaviourism. *Human Development*, 1976, 19, 99–107.

7. Skinner, B.F., *Science and Human Behaviour*. Macmillan, 1953.

8. Both these experiments are reported by A.R. Luria in his *The Making of Mind*. Harvard University Press, 1979, 125.

9. Tolman, E.C., Cognitive maps in rats and men. *Psychological Review*, 1948, 55(4), 189–208. For a most interesting comment see Krechevsky, I., Hypotheses in rats. *Psychological Review*, 1932, 39, 516–32. When I note the date of publication of this paper, I feel a sense of awe and affection for scholars such as these who have made a contribution to our groping attempts to understand the human condition. For an allied matter, associationism, see Jenkins, J.J., Remember that old theory of memory? Well, forget it! *American Psychologist*, 1974, 29, 785–95.

10. It is common to find scholars who claim that a meaning is simply the expression of a certain physical state of the brain, or a derivative of 'a language of the brain'. For clear comment on this matter see Harris, R., The grammar in your head. In *Mindwaves*. Blakemore, C., *et al.* (eds) Blackwell, 1987.

11. See *Science and Beyond*. Rose, S. and Appignanesi, L. (eds) Basil Blackwell, 1986.

12. Bransford, J.D., *Human Cognition*. Wadsworth, 1979, 254. The writer notes the work of Anita Willis here with developmentally delayed children. She found that a behaviour modification approach, in the absence of an attempt to understand what this approach meant for the children, led to poor results. For an example of the simplification and manipulation inherent in therapies based on a behaviourist approach, particularly helpful because it is more sophisticated than many, see Hunt, H.F., Prospects and possibilities in the development of behaviour therapy. In *The Role of Learning in Psychotherapy*. Porter, R. (ed.) J. & A. Churchill, 1968. The discussions that follow this paper, and those between pages 320 and 328, are also helpful.

13. Quoted in Cohen, B.I., *Franklin and Newton*. American Philosophical Society, 1956. For the need to use hypothetical constructs if one is to make progress see Sanford, N., Will psychologists study human problems?, *American Psychologist*, 1965, 20, 192–202.

14. In investigating young children, Bower concluded that 'not only that much of an infant's learning cannot be accounted for by the notion of reinforcement, but that his behaviour becomes inexplicable when that notion is applied'. See Bower, T.G.R., *The Rational Infant*. W.H. Freeman, 1989. For examples which show that even animals have an 'inner state' see Breland, K. and Breland, M., The misbehavior of organisms. *American Psychologist*, 1961, 16, 681–4.

15. For findings which indicate that humans do not hear sentences but the meaning of sentences see again Jenkins, cited earlier, Remember that old theory of memory? Also Bransford, J.U. and Franks, J.J., The abstraction of linguistic ideas. *Cognitive Psychology*, 1971, 2, 331–50; and Bransford, J.D. and Franks, J.J., The abstraction of linguistic ideas: a review. *Cognition*, 1972, 1, 211–49. Also Sachs, J.S., Recognition memory for syntactic and semantic aspects of connected discourse. *Perception and Psychophysics*, 1967, 2, 437–42. Also relevant is the finding by Keenan and her associates that our ability to remember seems to depend on 'the degree to which a statement conveys information about a speaker's intentions, beliefs, and attitudes toward the listener'. Keenan, J.M., *et al.*, Pragmatics in memory. In *Memory Observed*. Neisser, U. (ed.) W.H. Freeman, 1982. This is an excellent book on memory, and I believe it lends support to the thesis that mental functioning is largely abstract. Some of these findings on memory were anticipated by F.C. Bartlett in his *Remembering*. Cambridge University Press, 1932. A personal observation might be in order here. I happen to speak a few languages, was once trying to remember a man's name, and could not. All of a sudden, the German word *Schneider* came into my

head. In English, this means 'tailor'. I then remembered the man's name; it was *Chayat*, the Hebrew word for 'tailor'! My younger daughter has sometimes shown that she understands the meaning of a phrase in a foreign language, is sometimes able to use it correctly, yet sometimes finds it difficult to translate it into English. See also Frankl, V.E., *Man's Search for Meaning*. Beacon Press, 1962. Often reprinted. I am unable to see how behaviourists could account for the kind of material Frankl provides.

16. Lepper, M.R. and Greene, D., *The Hidden Costs of Reward*. Lawrence Erlbaum, 1978.
17. For a review of research and detailed comment see Deci, E.L. and Ryan, R.M., *Intrinsic Motivation and Self Determination in Human Behaviour*. Plenum Press, 1985. See also De Charms, R., From pawns to origins: towards self-motivation. In *Psychology and Educational Practice*. Lesser, G.S. (ed.) Scott, Foresman, 1971.
18. See again Donaldson, M., *Children's Minds*. Fontana, 1978.
19. Quoted in *Teacher Learning*. Dow, G. (ed.) Routledge, 1982.
20. Their work is noted by Lepper and Greene, *Hidden Costs*, cited earlier.
21. Fransson, A., On qualitative differences in learning: iv Effects of intrinsic motivation and extrinsic test anxiety on process and outcome. *British Journal of Educational Psychology*, 1977, 47, 244–57.
22. This research is also noted by Lepper and Greene, *Hidden Costs*, cited earlier.
23. Kavanau, E.T., Compulsory regime and control of environment in animal behaviour, I: Wheel-running. *Behaviour*, 1963, 20, 251–81. I have seldom seen laboratory findings on small animals with more striking implications for learning and teaching. Note the date of publication! For a review of research on the question of personal control and how it affects a learner's progress, see Stipek, D.J. and Weisz, J.R., Perceived personal control and academic achievement. *Review of Educational Research*, 1981, 51(1), 101–37. Most of this offers strong support for the position taken in this section.
24. Noted by Lepper and Green, *Hidden Costs*, cited earlier.
25. Nisbett, R. and Ross, L., *Human Inference*. Prentice-Hall, 1980, 129. See also Mack, A., Inattentional blindness: looking without seeing. *Current Directions in Psychological Science*, 2003, 12(5), 180–4. Also Eich, E., Memory for unattended events: remembering with and without awareness. *Memory and Cognition*, 1984, 12(2), 105–11.
26. I should perhaps own that this is a fancy figure of speech I sometimes used in class. Unfortunately, I never had the pleasure of meeting Albert Einstein.
27. This is the date of publication of J.B. Watson's *Psychological Care of the Infant and Child*. W.W. Norton, 1928; reprinted by Arno Press, 1972. Nobody should adopt a behaviourist approach without having read this work for it is surely important to examine the likely ends before one adopts any means. I believe the mechanistic triteness of this book is its most striking feature. It also seems to me that the picture conveyed of Watson as a parent, in Cohen, D., *J.B. Watson*, Routledge, 1979, is pathetic and a poor recommendation for his position.
28. A good introduction to the social factors that influence the behaviour of learners is Bronfenbrenner, I.J., The origins of alienation. *Scientific American*, 1974, 231, 53–61. See also *Producing and Reducing Dissatisfaction*. Booth, T., *et al.* (eds) Open University Press, 1987. For a readable account of some noteworthy schools see Lipsitz, J., *Successful Schools for Young Adolescents*. Transaction Books, 1984. See also Gerbner, G., Teacher image in mass culture: symbolic functions of the 'hidden curriculum'. In *Communications Technology and Social Policy*. Gerbner, G. (ed.) John Wiley, 1973.
29. I should like to be able to recommend an introductory book on gestalt psychology but I cannot.
30. For an unusual example see Shanon, B., The polyglot mismatch and the monolingual tie. *New Ideas in Psychology*, 1984, 2(1), 75–9.
31. See Bransford, J.D. and McCarrell, N.S., A sketch of a cognitive approach to comprehension: some thoughts about understanding what it means to comprehend. In *Cognition*

and the Symbolic Process. Vol. 1. Weimer, W.B. and Palermo, D.S. (eds) Lawrence Erlbaum, 1974.

32. These statements are made by the economist Samuelson, and I am indebted to Lars-Owe Dahlgren for them. See Dahlgren's chapter, Outcomes of learning. In *The Experience of Learning*. Marton, F., *et al.* (eds) Scottish Academic Press, 1984. See also Saljo, R., *Learning in the Learner's Perspective I* and *II*. Institute of Education, University of Göteborg, 1979. I feel much in sympathy with these Scandinavians.

33. A study in which beginners and experts are compared concludes: 'experts categorise problems by laws of physics, and novices by surface features'. Chi, M., *et al.*, Categorisation and representation of physics problems by experts and novices. *Cognitive Science*, 1981, 5, 121–52.

34. Köhler, W., *The Mentality of Apes*. Vintage Books, 1956, first published 1917. I believe this work is of central interest to teachers, and indeed to anyone interested in learning.

35. See Birch, C., The relation of previous experience in insightful problem solving. *Journal of Comparative Psychology*, 1945, 38, 367–83.

36. Köhler, *Mentality of Apes*, 120, cited earlier.

37. I use the word 'afford' in James Gibson's sense. See his *The Senses Considered as Perceptual Systems*. Houghton Mifflin, 1966. For a helpful comment on the implications of Gibson's work see Mace, M., Ecologically stimulating cognitive psychology: Gibsonian perspectives. In Weimer and Palermo, *Cognition and the Symbolic Process*, cited earlier. Also Reed, E.S., James Gibson's ecological approach to cognition. In *Cognitive Psychology in Question*. Costall, A., *et al.* (eds) Harvester Press, 1987. For criticism see Ullman, S., Against direct perception. *Behavioural and Brain Sciences*, 1980, 3, 373–415.

38. For a searching analysis of Köhler's findings, see Schiller, P.H., Innate constituents of complex responses in primates. *Psychological Review*, 1952, 59(3), 177–91. Schiller also has interesting things to say about the effects of extrinsic rewards on learning. For a detailed discussion of animal thinking and a wide review of the literature see Walker, S., *Animal Thought*. Routledge, 1983. For an account of interesting experiments and their implications in this context see Premack, D. and Woodruff, G., Does the chimpanzee have a theory of mind?, *Behavioral and Brain Sciences*, 1978, 1(4), 515–26.

39. Menzel found that the chimpanzees he observed learnt to use a pole as a ladder in hundreds of different circumstances. And he concluded that his observations 'fail to support the contention that primate tool using can be reduced to certain "innate movement patterns" and that seemingly intelligent performance is the chance occurrence of one of these movement patterns in a situation where it is likely to be reinforced'. See Menzel, E.W., Spontaneous invention of ladders in a group of young chimpanzees. *Folia Primatologica*, 1972, 17, 87–106.

40. One finding states: 'our experiment demonstrates unequivocally the capacity of rats to store an abstract description of a pattern: they do not merely store a list of the feature detectors fired by an input picture'. Sutherland, N.S. and Williams, C., Discrimination of checker-board patterns by rats. *Quarterly Journal of Experimental Psychology*, 1969, 21, 77–84.

41. This quotation is from Henri Poincaré's *The Foundations of Science*. Reprinted in *The Creative Process*. Ghiselin, B. (ed.) Mentor Books, 1952, 37.

42. For some striking examples see the work by Ghiselin noted above. See also Hadamard, J., *The Psychology of Invention in the Mathematical Field*. Princeton University Press, 1945. For other examples (not the argument of the book, which I find unconvincing) see Koestler, A., *The Act of Creation*. Hutchinson, 1964. See also the critical review of the latter book by Medawar, P.B., *The Art of the Soluble*. Penguin, 1967. For an excellent consideration of creativity beyond trivialities like doing one's own thing, see Jackson, P.W., *et al.*, The person, the product, and the response: conceptual problems in the assessment of creativity. *Journal of Personality*, 1965, 33, 309–29.

43. My comments on the nature of thinking all through this book are strongly influenced by the work of J. Krishnamurti. In addition to his *The First and Last Freedom*, Gollancz, 1969, see his *Commentaries on Living*. There are three series, variously published by Gollancz between 1965 and 1970.

44. Another writer who has introduced me to this way of viewing the world is Alan Watts. See his *Nature, Man and Woman*. Wildwood House, 1973. Watts and Krishnamurti might be followed by Lao Tsu, *Tao Te Ching*. The best (and most beautiful) edition I know is that by Gia Fu Feng and Jane English, Wildwood House, 1972. For fascinating and scholarly comment on this approach see Needham, J., *Science and Civilisation in China*, Vol. 2. Cambridge University Press, 1956. I strongly recommend this work.

45. Brown, G.S., *Laws of Form*. Allen & Unwin, 1969. Also Hunter, I.M., An exceptional memory. In Neisser, *Memory Observed*, cited earlier.

46. *Letters of John Keats*. Gittings, R. (ed.) Oxford University Press, 1970, 43.

47. Readers might like to see the source from which I take this use of the word 'resonate': 'Scholars of old time said that the mind is originally empty, and only because of this can it respond to natural things without prejudice. . . . Though everything resonates with the mind, the mind should be as if it had never resonated, and things should not remain in it. But once the mind has received (impressions of) natural things they tend to remain and not to disappear, thus leaving traces in the mind. (These affect later seeing and thinking . . .).' Needham, *Science and Civilisation*, noted above, 89.

48. The position adopted here is very different from that of those who hold that the human mind 'constructs' reality. It is true that the process of socialization, and social phenomena in general, shape our perception of reality to a very large extent, but that is a far cry from believing that we construct reality. I return to this important matter in a later chapter.

49. Spencer Brown writes about this vividly. See *Laws of Form*, cited earlier, 95.

Chapter 3 The Learning Process (pages 55–60)

1. Carroll, J.M. and Mack, R.L., Actively learning to use a word processor. In *Cognitive Aspects of Skilled Typewriting*. Cooper, W.E. (ed.) Springer-Verlag, 1983. There is a great deal to be learnt from this work. One of its concerns is how manuals should be written. The best manual I have come across is that by John Muir and Josh Gregg, *How to Keep Your Volkswagen Alive*. Santa Fe, NM, John Muir, 1969.

2. Feynman, R., *Surely You're Joking Mr Feynman!* Norton, 1985. This book is uneven, but there are many other enlightening and amusing passages in it.

3. Sacks, J.S., Recognition memory for syntactic and semantic aspects of connected discourse. *Perception and Psychophysics*, 1967, 1(9), 437–42. With regard to the general argument in this chapter, it might be argued that the concept of 'reinforcement' provides a better account of learning than the notion of 'hypothesis testing'. For experimental findings and a discussion which suggest the contrary, see Levine, M., Hypothesis theory and non-learning despite ideal S-R reinforcement contingencies. *Psychological Review*, 1971, 78(2), 130–40. For an excellent description of this process in medical education see Barrows, H.S. and Tamblyn, R.M., *Problem-Based Learning: An Approach to Medical Education*. Springer-Verlag, 1980.

4. Jenkins, Remember that old theory of memory?, cited earlier. The implications of Jenkins' paper are much greater than suggested in my text, and that is why I refer to it here for the third time.

5. Craik, F.I.M. and Tulvig, E., Depth of processing and retention of words in episodic memory. *Journal of Experimental Psychology: General*, 1975, 104(3), 268–94.

6. For comment on the words 'meaning' and 'understanding', and the difficulty of defining and measuring the extent to which a learner has understood the meaning of something, see Ormell, C.P., The problem of analysing understanding. *Educational Research*, 1979, 11(1), 32–8.

7. Elstein, A.S., *et al.*, Methods and theory in the study of medical inquiry. *Journal of Medical Education*, 1972, 47, 85–92. See also Barrows and Tamblyn, *Problem-Based Learning*, cited earlier. When one compares the findings of this research with that done on children, the similarity is remarkable. It seems that how very young children solve problems (e.g. how to balance a piece of wood across a beam) is basically the same as how medical practitioners go about making a diagnosis, that is, by forming and testing hunches. See Karmiloff-Smith, A. and Inhelder, B., If you want to get ahead, get a theory. *Cognition*, 1974, 3(3), 195–212. I trust that readers will see that the title of this paper summarizes much that I have written about theories in my text. See also Bower, *The Rational Infant*, cited earlier. I suggest that findings like the above support my contention that people of all ages learn in basically the same way.
8. Polanyi, M., *Personal Knowledge*. Routledge & Kegan Paul, 1958, 101. Polanyi is out of fashion at present, perhaps because he placed much emphasis on the traditional.

Chapter 4 Talking and Feeling (pages 62–74)

1. Polanyi, cited above, 54. For additional comment on the implication of the concept 'tacit' see Turvey, M.T., Construction theory, perceptual systems, and tacit knowledge; and Franks, J.J., Toward understanding understanding. Both in Weimer and Palermo, *Cognition and the Symbolic Process*, cited earlier.
2. Holt, J., *How Children Learn*. Penguin, 1970, 161. I have learnt a good deal from this writer, but perhaps I should mention what I consider to be two fundamental errors in his work: a) that children are better off not going to school; and b) the emphasis he places on individual needs. The latter is characteristic of many Western writers.
3. A good way to begin considering the place of language in education is to read Labov, W., The logic of non-standard English. In *Language and Poverty*. Williams, F. (ed.) Markham Publishing, 1970. For an excellent introduction to the relationship between thought and language, see Slobin, D.I., *Psycholinguistics*, 2nd edn. Scott, Foresman, 1979. For an early, succinct and helpful description of the nature of language see Hockett, C.F., Animal 'languages' and human language. In *The Evolution of Man's Capacity for Culture*. Spuhler, J.A. (ed.) Wayne State University Press, 1965.
4. Rogers, C.R., *On Becoming a Person*. Constable, 1967, 273.
5. Much of this was of course known to Freud. See his The unconscious. In *On Metapsychology: The Theory of Psychoanalysis*, Vol. 11. Penguin Freud Library, 1984.
6. See Hendrix, G., A new clue to transfer of training. *Elementary School Journal*, 1947, 48, 197–208; also her Prerequisites to meaning. *Mathematics Teacher*, 1950, 43, 334–9. Also, Learning by discovery. *Mathematics Teacher*, 1961, 54, 290–9. Notice the dates of publication! For highly perceptive comment on this matter see Katona, G., *Organising and Memorising*. Hafner, 1967, first published 1940. It is a shame that this work is not better known. For further thoughtful comment see Hilgard, E.R., *et al.*, Rote memorization, understanding, and transfer. *Journal of Experimental Psychology*, 1953, 46(4), 288–92. Also Haslerud, G.M. and Meyers, S., The transfer value of given and individually derived principles. *Journal of Educational Psychology*, 1958, 49, 293–9. And Wittrock, M.C., The learning by discovery hypothesis. In *Learning by Discovery: A Critical Appraisal*. Shulman, L.S., *et al.* (eds) Rand McNally, 1966. And Worthen, B.R., A study of discovery and expository presentation: implications for teaching. *Journal of Teacher Education*, 1968, 19, 223–42. Two further interesting comments are Kersh, B.Y., The adequacy of meaning as an explanation for the superiority of learning by independent discovery. *Journal of Educational Psychology*, 1958, 49(5), 282–92; and The motivating effect of learning by directed discovery. *Journal of Educational Psychology*, 1962, 53(2), 65–71. All these were written some time ago, but are still highly pertinent. For a thoughtful and practical analysis of what is involved in 'problem-based learning', applied to a university setting but having general applicabil-

ity, see Schmidt, H.G., Problem-based learning: rationale and description. *Medical Education*, 1983, 117, 11–16. There are studies of this matter which suggest that expository methods result in learners gaining marks in tests as high as those obtained by learners taught by discovery methods, but that is not what is under discussion here. It should also be noted that most of those who have conducted research on this topic appear to believe that teachers can apply discovery methods if only asked to do so and given some training in their use. In my experience, nothing could be further from the truth, and a chapter on this follows. But I would emphasize that neither the 'discovery' method, nor indeed any 'method', is advocated in this book. All such terms are trite. I should perhaps add that the samples used by Hendrix are small, but her findings are supported by other researchers. D.P. Ausubel drew my attention to the work of Hendrix, and he was critical of it. See his Learning by discovery: rationale and mystique. *Bulletin of the National Association of Secondary School Principals*, 1961, 45, 18–58. Unfortunately, I found his work largely unhelpful. Also of interest here is Kubie, L., The psychotherapeutic ingredient in the learning process. In *The Role of Learning in Psychotherapy*. Porter, R. (ed.) J. & A. Churchill, 1968. For later work see Margetson, D., Why is problem-based learning a challenge? In *The Challenge of Problem-Based Learning*. Boud, D. and Feletti, G. (eds) Kogan Page, 1991.

7. The outlook of a 'liberal' like Rogers, in its focus on the individual, ends up being very similar to the views of those on the radical right, eventually resulting, in my estimation, not only in the neglect of family and community, but also in their destruction, and, with that, the ultimate destruction of the individual.

8. The most suggestive examples I know are to be found in some of the literature on Zen Buddhism. See for example Watts, A., *Psychotherapy East and West*. Penguin, 1973.

9. For examples of laboratory research into problem solving see Johnson-Laird, P.N. and Wason, P.C., *Thinking*. Cambridge University Press, 1977. And Wason, P.C. and Johnson-Laird, P.N., *Psychology of Learning: Structure and Content*. Batsford, 1972. For further comment see Cheng, P.W. and Holyoak, K.J., Pragmatic reasoning schemas. *Cognitive Psychology*, 1985, 17, 391–416. For a brief introduction see Kahney, H., *Problem Solving: A Cognitive Approach*. Open University Press, 1986. While reading work of this kind, I often found myself thinking that, if a creature from another planet came across it, the image that creature would form of a human being would resemble a pocket calculator. But then, as Spinoza pointed out, not only God creates man in 'his' own image.

10. See Jerome Bruner's reflections in his *In Search of Mind*. Harper & Row, 1983. For comment on the neglect of feelings in much psychological literature see Frosh, S., *Psychoanalysis and Psychology*. Macmillan, 1989. I turn to this matter again more substantially in a later chapter.

11. The last reason was prompted by a suggestion in one of George Steiner's essays; some of the others were suggested by E.M. Forster in one of his essays.

12. I have here in mind especially the work of Karl Popper. For an application of it in medical education see Campbell, E.J.M., Clinical science. *Clinical Science and Molecular Medicine*, 1976, SI, 1–7.

13. See Dreyfus, H.L. and Dreyfus, S.E., The mistaken psychological assumptions underlying the belief in expert systems. In *Cognitive Psychology in Question*. Costall, A., *et al*. (eds) Harvester Press, 1987.

14. Any attempt to simulate human thinking with a computer, which ignores the aesthetic dimension, is sterile. See Heisenberg, W., Science and the beautiful. In *Quantum Questions*, cited earlier; and Polanyi, M., *The Study of Man*. University of Chicago Press, 1959. I could list offhand a dozen works by eminent scientists that stress the importance of the aesthetic dimension in their work.

15. Royston, R., An analysis of intellectual dysfunction. *British Journal of Psychotherapy*, 1995, 12(1), 15–28. The psychoanalytic metaphysics aside, the writer illuminates well how many people, with a need 'not to know', are unable to assimilate new material, and hence experience difficulties with study.

16. Readers who find these comments absurd or interesting might like to consider the remarkable opening pages of Harding, D.E., On having no head. In *The Mind's I*. Hofstadter, D., *et al.* (eds) Harvester Press, 1981. I believe the thrust of most of the rest of this book is mistaken. See also Spencer Brown for a fascinating account of the process of discovery in mathematics *(Laws of Form*, 95, cited earlier). Nothing could be less like how a computer works.

17. In view of Piaget's eminence, I should perhaps note that there are no references to his work in these notes because for years I found his work uncongenial. I eventually came to appreciate the questions he raised, but, by then, I had almost completed this manuscript. For comment on Piaget's work see Kuhn, D., The application of Piaget's theory of cognitive development to education. *Harvard Educational Review*, 1979, 49(3), 340–60. See also Phillips, D.C. and Kelly, M.E., Hierarchical theories of development in education and psychology. *Harvard Educational Review*, 1975, 45(3), 351–75. And Sugarman, S., *Piaget's Construction of the Child's Reality*. Cambridge University Press, 1987. For further comment see *Cognitive Development to Adolescence*. Richardson, K. and Sheldon, S. (eds) Lawrence Erlbaum, 1990. Also *The Epigenesis of Mind*. Carey, S. and Gelman, R. (eds) Lawrence Erlbaum, 1991.

18. For a lively account of the development of cognitive psychology see Baars, B.J., *The Cognitive Revolution in Psychology*. Guilford Press, 1986. The interviews with Jenkins and Weimer make for exciting reading and are about the best introduction to the study of academic psychology I know. For a comment on the way cognitivism is a part of Western ideology see Sampson, E.E., Cognitive psychology as ideology. *American Psychologist*, 1981, 36(7), 730–43. See also Prilleltensky, I., On the social and political implications of cognitive psychology. *The Journal of Mind and Behavior*, 1990, 11(2), 127–36. For a general critique of much academic psychology (without the distortions often found in sociological accounts) see Sarason, S.B., *Psychology Misdirected*. Free Press, 1981. Also Williams, S.M., *Psychology on the Couch*. Harvester Press, 1988.

19. Finkelman writes: 'A theory purporting to explain some aspect of psychological functioning is advanced. Experiments are performed to test the theory, with conflicting results. More experiments are performed, each one adding less to any genuine understanding of the phenomenon. Finally psychologists become frustrated (and bored) by their inability to make progress, and study of the issue ceases.' Finkelman, D., Science and psychology. *American Journal of Psychology*, 1978, 91(2), 179–99. Readers might like to compare the above with the following comment regarding the seventeenth century: 'An "Explanation" may perhaps be roughly defined as a restatement of something – event, theory, doctrine, etc. – in terms of current interests and assumptions. It satisfies, as explanation, because it appeals to that particular set of assumptions, as superseding those of a past age or of a former state of mind. . . . All depends upon our presuppositions, which depend in turn upon our training, whereby we have come to regard (or to feel) one set of terms as ultimate, the other not.' Willey, B., *The Seventeenth-Century Background*. Penguin Books, 1962, 10. See also Jerome Bruner's Herbert Spencer Lecture, Psychology and the image of man. In *The Times Literary Supplement*, 17 December 1976. See also the same writer's *In Search of Mind*, cited earlier.

20. For comment on how highly integrated are organisms and environment see Lewontin, R.C., Genes, environment, and organisms. In *Hidden Histories of Science*. Silvers, R.B. (ed.) A New York Review Book, 1995. The lovely phrase, 'encapsulated in a bag of skin', belongs to Watts, A., *The Book. On the Taboo Against Knowing Who You Are*. Pantheon Books, 1966.

21. In 1950, Turing wrote a paper, considered a classic, entitled Computing machinery and intelligence. It is, I think, a sign of our times that this writer argued that a valid test of computer intelligence would occur if a judge were unable to differentiate between a computer and a human being giving a reply, if the computer, human and judge were in

separate rooms, and the human used a typewriter. This paper has often been reprinted, and was discussed in Anderson, A.R., *Minds and Machines*. Prentice-Hall, 1964. Compare this with, Sacks, O., *Awakenings*. Picador, 1982, 207.

22. See for example *Applications of Cognitive Psychology: Problem Solving, Education and Computing*. Benger, D.A., *et al.* (eds) Lawrence Erlbaum, 1987. The most useful contributions (e.g. by Trowbridge on the best number of learners to each terminal) have nothing to do with cognitive psychology but report straightforward educational research. For a discussion of cognitivism by a large number of scholars see Haugeland, J., The nature and plausibility of cognitivism. *Behavioral and Brain Sciences*, 1978, 2, 215–60. Again, I do not think teachers will find anything useful in these forty-five closely printed pages. A notable exception to the general unhelpfulness of cognitive psychology for teachers is the collection by Weimer and Palermo, *Cognition and the Symbolic Process*. In this, I found the contribution by Weimer, Overview of a cognitive conspiracy: reflections on the volume, exceptionally helpful. Also interesting is his Ambiguity and the future of psychology. In Weimer, W.B. and Palermo, D.S. (eds) *Cognition and the Symbolic Process*, Vol. 2. Lawrence Erlbaum, 1982. I did not learn as much from his Hayek's approach to the problems of complex phenomena: an introduction to the theoretical psychology of *The Sensory Order*. Writing of this kind suggests that what we now have in the West, and increasingly as countries develop, is the best of all possible worlds. It is interesting that Polanyi, Popper and Hayek – to whose writings Weimer frequently refers – seem to share a basic political and philosophic outlook, perhaps grounded in a reaction to Central European utopian totalitarianism. This might be compared with, say, Lewontin, R.C., Organism and environment. In *Learning, Development and Culture*. Plotkin, H.C. (ed.) Wiley, 1982. As I was correcting the page proofs of this book, I was sent a copy of Benny Shanon's *The Representational and the Presentational: An Essay on Cognition and the Study of Mind*. Harvester Wheatsheaf, 1993. I was relieved and delighted to find someone who shares my disquiet about cognitivism, and is also able to muster a scholarly critique of it. I had better add that an attractively written work in the cognitive tradition is Bransford, J., *Human Cognition*. Wadsworth Publishing, 1979. This contains many practical findings that teachers might find useful.

23. For some light on how journal papers are selected, see Standing, L. and McKelvie, S., Psychological journals: a case for treatment. *Bulletin of the British Psychological Society*, 1986, 39, 445–50. Also Stacey, B.G., The uses of psychology journals. *The Psychologist*, 1993, 6, 12–15.

24. See for example *Psychotherapy Process*. Mahoney, M. J. (ed.) Plenum Press, 1980. The most interesting contributions (e.g. those by Mahoney, Arnkoff, Neisser, Weimer, and the Maxwells) are all directly or implicitly critical of the cognitive position. Also critical are Coyne, J.C. and Gotlib, I.H., The role of cognition in depression: a critical appraisal. *Psychological Bulletin*, 1983, 94(3), 472–505. See also Persons, J.B., *et al.*, Mechanisms of action of cognitive therapy: with reference to relative contributions of technical and interpersonal interventions. *Cognitive Therapy and Research*, 1985, 9(5), 539–51. See also Coyne, J.C., A critique of cognitions as causal entities with particular reference to depression. *Cognitive Therapy and Research*, 1982, 6(1), 3–13. Also Frank, J.D., Psychotherapy: the restoration of morale. *American Journal of Psychiatry*, 1974, 131(3), 271–4. For a most valuable contribution see Scovern, A.W., From placebo to alliance. In *The Heart and Soul of Change*. Hubble, A.M., *et al.* (eds) American Psychological Association, 1999. Also Roberts, A.H., The power of non-specific effects in healing. *Clinical Psychology Review*, 1993, 13, 375–91. And Stern, D.N., *et al.*, Non-interpretive mechanisms in psychoanalytic therapy. *International Journal of Psychoanalysis*, 1998, 79, 903–21. Also most valuable is Karasu, T.B., The specificity versus non-specificity dilemma: toward identifying therapeutic change agents. *American Journal of Psychiatry*, 1986, 143(6), 687–95. All these are exceptional contributions to a large literature; and all convey that what is most helpful in psychotherapy

is experience, not insight. The basic fault of the cognitive model is that it is unable to account for psychopathology. I believe the same is true of family systems theory and social psychology in general. Whatever the case, as these approaches are based on language and cognition, rather than on experience, they run counter to the basic thesis of this book.

25. I have come to believe that all discussion about change in the course of psychotherapy that does not focus on the sense of self is deeply mistaken. See for example Bretherton, I., From dialogue to internal working models: the co-construction of self in relationship. In *Memory and Affect in Development*. Nelson, C.A. (ed.) Lawrence Erlbaum, 1993. For a most valuable if sometimes dense analysis of these matters see De Waele, M., A clinical concept of the self: the experiential being. *British Journal of Medical Psychology*, 1995, 68, 223–42. The writer concludes that psychotherapy is successful to the extent that a client feels capable of becoming aware of all his or her experiences, so that they become a part of that person's slowly strengthening sense of self, which in turn will enable that person to assimilate new experiences. Also pertinent here is the work of Brown and his associates, who found that the development of self-esteem is related to having had close relationships, and that the onset of depression is related to having a low sense of self-esteem. The severity of the depression is exacerbated when it is coupled with current difficulties, and is mitigated when one has close relationships, especially with one person. Recovery from depression is likewise strengthened by the extent to which self-esteem is positive. Brown, G.W., *et al.*, Self-esteem and depression, II. *Social Psychiatry and Psychiatric Epidemiology*, 1990, 25, 225–34. In the same issue, see also the same writers' Self-esteem and depression, III, 235–43; and Self-esteem and depression, IV, 244–9. For a valuable paper on what ensues in psychotherapy when the sense of self is fragile, see Guntrip, H., Ego-weakness and the hard core of the problem of psychotherapy. *British Journal of Medical Psychology*, 1960, 33, 163–84. Kihlstrom writes: 'in order for ongoing experiences . . . to become conscious, a link must be made between their mental representation and some mental representation of the self as agent'. Kihlstrom, J.F., The cognitive unconscious. *Science*, 1987, 237, 1445–52.

26. It is interesting to recall here two quite independent findings. One is that progress in psychotherapy depends only marginally on the orientation of the therapist. The second is that progress in psychotherapy is beneficially affected by the extent to which the therapist believes in the validity of the orientation that he or she favours!

Chapter 5 Perception (pages 75–81)

1. For comment on the word 'coded' see Bower, T., *The Perceptual World of the Child*. Fontana, 1977, 65. For a review of the evidence on acquiring sight, see Singer, W., Learning to see: mechanisms in experience-dependent development. In *The Biology of Learning*. Marler, P., *et al.* (eds) Springer Verlag, 1984.

2. I first came across the concept of 'schemas' in Frederic Bartlett's delightful book *Remembering*. Cambridge University Press, 1932. I am very much indebted to him. I have been strongly influenced in my understanding of the application of the notion of schemas to learning and teaching by Abercrombie, M.L.J., *The Anatomy of Judgement*. Free Association Books, 1989; first published 1960. For an excellent description of what has been recently considered salient about 'schemas' see Brewer, W.F., *et al.*, The nature and function of schemas. In *Handbook of Social Cognition*. Vol 1, Wyer, R.S., *et al.* (eds) Lawrence Erlbaum, 1984. In the same volume, see the chapter by Rumelhart, D.E., Schemata and the cognitive system. This contains illuminating comments on the application of the concept of schemas to problem solving. For a fascinating illustration of the way in which 'a set' of schemas can help to determine what we see, see Rosenhan, D.L., On being sane in insane places. *Science*, 1973, 179, 250–8. Rosenhan persuaded eight ordinary people to visit a variety of hospitals with the complaint that they were hearing voices that

said 'empty', 'hollow' and 'thud'. All were diagnosed as schizophrenic and hospitalized, and, although all of them then behaved as they usually did, none were discovered to be 'normal'. Indeed, the staff interpreted their normal behaviour as indicating abnormality. For a helpful overview of the concept of schema see Fiske, S.T., *et al.*, What does the schema concept buy us? *Personality and Social Psychology Bulletin*, 1980, 6(4), 543–57. Another example of the concept of schemas lies in this – that, over the years, people build a picture of the kind of place they believe the world is. Should they then experience a catastrophe that requires an alteration in their outlook, for example that the world is a less just place than they had believed, a change must take place in their schemas. This can take a great deal of time, and can also be very painful. See Janoff-Bulman, R., Assumptive worlds and the stress of traumatic events: applications of the schema construct. *Social Cognition*, 1989, 7(2), 113–36. For more recent work see Merzenich, M.M., *et al.*, Cortical plasticity and memory. *Current Opinion in Neurobiology*, 1993, 3, 187–96. For another application of the concept see Rumelhart, D.E., *Understanding Understanding*. Centre for Human Information Processing, University of California, 1981.

3. I refer here again to Oakley, D.A., Cognition and imagery in animals. In Oakley, D.A. (ed.) *Brain and Mind*. Methuen, 1985.
4. This illustration is taken from Dallenbach, K.M., A puzzle picture with a new principle of concealment. *American Journal of Psychology*, 1951, 64, 431–3. Reproduced with permission.
5. Gregory, R.L., *Eye and Brain*. Weidenfeld & Nicolson, 1979.
6. Tom Bower shows how a child deprived of visual stimulus in the early months of life may never learn how to see, even when it has optimal conditions to do so later in life. See his *The Perceptual World of the Child*. Fontana, 1977. Readers might wonder what happens when a person has intact eyes but sustains an injury in the part of the brain responsible for seeing. For an account, with fascinating implications, see Weiskrantz, L., *Blindsight*. Oxford University Press, 1986. See also Singer, W., Learning to see: mechanisms in experience-dependent development. In *The Biology of Learning*. Marler, P., *et al.* (eds) Springer Verlag, 1984.
7. For important differences between seeing, and hearing language, see the contribution by Turvey, M. T., in *Cognition and the Symbolic Process*. Weimer, W.B. and Palermo, D.S. (eds) Lawrence Erlbaum, 1982.
8. Boas is quoted to the effect that, when anthropologists first encountered so-called primitive people, and attempted to write those people's language with the letters of their own language, they often jotted down sounds that were irrelevant, and left out sounds that were important. What their jottings most clearly revealed was what their own native language happened to be (e.g. English, French, German). See Proffit, D.R. and Halwes, T., Categorical perception: a contractual approach. In *Cognition and the Symbolic Process*. Vol. 2, cited earlier.
9. See Buckhout, R., Eyewitness testimony; and Neisser, U., John Dean's memory: a case study. Both in *Memory Observed*. Neisser, U. (ed.) W.H. Freeman, 1982.

Chapter 6 Where are the Answers? (pages 83–86)

1. Plato, *Protagoras & Meno*. Penguin, 1964.
2. Brown, S., *Laws of Form*. Allen & Unwin, 1969.
3. Blakemore, C., *Mechanics of the Mind*. Cambridge University Press, 1977. Memory must have a physiological basis in the brain. For example, it has been found that, when rats have been trained to do a certain task, and when the brains of these rats are then injected into the brains of untrained rats, the untrained rats acquire the ability of the rats that had been trained! See Ungar, G., *et al.*, Chemical transfer of learned fear. *Nature*, 1968, 217, 1259–61.
4. For a review of research in this area see Mayes, A., The physiology of memory. In *Aspects of Consciousness*. Vol 2. Underwood, G., *et al.* (eds) Academic Press, 1981. For a wide-ranging

and highly technical review of the research see Chapouthier, G., Protein synthesis and memory. In *The Physiological Basis of Memory*. Deutsch, J.A. (ed.) Academic Press, 1983. For further technical comment in the same volume see the contribution by Deutsch, J.A., The cholinergic synapse and the site of memory. The question Blakemore raised appears to be still unanswered. For important comment on how an experience must be processed – and perhaps slept on – before it becomes a memory see Bloch, V., Brain activation and memory consolidation. In *Neural Mechanisms of Learning and Memory*. Rosenzweig, M.R., *et al.* (eds) MIT Press, 1978.

5. Again, see Weimer, W.B., Psycholinguistics and Plato's paradoxes of the *Meno. American Psychologist*, 1973, 28, 15–33. I had not seen this paper 'til I read of it in Baars's book, *The Cognitive Revolution in Psychology*. Guilford Press, 1986, cited earlier. I thought it one of the most interesting contributions to the study of learning I had come across. I also found it strange to think I had in part been trying to retrace a route Plato had traversed long ago.

6. Sinnott, E.W., *Matter, Mind and Man*. Allen & Unwin, 1937, 43.

7. Schrödinger, E., *What Is Life?* and *Mind and Matter*. Cambridge University Press, 1967. Readers might see how far removed this position is from the one which postulates that the human mind 'constructs' reality. Or consider the following comment by Louis de Broglie, who won the Nobel prize for physics in 1929: '. . . in order that humanity should have been able to adapt itself to live in the world which surrounds us, it would undoubtedly be necessary that there should be already between this world and our mind some analogy in structure; if that had not been so, perhaps humanity would not have been able to survive. Well, it would have disappeared, that is all!' In *Quantum Questions*. Wilber, K. (ed.) Shambhala, 1984, 118. I shall return to this important matter at the end of this book.

8. Gibson, J., *The Senses Considered as Perceptual Systems*. Houghton Mifflin, 1966, 267. Gibson also wrote: 'If what things afford is specified in the light, sound, and odour around them, and does not consist of the subjective memories of what they have afforded in the past, then the learning of new meanings is an education in attention rather than an accrual of associations.'

9. See for example *Language and Learning*. Piattelli-Palmarini, M. (ed.) Routledge, 1980, especially the contributions by Chomsky, Fodor and Sperber.

Chapter 7 Why Only Living Things Can Learn (pages 90–94)

1. Reynolds, B., Reductionism in literary theory. In *Reductionism in Academic Disciplines*. Peacocke, A. (ed.) SRHE and NFER-Nelson, 1985, 79.

2. For vivid illustrations see Laing, R.D., *The Divided Self*. Penguin, 1965.

3. Weckowicz, T.E., Depersonalisation-derealisation syndrome and perception: a contribution of psychopathology to epistemology. In *The Psychology of Knowing*. Royce, J.R., *et al.* (eds) Gordon & Breach, 1972.

4. For help with this insight I am indebted to Gustavo Delgado-Aparicio in a personal communication. See Damasio, A., *Descartes' Error*. Putnam's Sons, 1994. I believe it is symptomatic of what I write about that, among other things, Damasio deplores how, in the case of emotional distress, the focus of attention in medicine is on the brain, not the mind. In all, I found this book as felicitous as its title. See also Oatley, K., The importance of being emotional. *New Scientist*, 19 August 1989, 33–6. In conjecturing that we gain our basic sense of self from the early experience of sensing that we exist in the mind of a parent or other significant person, I express a position similar to that of Vygotsky when he noted the social origins of speech. See Wertsch, J.V., From social interaction to higher psychological processes: a clarification and application of Vygotsky's theory. *Human Development*, 1979, 22, 1–22. The focus on the individual in the West can blind one to the interactive origin of human development.

5. See Zajonc, R.B., Feeling and thinking. *American Psychologist*, 1980, 35(2), 151–75. See also the early and fascinating paper by Morton Prince, Can emotion be regarded as energy? In

Feelings and Emotions: The Wittenberg Symposium. Reymert, M.L. (ed.) Clark University Press, 1928.

6. See Claxton, G., The light's on but there's nobody home. This is a clear argument in support of the belief that our ego is a fiction. In *Beyond Therapy.* Claxton, G. (ed.) Wisdom Publications, 1986.

7. I am indebted to Benjamin Lee Whorf here. I take this opportunity to note my debt to my late friend George Stern for drawing my attention to his important work. It is interesting to see how Whorf and Vygotsky complement each other so well. See especially the last four chapters in Whorf's *Language, Thought and Reality.* Carroll, J.B. (ed.) MIT Press, 1973. First published 1956. For some glimpses of what the state 'behind' language might involve see Luria, A.R., *The Mind of a Mnemonist.* Harvard University Press, 1968. Also helpful is Brewer, W.F., The problem of meaning and the interrelations of the higher mental processes. In *Cognition and the Symbolic Process*, cited earlier. For more recent comment see *Thought without Language.* Weiskrantz, L. (ed.) Oxford University Press, 1988, especially the contributions by Premack, Schacter, Horn, Kertesz and Bisiach.

8. For an introduction to the thinking of the deaf see Furth, H.G., *Thinking without Language.* Free Press, 1966. Also Meyers, R., Relation of thinking and language. *Archives of Neurology and Psychiatry*, 1948, 60, 119–39. See also Slobin, D.I., *Psycholinguistics*, 2nd edn, cited earlier.

9. For this example and several others, I am indebted to Gendlin, E.T., A theory of personality change. In *Personality Change.* Worchel, P., *et al.* (eds) Wiley, 1964. Also the same writer's Focusing. *Psychotherapy*, 1961, 6(1), 4–15. For further comment see Wickens, D.D., Encoding categories of words: an empirical approach to meaning. *Psychological Review*, 1970, 77, 1–15. A letter from Einstein is also pertinent here. It is reproduced in Hadamard, J., *The Psychology of Invention in the Mathematical Field.* Dover, 1954.

10. Quoted in Brown, R. and McNeill, D., The tip of the tongue phenomenon. *Journal of Verbal Learning and Verbal Behavior*, 1966, 5, 325–37. These writers note that 'the whole word is represented in *abstract form recall'.* Emphasis in the original.

11. MacLean, P.D., The evolution of three mentalities. In *Human Evolution: Biosocial Perspectives.* Washburn, S.L., *et al.* (eds) Benjamin/Cummings Publishing Company, 1975. The figures in my text are amended from this work. Also MacLean, P.D., On the origin and progressive evolution of the triune brain. In *Primate Brain Evolution.* Armstrong, E., *et al.* (eds) Plenum Press, 1982. And MacLean, P.D., The triune brain, emotion, and scientific bias. In *The Neurosciences: Second Study Program.* Schmitt, F.O. (ed.) Rockefeller University Press, 1970. For a recent comment on the term 'limbic', see Damasio, A.R., Emotion and the human brain. In *Unity of Knowledge.* Damasio, A.R., *et al.* (eds) New York Academy of Sciences, 2001. For a wide-ranging review that lends some support for MacLean's approach see Rozin, P., The psychobiological approach to human memory. In *Neural Mechanisms of Learning and Memory.* Rosenzweig, M.R., *et al.* (eds) MIT Press, 1976.

Chapter 8 Two Memories (pages 97–108)

1. For a review of memory structures see Squire L.R., *et al.*, The structure and organisation of memory. *Annual Review of Psychology*, 1993, 44, 453–95. Also Lewicki, P., *et al.*, Nonconscious information processing and personality. In *How Implicit is Implicit Learning?* Berry, D.C. (ed.) Oxford University Press, 1997. What I have been calling 'schemas' these writers call 'encoding algorithms'. Perner and his associates make a distinction between 'knowing' something, and being able to 'remember' something. When we 'know' something, we may have no recollection of how we know; whereas, in the case of remembering, we are also aware of having had the experience that has led to our knowing. They go on to explain the phenomenon of childhood amnesia by noting that the latter capacity does not develop till about the age of four. See Perner, J., *et al.*, Episodic memory and

autonoetic consciousness: developmental evidence and a theory of childhood amnesia. *Journal of Experimental Child Psychology*, 1995, 59, 516–48. For a critical review of the experimental findings on implicit memory see Schacter, D.L., Implicit memory: history and current status. *Journal of Experimental Psychology: Learning, Memory and Cognition*, 1987, 13(3), 501–18. LeDoux shows that the pathways in the brain that create our feelings of fear in response to a fear-provoking situation are much faster than the pathways to the thinking parts of our brain. This makes for safety, for an immediate sense of fear, rather than thinking about its cause, would prompt us to an immediate action like freezing or running, and thus help us to elude or escape from that which has caused our fear. In line with evolutionary theory, such a process would be selected, for it has a survival value. Thus, fear conditioning is not only quick, but will also tend to last. In fact, there is little forgetting when it comes to conditioned fear. However, it can become extinct. For example, a person might have had a fearful experience in a lift, and hence becomes fearful every time he or she enters one. That person might nevertheless continue using a lift; and, if nothing fearful again occurs, that person's fear is likely to become extinct. But, should anything of a fearful nature again occur in a lift, the fear that that person originally experienced may be re-experienced. Roughly speaking, our emotional reactions are located in the amygdale, while our more thoughtful responses are located in the hippocampus. Further, we are unable to access our conscious memories before about the age of two or three, because the hippocampus only develops after this age. Recent findings suggest that it is not so much the hippocampus that develops later, but the ancillary areas that support its functions. For details see LeDoux, J., *The Emotional Brain*. Simon & Schuster, 1996.

2. Tulving, E., Précis of Elements of episodic memory. *The Behavioral and Brain Sciences*, 1984, 7, 223–68. For a masterly review of what is often called 'episodic memory', that is, the ability to recall a memory of personally relevant matters, made possible by what the writers term 'autonoetic consciousness', see Wheeler, M.A., *et al.*, Toward a theory of episodic memory. *Psychological Bulletin*, 1997, 121(3), 331–54.

3. For wide-ranging comment on memory systems see Rozin, P., The psychobiological approach to human memory. In *Neural Mechanisms of Learning and Memory*, cited earlier. Also Oakley, D.A., The varieties of memory: a phylogenetic approach. In *Memory in Animals and Humans*. Mayes, A. (ed.) Van Nostrand Reinhold (UK), 1983. Also Weiskrantz, L., Neuropsychology and the nature of consciousness. In *Mindwaves*. Blakemore, C., *et al.* (eds) Blackwell, 1987. And Schacter, D.A., *et al.*, Access to consciousness. In *Thought without Language*. Weiskrantz, L. (ed.) Clarendon Press, 1988.

4. It is more accurate to say that 'the left hemisphere achieves superiority in the utilization of a multiplicity of descriptive systems which are fully formed in an individual's cognitive repertoire'. The right hemisphere is 'most crucial in the processing of materials to which none of the descriptive systems pre-existing in a subject's cognitive repertoire is readily applicable, and in assembling new descriptive systems'. See Goldberg, E. and Costa, L.D., Hemispheric differences in the acquisition and use of descriptive systems. *Brain and Language*, 1981, 14, 144–73.

5. See Oakley, D.A. and Eames, L.C., The plurality of consciousness. In *Brain and Mind*. Oakley, D. (ed.) Methuen, 1985.

6. Goldstein, K., *Human Nature in the Light of Psychopathology*. Schocken Books, 1963. First published 1939! Geschwind notes that Goldstein had reported such findings as early as 1908!! See Geschwind, N., The perverseness of the right hemisphere. *Behavioral and Brain Sciences*, 1981, 4, 106–7. Freud noted the same phenomenon but explained it via the concept of 'repression'. See Freud's The unconscious. In *On Metapsychology. The Theory of Psychoanalysis*, Vol. II. Penguin Freud Library, 1984, 199. See also Schachtel, E.A., On memory and childhood amnesia. In *Memory Observed*. Neisser, U. (ed.) W.H. Freeman, 1982. I thought this a fascinating paper, among other things because it points to the limitations of language. For an interesting comment on the way psychoanalytic and

sociobiological ideas sometimes converge see Badcock, C.R., *The Problem of Altruism*. Blackwell, 1986.

7. LeDoux, J.E., Brain, mind and language. In *Brain and Mind*, cited earlier, 206. As noted, a child's earliest experiences take place before the speech centres in its brain have developed. If so, early experiences are likely to be coded in a form not accessible to the speaking part of the brain when speech develops. The result is that these early experiences will probably remain unconscious, even though they will affect this child's behaviour as it grows older. The second quotation in my text is from Josef, R., The neuropsychology of development: hemispheric laterality, limbic language, and the origin of thought. *Journal of Clinical Psychology*, 1982, 33(1), 4–33. For a searching review of these matters see Schore, A.N., Effects of a secure attachment relationship on right brain development, affect regulation, and infant mental health. *Infant Mental Health Journal*, 2001, 22(1–2), 7–66. The third quotation in my text is from Squire, L.R., Biological foundations of accuracy and inaccuracy in memory. In *Memory Distortion*. Schacter, D.L. (ed.) Harvard University Press, 1995. See also Howe, M.L., *et al.*, How can I remember when 'I' wasn't there: long-term retention of traumatic experiences and the emergence of the cognitive self. *Consciousness and Cognition*, 1994, 3, 327–55. See also Volpe, B.T., *et al.*, Information processing of visual stimuli in an 'extinguished' field. *Nature*, 1979, 282, 722–4. Also Gazzaniga, M.S., Right hemisphere language following brain bisection: a 20-year perspective. *American Psychologist*, 1983, 38, 525–37. In an earlier publication Gazzaniga and Sperry (Language after section of the cerebral commissures. *Brain*, 1967, 90, 131–48) stated that the right hemisphere is conscious. The discussion hinges on a definition of the term 'conscious'. In using that term, I have in mind Bartlett's notion of the organism's 'capacity to turn around upon its own schemata and to construct them afresh'. In another publication, we find 'while nonhumans may be found to be aware and even self-aware, they are nevertheless not aware in the unique ways and to the extent made possible by the human verbal system'. LeDoux, J.E., *et al.*, Beyond commissurotomy: clues to consciousness. In *Handbook of Behavioural Neurobiology and Neuropsychology*. Vol. 2. Gazzaniga, M.S. (ed.) Plenum, 1979. See also Marin, O.S.M., *et al.*, Origins and distribution of language. Also in the previous publication. For comment on how the left hemisphere tends to interfere with the right hemisphere's attempts to deal with verbal stimuli, see Levy, J., *et al.*, Expressive language in the surgically separated minor hemisphere. *Cortex*, 1971, 7, 49–58. Also Levy, J., Possible basis for the evolution of lateral specialisation of the human brain. *Nature*, 1969, 224, 614–15. For a review see Galin, D., Implications for psychiatry of left and right cerebral specialisation. *Archives of General Psychiatry*, 1974, 31, 572–83. For a general review of the topic of hemisphere differences see Springer, S.P., *et al.*, *Left Brain, Right Brain*, 3rd edn. W.H. Freeman, 1989. For a brief and clear review, see Nebes, R.D., Hemispheric specialization in commissurotomized man. *Psychological Bulletin*, 1974, 81(1), 1–14. For a masterly review of language and the brain see N. Geschwind's paper in *Science*, 1970, 170, 940–4. For a clinical case, in which the loss of the right hemisphere in a man with a right hemisphere speech centre is described, see Smith, A., Speech and other functions after left (dominant) hemispherectomy. *Journal of Neurology, Neurosurgery and Psychiatry*, 1966, 29, 467–71.

8. See Ley, R.A., *et al.*, Consciousness, emotion, and the right hemisphere. In *Aspects of Consciousness*, Vol. 2, cited earlier. Also Schwartz, A.E., *et al.*, Right hemisphere lateralisation for emotion in the human brain: interaction with cognition. *Science*, 1975, 190, 280–8. Also Jackeim, H.A., *et al.*, Emotions are expressed more intensely on the left side of the face. *Science*, 1978, 202, 434–6. See also Schore, A.N., Effects of a secure attachment relationship on right brain development, affect regulation, and infant mental health. *Infant Mental Health Journal*, 2001, 22(1–2), 7–66.

9. The best single source of evidence I know for this assertion is to be found in the correspondence on 'The Cyril Burt Affair' published in various issues of the *Bulletin of the British Psychological Society* from January 1977.

10. For an early comment on this see Freud's *The Ego and the Id*, cited earlier.
11. Spinetta, J.J. and Rigler, D., The child-abusing parent. *Psychological Bulletin*, 1972, 77(4), 296–304. See also Lewis, D.O., *et al.*, Toward a theory of the genesis of violence: a follow-up study of delinquents. *Journal of the American Academy Of Child and Adolescent Psychiatry*, 1989, 28(3), 431–6. See also Wisdom, C.S., The cycle of violence. *Science*, 1989, 244, 116–65.

Chapter 9 Explaining and Experiencing (pages 109–122)

1. Nisbett, R.E. and Wilson, T.D., Telling more than we can know: verbal reports on mental processes. *Psychological Review*, 1977, 84, 231–59. But see Smith, E.R. and Miller, F.D., Limits on perception of cognitive processes. *Psychological Review*, 1978, 85(4), 355–62. For further comment see Natsoulas, T., Conscious perception and the paradox of blind-sight. In *Aspects of Consciousness*, Vol. 3. Underwood, A., *et al.* (eds), cited earlier. For a review, see Dixon, N.F., *Subliminal Perception: The Nature of a Controversy*. McGraw-Hill, 1971. For an empirical test of the psychoanalytic contribution see Silverman, L.H., Psychoanalytic theory: the reports of my death are greatly exaggerated. *American Psychologist*, 1976, 31, 621–37.
2. For an introduction to this topic and helpful references see Wilkinson, A., *The Foundations of Language*. Oxford University Press, 1971. For comments which indicate that the kind of grammar taught in school is seldom the kind of grammar used to produce language, see Slobin, *Psycholinguistics*, cited earlier. Perhaps I should note here my belief that it is most important for learners to know how to spell and punctuate accurately, but for a finding which suggests that such learning is powerfully a matter of suitable exposure, rather than teaching, see Pronko, N.H., On learning how to play the violin at the age of four without tears. *Psychology Today*, 1969, 2, 52–7.
3. See Frith, C.D., Consciousness, information processing and schizophrenia. *British Journal of Psychiatry*, 1979, 134, 225–35. Also Frith, C.D., *The Cognitive Neuropsychology of Schizophrenia*. Psychology Press, 1999. Schizophrenia does not appear to have much to do with teaching, but we often gain insights into the usual when we consider the unusual.
4. Vygotsky, L.S., *Mind in Society*. Cole, M., *et al.* (eds) Harvard University Press, 1978, explained this well years ago.
5. Although I find his writing opaque, I am indebted to F.M. Alexander here. See his *The Use of the Self*. Gollancz, 1985. First published 1932. For comment on the work of Alexander see Jones, F.P., *Body Awareness in Action*. Schocken Books, 1976.
6. Compare this formulation with the one suggested by Newcomb, T.M., Persistence and regression of changed attitudes; long-range studies. *Journal of Social Issues*, 1963, 19, 3–14.
7. See Simon, H.A., The shape of automation, first published in 1960, and reprinted in *Perspectives on the Computer Revolution*. Pylyshyn, Z.W. (ed.) Prentice-Hall, 1970. For an introduction to artificial intelligence see Boden, M.A., *Artificial Intelligence and Natural Man*. Harvester Press, 1977. I began reading this work with interest and admired the writer's clear writing and sympathetic intelligence. However, as I continued, I became increasingly uneasy. I kept thinking of a character named Bledyard in Iris Murdoch's novel *The Sandcastle* (1954) and the way a female character describes him (in the Penguin edition, 81). She wrote: 'He argues insistently and coherently and with the appearance of logic – but somehow it's just all wrong, there's some colossal distortion.' I had better quote another character's reply: 'One has to ask oneself now and then whether it isn't one's own vision that is distorted.' I sense the same 'distortion' in other accounts of artificial intelligence I have read, and readers must make up their own minds. I have been much helped here by Joseph Weizenbaum's highly readable *Computer Power and Human Reason*. Penguin, 1984. Also Landauer, T.K., *The Trouble with Computers*. MIT Press, 1995.

8. It was E. Fromm who first drew my attention to these steps, but I am unfortunately unable to recall where.

9. For an early, but clear and concise introduction to marital problems, see Dominian, J., *Marital Breakdown*. Penguin, 1969. For a more detailed treatment see Dicks, H.V., *Marital Tensions*. Routledge, 1967. Both cite much data that links divorce with early experiences. For a more recent popular account see Clulow, C., *et al.*, *Marriage Inside Out*. Penguin Books, 1989. For a comment written with grace and warmth see Mellen, S.L.W., *The Evolution of Love*. W.H. Freeman, 1981. For further scholarly comment see Block, J., *et al.*, Parental functioning and the home environment in families of divorce: prospective and current analyses. *Journal of the American Academy of Child and Adolescent Psychiatry*, 1988, 27(2), 207–13. For a more recent review see Cherlin, A.J., *Marriage, Divorce, Remarriage*. Harvard University Press, 1992. For sex differences in marriage see Hu, Y., *et al.*, Mortality differentials by marital status: an international comparison. *Demography*, 1990, 27(2), 233–50. Also Wood, W., *et al.*, Sex differences in positive well-being: a consideration of emotional styles and marital status. *Psychological Bulletin*, 1989, 106(2), 249–64. See also Mastekaasa, A., Marital status and subjective well being: a changing relationship? *Social Indicators Research*, 1993, 29, 249–76. This writer questions research which suggests that being married has ceased to contribute to well-being. And Popenoe, D., American family decline, 1960–1990: a review and appraisal. *Journal of Marriage and the Family*, 1993, 55, 527–55. This writer notes that, over the past 50 years, families have tended to become smaller, less stable, and to last for a short time; and that this suggests that many people have become less willing to invest time, money and energy in them, and appear to prefer to invest these in themselves. Although learning does not appear to have anything to do with marriage, I provide the above references for two reasons. One, because the available evidence strongly suggests that marital stability has much to do with early learning; and two, because learning certainly is affected by well-being, and well-being, in turn, is affected by rewarding close relationships.

10. Freud, S., The unconscious. In *On Metapsychology*. The Pelican Freud Library, Vol. 11. Penguin Books, 1984, 177–8. I earlier noted that it is unnecessary to invoke the term 'repression' to explain why we are unaware of something painful we have experienced. One could instead assume that, when an experience is for some reason pushed aside, and then not thought about, people cease in time to be consciously aware of it. For this argument see Erdelyi, M.H., Repression, reconstruction, and defence. In *Repression and Dissociation*. Singer, J.L. (ed.) University of Chicago Press, 1990. In the same volume, see also Bower, G.H., Awareness, the unconscious, and repression. See also Perry, C., *et al.*, Mental processing outside of awareness: the contributions of Freud and Janet. In *The Unconscious Reconsidered*. Bowers, K.S. and Meichenbaum, D. (eds) John Wiley, 1984. For further comment on the concept of repression see Erdelyi, M.H., Repression: the mechanism and the defence. In *Handbook of Mental Control*. Wegner, D.M., *et al.* (eds) Prentice-Hall, 1993. Also Davis, P.J., *et al.*, Repression and the inaccessibility of affective memories. *Journal of Personality and Social Psychology*, 1987, 52(1), 155–62. I note these works because all throw light on the processes that take place in our minds, and that is relevant to learning.

11. All this was of course clear to Freud. See his *The Ego and the Id*, cited earlier. In this, we see Freud attempting to grope his way towards an understanding of mental functioning, but still hamstrung by the materialistic conceptions of his time. He was clearly wrong about many things, but then, only mediocrities are always right.

12. Bowlby, J., On knowing what you are not supposed to know and feeling what you are not supposed to feel. *Canadian Journal of Psychiatry*, 1979, 24(5), 403–8. To any reader interested in such things, I would warmly recommend John Bowlby's *The Making and Breaking of Affectional Bonds*. Tavistock, 1979. I would add that I believe that this writer's *Attachment and Loss* (Vols 1, 2 and 3; Penguin, 1971–81) is the single most important contribution to the topic of human development and relations published in the last 50 years.

13. For a vivid description of a person who does not know what she is feeling see Chekhov's short story, The Princess. In *The Oxford Chekhov*. Vol. 5. Oxford University Press, 1970. See also Eagle, M., Psychoanalysis and the personal. In *Mind, Psychoanalysis and Science*. Clark, P., *et al.* (eds) Blackwell, 1988. Unfortunately, some of the other contributors to this volume attack Freud viciously and, I think, largely pointlessly. For perceptive comments on these matters see Eagle, M.N., *Recent Developments in Psychoanalysis*. McGraw-Hill, 1984.

14. Examples can be found in Boden, *Artificial Intelligence*, cited earlier.

15. Sacks, O., *The Man Who Mistook His Wife for a Hat*. Pan Books, 1986, 12. Compare the words quoted by Sacks with those supplied by Boden in her paper, Does artificial intelligence need artificial brains? In *Science and Beyond*. Rose, S., *et al.* (eds) Blackwell, 1986. Boden notes how a computer, simulating human intelligence, might pose a question, and uses these words to convey this: 'I don't know just what that thing is – but it's about a foot long, with an undulating spotted surface slanting away from the ground.' Because so much of Boden's reasoning is by analogy, the really interesting questions are lost. For example, how could one program a computer to have a sense of 'I'? For a lucid criticism of the notion of artificial intelligence see Wall, P.D. and Safran, J.N., Artefactual intelligence. In *Science and Beyond*, cited above. For helpful comment on the way much current discussion on these matters is befuddled by reasoning based on false analogies, see Hacker, P., Languages, minds and brains. In *Mindwaves*. Blakemore *et al.* (eds), cited earlier. One might here ask how one could model on a computer the reactions of a patient with Parkinson's when given L-Dopa. Interestingly enough, the description that Sacks provides ties in with much of Freud's work. It even helps to clarify Georg Groddeck's *The Book of the It*. Vintage Books, 1961. The mind boggles when one thinks what might happen should an attempt be made to simulate this on a computer.

16. In addition to the work of Gendlin cited earlier, see Rangell, L., Psychoanalysis, affects, and the human core. *Psychoanalytic Quarterly*, 1962, 36, 172–202. Also Welwood, J., Unfolding of experience: psychotherapy and beyond. *Journal of Humanistic Psychology*, 1982, 22, 91–104. See also the same writer's collection, *Awakening the Heart*. Shambhala, 1983. See also Janov, A., *The Primal Scream*. Abacus, 1973. Janov makes mistakes, but, in line with everything in my text, I believe his emphasis on the need to experience is most important. Another work of interest here is *The Role of Learning in Psychotherapy*. Porter, R. (ed.) J. & A. Churchill, 1968, especially the contributions by Sackett and Kubie.

17. Forster, E.M., *Aspects of the Novel*. Penguin, 1970.

18. In Strupp, H.H., *et al.*, Psychotherapy experience in retrospect. *Psychological Monographs: General and Applied*, 1964, 78(11), whole no 588. And Whitehorn, J.C. and Betz, B.J., A study of psychotherapeutic relationship between physicians and schizophrenic patients. *American Journal of Psychiatry*, 1954, 321–31. See also Gelso, C.J. and Carter, J.A., The relationship in counselling and psychotherapy. *Counselling Psychologist*, 1985, 13(2), 155–243. For an early review of research and perceptive comment see Frank, J.D., *Persuasion and Healing*. Schocken Books, 1963. These are early papers, but most perceptive.

19. See Dinnage, R., *One to One: Experiences of Psychotherapy*. Penguin, 1989, 50. This is a collection of interviews with people who underwent psychotherapy, and one catches one's breath at the sheer *personal* ineptitude of some of the therapists, as well as the damage this does to clients. This closely parallels my own experience as a client and practitioner. Few situations have raised my hair as much as hearing a wacky therapist present the case of one of his or her patients, and no amount of mere training overcomes this problem. For readers interested in these matters, I note the following works. For an early, brief and still perceptive introduction to psychotherapy, see Storr, A., *The Integrity of the Personality*. Penguin, 1972. Basch, M.F., *Doing Psychotherapy*. Basic Books, 1980. Malan, D.H., *Individual Psychotherapy and the Science of Psychodynamics*. Butterworth, 1978. Peterfreund, E., *The Process of Psychoanalytic Therapy*. Analytic Press, 1983. (I thank Emmy Gut for first drawing my attention to the foregoing.) For clients who have certain

attributes, short-term psychotherapy can be of value. See the following works: *Short-Term Dynamic Psychotherapy*. Davanloo, H. (ed.) Jason Aronson, 1992. Mann, J., *Time-Limited Psychotherapy*. Harvard University Press, 1973. Sifneos, P.E., *Short-Term Anxiety-Provoking Psychotherapy*. Basic Books, 1992. *Handbook of Short-Term Dynamic Psychotherapy*. Crits-Christoph, P. and Barber, J.P. (eds) Basic Books, 1991. For essential background reading see Ellenberger, H.F., *The Discovery of the Unconscious*. Basic Books, 1970. See also Suttie, I., *The Origins of Love and Hate*. Free Association Books, 1988. Unfortunately, the writer died before his book was published, and this might explain why this work is not as well written as well it might be. I believe it contains important observations for anyone interested in human development.

20. In his *The Theory and Practice of Group Psychotherapy*, Basic Books, 1985, Irving Yalom notes the following: that, when clients are asked to evaluate their experience of therapy, they tend to say that they learnt the most from interactions in the group, not the interpretations of the therapist; and that, when they mention a therapist, it is more in terms of who she is, rather than what she has said. This finding surely questions the emphasis this writer places on the cognitive element in therapy.

21. Oliver, W.A., Teachers' educational beliefs versus their classroom practice. *Journal of Educational Research*, 1953, 47, 47–55. Note the early date of publication, and yet how pertinent the finding still is.

22. Combs, A.W. and Soper, D.W., The helping relationship as described by 'good' and 'poor' teachers. *Journal of Teacher Education*, 1963, 14, 64–7.

23. Gonnella, J.S., *et al.*, Evaluation of patient care: an approach. *Journal of the American Medical Association*, 1970, 214(11), 2040–3.

24. Shakespeare, W., *Hamlet*. I, iii. c.1601.

25. Shakespeare, W., *The Merchant of Venice*. I, ii. c.1597.

26. I refer again to Vygotsky's *Thought and Language*. MIT Press, 1962. Long after Vygotsky had died, his colleague Luria wrote: 'It is no exaggeration to say that Vygotsky was a genius. Through more than five decades of science, I never again met a person who even approached his clearness of mind, his ability to lay bare the essential structure of complex problems, his breadth of knowledge in many fields, and his ability to foresee the future development of his science.' In Luria, A.R., *The Making of Mind*. Harvard University Press, 1979, 38.

27. I am again indebted to the marvellous last four chapters in Whorf, B.L., *Language, Thought and Reality*. Whorf is often read as if supporting the relativist position, but I believe that this misses the essential point of his work. See also Fromm, E., *Beyond the Chains of Illusion*. Simon & Schuster, 1962.

28. Bartlett, F., *Remembering*. Cambridge University Press, 1932, 207.

29. Quoted by Luria in his *The Making of Mind*, cited earlier. Luria also draws attention to the fact that, in his work with brain-damaged patients, Kurt Goldstein had noted years ago that the most basic forms of speech are not individual words, but the formulation of ideas as whole propositions. He adds that Goldstein had noted that these are always bound up with the motives of people and the conditions in which they find themselves.

30. I believe it is impossible to write sensible psychology unless it incorporates an awareness of material of the kind to be found in works like Lynch, J.J., *The Broken Heart*. Harper & Row, 1977; and Totman, R., *The Social Causes of Illness*. Pantheon Books, 1979. The political and economic context is obviously also very important.

Chapter 10 A Theory of Learning (pages 123–125)

1. See the striking Summary at the end of John Holt's *How Children Fail*. Penguin, 1969, rev. edn, 1987. Jerome Bruner also has a good chapter on this matter entitled On coping and defending. In his *Toward a Theory of Instruction*. Norton, 1968.

2. This is a paraphrase from J. Krishnamurti. It is an observation often found in his work.

3. For comments on this mystery, see the following classics, all by eminent scholars, and all still eminently readable: Eiseley, L., *The Immense Journey*. Vintage, 1946. Dobzhansky, T., *The Biology of Ultimate Concern*. Fontana, 1971. Dubos, R., *The Torch of Life*. Simon & Schuster, 1962. Hardy, A., *The Living Stream*. Collins, 1965. Waddington, C.H., *The Nature of Life*. Unwin Books, 1961.

Part II Teaching

Chapter 11 The Transmission Method and an Alternative Approach (pages 131–137)

1. The illustration of a schoolroom is taken from Wertheimer, M., *Productive Thinking*. Greenwood Press, 1978. For perceptive comments on the quality of teaching in colleges, see Klapper, P., The professional preparation of the college teacher. *Journal of General Education*, 1959, 3, 228–44. Notice date of publication and compare with the current situation.

2. Katona, G., *Organising and Memorising*. Hafner, 1967. Also Hohn, F.E., Teaching creativity in mathematics. *Arithmetic Teacher*, 1961, 8, 102–6. And Good, T.L. and Grouws, D.A., Teaching effectiveness in fourth grade mathematics class-rooms. In *The Appraisal of Teaching: Concepts and Process*. Borich, G.D., *et al.* (eds) Addison-Wesley, 1977.

3. Rogers, C.R., Personal thoughts on teaching and learning. In Rogers, *On Becoming a Person*, cited earlier.

4. In Wragg, E.C., *Classroom Teaching Skills*. Croom Helm, 1984.

5. Miller, A., Depression and grandiosity as related forms of narcissistic disturbances. *International Review of Psycho-Analysis*, 1979, 6, 61–76.

6. Abercrombie, M.L.J., *The Anatomy of Judgement*. Free Association Books, 1989. First published 1960.

7. There is a great deal of research in which 'the lecture method' is compared with 'the discussion method'. None that I have seen would answer the question I have posed; and I believe that all of this research is highly unsatisfactory, and for mainly three reasons. One, there is no such thing as a 'discussion method', and an attempt to practise such a thing would result in trivialities. Two, it takes a great deal of practice over many months before anyone can learn how to apply any new 'method' and in none of this research is there an indication that this has been done. And three, such research leaves out all the important details and results in mere number crunching. For an early example of such research, see Costin, F., Lecturing versus other methods of teaching: a review of research. *British Journal of Educational Technology*, 1972, 1(3), 4–31.

Chapter 12 Research into Teaching (pages 139–143)

1. See Smith's Introduction in *Research in Teacher Education: A Symposium*. Smith, B.O. (ed.) Prentice-Hall, 1971. See also Saadeh, I.Q., Teacher effectiveness or classroom efficiency: a new direction in the evaluation of teaching. *Journal of Teacher Education*, 1970, 21, 73–91. Saadeh showed why much research into teaching has yielded little, but his conclusions strike me as opaque. See also Mitzel, H.E., Teacher effectiveness. In *Encyclopedia of Educational Research*. Harris, C.W. (ed.) 1960, 1481–6. For a more recent account of teacher training, mostly based on the 'skills' or 'experience' approach, see *Teacher Education in the Classroom: Initial and In-service*. Ashton, P.M.E., *et al.* (eds) Croom Helm, 1983. For work which shows how even carefully conducted classroom research often yields little of value, see Medley, D.M. and Mitzel, H.E., Some behavioural correlates of teacher effectiveness. *Journal of Educational Psychology*, 1959, 50(6), 239–46. The only thing these researchers

were able to establish with some certainty is that there is little relationship between how well a teacher teaches, and how effective that teacher's superiors believe he or she is. Few practising teachers will be surprised! For a detailed review of research into teaching see Dunkin, M.J. and Biddle, B.J., *The Study of Teaching.* Holt, Rinehart & Winston, 1974. As with much so-called 'empirical' work, it contains a mass of data without, as far as I could see, a theory to give the reader a sense of direction. At risk of sounding overcritical, I will add that, in preparing this book, I got next to nothing from wading through scores of works on research into teaching, and concluded that it had far more to do with the need for academics to 'make the grade' than helping anyone in their practice.

2. For a brief account of classroom research see Hopkins, D., *A Teacher's Guide to Classroom Research.* Open University Press, 1985. For a succinct comment on the difficulty of doing classroom research see Travers, R.M., Criteria of good teaching. In *Handook of Teacher Evaluation.* Millman, J. (ed.) Sage, 1981. A work that has influenced me is Hamilton, D. and Delamont, S., Classroom research: a cautionary tale. In *Beyond the Numbers Game.* Hamilton, D. (ed.) Macmillan, 1977. But see *Controversies in Classroom Research.* Hammersley, M. (ed.) Open University Press, 1986. And *Case Studies in Classroom Research.* Hammersley, M. (ed.) Open University Press, 1986. Also helpful are Erickson, F., Qualitative methods in research on teaching; and especially Biddle, B.J. and Anderson, D.S., Theory, methods, knowledge, and research on teaching. Both in *Handbook of Research on Teaching.* Wittrock, M.C. (ed.) Macmillan, 1986. Though hard to apply to education, I have a hankering for the approach expressed long ago by Platt, J.R., Strong inference. *Science,* 1964, 146, 347–53. I would recommend these works only to readers especially interested in such things.

3. For a superb review of what is involved in meta-analysis in educational research see Slavin, R.E., Meta-analysis in education: how has it been used? *Educational Researcher,* 1984, 13(8), 6–15. See also the discussions that follow. All these indicate primarily two things: a) that meta-analysis tends to produce highly dubious results; and b), that much educational research is a part of the pulp/academe industry and of little relevance to teachers.

4. Rosenshine, B.V. and Furst, J., *Teacher Behaviour and Student Progress.* NFER, 1971. For another, very early, review of research, which largely supports the position outlined in this book, see Soar, R.S., Teacher behaviour related to pupil growth. *International Review of Education,* 1922, 18, 508–28. See also Rosenshine's contribution in *Research in Teacher Education: A Symposium,* cited earlier. See also the same writer's review of research, Content, time and direct instruction. In *Research on Teaching.* Peterson, P.L., *et al.* (eds) McCutchan, 1979. For a response, see Peterson's chapter in the same publication, Direct instruction reconsidered. A more recent review of research on teaching advocates being directive in teaching. See Rosenshine, B. and Stevens, R., Teaching function. In *Handbook of Research on Teaching,* cited earlier. See also Good, T.L., Classroom research: a decade of progress. *Educational Psychologist,* 1983, 18(3), 127–44. It is unclear whether this trend reflects better research, or a change in educational fashions, for, although learners may gain more knowledge when directed closely, I suspect they are less likely to achieve 'real' understanding in that way. I would again note that I found most of the above works highly unrewarding, and would explain this by saying that none are embedded in a theory of learning. In short, they are atheoretical, and based on the mistaken belief that understanding comes about as a result of accumulating data.

5. Sarason, I.G., The effects of anxiety and threat on the solution of a difficult task. *Journal of Abnormal and Social Psychology,* 1961, 62, 165–8. Also Thelen, H.T., Experimental research towards a theory of instruction. *Journal of Educational Research,* 1951, 45, 89–136. These are early works but cogent and still applicable.

6. A work with many helpful suggestions on how to teach English in a non-didactic way is Elbow, P., *Writing without Teachers.* Oxford University Press, 1973. See also Klippel, F., *Keep Talking.* Cambridge University Press, 1984. And Rinvolucri, M., *Grammar Games.* Cambridge University Press, 1986.

Chapter 13 Clarity, Enthusiasm and Variety (pages 145–150)

1. Bransford, J.D., *Human Cognition*. Wadsworth. 1979, 119. The author notes interesting work by Pollchik on the value of giving examples. This is one of the few works with a cognitive approach that I found helpful.
2. Some of these comments are based on Fowler, H.W. and Fowler, F.G., *The King's English*. Oxford University Press, 1973, 11.
3. Leavitt, H.J. and Mueller, R.A.H., Some effects of feedback on communication. *Human Relations*, 1951, 4, 401–10. Again, note date of publication.
4. Stuart, S., *Say*. Nelson. 1969. This is an early but lively account, by a teacher of English, about his discomfort with the transmission method of teaching and how he moved away from it.
5. Winnicott, D.W., *The Child, the Family, and the Outside World*. Penguin, 1964. Also Greenson, R.R., On enthusiasm. *Journal of the American Psychoanalytic Association*, 1962, 10, 3–21.
6. Kounin, J.S., *Discipline and Group Management in Classrooms*. R.E. Krieger, 1977. For a more readable account see Kounin, J.S., An analysis of teachers' managerial techniques. In *The Social Psychology of Teaching*. Morrison, A., *et al*. (eds) Penguin, 1972. For a comment on Kounin's work see Brophy, J.E. and Evertson, C.M., Teacher behaviour and student learning in second and third grades. In *The Appraisal of Teaching: Concepts and Process*. Borich, G.D., *et al*. (eds) Addison-Wesley, 1977. For tips on classroom management in schools see Marland, M., *The Craft of the Classroom*. Heinemann, 1975. Also Wragg, E.C., *Classroom Teaching Skills*. Croom Helm, 1984.
7. For a comment on the concept of 'habituation' see Bower, *The Perceptual World of the Child*, cited earlier, 25. Also Humphrey, N.K. and Keeble, G.R., How monkeys acquire a new way of seeing. *Perception*, 1976, 5, 51–6.
8. Montgomery, E.C., Exploratory behaviour as a function of similarity of stimulus situations. *Journal of Comparative Physiological Psychology*, 1953, 46, 129–33. And Berlyne, D.E. and Slater, J., Perceptual curiosity, exploratory behaviour, and maze learning. *Journal of Comparative Physiological Psychology*, 1957, 50, 228–32. Also Maddi, S.R., Affective tone during environmental regularity and change. *Journal of Abnormal and Social Psychology*, 1961, 62, 338–45. These are again all early papers but still highly relevant.

Chapter 14 Indirectness, Opportunities and Fit (pages 152–156)

1. The term 'village idiot' is highly questionable if not worse. But this story is based on a tale I heard many years ago when such a term was considered less offensive than it rightly is now, and I use it in an attempt to convey the flavour of those times. The term implies feeble-mindedness, and a certain attitude toward it, and for this I cannot think of a modern equivalent.
2. For some answers, see Brown, N.O., *Life against Death*. Wesleyan University Press, 1959, often reprinted. Also Macfarlane, A., The root of all evil. In *The Anthropology of Evil*. Parkin, D. (ed.) Basil Blackwell, 1985. Also Heilbronner, R.L., *The Quest for Wealth*. Simon & Schuster, 1956. See also Kasser, T., *et al*., The relations of maternal and social environments to late adolescents' materialistic and pro-social values. *Developmental Psychology*, 1995, 31(6), 907–14. These writers found that teenagers who are materially oriented tend to have mothers who do not support emotional growth and self-expression, but favour financial success.
3. For comments on the nature of analogies and their place in learning see Gick, M.L. and Holyoak, K.J., Schema induction and analogical transfer. *Cognitive Psychology*, 1983, 15, 1–38.
4. For comment on the place of imagination in teaching see Egan, K., *et al*. (eds) *Education and Imagination*. Open University Press, 1988.

5. Egan, K., *Teaching as Storytelling*. Routledge, 1988. Among other things, the author questions the assumption that young children are unable to think in an abstract way.
6. Bower, G.H. and Clark, M.C., Narrative stories as mediators for serial learning. *Psychonomic Science*, 1969, 14(4), 181–2.
7. See for example Watson, J.D., *The Double Helix*. Penguin Books, 1970. The author shows vividly how the scientists involved in the discovery here described, engaged in an almost incessant process of discussion. I would have thought this brief and engaging book essential reading for any science teacher, indeed anyone engaged in teaching.
8. Quoted in Koestler, A., *The Sleepwalkers*. Penguin Books, 1968, 399. This is again a popular and highly readable account of how discoveries are often made in science. For a judicious review, see Graubard, M., The Sleepwalkers: its contribution and impact. In *Astride the Two Cultures: Arthur Koestler at 70*. Harris, H. (ed.) Random House, 1976.
9. For a scholarly plea for better science teaching see Pollack, R., Some practical suggestions for teaching science in the liberal arts. In *Unity of Knowledge*. Damasio, A.R., *et al.* (eds) New York Academy of Sciences, 2001.

Chapter 15 Theory and Practice (pages 160–167)

1. See Inagaki, K. and Hatano, G., Amplification of cognitive motivation and its effects on epistemic observation. *American Educational Research Journal*, 1977, 14(4), 485–91. Also Nisbet, J. and Shucksmith, J., *Learning Strategies*. Routledge, 1986. And Entwistle, N., Learning from the experience of studying. In *Learning to Teach: Psychology in Teacher Training*. Francis, H. (ed.) Falmer Press, 1985.
2. A particularly good illustration of learning material, and an evaluation of its use compared with didactic teaching, is Brewer, I.M., *Learning More and Teaching Less*. SRHE and NFER-Nelson, 1985. Also Monk, G.L., Student engagement and teacher power in large classes. In *Learning in Groups*. Boulton, C., *et al.* (eds) Jossey-Bass, 1983.
3. Lifson, T., A comparison between lectures and conference methods of teaching physiology. *Journal of Medical Education*, 1956, 31(6), 376–82.
4. West, M., *et al.*, Medical students' attitudes toward basic sciences. *Medical Education*, 1982, 16, 188–91. Also Neame, R.L.B., How to construct a problem-based course. *Medical Teacher*, 1981, 3(3), 94–9.
5. Anderson, R.C. and Biddle, W.B., On asking people questions about what they are reading. In *The Psychology of Learning* and *Motivation*. Bower, G.H. (ed.) Academic Press, 1975.
6. For an excellent description of good and poor teaching based on worksheets see Mixed ability teaching at Beachside Comprehensive. In Ball, S., *Beachside Comprehensive*. Cambridge University Press, 1981.
7. Finkel, D.L. and Monk, G.S., Teachers and learning groups: dissolution of the Atlas complex. In Boulton, C. *et al.*, *Learning in Groups*. Also Thelen, N.A., Some classroom quiddities for people-orientated teachers. In *The Psychology of Open Teaching and Learning*. Silberman, M.L., *et al.* (eds) Little, Brown, 1972.

Chapter 16 Reflections on Educational Technology (pages 169–188)

1. See Musgrave, A., The ultimate argument for scientific realism. In *Relativism and Realism in Science*. Nola, R. (ed.) Kluwer Academic Publishers, 1988. On my last day of work on this revised manuscript, and the day before I was to send it to the publisher, I came across Blackmore, J.T., A new conception of epistemology and its relation to the methodology and philosophy of science. *Methodology and Science*, 1984, 14(2), 95–126. Much in this paper expresses better than I am able what I often wish to say.
2. Malone, T.W., Toward a theory of intrinsically motivating instruction. *Cognitive Science*, 1981, 4, 333–69. I am much obliged to this writer.

3. Weizenbaum, J., The myths of artificial intelligence. In *The Information Technology Revolution*. Forrester, T. (ed.) Basil Blackwell, 1985. For comment on the decline in American educational attainments see National Commission on Excellence in Education, A nation at risk. In *Kaleidoscope: Readings in Education*, 5th edn. Ryan, K. and Cooper, J.M. (eds) Houghton Mifflin, 1988. This book contains many useful articles.

4. For further comment see Dede, C., Educational and social implications. In *The Information Technology Revolution*, cited above.

5. Ritzer, G., *The McDonaldization of Society*. Pine Forge Press, 1993.

6. Sirotnik, K.A., What goes on in classrooms? In *The Curriculum: Problems, Politics, and Possibilities*. Beyer, L.E., *et al.* (eds) State University of New York Press, 1998.

7. For comment on the difference between interacting with people and interacting with a computer, see Bench-Capon, T.J.M., *et al.*, People interact through computers not with them. *Interacting With Computers*, 1989, 1(1), 31–42. Also Ihde, D., A phenomenology of man–machine relations. In *Work, Technology, and Education*. Feinberg, W., *et al.* (eds) University of Illinois Press, 1975. See also Noble, D.D., The regime of technology in education. In *The Curriculum: Problems, Politics, and Possibilities*. Beyer, L.E., *et al.* (eds) State University of New York Press, 1998. Any comment on educational technology that does not include a consideration of the points that Noble raises is, I believe, dangerous nonsense. See also Bonnett, M., Computers in the classroom: some values issues. In *Information Technology and Authentic Learning*. McFarlane, A. (ed.) Routledge, 1987. Also Lepper, M.R., Microcomputers in education: motivational and social issues. *American Psychologist*, 1985, 40 (1), 1–18. Also Clark, R.E., Reconsidering research on learning from media. *Review of Educational Research*, 1983, 53(4), 445-59. Also Zuckerman, D.M., *et al.*, Television viewing, children's reading, and related classroom behavior. *Communication*, 1980, 30(1), 166–74. Observations such as the above become important when one recalls the decline in basic literacy and numeracy in some developed countries, especially the USA. On the latter, see also Copperman, P., The decline of literacy. *Communication*, 1980, 30(1), 113–22.

8. See Shaw, R.E., *et al.*, Abstract conceptual knowledge: how we know what we know. In *Cognition and Instruction*. Klahr, D. (ed.) Lawrence Erlbaum, 1976. For early and highly scholarly work on what is involved in an 'abstract mode' of thinking see Goldstein's contribution in *A History of Psychology in Autobiography*. Vol. 5. Boring, E.G., *et al.* (eds) Appleton-Century-Crofts, 1967. For a more technical description see Goldstein, K. and Scheerer, M., Abstract and concrete behaviour: an experimental study with special tests. *Psychological Monographs*, 1941, 53, 2; whole number 239. See also Hayek, F.A., The primacy of the abstract. In *Beyond Reductionism*. Koestler, A., *et al.* (eds) Hutchinson, 1969. See also Egan, K., *Teaching as Storytelling*. Routledge, 1988. As previously noted, this author questions the assumption that young children are unable to think in an abstract way.

9. Havelock, E., The coming of literate communication to western culture. *Journal of Communication*, 1980, 30, 90–7.

10. Havelock, E.A., *Preface to Plato*. Basil Blackwell, 1963. I believe this work is essential reading.

11. For some of what I note in my text I am much indebted to the first part of Postman, N., *Teaching as a Conserving Activity*. Delacorte Press, 1979.

12. Tan, S.C., The effects of incorporating concept mapping into computer-assisted instruction. *Journal of Educational Computing Research*, 2000, 23(2), 113–31.

13. For incisive comment on the underlying implications of consumerism see the contributions in *The Culture of Consumption*. Fox, R.W. and Lears, T.J.J. (eds) Pantheon Books, 1983. For brief and often vivid comment on the psychological effects of shopping see Tauber, E.M., Why do people shop? *Journal of Marketing*, 1972, 36, 46–59.

14. Tierney, R.J., *et al.*, The effects of reading and writing upon thinking critically. *Reading Research Quarterly*, 1989, 24(2), 134–69. See also Eckhoff, B., How reading affects children's writing. *Language Arts*, 1983, 60(5), 607–16. For more general comments see

Campbell, B., Word processing in school. In *Teachers, Computers and the Classroom*. Reid, I., *et al.* (eds) Manchester University Press, 1985. Also Bork, A., Computers and the future of education. *Computer Education*, 1984, 8(1), 1–4. Also Tait, K., *et al.*, Some experiences in using a computer-based learning system as an aid to self-teaching and self-assessment. *Computer Education*, 1984, 8(3), 271–8. See also Davidson, J., *et al.*, A preliminary study of the effect of computer-assisted practice on reading attainment. *Journal of Research in Reading*, 1996, 19(2), 102–10. For roughly the same conclusions see Reitsma, P., Reading practice for beginners: effects of guided reading, reading while listening, and independent reading with computer-based speech feedback. *Reading Research Quarterly*, 1988, 23(2), 219–35. For comment on how the use of educational technology sometimes increases the motivation to learn see Underwood, J.D.M., A comparison of two types of computer support for reading development. *Journal of Research in Reading*, 2000, 23(2), 136–48. Also Dalton, D.W., *et al.*, The effects of word processing on written composition. *Journal of Educational Research*, 1987, 80(6), 338–45. These writers found that word processors helped able learners much less than less able ones. See also Jones, C. and Fortescue, S., *Using Computers in the Language Classroom*. Longman, 1987. This is an attractively designed book with many practical suggestions.

15. Latcham, C., Failure: the key to understanding success. *British Journal of Educational Technology*, 2005, 36(4), 665–7. For further implications of computer use see Rogers, L., *et al.*, Developing successful pedagogy with information and communications technology: how are science teachers meeting the challenge? *Technology, Pedagogy and Education*, 2004, 13(3), 287–305. Also Olson, J., Teacher influence in the classroom: a context for understanding curriculum transition. *Instructional Science*, 1981, 10, 259–75. This writer sympathetically and perceptively indicates why a transition to a new form of teaching can be very difficult. For comment on how educational technology cannot simply be introduced in the absence of changes in organization and teaching styles see Dawson, K., *et al.*, Conditions, processes and consequences of technology use: a case study. *Technology, Pedagogy and Education*, 2004, 13(1), 61–82. I believe that the single most important feature of educational technology is that, when properly used, it moves teachers away from didactic teaching, and encourages them to focus on learning. For valuable comments on this change of roles see Fisher, E., The teacher's role. In *Language, Classrooms and Computers*. Scrimshaw, P. (ed.) Routledge, 1993. See also Whitworth, A., The politics of virtual learning environments: environmental change, conflict, and e-learning. *British Journal of Educational Technology*, 2005, 36(4), 685–91.

16. Alexandre, L., Television Marti: electronic invasion in the post-cold war. *Media, Culture and Society*, 1992, 14, 523–40.

17. For further comment see Hawkridge, D., *New Information Technology in Education*. The Johns Hopkins University Press, 1983. Also Webster, F., *Theories of the Information Society*. Routledge, 1995.

18. For a review of the less happy implications of exchanging emails in an educational setting see Fabos, B., *et al.*, Telecommunication in the classroom: rhetoric versus reality. *Review of Educational Research*, 1999, 69(3), 217–59.

19. Dillon, A., *et al.*, Human factors of journal usage and design of electronic texts. *Interacting with Computers*, 1989, 1(2), 183–9. Also McKnight, C., *et al.*, *Hypertext in Context*. Cambridge University Press, 1991. Also Berg, van den S., *et al.*, Effects of educational settings on student responses to structured hypertext. *Journal of Computer-based Instruction*, 1991, 18(4), 118–24. The latter writers do not even allude to my basic criticisms.

20. See Underwood, J., *Technology, Pedagogy and Education*, 2004, 13(2), 135–45.

21. Heisenberg, W., *The Physicist's Conception of Nature*. Greenwood Press, 1970, 21.

22. An excellent and subtle reminder of what is involved in being 'simple' is provided by Milne, A.A., *Winnie-the-Pooh*. With the original line drawings by E.H. Shepard. Many times reprinted, and warmly recommended.

Chapter 18 Communicating and Participating (pages 195–202)

1. Rogers, C., *On Becoming a Person*. Constable, 1967. Also his *Client-Centred Therapy*. Houghton Mifflin, 1951. Also Yalom, I., *Theory and Practice of Group Psychotherapy*. Basic Books, 1985. For helpful comments on what goes on in many discussions, see Lomov, B.F., Psychological processes and communication. *Soviet Psychology*, 1978, 17, 3–22. Also Kol'tsova, V.A., Experimental study of cognitive activity in communication. *Soviet Education*, 1978, 17, 23–38. And Inagaki, K., Facilitation of knowledge integration through classroom discussion. *Quarterly Newsletter of the Laboratory of Comparative Human Cognition*, 1981, 3(2), 26–8.

2. Christensen, C.M., Relationship between pupil achievement, pupil affect-need, teacher warmth, and teacher permissiveness. *Journal of Educational Psychology*, 1960, 51(3), 169–74. This is an early but most perceptive contribution. For an early review of research see Ripple, R.W., Affective factors influence classroom learning. *Educational Leadership*, 1965, 22, 476–80.

3. John Holt has some vivid descriptions of this. See his *How Children Fail*. Penguin, 1969, rev edn 1987.

4. Johnson, D.W., Student–student interaction: the neglected variable in education. *Educational Researcher*, 1981, 10(1), 5–10. I am also again greatly indebted to Jane Abercrombie, *The Anatomy of Judgement*. Free Association Books, 1989. For comment on the way classroom topography reflects ideas about learning and teaching, see Getzels, J.W., Images of the classroom and visions of the learner. *School Review*, 1974, 82, 527–40.

Chapter 19 Interacting (pages 205–209)

1. For the importance of learning something well, before one goes on to something new, see Rosenshine, B.V., Content, time, and direct instruction. In *Research On Teaching*. Peterson, P.L., *et al*. (eds) McCutchan, 1979.

2. See Collier, K.G., Peer-group learning in higher education: the development of higher order skills. *Studies in Higher Education*, 1980, 5(1), 55–62. For some helpful tips on how to facilitate group work when teaching adult literacy classes see *Teaching Groups: A Basic Education Handbook*. London: Adult Literacy and Basic Skills Unit, 1982.

3. Though early, the following have helpful suggestions on how to encourage learner participation: Barnes, D., *Language, the Learner and the School*. Penguin, 1969. Bridges, D., The silent student in small group discussion. *Education for Teaching*, 59–66, 1975; Smith, B., The noisy tutor in small group discussion. *Education for Teaching*, 1976, 35–8. Seal, C., The discussion group. *Journal of Further and Higher Education*, 1977, 1(1), 22–5. Seal, C., Two views of discussion groups. *Journal of Further and Higher Education*, 1980, 4(1), 51–9. Beattie, G.W., The dynamics of university tutorial groups. *Bulletin of the British Psychological Society*, 1982, 35, 147–50. Flanders, N.A., *Analysing Teaching Behaviour*. Addison-Wesley, 1970. For suggestions on how to facilitate discussions when teaching a foreign language see Ur, P., *Discussions That Work*. Cambridge University Press, 1981. My greatest debt is again to Jane Abercrombie (*The Anatomy of Judgement*, cited earlier), but two serious omissions in her work might be noted. First, although she discussed the difficulties students experience when they have a teacher who is not didactic, she did not note that teachers also have trouble when they attempt to move from a didactic to a less didactic approach. This omission is important because I found that some teachers who find non-didactic teaching difficult often blame their learners for this difficulty. Second, she did not note that even a two-sentence exchange can sometimes serve the same purpose as a 'free group discussion'.

4. Rowe, M.B., Wait-time and rewards as instructional variables, their influence on language, logic, and control: Part One: Wait-time. *Journal of Research in Science Teaching*, 1974, 11(2), 81–94. I thought this a valuable paper written in an unfortunate style.

5. In a review of research on questioning, it has been found that using 'higher cognitive questions has a positive effect on student achievement'. See Redfield, D.L. and Rousseau, E.W., A meta-analysis of experimental research on teacher questioning behaviour. *Review of Educational Research*, 1981, 51(2), 237–45. For further research and a sustained discussion see Marton, F. and Saljo, R., On qualitative differences in learning: 1 – outcome and process; and symposium: learning process and strategies; 2 – outcome as a function of the learner's conception of the task. *British Journal of Educational Psychology*, 1976, 46, 4–11 and 115–27. See also Watkins, D., Depth of processing and the quality of learning outcomes. *Instructional Science*, 1983, 12, 49–58. For other findings see Entwistle, A. and Entwistle, N., Experiences of understanding in revising for degree examinations. *Learning and Instruction*, 1992, 2, 1–22. See also Hammersley, M., The organisation of pupil participation. *Sociological Review*, 1974, 22, 355–68; and the same writer's *Case Studies in Classroom Research*. Open University Press, 1986.

Chapter 20 Discussing (pages 213–222)

1. Tizard, B. and Hughes, M., *Young Children Learning*. Fontana, 1984, 200.
2. In discussing the change in people's thinking during the period commonly called the Renaissance, Wayland Young noted: 'The mystery does not lie in the fact that they found answers; it lies in the fact that they asked the questions which had not been asked for thousands of years. And this is a matter of feeling, not knowledge. The difference between asking a question and not asking it, is quite a different kind of difference from that between finding the answer and not finding it. Whether you can answer it, is a matter of intelligence and perseverance. But whether you ask it in the first place, is a matter of emotion. What emotion? I would say the feeling of being authorized to ask it, the feeling that one is allowed to inquire, and that things and people will not bite if you look closely at them.' Young, W., *Eros Denied*. Corgi Books, 1967, 78. These comments are also highly pertinent to the last chapter in this book.
3. For an illuminating analysis of the personal experiences I have recounted here see Saljo, R., *Learning in the learner's perspective I and II*. Institute of Education. University of Göteborg, 1979.
4. Bartley, W.W. III, *The Retreat to Commitment*. Open Court, 1984. A most important work.
5. Keller, W.D., On teaching and learning. In *Excellence in University Teaching*. Burton, T.H., *et al.* (eds) University of South Carolina Press, 1975.
6. My use of the word 'open' is prompted by the work of Sidney Jourard. See his *The Transparent Self*. Van Nostrand Reinhold, 1971.
7. Yalom, I., *The Theory and Practice of Group Psychotherapy*. Basic Books, 1985, 386.
8. Wispé, L.G., Evaluation of section teaching methods in the introductory course. *Journal of Educational Research*, 1951, 45, 161–85. Wispé's research was done long ago, so the percentages she reported would probably be somewhat different today. Though an early work, it is one of the better papers on this topic that I know. However, I believe it suffers from a fundamental flaw. Although Wispé distinguished between experienced teachers and graduate students acting as instructors, none of the teachers involved had any systematic training in teaching. But then, nearly everyone who does this kind of research seems to take it as self-evident that effective teaching does not require systematic study and much practice.
9. An early but good introduction to this large topic is McLeish, J., *The Lecture Method*. Cambridge Monographs on Teaching Methods, No.1. Cambridge Institute of Education, 1968. Another early but perceptive introduction is Frenkel-Brunswick, E., Personality theory and perception. In *Perception: An Approach to Personality*. Blake, R.R., *et al.* (eds) Ronald Press, 1951. Also still worth reading is *The Authoritarian Personality*. Adorno, T.W., *et al.* (eds) Norton, 1969.

10. I still haven't quite got over my surprise at finding that this is so. My education began with *Knowledge and Control*. Young, M.F.D. (ed.) Collier-Macmillan, 1971.
11. An early work, but still worth reading, is Erikson, E.H., *Childhood and Society*. Hogarth Press, 1965. Many times reprinted.

Chapter 21 Difficult Lessons (pages 223–231)

1. Salzberger-Wittenberg, I., *The Emotional Experience of Learning and Teaching*. Routledge, 1983.
2. For some glimpses of adult learners see Marsh, J., The boredom of study: a study of boredom. *Management Education and Development*, 1983, 14(2), 120–35. The picture presented is totally unlike that which is fashionable in current writing on adult education. See also the first half of Otty, N., *Learner Teacher*. Penguin, 1972.
3. Haste, H., Beyond the barriers. *The Psychologist*, 1990, 3(5), 212–14.
4. The following early paper is still surprisingly relevant here: Cooper, E. and Jahoda, M., The evasion of propaganda: how prejudiced people respond to anti-prejudice propaganda. *Journal of Psychology*, 1947, 23, 15–25.
5. Lindsay, J., *Cezanne: His Life and Art*. Evelyn, Adams and Mackay, 1969, 163 and 160.
6. Planck, M., *Scientific Autobiography and Other Papers*. Williams & Norgate, 1950, 19. See also Barber, B., Resistance by scientists to scientific discovery. *Science*, 1961, 134, 596–602.
7. Freud, S., *Group Psychology and the Analysis of the Ego*. In Freud, *Civilisation, Society and Religion*. Pelican Freud Library, Vol. 12, 1985.
8. Bion, W.R., *Experience in Groups*. Tavistock, 1961. I found Bion's writing opaque, and busy teachers will find the material most relevant to them on 29–75. A good introduction to the work of Bion is Rioch, M.J., The work of Wilfred Bion on groups. *Psychiatry*, 1970, 33, 56–66. A helpful work, which applies the work of Bion to classroom interaction, is Mann, R.D., *The College Classroom*. Wiley, 1970. For an early criticism of Bion's work, as well as much psychoanalytic writing, see Sherwood, M., Bion's experiences in groups: a critical review. *Human Relations*, 1964, 15, 113–30. For the idea of 'forming, storming, norming, and performing', see Tuckman, B.W., Developmental sequence in small groups. *Psychological Bulletin*, 1965, 63(6), 384–99.
9. See Grünbaum, A., Epistemological liabilities of the clinical appraisal of psychoanalytic theory. *NOÛS*, 1980, 14, 307–85. This is a superb paper, and essential reading on this topic. See also the same writer's fine Précis of The Foundations of Psychoanalysis: a Philosophical Critique. *The Behavioral and Brain Sciences*, 1986, 9, 217–84.
10. For helpful comments on such matters see Horwitz, L., Projective identification in dyads and groups. *International Journal of Group Psychotherapy*, 1983, 33(3), 259–79.
11. See Yalom, *Theory and Practice of Group Psychotherapy*, cited earlier. Although it is obviously important to distinguish between therapy and teaching, I think teachers will find this work useful.
12. An example of such writing is *School and Society*. Cosin, B.R., *et al.* (eds) Open University and Routledge, 1971. A better collection is *The Process of Schooling*. Hammersley, M. and Woods, P. (eds) Open University Press, 1976.

Chapter 22 Learning a New Approach (pages 235–237)

1. See Solomon, G. and McDonald, F.J., Pre-test and post-test reactions to self-viewing one's teaching performance on video tape. *Journal of Educational Psychology*, 1970, 4, 280–6. For further references see Wragg, E.C., *A Review of Research in Teacher Education*. NFER-Nelson, 1982.
2. Alexander, F.M., *The Use of the Self*. Gollancz, 1985, 33. Long after I had completed this manuscript, I came across Leon Festinger's paper, Behavioural support for opinion change.

Public Opinion Quarterly, 1964, 28, 404–17. In this he noted: 'All in all, we can detect no effect on behaviour, of a clear and persistent change in opinion brought about by a persuasive communication.' Corey reported something similar in an even earlier paper. See Corey, S.M., Professed attitudes and actual behaviour. *Journal of Educational Psychology*, 1931, 28, 271–80. Notice how those findings flatly contradict common assumptions, and echo much that has been noted all through this book.

3. If the argument in this chapter, and the evidence cited in its support, is reasonably sound, it must have important implications for teacher training. Among other things, the argument implies that having suitable information, finding it relevant, having experiences and reflecting on them are insufficient to bring about appropriate practice. I have also frequently noticed that even a genuine commitment to, or ability to discuss what is held to be most advisable, is no indicator that one is able to teach in a manner consonant with those views. On the contrary: I frequently found that the people who speak most persuasively often do not behave in line with what they say. Nor are one-day workshops of any use in furthering a new approach unless the participants are already well advanced in those directions. For a review of the difficulties of change see Fullan, M.G., *The New Meaning of Educational Change*. Cassell, 1991.

4. I note here that I found reading John Holt's *How Children Fail* did more to change the attitude of student-teachers toward teaching adults than any book on teaching adults they happened to come across. The works by Abercrombie and Rogers I cited earlier also usually had a big impact on them. This was especially the case with many instructors who were not graduates. The minds of some of these student-teachers seemed to blossom with the wider implications of these writers' work, especially after having been exposed to years of the fatuous skill-based approach. For some evidence for these comments see Patricia Wilson's *Anti-natal Teaching*. Faber & Faber, 1990. I mention the latter work in part because an inspector once reported that the reading I recommended 'does not reflect current practices in adult and continuing education and the concentration on early childhood and child psychology is of little relevance'. (DES, Report T216/51/0270, 299/88.)

Chapter 23 Variations on a Theme (pages 243–247)

1. For suggestions in a school setting see Klrk, R., *Learning in Action*. Blackwell, 1987. For early applications to a Peace Corps training programme, see Harrison, R. and Hopkins, R.L., The design of cross-cultural training: an alternative to the university model. *Journal of Applied Behavioural Science*, 1967, 3, 431–60.

2. As some readers may have missed a reference to what is commonly called 'non-verbal communication' or 'body language', I should perhaps admit that I have not found the material I have read on this topic very helpful in teaching.

3. Haramati, S., *Three Who Preceded Ben-Yehuda*. Jerusalem: Yad Izhak Ben-Zvi Publications, 1978. See the section on my grandfather Baruch Mitrani.

4. For an introduction, see van Ments, M., *The Effective Use of Role-Play*. Kogan Page, 1984. See also Mann, R.D., *The College Classroom*. John Wiley, 1970. For a collection of educational games for all ages see Brandes, D. and Phillips, H., *Gamesters' Handbook*. Hutchinson, 1977. Often reprinted.

Chapter 24 Overview (pages 251–252)

1. I should perhaps have noted by now that, although I have often referred to the need to have a theory if one has to deal with a complex matter, and although I have attempted to describe the characteristics of a good theory, there has been nothing about how a discovery is occasionally arrived at. That is a completely different story!

2. The effects of a culture on the people who are born in it are important, and here are three reasons: a) one is no more consciously aware of these effects than one is aware of the schemas that help one to walk down a flight of stairs; b) the behaviours characteristic of that culture will tend to seem self-evidently appropriate to the people in it; and c) such behaviour will often override rational considerations. For examples see Turnbull, C.G., *The Mountain People*. Jonathan Cape, 1973. Hart, C.W.M., et al., *The Tiwi of North Australia*. Holt, Rinehart & Winston, 1960. Gilsenan, M., *Lords of the Lebanese Marches: Violence and Narrative in an Arab Society*. I.B. Tauris Publishers, 1996. Titmuss, R.M., *The Gift Relationship: From Human Blood to Social Policy*. George Allen & Unwin, 1970. Macfarlane, A., *The Culture of Capitalism*. Basil Blackwell, 1987. Donald, M., *A Mind So Rare*. Norton, 2001. Doi, T., *The Anatomy of Dependence*. Kodansha International, 1981. Diekstra, R.F.W., The epidemiology of suicide and parasuicide. *Archives of Suicide Research*, 1996, 2, 1–29. Inglehart, R., *Culture Shift in Advanced Industrial Society*. Princeton University Press, 1990, especially Chapter 1. Also Blok, A., *The Mafia of a Sicilian Village, 1860–1960*. Polity Press, 1974. The latter book provides a description of economic and social factors, but the end result is to show that the phenomenon of 'mafia' arises in a context in which people lack a sense of mutual trust. It is one stark illustration of how people *become* who they are. For a clear and elegant exposition of the powerful effects of cultural evolution see Short, R.V., Man, the changing animal. In *Physiology and Genetics of Reproduction*. Part A. Coutinho, E.M., et al. (eds) Plenum Press, 1973. The effect that a culture can have on a people is a most important topic and I must resist the temptation to provide more references.

Chapter 25 Why Teach? (pages 255–274)

1. I here found helpful the first 50 pages of Postman, N., *The End of Education*. Alfred A Knopf, 1996.
2. My source is Plato, *The Republic*. Ferrari, G.R.F., editor; and Griffith, T., translator. Cambridge University Press, 2000, 220.
3. Jungk, R., *Brighter Than a Thousand Suns*. Penguin Books, 1960.
4. There is a huge literature on the questions raised here, and I cite a small part of what I have read and found valuable. I admire especially Bunge, M., A critical examination of the new sociology of science: Part 1. *Philosophy of the Social Sciences*, 1991, 21(4), 524–60; and Bunge, M., A critical examination of the new sociology of science: Part 2. *Philosophy of the Social Sciences*, 1992, 22(1), 46–76. Also valuable is Bartley, W.W., III, Philosophy of biology versus philosophy of physics. In *Evolutionary Epistemology, Rationality, and the Sociology of Knowledge*. Radnitzky, G., et al. (eds) Open Court, 1987. I also found engaging and helpful Philips, D.C., *Philosophy, Science, and Social Inquiry*. Pergamon Press, 1987. The next writer cited illustrates her thesis practically through journalism: Lichtenberg, J., In defence of objectivity. In *Mass Media and Society*. Curran, J., et al. (eds) Edward Arnold, 1991. See also Pyle, A., The rationality of the chemical revolution. In *After Popper, Kuhn and Feyerabend*. Nola, R., et al. (eds) Kluwer Academic Publishers, 2000. Also Laudan, L., *Progress and Its Problems*. Routledge & Kegan Paul, 1977. And Goodman, L.E., Six dogmas of relativism. In *Cultural Relativism and Philosophy*. Dascal, M. (ed.) E.J. Brill, 1991. I believe Goodman makes a serious mistake to state that everything in a language is translatable; nevertheless, the fact that nuances are not always translatable is no support for the notion of paradigms. For two examples of the relativist position see Latour, B. and Woolgar, S., *Laboratory Life: The Social Construction of Scientific Facts*. Sage, 1979; and *Psychology and Postmodernism*. Kvale, S. (ed.) Sage, 1992. For reasons given in my text, I found both hopelessly inadequate. A recent exposition of the so-called 'strong position' in the sociology of knowledge is Bloor, D., *Knowledge and Social Imagery*, 2nd edn. University of Chicago Press, 1991. I did my best to read this, but even-

tually laid it aside. Nowhere in this book is there any indication of breathing people trying to do anything, of any hint that might help people to do anything, or of some contribution however vague that might help people to understand something. The only time people are mentioned is as disputants in a debate that seems to me remote from reality. When people are mentioned who disagree with the author, one has the sense of ships passing in the night. The best known, if now rather dated, exposition of the relativist position is probably Berger, P.L. and Luckman, M., *The Social Construction of Reality: A Treatise on the Sociology of Knowledge*. Penguin Books, 1966. Much of this strikes me as nonsensical. In support of the idea that all scientific explanations are social constructs, some writers cite Kuhn, T.S., *The Structure of Scientific Revolutions*, 2nd edn. University of Chicago Press, 1970. For a careful analysis that illustrates why the notion of 'revolutions' in science is quite mistaken see Elie Zahar's two fine papers, Why did Einstein's programme supersede Lorents's: 1 and 2. *British Journal of the Philosophy of Science*, 1973, 24, 95–123 and 223–62. For a comment on these papers that misses the main points see Feyerabend, P., Zahar on Einstein. *British Journal of the Philosophy of Science*, 1974, 25, 25-8. For many genial comments on these matters see Bronowski, J., *The Origins of Knowledge and Imagination*. Yale University Press, 1978. I hold back from citing more works and must hope that I have supplied enough to enable interested readers to pursue this most important topic if they wish to.

5. There is again a large literature on this topic, and the single best work I know (and one that is seldom cited) is Maltitz, Horst, v., *The Evolution of Hitler's Germany*. McGraw-Hill, 1973. I salute this writer! Also recommended, *Survivors, Victims, and Perpetrators*. Dimsdale, J.E. (ed.) Hemisphere Publishing, 1980; Marrus, M.R., *The Holocaust in History*. Penguin Books, 1989. One of the virtues of the latter book is that it places the Holocaust in a historical perspective. For highly perceptive comments on this literature, and a judicious bibliography, see Ascheim, S.E., Small forays, grand theories and deep origins. In *Reshaping the Past*. Frankel, J. (ed.) Oxford University Press, 1994. See also *The Good Old Days: The Holocaust As Seen by Its Perpetrators and Bystanders*. Klee, E., et al. (eds) Konecky & Konecky, 1988. For a gripping personal account see Levi, P., *If This is a Man* and *The Truce*. Abacus, 1978. For the aftermath see Bar-On, D., *Legacy of Silence: Encounters with Children of the Third Reich*. Harvard University Press, 1989. Again, I must resist the temptation to cite more works.

6. For an excellent account of what is involved for something to become 'a fact', see Micale, M.A., On the 'disappearance' of hysteria. *Isis*, 1993, 84, 496–526.

7. Miringoff, M., et al., *The Social Health of the Nation*. Oxford University Press, 1999. I regret that I do no justice to this splendid work. Also Wilkinson, R.G., *Unhealthy Societies*. Routledge, 1996.

8. Schlesinger, P., *Putting 'Reality' Together*. Methuen, 1987. See especially the introductory essay.

9. Quoted by Ken Wilber in the introduction to his collection *Quantum Questions*. Shambhala, 1984.

10. This quotation appears in, Brown, J.R., *The Laboratory of the Mind*. Routledge 1991. As it is common to hear talk of 'paradigms' and 'revolutions' in science after the work of Kuhn, T., *The Structure of Scientific Revolutions*, 2nd enlarged edn, University of Chicago Press, 1970, here is Holton who refers to Einstein in respect of 'revolutions' like this: 'As for being labelled a great revolutionary . . . Einstein took every opportunity to disavow it. He saw himself as essentially a continuist, and had specific ideas on the way scientific theory developed by evolution'. Holton, G., *Einstein, History, and Other Passions*. American Institute of Physics, 1995, 6. See also Holton, G., *Thematic Origins of Scientific Thought: Kepler to Einstein*. Harvard University Press, 1988, 197. Here Holton writes that Einstein dismissed 'all talk of revolution when applied to his work or to that of other modern scientists. Such characterization, he caustically remarked once, gives the impression that science

progresses by acts "somewhat like the *coups d'état* in some of the smaller, unstable republics".'

11. Quoted on page 153 in the collection by Wilber noted above. See also the contribution by the Maxwells in *Psychotherapy Process*. Mahoney, M.J. (ed.) Plenum Press, 1980.

12. Heisenberg, W., *Physics and Beyond*. Allen and Unwin, 1971. Heisenberg also notes that scientists sometimes find they have at last grasped that a simple relationship exists in the mass of facts they have been examining. They then often go on to say that they are aware that this relationship must always have existed, and is not simply the product of the theories they hold. This follows from the fact that the new relationship that has been discovered often forces a change in the nature of the theory with which they began. For example, Newton's equations express the movement of the planets much more fully and correctly then did Ptolemy's. Newton's equations, so to speak, appear to come closer to describing nature's construction. Heisenberg, W., *Physics and Beyond*. Harper & Row, 1971, 212. Or see Schrödinger, E., *My View of the World*. Cambridge University Press, 1964. For fascinating comments on these matters, see also the autobiographical section in *Albert Einstein: Philosopher Scientist*. Schlipp, P.A. (ed.) Open Court, 1970. Everything these eminent scientists say is in direct contradiction to the relativist position. Notice also that scientists from countries with a culture quite different from that common in the West accept the orientation taken by the scientists I have quoted.

13. The source here is the short and easily accessible account of this man's work, Kelly, G.A., *A Theory of Personality: The Psychology of Personal Constructs*. W.W. Norton, 1963, 135. The quotation I provide is typical of this man's views, and many similar could be given.

14. I write those words thinking of my first degree in psychology, for this idea of 'negotiating' was what the course team actually advocated. But then, such a position was inevitable since the course was based on the premise that human beings 'construe' their reality. I was even informed on that course that people who adhere to the belief that 'the truth' exists do so because they are unable to relinquish the safety of having such a belief! Among many other inanities, I was also taught on that course that, if a child's ability to acquire its native language is largely innate, then there is nothing to study about the acquisition of language. This is like saying that, if the working of the heart is largely innate, then there is nothing to study about how hearts function. The work of John Bowlby was derided; and the main form of psychotherapy considered was 'Family Systems Theory'. I suspect that this approach was favoured because it has nothing to say about why some people become severely emotionally distressed in the first place, and because it is so impersonal and intellectual. (See Pam, A., Family systems theory: a critical view. *New Ideas in Psychology*, 1993, 11(1), 77–94.) The grinding of axes on that course was so loud it obliterated serious scholarly discourse; and it was autocratic especially as, on the surface, it appeared to be egalitarian. That course provided one of the worst experiences of my professional life. The first edition of this book was, in part, written in refutation of it.

15. Pennebaker, J.W., *et al*., Disclosure of traumas and immune function: health implications for psychotherapy. *Journal of Consulting and Clinical Psychology*, 1988, 56(2), 239–45. Also Pennebaker, J.W., *et al*., Cognitive, emotional, and language processes in disclosure. *Cognition and Emotion*, 1996, 10(6), 601–26. These writers found that only those who wrote about both the facts of their trauma, as well as their emotional responses to them, showed long-term health benefits. Further, in contrast to people who attempted to put a positive gloss on things, and whose health did not improve, the people who disclosed pain felt low immediately afterwards but their health improved in the long run. See also Pennebaker, J.W., Putting stress into words: health, linguistic, and therapeutic implications. *Behavioural Research and Therapy*, 1993, 31(6), 539–48. Among other things, the writer found that when people disclose negative emotions, and also develop a clear cognitive storyline in doing so, their physical and mental health improve. See also Dattore, P.J., *et al*., Premorbid personality differentiation of cancer and non-cancer groups: a test of the

hypothesis of cancer proneness. *Journal of Consulting and Clinical Psychology*, 1980, 48(3), 338–94. Also pertinent here is the work of Harvey and associates. They found that what they call 'account-making' helps people who have suffered trauma. They refer to the research of Silver who found that women who were able to make some sense of their experience of rape reported less psychological distress, better social adjustment, higher levels of self-esteem, and a greater resolution of their painful experience. These writers also found that confiding in others relatively early after the experience of trauma (that is, within a year), is positively related to later adjustment, but only if that confiding is to someone whose response is felt to be empathic, non-judgemental, consoling and under-standing. Harvey, J.H., *et al.*, Coping with sexual assault: the roles of account making and confiding. *Journal of Traumatic Stress*, 1991, 4(4), 515–31. I hold back from citing more of this literature, and all of it contradicts a relativistic view.

16. See Broszat, M., *The Hitler State*. Longman, 1981. Also Kershaw, J., *The Nazi Dictatorship*, 3rd edn. Arnold, 1993.

17. For some of these ideas I am much indebted to Bellah, R.N., *et al.*, *Habits of the Heart*. University of California Press, 1985.

18. Rescher, N., *Nature and Understanding*. Oxford University Press, 2000. See especially the chapter entitled The intelligibility of nature. Also Rescher, N., *Satisfying Reason*. Kluwer, 1995. For comment on 'deconstruction' see Chapter 11. And Rescher, N., *Rationality*. Clarendon Press, 1988. I am greatly indebted to Rescher, and draw attention especially to the lucidity of his writing. See also Wheeler, J.A., The universe as home for man. *American Scientist*, 1974, 62, 683–91. Here I should perhaps note that I am aware of the limitations of what is often called a sociobiological approach. See Gould, S.J., Exaptation: a crucial tool for evolutionary psychology. *Journal of Social Issues*, 1991, 47(3), 43–65. For a scholarly review of the socio-biological approach see Archer, J., Human sociobiology: basic concepts and limitations. *Journal of Social Issues*, 1991, 47(3), 11–26. For an engaging and scholarly review of the contrast between the biological and the cultural view see Kuper, A., *The Chosen Primate: Human Nature and Cultural Diversity*. Harvard University Press, 1994. Also Sahlins, M., *The Use and Abuse of Biology*. Tavistock Publications, 1977. And Bock, K., *Human Nature and History: A Response to Sociobiology*. Columbia University Press, 1980.

19. Schrödinger, E., *What Is Life?* and *Mind and Matter*. Cambridge University Press, 1967. For later comment on the likely relationship between mind and nature see Brown, J.R., *The Laboratory of the Mind*. Routledge, 1991.

20. See Wegner, D.M., *et al.*, Apparent mental causation: sources of the experience of the will. *American Psychologist*, 1999, 54(7), 480–92. Also Libet, B., Unconscious cerebral initiative and the role of conscious will in voluntary action. *The Behavioral and Brain Sciences*, 1985, 8, 529–66. And Baumeister, R.F., *et al.*, Consciousness, free choice, and automaticity. In *The Automaticity of Everyday Life: Advances in Social Cognition*. Vol. 10. Wyer, Jr., R.S. (ed.) Lawrence Erlbaum, 1997. Also Norman, D.A., *et al.*, Attention and action: willed and auto-matic control of behaviour. In *Consciousness and Self-Regulation*. Vol. 4. Davidson, R.J., *et al.* (eds) Plenum Press, 1976. Also Velmans, M., Is human information processing con-scious? *Behavioral and Brain Sciences*, 1991, 14, 651–726. See especially the Commentaries by Bowers, Dixon, Kinsbourne, Libet, Mandler, Mangan, Underwood and Wilson.

21. See Lewontin, R.C., Organism and environment. In *Learning, Development, and Culture*. Plotkin, H.C. *et al.* (eds) John Wiley, 1982. Also and especially, Meaney, M.J., Nature, nurture, and the disunity of knowledge. In *Unity of Knowledge*. Damasio, A.R., *et al.* (eds) New York Academy of Sciences, 2001.

22. Metzinger, T., The problem of consciousness. In *Conscious Experience*. Metzinger, T. (ed.) Schonlingh, 1995. I found this an exceptionally lucid and perceptive work. Anyone ser-iously interested in learning and teaching must eventually grapple with the nature of con-sciousness. Attempts to reduce consciousness to activity in the brain strike me as highly unsatisfactory, and earlier works on this topic that I have found helpful include the

following: *Brain and Conscious Experience*. Eccles, J.C. (ed.) Springer Verlag, 1966, especially the contributions by Sperry and Thorpe; *Body and Mind*. Rieber, R.W. (ed.) Academic Press, 1980, especially the contributions by Hankoff, Irani, Bakan and Kinsbourne; *Consciousness and the Physical World*. Josephson, B.D. and Ramachandran, V.S. (eds) Pergamon Press, 1980, especially the contributions by Humphrey and Barlow; *Consciousness and the Brain*. Globus, G.G., *et al.* (eds) Plenum Press, 1976, especially the contribution by Maxwell; *Dimensions of Mind*. Hook, S. (ed.) New York University Press, 1960, especially the contributions by Price, Ducasse and Hintz. Also Sperry, R.W., A modified concept of consciousness. *Psychological Review*, 1969, 76, 532–6. And Kihlstrom, J.F., The continuum of consciousness. *Consciousness and Cognition*, 1993, 2, 334–54. And Popper, K., Three worlds. In *The Tanner Lectures on Human Values*, Vol. I. McMurrin, S.M. (ed.) University of Utah Press, 1980.

23. Rescher, N., *Satisfying Reason*. Kluwer Academic Publishers, 1995. For how talk of 'postmodernism' and 'deconstructionism' obscure understanding see Herf, J., How the culture wars matter. In *Higher Education Under Fire*. Bērubē, M., *et al.* (eds) Routledge, 1995.

24. Lest the above sound contrived, I note that most of the contributions in, to take one example, *Psychology and Postmodernism*, Kvale, S. (ed.) Sage, 1992, are mere polemics, with the exception of the contribution by Seth Chaiklin. One reaches the latter's contribution like someone coming across a pool of fresh water in an arid land. Even the English in which it is written suddenly sounds alive. Not only are we never told by the other contributors how one might concretely do anything; the only tool they give us, to help us to decide whether what we are doing is stupid or sound, is to see whether it 'works'. That is like using a hammer to open a tin of beans. This will 'work', but there are better ways of doing things.

25. For fascinating comment on the effect of a focus on self, see Titmuss, R.M., *The Gift Relationship: From Human Blood to Social Policy*. George Allen & Unwin, 1970. Macfarlane, A., *The Origins of English Individualism*. Basil Blackwell, 1978. Popenoe, D., American family decline, 1960–1990: a review and appraisal. *Journal of Marriage and the Family*, 1993, 55, 527–55. For illuminating comments on how individualism is often no more than 'genuine, imitation teak veneer' covering an underlying selfishness, see Hsu, F.L.K., Rugged individualism reconsidered. In that writer's *Rugged Individualism Reconsidered: Essays in Psychological Anthropology*. University of Tennessee Press, 1983. Also Sandel, M.J., The procedural republic and the unencumbered self. *Political Theory*, 1984, 12(1), 81–96. Also Solomon, M.F., *Narcissism and Intimacy*. Norton, 1989. For further comment on the phenomenon of individualism see Spence, J.T., Achievement American style: the rewards and costs of individualism. *American Psychologist*, 1985, 40(12), 1285–95. For an early view of the high costs of individualism from a military perspective see Spindler, G.D., American character as revealed by the military: descriptions and origins. *Psychiatry*, 1948, 11, 275–81. Also Guisinger, S., *et al.*, Individuality and relatedness. *American Psychologist*, 1994, 49(2), 104–11. Also Sampson, E.E., The debate on individualism. *American Psychologist*, 1988, 43(1), 15–22. And Albee, G.W., The Protestant ethic, sex, and psychotherapy. *American Psychologist*, 1977, 32, 150–61. See also Conger, J.J., Freedom and commitment, *American Psychologist*, 1981, 36(12), 1475–84. The latter is a fine paper and conveys much that I would want to say if I had the space. I must resist adding further works, and will close by noting Spindler, G.D., *et al.*, Anthropologists view American culture. *Annual Review of Anthropology*, 1983, 12, 49–78. This is an excellent review of work done on this topic, and provides a detailed bibliography. Notice, alas, that almost none of these works is by a British author.

26. Whitehead, A.N., *The Aims of Education and Other Essays*. Williams & Norgate, 1946, 18. Some readers might have noticed that, with the exception of Plato, this is one of the few references to a work by a philosopher in this book. This is not an oversight. Human beings live in two worlds: in their head, and in the outside world, and getting the balance

between them right isn't always easy. It seems to me that most philosophers and sociologists have that balance wrong: they are too much in their heads. For another view of what the aim of education might be see Chomsky, N., Toward a humanistic conception of education. In *Work, Technology, and Education*. Feinberg, W., *et al*. (eds) University of Illinois Press, 1975.

27. See Bushman, B.J., *et al*., Media violence and the American public: scientific fact versus media misinformation. *American Psychologist*, 2001, 56(6/7), 477–89. Some American psychologists take a broad view, as is the case in this splendid paper, and this is unlike most contemporary British psychologists, who appear to see psychology as a technology rather than a science.

28. Furedi, F., *Where Have All the Intellectuals Gone?* Continuum, 2004.

29. I was pleased to find that my views are often similar to those that E.M. Forster expressed in his article, 'What I believe'. This appears in his collection of essays, *Two Cheers for Democracy*. Edward Arnold, 1951.

30. Warnock, M., The neutral teacher. In *Philosophers Discuss Education*. Brown, S.C. (ed.) Macmillan, 1975. I found this writer's comments not only valuable but also refreshingly readable! I put it like that because I must have tried reading the work of dozens of philosophers while working on this manuscript, and almost always found them arid and ultimately pointless. The extent to which their work tends to focus merely on what others have said is amazing among grown-ups, and often amounts to no more than gossip. No wonder philosophy tends to go round and round in circles. See also the contribution which follows that by Warnock, that by Norman, R., The neutral teacher?

31. Wald, G., Life and mind in the universe. *International Journal of Quantum Chemistry: Quantum Biology Symposium* 1984, 11, 1–15.

32. I am indebted here to Barrett, W., *The Illusion of Technique*. Doubleday, 1978. See especially the section entitled 'Afternoon', 140.

33. I should perhaps also divulge that Square Root is, as one might say, a second cousin of Kongor's. For a genial introduction to that engaging creature, see Lefrançoise, G., *Psychological Theories and Human Learning: Kongor's Report*. Brooks/Cole, 1972.

34. For detailed and scholarly comment on child abuse in the UK (and partly in the USA), see *The Child Protection Handbook*. Wilson, K., *et al*. (eds) Bailliere Tindall, 2002.

35. For details on the incidence of divorce see Martin, T.C., Recent tends in marital disruption. *Demography*, 1989, 26(1), 37–51. These writers estimate that second marriages in the USA are 25 per cent more likely to end in divorce than first marriages. Also Booth, A., *et al*., Starting over: why remarriages are more unstable. *Journal of Family Issues*, 1992, 13(2), 179–94. Also Wilson, B.F., *et al*., Remarriages. *Journal of Family Issues*, 1992, 13(2), 123–41. And Walker, K.N., *et al*., Remarriage after divorce: a review. *Social Casework*, May 1977, 276–85. Also Dean, G., *et al*., Marital homogamy the second time around. *Journal of Marriage and the Family*, 1978, 40, 559–70. Also McCranie, E.W., *et al*., Personality and multiple divorce: a prospective study. *Journal of Nervous and Mental Disease*, 1986, 174(3), 154–61. And Counts, R.M., Second and third divorces: the flood to come. *Journal of Divorce and Remarriage*, 1991, 17(1/2), 193–200.

36. Sherrington, C., *Man on His Nature*. Cambridge University Press, 1940, especially Chapter 10: Earth's alchemy. At this point, I refer to what is often called the 'mind–body' problem. As this takes one beyond the remit of this book, I reluctantly note only two references to it. Nagel, T., What is it like to be a bat? In *Mortal Questions*. Cambridge University Press, 1979. And for a clear review of the relevant literature, Güzeldere, G., Consciousness: what it is, how to study it, what to learn from its history. *Journal of Consciousness Studies*, 1995, 2(1), 30–51.

37. One often comes across the notion of 'critical thinking' in the literature on teaching and, as what is meant by the term is not immediately clear, it might be helpful to compare that notion with another commonly used in discussions about teaching, namely, 'problem

solving'. If one compares in this way, one soon finds that, when we think critically, we ask ourselves how valid is a statement. But when we attempt to solve a problem we ask ourselves how this matter can be solved. It follows that, when we think critically we examine the matter at hand in terms of the evidence given for it, and we compare that against some sort of a standard that we have in our head. In other words, when we think critically we make a sustained attempt to examine a particular matter in the light of the evidence given for it, and what we know about the matter. This is not quite the same as having a cast of mind that often sees questions, but it is sufficiently close to suggest that the two have a good deal in common. See Beyer, B.K., Critical thinking: what is it? *Social Education*, 1985, 49(4), 270–6.

38. Dinnage, R., *One to One: Experiences of Psychotherapy*. Penguin, 1988, 82.

39. Fowles, J., The enigma. In this writer's collection of short stories, *The Ebony Tower*. Little, Brown, 1974. See also this writer's *The Collector*. Jonathan Cape, 1963. See also Maslow, A.H., The need to know and the fear of knowing. *The Journal of General Psychology*, 1963, 68, 11–125. And Bowlby, J., On knowing what you are not supposed to know and feeling what you are not supposed to feel. *Canadian Journal of Psychiatry*, 1979, 24(5), 403–8. For a superb fictional description of a man who does not want to know see Ishiguro, K., *The Remains of the Day*. Faber & Faber, 1989. But not only do certain individuals prefer 'not to know'. Thus the author C.R. Badcock, in his *The Problem of Altruism*. Blackwell, 1986, 13, writes that 'sociology as a so-called "science" contains little or nothing in the way of genuine scientific insight but in reality functions as a vast, defensive elaboration'. If that comment sounds outlandish, recall that the bulk of sociological writing is characterized above all by its impersonality. Why is that the case? The single best account of a character that 'did not want to know', and the effect that this had on those around her is, I think, supplied by Shakespeare in his portrayal of Hamlet's mother, Gertrude.

40. For some empirical indicators that some people are more open to their experiences than others see Green-Hennessy, S., *et al*., Openness in processing social information among attachment types. *Personal Relationships*, 1998, 5, 449–66. See also Heatherton, T.F., *et al*., Binge eating as escape from self-awareness. *Psychological Bulletin*, 1991, 110(1), 86–108. Also Crisp, A.H., *et al*., Jolly fat: relationship between obesity and psychoneurosis in the general population. *British Medical Journal*, 1976, 1, 7–9. The authors write, 'the main themes that emerge are that both obesity . . . and the overeating of obese people may sometimes be a protective mechanism against the experience and display of anxiety and depression'.

41. I would suggest in closing a new curriculum for schools, and it might be called The Mass Media. This would consist of an examination of the *underlying* content and form that topics take in the mass media; and this would, I think, reveal how this media indirectly reveals and shapes much that is amiss with our world. It would be similar to a problem-based course in medical school in that, by beginning with a problem, one is led towards the need to learn basics.

Index

abstract 175, 176, 181
Adam 151
aesthetics 70
aids 188
aims 191
appearance 257
appraisal 158
Asiago 90
assessment 193
assignments 193, 215

behaviour modification 39
Behaviourists 33
blackcurrants 48
brainstorming 212
Brewster's angle 56

case study 164
citations 275
cognitivism 72
community 144, 223, 265
competence 11, 138
computer 70, 90, 119, 174, 182
computer games 169
computer literate 170
consciousness 53, 72, 86, 271
constructivism 261
corrections 144, 198
creative 225
criticism 87, 142
culture 235

Descartes, R. 92
dictating 206, 214
dietician 239

dignity 30
direct method 1
discipline 6, 218
discovery 53

emancipatory 172
evaluation 188
Eve 151
evidence 217
exist 92

facts 55, 257
fear 29
feeling 71, 92, 121
felt meanings 93
films 176, 181
financial 171, 182

Gestalt 46
grammar 109
groups 227
gumdrop 205

happiness 13, 269
hedgehogs 119
horticulture 247
humour 44, 206, 219, 230
hypertext 187

ice-breaker 244
ice-floes 210
imagination 154, 161, 170
individualism 264
inflation 174
information 185, 186

insight 52
integrity 29, 261
internet 185

Jesus 13

lesson plan 191
love 274

mass media 150, 172, 181, 256, 318
meaning 40, 58, 63
medical education 120
memory 97
money 45, 181
mystery 40

nature 17, 47, 51, 54, 72, 85, 189, 251, 264, 266
Newton, I. 40
note taking 214

objectives 191
oral 178

pattern 46, 47
personal 65, 89
Pinot Noir 162
Plato 83, 256
preparation 190
primula 164
print 181
problem-solving 68
profession 14, 274
projector 173
proof 126

quiz show 185

rational 258
reflection 10
relativism 81, 257
relevance 29
revision 205
rewards 41

responsibility 151
role-play 245
rote learning 3, 57, 58, 59
rules 110

schema 75
science 156
self 13, 124, 265, 269
skill 11, 138
Sassoon, S. 164
silence 207, 208
simplicity 188, 275
social construct 231
Socrates 13
solidarity 266
sound effects 181
spaghetti 256
student-centred 11
syllabus 8

tacit 63
talk 24
technique 196, 255
textbooks 162
the news 176, 186
theory 10, 15, 125
thinking 52, 209
topography 201
transfer of learning 66, 133
transmission method 7
truth 262, 272
tv 179, 265

understanding 52
university 14, 56, 119

values 30, 254, 265
vision 188

war 186
wealth 259
Winch, S. 23
workshops 9
writing 69